The Solidarity Encounter

The Solidarity Encounter
Women, Activism, and Creating Non-colonizing Relations

Carol Lynne D'Arcangelis

UBCPress · Vancouver · Toronto

© UBC Press 2022

All rights reserved. No part of this publication may be reproduced, stored in a retrieval system, or transmitted, in any form or by any means, without prior written permission of the publisher, or, in Canada, in the case of photocopying or other reprographic copying, a licence from Access Copyright, www.accesscopyright.ca.

31 30 29 28 27 26 25 24 23 22   5 4 3 2 1

Printed in Canada on FSC-certified ancient-forest-free paper (100% post-consumer recycled) that is processed chlorine- and acid-free.

Library and Archives Canada Cataloguing in Publication
Title: The solidarity encounter : women, activism, and creating non-colonizing relations / Carol Lynne D'Arcangelis.
Names: D'Arcangelis, Carol Lynne, author.
Description: Includes bibliographical references and index.
Identifiers: Canadiana (print) 20220198489 | Canadiana (ebook) 20220203385 | ISBN 9780774863810 (hardcover) | ISBN 9780774863865 (paperback) | ISBN 9780774864404 (PDF) | ISBN 9780774864503 (EPUB)
Subjects: LCSH: Anti-racism—North America. | LCSH: North America—Race relations. | LCSH: Women political activists—North America. | LCSH: Minority women activists—North America. | LCSH: Women, White—North America—Attitudes. | LCSH: Social justice—North America. | LCSH: Social action—North America.
Classification: LCC HT1563 .D37 2022 | DDC 305.80097—dc23

Canada

UBC Press gratefully acknowledges the financial support for our publishing program of the Government of Canada (through the Canada Book Fund), the Canada Council for the Arts, and the British Columbia Arts Council.

This book has been published with the help of a grant from the Canadian Federation for the Humanities and Social Sciences, through the Awards to Scholarly Publications Program, using funds provided by the Social Sciences and Humanities Research Council of Canada.

Printed and bound in Canada by Friesens
Set in Segoe and Warnock by Apex CoVantage, LLC
Copy editor: Lesley Erickson
Proofreader: Jesse Marchand
Indexer: Cheryl Lemmens
Cover designer: Gabi Proctor, DesignGeist

UBC Press
The University of British Columbia
2029 West Mall
Vancouver, BC V6T 1Z2
www.ubcpress.ca

To my mother, Caroline, whose fierce love, kind nature, appreciation of food, and penchant for dancing on tables remain unparalleled in my life.

Contents

Preface / viii

Acknowledgments / xii

Introduction / 3

1. The Spectrum of Proximity: White Women, Solidarity, and Settler/Liberal Self-Making / 37

2. Transgressing Cherished Spaces: Indigenous Women on the Impulse to Solidarity / 77

3. Risky Romanticization: Cultural Difference, National Belonging, and Indigenous Resistance / 111

4. Claiming Exceptionalism as the Rule: "Good/White Settler Allies" and the Politics of Declaration / 154

5. Rewriting Colonial Scripts: Toward Non-colonizing Solidarity / 195

Notes / 225

References / 237

Index / 257

Preface

A brilliant sun streams through the room's tall windows. I am at an event hosted by First Nations House at the University of Toronto. It is the early 2000s. We are upwards of fifteen people gathered in a circle, at ease, yet riveted by the conversation. The speaker is mixed-race nehiyaw iskwew (Cree woman) scholar-activist, author, and artist Robyn Bourgeois and the topic colonial constructions of Indigenous women as disposable. It is my introduction to the issue of missing and murdered Indigenous women, girls, and two-spirit people (MMIWG2S) across what many now call Canada.

Bourgeois' stark, impassioned critique provoked my anger and activist impulses, which are, not incidentally, among the white settler reactions to Indigenous struggles that I scrutinize in this book. Not long after, I became a non-Indigenous member of No More Silence (NMS), a group of Indigenous women and non-Indigenous women dedicated to raising awareness about the issue. I have stayed connected ever since. In the intervening years, public awareness of MMIWG2S people has increased exponentially, thanks to decades of organizing by Indigenous "warrior women" (Bourgeois 2014), so much so that the Trudeau government finally launched a public inquiry into the matter in 2015. At the time, however, the topic rarely made it onto the public radar and was certainly new to me. That talk at First Nations House became a defining moment of my next decade, ultimately propelling me to research what I call the solidarity encounter between Indigenous women and white women in a contemporary Canadian context.

Immersed in the realm of Indigenous–non-Indigenous political solidarity, I soon became familiar with what was supposed to undergird our social-justice imaginaries; in the activist spaces I frequented, we were expected to valorize and act on an anticolonial analysis of Canadian settler state institutions. I also internalized the oft-repeated refrain, of Indigenous and non-Indigenous voices alike, that non-Indigenous allies should take direction from the Indigenous protagonists in our midst. I also frequently heard it said that establishing friendships with Indigenous peoples and communities is a prerequisite for political solidarity work, and I recall my increasing unease with this assumed truism – another element of my experience that shapes this research. I became well versed in widespread Indigenous critiques of the saviour mentality said to drive many non-Indigenous allies, especially white women. I therefore became hypervigilant about my position in the work as a "white settler woman," which I define as a non-Indigenous woman of European descent whose whiteness goes without comment in most settings. All of this to say, I could talk the talk!

Nevertheless, something was niggling at me as I faced the apparent intractability of settler colonialism: how do everyday interactions between Indigenous and non-Indigenous people reproduce colonial power structures – especially when allies are supposed to know better? In other words, the connection between the micro and the macro continued to elude me. I could not figure out, let alone explain, how white women embody and enact colonialism in everyday activist spaces. On a personal level, I frankly did not grasp how my own, seemingly individual, good intentions might help shore up collective white privilege. And so, I became curious about how white settler colonial power relations – whether reproduced or contested – play out in the solidarity encounter and, in particular, how white women within that encounter negotiate our structurally dominant position as settlers. With these initial thoughts, I spoke with thirteen Indigenous women and eleven white women about their experiences of solidarity work.

To be more explicit, this book is underscored by an unapologetically political rationale – my modest offering to the tradition of activist scholarship derived "through active engagements with, and in the service of, progressive social movements" (Sudbury and Okazawa-Rey 2009, 3). In it, I reflect on my interactions with Indigenous women and white women solidarity practitioners to yield what I hope is useful knowledge for our ongoing social movement organizing. Indeed, as an activist-turned-scholar, I embrace the notion that theory can and does connect directly and intimately to practice. As Mississauga Nishnaabeg scholar, activist, and artist Leanne Betasamosake Simpson (2017, 20) notes in a scathing critique of Western approaches to knowledge production that would neatly separate thinking and doing, "theory and praxis, story and practice are interdependent, cogenerators of knowledge." This work represents my reading of a small slice of the knowledge produced by Indigenous women and white women through their engagement with and stories of solidarity work.

Always the aspiring scholar-activist, I take direction from feminist social movement scholar Janet Conway (2004, 6) who advises scholars involved in social-justice movements to think of themselves first and foremost as "an activist knower-practitioner among other knower-practitioners." At the same time, she situates scholar-activists as uniquely positioned to assess social movement dynamics without idealizing those dynamics. I take up this challenge by theorizing a particular realm of activist practice – the solidarity encounter between Indigenous women and white women in the Greater Toronto Area (GTA), in Ontario, Canada – with a hope to facilitate our collective move toward non-colonizing forms of solidarity.

In many ways, my scholarly concerns are autobiographical, emerging directly out of my work with NMS and indirectly out of my involvement since the 1990s in initiatives for social justice and human rights in the United States, Central America, and Canada. However, I deliberately chose narrative ethnography, in conjunction with participant interviews, to limit the space I allot to my story. This approach not only helps me avoid the snare of white solipsism – that is, navel-gazing tendencies or "the tendency to think, imagine and speak as if whiteness described the world" – but also to highlight the collective, structural nature of white settler privilege (Rich 1979, 299). I make judicious use of my beliefs, fantasies, and desires as a white woman attempting solidarity with Indigenous women to shine the spotlight on white settler women's collective subjectivity and investments in solidarity. In other words, I argue that what can seem like essentially personal or individual anxieties, motivations, and desires are not only that: they are collective, a consequence of ongoing settler colonial power dynamics. I hope that a fuller understanding of the inseparability of the individual and collective will assist white women in our roles and responsibilities related to fostering non-colonizing solidarity. Nevertheless, this book is eminently personal, reflecting as it does my perspectives as a white woman and my efforts to hold myself accountable – to Indigenous women and white women alike – for rendering the collective forces at play.

Let me be clear: this book is not about white women failing to get solidarity right or lacking political convictions or commitment. Instead, it draws on diverse women's insights and experiences to offer a perspective on the complexities of solidarity work and its vital importance, despite the challenges.

Acknowledgments

So many relations and relationships have sustained me during this journey. When I began researching the solidarity encounter, I was living in Tkaronto (Toronto), the traditional territory of several Indigenous nations, including the Mississaugas of the Credit, Anishinaabe, Chippewa, Haudenosaunee, and Wendat peoples. Currently, I live, love, and work in St. John's on the island of Ktaqmkuk (Newfoundland), translated from L'nui'simk as "far across place." Ktaqmkuk is the ancestral homelands of the Beothuk and the traditional territory of the Ktaqamkukewe'k Mi'kmaq, including the Qalipu and Miawpukek First Nations. I would also like to recognize the Inuit of Nunatsiavut and NunatuKavut and the Innu of Nitassinan, and their ancestors, as the original people of Labrador. I offer these land acknowledgments as part of my ongoing commitment to non-colonizing solidarity and decolonizing settler colonialism in the nation-state known as Canada.

This research would simply not have been possible without the participants: those who chose to be identified by their real names, Zainab Amadahy (Cherokee, Seminole), Ruth Green (Kanien'kehá:ka), Lee Maracle (Stó:lō/Métis), Rebeka Tabobondung (Anishinaabe) and Wanda Whitebird (Mi'kmaq); and the nineteen other women who remain anonymous. Thank you for trusting me with your knowledge. A big shout-out to my friends and comrades in struggle at No More Silence past and present, including Audrey, Barbara, Carmen, Cass, Darlene, Doreen, Gloria, Jen, Krista, Selina, Sheryl, Stephanie, and Wanda and the many others who have supported the work. A special thanks to my friend, the incomparable Audrey Huntley, whose sincerity, intelligence, political acumen, and dedication to justice continually inspire me. Thanks also to the Native Canadian Centre of Toronto and First Light: St. John's Friendship Centre.

I join many others in acknowledging the recent passing of Lee Maracle (1950–2021). I am grateful to have benefited from her generous spirit, fierce intellect, and good humour. Thank you for sharing your wisdom; it is a pillar of my argument.

This book has benefitted immensely from the guidance of Sherene Razack, Rauna Kuokkanen (Sámi), and Jean-Paul Restoule (Anishinaabe). Your encouragement and constructive critique have served me well to this day. Thanks also to Bonnie McElhinny, Angela Miles, Kiran Mirchandani, Martin Cannon (Kanien'kehá:ka) and the late Roger Simon for your guidance in course work and beyond. During my graduate program, I was the beneficiary of an Ontario Graduate Scholarship and CGS Doctoral Scholarship from the Social Sciences and Humanities Research Council. Additionally, thank you for the camaraderie and support of all my fellow OISE/UT students and Robarts Library buddies, including Tannis Atkinson, Robyn Bourgeois, Sara Carpenter, Arun Chaudhuri, Valerie Damasco, John Doran, Rob Heynen, Dan Hill, Hang-Sun Kim, Yu Kyung Kim-Cho, Adil Mawani, Arie Molema, Lori Neale, Adam Perry, Sheila Stewart, and many others. Thanks also to Chris Hiller for your compassionate listening over coffee at Trent University in 2010.

For much of my time researching this book, I lived in a tight-knit community at 35 Charles Street West (U of T Student Family Housing) with my partner and daughter. This community included, in alphabetical order, Sheila Batacharya, Prasad Bidaye, Soma Chatterjee, Asia Cichocka, Vichi and Cristian Ciocani, Praśanta Dhar, Alon Eisenstein, Mete and Jitka Eryilmaz, Rochelle Johnston, Anupama Mohan, Mandeep Kaur Mucina and Devi Dee Mucina, Jeff Myers, Ajamu Nangwaya, Adwoa Onuora, Neta Raz, Suddhaseel Sen, Lukasz Sicinski, Koen Van Rossum, and Brenda Wastasecoot. I carry vivid images and fond memories of our time together. Know that your support was indispensable to my well-being. Thanks also to the friends I've made in St. John's since coming here in 2013, especially Stacy Gardner and her son, Cohen. Without you, I would have little social life – or social media presence!

I would also like to mention my colleagues at Memorial University in the Department of Gender Studies. I could not ask for a better place to work. Thanks to Joan Butler (now retired), Juanita Lawrence, and Audrey O'Neil for keeping the department afloat, sometimes in very choppy waters. Thanks to Katherine Side for the idea of guest lecturing in each other's classes. Thanks to Pat Dold for your assurances that things would be fine. Thanks to Jennifer Dyer for your reassurances, exemplary positivity and infectious laugh, and many useful comments on my work. Thanks to Giovanna del Negro and Harry Berger for your great taste in music, good energy, and delectable food. Thanks to Vicki Hallett for your wry humour, quick wit, and bearing witness to my less confident moments. Thanks to Sonja Boon for our long walks, inspiring conversations, Costco-sharing ventures, and so much more. Thanks to Christina Doonan for your kindness, abiding faith in my abilities, intellectual prowess, and willingness to read multiple draft chapters. Thanks to other Memorial colleagues, including Amanda Bittner and Isabelle Côté, for instituting Writing Boot Camps on campus; Jennifer Selby, for being my steadfast writing companion for several years; and Shannon Hoff, for inviting me to help organize the philoSOPHIA Conference. Thanks to Mario Blaser for sending students my way and for welcoming me into the Argentinian fold. Gracias, Carolina Tytelman, for offering friendship and introducing me to the Spanish Book Club when I needed it most. Thanks to Alec Brookes for your sensitivity and soulful philosophical musings, anytime, anywhere, and to Elise Thorburn for your indefatigable spirit. I also extend much appreciation to my students whose *ah-ha* moments are the main reason I stay on (the academic) course. A special thanks to Joanne Harris for a stellar presentation on our panel for the NORA Conference and also to Lesley Butler and Emily Murphy for copy-editing an earlier version of this book.

A heartfelt thank you to the UBC Press team – Darcy Cullen, Meagan Dyer, Nadine Pedersen, and Carmen Tiampo – for seeing the merit of my work and helping me bring it to fruition. Thanks also to copy editor Lesley Erickson, cover designer Gabi Proctor, proofreader Jesse Marchand, and indexer Cheryl Lemmens. On a related note, I would like to acknowledge the financial support of Memorial University's Publications Subvention Grant towards indexing costs.

I am indebted to Victoria Freeman as a friend and colleague who generously read versions of the book and counselled me at several points along the way. A special thanks to my mentor, colleague, and friend Janet Conway. You continue to buoy me with your political astuteness, intellectual insights, and confidence in my work.

To my brother Raymond, I owe you for my fondness of all things outdoors. To my siblings Mary Anne and Chancy, for my gravitation to all things musical. To my sister Annette, my adoration, appreciation, and affection for you are beyond measure. To my parents who have passed, Caroline and Chancy (Nocenzio), I hope I have made you proud. To others in my far-away family, please know that I carry within me your intense zest for life. Finally, I am blessed to have my partner, Dennis, and our daughter, Marlena, in my life. Dennis, thanks for being the most honest person I know. I am grateful for all that you do and all that you are. Marlena, you light up my world. I love and thank you both with all my heart.

The Solidarity Encounter

Introduction

> The most fundamental principle in the search for a new political ontology for being together in the world is the relationship between the "self" and "other."
> — MAKERE STEWART-HARAWIRA, "PRACTISING INDIGENOUS FEMINISM: RESISTANCE TO IMPERIALISM"

This book is about the everyday self–other relationships of political solidarity in a particular setting: the solidarity encounter between Indigenous women/feminists and white women/feminists[1] in the Greater Toronto Area (GTA).[2] This bold claim of Māori-Scots scholar Makere Stewart-Harawira that appears in the epigraph (2007, 134) has been a guiding beacon throughout my research journey, as has more recently the National Inquiry into Missing and Murdered Indigenous Women and Girls. Its final report is unequivocal: "Finding self-determined solutions for addressing the crisis of missing and murdered Indigenous women, girls, and 2SLGBTQQIA people [hereafter MMIWG2S people][3] means conceptualizing rights as founded in all relationships ... and understanding that at the centre of it all, we begin with our relationships to each other" (NIMMIWG 2019, 12).

I have long been determined to expose solidarity's relational pitfalls – that is, to figure out what remains colonial about intersubjective (self–other) dynamics in solidarity work – but always with the goal of enhancing its possibilities. To do that, in this book, I concentrate on one side of the self–other equation:

white settler women's "self-making" projects, or the ways we form our identities and make sense of being white women in solidarity spaces. I soon realized that illuminating these self-making processes required the perspectives of both white women and Indigenous women. Accordingly, I spoke to thirteen Indigenous women and eleven white women "activist knower-practitioners" about their experiences of solidarity work (Conway 2004). The result is a qualitatively based theory of intersubjective relations in the solidarity encounter from my vantage point as a white feminist scholar-activist. With this intervention into theory, I humbly offer an intervention into practice. I hope that looking at what has gone wrong – and right – in solidarity encounters can be a precursor to further non-colonizing relations, a point I crystallize in the final chapter.

Admittedly, not everyone will share my perspective. Canada is undisputedly a white settler context. Colonialism is in the air we breathe and a large part of who we are and are constantly becoming. We are caught in what geographer Derek Gregory (2004, xv) calls the "colonial present," where "constellations of power, knowledge, and geography ... continue to colonize lives all over the world."[4] Solidarity encounters are no different: they are microcosms of the colonial relations that saturate society more broadly. In the spirit of literary and cultural studies scholar Mary Louise Pratt (1991, 2008), we can also think of solidarity encounters as colonial contact zones where subjects, meaning making, and power relations take place. Contact zones involve inequalities that remain long after the initial contact between two or more societies, and so Indigenous–non-Indigenous political solidarity is as fraught as it is necessary. With that in mind, I propose the somewhat paradoxical idea that we *can* do solidarity in non-colonizing ways. I offer this analysis of the perils and possibilities of solidarity encounters to enrich dialogue already underway in other academic and activist endeavours.[5]

As an attentive reader, you will have already noted my use of "non-colonizing" rather than "decolonizing." This requires some explanation. I had peppered my research proposal more or less equally with both terms before Stó:lō/Métis scholar, writer, and activist Lee Maracle, at the time a traditional teacher affiliated with First Nations House at the University of Toronto, pushed for clarity. After reading the proposal, she chided good-humoredly, "Do you mean decolonizing or non-colonizing? Decide!" And so I did. Before reviewing any of the literature, my intuition told me that non-colonizing was the less presumptuous choice – a kind of Hippocratic Oath for non-Indigenous allies who vow to stop doing colonial harm in their everyday interactions. I then found Eve Tuck (Unangax̂) and K. Wayne Yang's (2014, 812) now widely cited critique of social-justice initiatives that use decolonization and its derivatives as a metaphor for things unrelated to Indigenous self-determination. I also drew inspiration from postcolonial feminist Chandra Mohanty's (2003) belief in the possibility of non-colonizing transnational feminist solidarity across borders. Mohanty does not so much define the concept as describe what is necessary for its fulfillment, namely, a commitment to decentring the self, engaging difference, and embracing "unsettled relationality" (Boudreau Morris 2017, 458). Perhaps Corey Snelgrove captures the essence of a non-colonizing approach, however, when he describes it as "a practice that does not reify colonization" (Snelgrove, Dhamoon and Corntassel 2014, 26). I have now come to think of non-colonizing as a precursor to decolonizing; it is the attitudes and actions that set the stage for a radical undoing of settler colonial structures. For a more precise or robust meaning of non-colonizing, that, dear reader, is the subject of this book.

Turning briefly to another definitional question, I know that making a categorical distinction between "Indigenous" and "settler" carries with it certain risks.[6] Nonetheless, following settler postcolonial scholars Anna Johnston and Alan Lawson (2000, 368), I believe that the lasting structural inequalities wrought by colonialism demand this analytical distinction. Besides, debates about the category settler can be a distraction (Snelgrove, Dhamoon, and Corntassel 2014) and risk ignoring the real effects of its power. I conceptualize Indigenous and settler as relational and "historically porous" categories (Morgensen 2011) that accord to the political demands of a particular colonial project. Finally, I acknowledge the specific histories, solidarity work, and intersubjective relations between people of colour and Indigenous nations in Canada – relations that lie beyond the purview of this book.[7]

While theorizing involves a certain level of abstraction, it is always place-based. In my case, I began generating ideas about the solidarity encounter while living in downtown Toronto in the early 2000s. As the largest metropolitan area in Canada, Toronto wields potent social, political, and economic influence over the rest of the country, often making it the target of resentment. In 2011, when I started interviewing participants for this research, the GTA was home to some 5.6 million people. The City of Toronto alone had a population of 2.6 million, about 19,270 (0.8%) of whom were Indigenous.[8] Unlike other Canadian cities, there are no urban First Nations reserves in the GTA. The closest is the Mississaugas of Scugog First Nation, located about 94 kilometres northeast of the city. However, Six Nations of the Grand River, the largest First Nations Reserve in Canada, is a relatively short 100-kilometre drive to the southwest.[9]

The Indigenous population in Toronto is a "multicultural, cosmopolitan and diasporic" group, the majority of whom arrived after the Second World War as "part of a postcolonial phenomenon arising from a history of oppression and dispossession," according to anticolonial scholar and historian Victoria Freeman (2010, 296–97). As a result, Indigenous people from many different nations call Toronto home, some of whom have mixed heritage and/or lost connections. Many others maintain strong relationships with family and friends through frequent travel back and forth to their reserves. While things have changed considerably since Freeman wrote "'Toronto Has No History!' Indigeneity, Settler Colonialism and Historical Memory," most non-Indigenous Torontonians still have little awareness of the city's Indigenous history or contemporary reality (Freeman 2010, 295–96). The combined effect of these demographics and the sociocultural narrative Freeman describes has been the relative invisibility of Toronto's diverse Indigenous inhabitants as Indigenous peoples; when noticed, they would have likely been seen as just another ethnic group.[10]

Due in no small part to the rich activist tradition of the Ontario Institute for Studies in Education (OISE) at the University of Toronto, I had a different perspective. For many years, my epicentre was the intersection of Yonge and Bloor Streets, a stone's throw from my apartment in University of Toronto (U of T) Student Family Housing. I rarely ventured beyond Davenport, with maybe a biannual excursion to Eglinton Avenue with my young daughter for some discount sandals. From this base, I explored the world of progressive Toronto, attending lectures, performances, and events hosted by groups including No One Is Illegal, the Ontario Coalition against Poverty, and Christian Peacemakers. In 2001, I even travelled with OISE folks to protest the Free Trade Area of the Americas in Quebec City. I also joined U of T's Indigenous Education Network, where I met like-minded people committed to promoting Indigenous education and research at OISE and fostering links with the broader community.

Flash forward to fall 2006. Stepping lightly over fraying antique carpets, past deep mahogany banisters, I entered a dimly lit, panelled room. I was nervous and quiet at my first No More Silence (NMS) meeting to organize the February 14 vigil for MMIWG2S people in Ontario.[11] As I quickly learned, Toronto (Tkaronto) is a hub of Indigenous social, cultural, political, and service organizations such as the Native Canadian Centre, the Native

Women's Resource Centre, Council Fire Native Cultural Centre, Na-Me-Res (Native Men's Residence), and Aboriginal Legal Services – all places I became familiar with through NMS.[12]

The Paradox of Political Solidarity in a Colonial Landscape

Since that time, Canadian public debate about the need to redefine Indigenous–non-Indigenous relations has grown exponentially. Discussions flared noticeably at several points in the last decade: in the wake of Idle No More in late 2012,[13] after the release of the final report of the Truth and Reconciliation Commission of Canada in 2015, and, most recently, after the publication of the final report of the National Inquiry into Missing and Murdered Indigenous Women and Girls in 2019.[14] Even Canada's 2017 sesquicentennial did not escape scrutiny. As Ojibwe film and pop culture critic Jesse Wente (2017) notes, "The timing was ripe for Canada's sesquicentennial to meet vocal resistance, its message recast, its meaning reframed." In the classroom, I still turn to Michif visual artist Christi Belcourt's 2017 narration of her poem "Canada, I can cite for you 150" as a powerful critique of mainstream celebrations of Canadian nationhood. Canada's "settler problem" has bubbled to the surface for an increasing number of settlers (Battell Lowman and Barker 2015; Mackey 2016; Regan 2010).

Of course, as Mississauga Nishnaabeg scholar, activist, and artist Leanne Betasamosake Simpson puts it, the elephant in the room – the matter of stolen land – looms ever larger in these discussions.[15] I recall listening to the CBC's "Ask Me Anything with Host Ali Hassan" on January 1, 2018, when Hassan asked CBC announcer Duncan McCue (Anishinaabe) about the one thing needed to further reconciliation. Without skipping a beat, McHugh identified the resolution of conflicts over land and resources as that one thing. Closer to home, the Indigenous activists I know consistently cite the dispossession of Indigenous lands and resources through sexual and gender violence as the root cause of the crisis of MMIWG2S people (INM Collective 2014; Konsmo and Pacheco 2016; NIMMIWG 2019; Simpson 2017; Smith 2005).[16] For these activists, stopping the murders and disappearances requires ending settler colonialism in Canada and the Indigenous–non-Indigenous hierarchies it sustains.

The message is clear and increasingly audible, and it includes settlers taking a proactive role in dismantling settler colonialism. The calls come from a variety of ideological quarters,[17] critiques of reconciliation discourse notwithstanding (Simpson 2011).[18] I tuned into these critiques early on in my research at a 2011 Reconciliation Symposium in Toronto when Kanien'kehá:ka (Mohawk) scholar Marlene Brant Castellano took the stage. The former chair of Indigenous studies at Trent University, Brant Castellano promptly admonished mainstream institutions and politicians who would use the language of reconciliation without the commitment to redress material inequities such as land dispossession. Instead, she exhorted listeners to prioritize Indigenous meanings and practices of reconciliation. My experiences in the solidarity contact zone – from public rallies to more intimate settings such as NMS meetings – attest to these doubts but also to the demand that non-Indigenous allies back Indigenous self-determination struggles by committing to solidarity work (King 2016; Kuokkanen 2012; Walia 2012). Take the email I received in 2011 from a prominent Indigenous woman activist in Toronto: "It is good to hear the organizations are uniting [around the February 14 event] ... Solidarity is one of the tools we need to bring awareness and to help promote safety nets for our beautiful women and their children, our future generations. We have to teach our children to work together so that things get done." Later that year, Sylvia Maracle (Kanien'kehá:ka) shared her vision of what non-Indigenous support for Indigenous self-determination would entail, namely, a new conversation in which settlers do not cast Indigenous peoples as deficient.[19] In these and many other ways, Indigenous peoples are insisting on and fostering Indigenous–non-Indigenous relationships in which settlers are not positioned as superior (LaRocque 2010). As Coast Salish scholar Rachel Flowers (2015, 34) writes, "There has and continues to be space offered by Indigenous peoples for settlers to align themselves with our struggles to support the transformation of the colonial relationship and constructing alternatives to it." For Flowers (2015, 35), it boils down to collective anticolonial resistance for a shared future on terms not "asymmetrically dictated" by settlers.

The Indigenous women interviewed for this book are no different. Despite the risks and challenges, they not only ask white women to engage in solidarity but also laud our efforts. Well aware of the complexities, several Indigenous participants stressed the importance of attempting solidarity. In fact, as I discuss in Chapter 2, several Indigenous women claimed that non-colonizing solidarity is not only possible, but also already underway, and that *not* to attempt solidarity is in itself a colonizing behaviour. The simple fact is that non-colonizing solidarity will not happen if people do not enter the fray. Put differently, these Indigenous women urge us to *care* about their lives. If history tells us anything, however, it is that good intentions can have disastrous consequences for those on the receiving end. Thus, it is important to appraise the positive and negative repercussions of white women's decisions to care about or help Indigenous women. In fact, throughout this book, I contemplate the ironic twist of a desire to help turned inward: white women can veer away from the political aim of dismantling colonial structures and turn exclusively toward the personal or individualistic aim of settler self-making projects.

I remind you that my purpose is not to repudiate white settler women's genuine desires and efforts to engage ethically with Indigenous women. In fact, I want to disentangle this righteous desire from the potentially damaging desire for legitimacy or belonging that can also operate in the solidarity encounter. Perhaps what I do best is convey the "messiness" of intersubjective relations in the solidarity encounter (D'Arcangelis and Huntley 2012). Clear amid that messiness, however, is a central challenge facing white women – how to be vigilant about the pernicious aspects of what I call "gendered colonial subjectivity" or white settler/liberal subjectivity in its gendered forms, broadly defined as white women's feelings, thoughts, actions, and identities in a colonial context. This challenge forms part of the paradoxical waters that all of us must navigate: how Indigenous peoples and settlers can work together to foster equitable relations in the inherently inequitable context of settler colonialism (D'Arcangelis and Huntley 2012). The effects of this paradox – existing in a seemingly inescapable colonial present – on solidarity relations require a more careful look, which is what I set out to do in this book.

Beginnings

I was alone with a powerhouse – a highly respected leader in what has become a more widespread MMIWG2S movement. Mustering up my nerve, I asked, "Do you think it would be okay if I did my dissertation about NMS?" Her nonchalant yes practically brought me to tears and a visceral sense of relief flooded my body. This, I thought, is solidarity embodied.

In retrospect, that interaction obviously brings to the surface many of the themes central to this book. It reflects the blend of social activism and academia that brought me to Toronto in 1999. After seven years in Central America, I chose OISE as the place to ponder my experiences in the so-called field. I have been straddling activism and academia ever since. My tears point to the nexus of motivations – some personal, some political, some guilt-ridden – that brought me to this solidarity encounter. The leader's response signalled not only generosity but also many Indigenous women's willingness to work with non-Indigenous allies. While I did not end up focusing exclusively on NMS, my experiences with the group plunged me into the research and found their way into this book.

My time with NMS taught me that white women need a better handle on the everyday interpersonal aspects of solidarity work if we are to neutralize the white saviour complex (Kempadoo 2015; Maurantonio 2017; Vera and Gordon 2003). I also knew we needed more experientially based research to gain this understanding. I converted these realizations into two research goals: mapping the challenges and tensions of solidarity work to the operation of gendered colonial subjectivity and developing a framework for non-colonizing solidarity, or interpersonal interactions that do not reproduce settler colonial structures. I decided interviews with solidarity practitioners were the best way to identify interactive patterns between women in the solidarity encounter. I was not disappointed. In speaking to participants and reading their narratives, certain problematic expressions, subtle and blatant, of white women's self-making stood out. In fact, while I intended to focus equally on solidarity perils and possibilities, charting the potentially damaging effects of this self-making was a more daunting task than anticipated. This is why I dedicate much of the book to unpacking the complex layers of the more perilous side of things.

My main finding is deceptively straightforward: the "white desire for proximity" to Indigenous Others can operate as a colonial impulse. That is, a colonizing relationship between Indigenous women and white women persists when white women get too close, figuratively or literally, to Indigenous women in ways that the latter deem invasive. The solidarity encounter of my theorizing is a space with multiple and overlapping boundaries, from material (physical) to intersubjective (interpersonal) to epistemic (about knowledge). As I explain more fully below, the idea of proximity is generative because it allows us to think about not only the kinds of spaces created through solidarity encounters but also the dynamics of those spaces (how white women might seek closeness) in different sociopolitical contexts. Writing this – then and now – reminds me that I am no stranger to proximity desires, as attested to by the personal exchanges I share in these pages.

But, I am getting ahead of the story. To set the record straight, I have never thought that white women go into solidarity encounters planning to reinforce settler colonial structures. If my experience is any indication, though, Indigenous women continue to have negative interactions in these encounters. Shining the spotlight on the white settler woman and her self-making is my attempt to square the facts. Drawing inspiration from

Ruth Frankenberg's (1993) groundbreaking work on white women and race,[20] I, too, see white women's lives as sites for reproducing and challenging colonialism.[21] To this end, I adapt critical whiteness scholar Barbara Heron's (1999, 41–42) question about Canadian women development workers in Africa: How do white women in Canada "negotiate and understand our positions in relations of power"?

I should clarify up front that I consider white settler women a heterogeneous category of women with diverse experiences and relative power.[22] For example, while class as a category came up infrequently in the interviews, Maracle cited it is an important factor in considering the scope of white women's privilege. In 2010, she generously agreed to meet me in her office to discuss my research, which was still in the proposal stage. I sat there listening intently, despite my nervous fidgeting. She began:

> If you are a poor white woman, you do not necessarily occupy a dominant position vis-à-vis someone like me ... What you have is illicit citizenship in my homeland. A privilege I do not have. A poor white woman has no access to its wealth, a subjugation we share, but all white women have the privilege of citizenship in a country they contributed [minimally] to constructing.

As this book's first order of business, I consider how white women engaged in solidarity work grapple with this structural privilege as settlers and what our thoughts and deeds indicate about the perils and promise of political solidarity.

Galvanized by the conversation with Maracle, my head was awash in questions. What happens when white women confront (or are confronted with) our settler status? How does white settler guilt affect solidarity efforts? Do white women in the solidarity encounter knowingly or otherwise imagine ourselves to be "autonomous independent individuals" (Moreton-Robinson 2000) capable of denying or transcending our complicity in settler colonialism? In short, to what extent are white women prepared to reckon with our settler status, that is, our membership in a structurally dominant collectivity? What might be the consequences for solidarity if and when we do? The likelihood that notions of liberal individualism were at play started to fascinate me.

Clearly, contemporary solidarity encounters do not occur in a historical vacuum. My initial research consisted of learning about this "white woman subject" of past colonial/imperial encounters as well as Indigenous women's views on the current state of affairs (D'Arcangelis 2015). My review of this literature fostered another important set of questions. What had become of the colonial roots of Western feminism (Yeğenoğlu 1998)? What if any "colonial continuities" (Heron 2007) exist in today's solidarity encounter? Are white women still apt to see ourselves as the "helpers" of more "oppressed" Indigenous women?

I have not always been skeptical of self-reflexivity. After all, in putting the white settler woman under the microscope, this research is effectively one giant exercise in self-reflexivity! However, as I put the literature in conversation with what I heard from participants, I became more dubious about the role of self-reflexivity in social-justice pursuits (D'Arcangelis 2018). Consequently, in this book, I take a critical stance on self-reflexivity and ask what (else) is required to right colonizing solidarity's wrongs. Lastly, I confronted this head-scratching problem: how can transformations at the micro level, such as self-transformations or interpersonal group dynamics, alter social relations at the macro level? In the spirit of dialogue, and with many questions remaining, I recount my journey into the complex undertaking of solidarity between Indigenous women and white women in a contemporary Canadian context.

The Impulse to Solidarity: Proximity and Its Discontents

Now I can return to the animating idea of this book, which is that a white desire for proximity to Indigenous Others can operate as a colonial impulse. That is to say, a colonial relationship between Indigenous women and white women persists in part when white women get too close, figuratively or literally, to Indigenous women in ways deemed invasive by the latter. Moreover, the boundaries in question can be material, intersubjective, or epistemic.

There are several theoretical claims wrapped up in this finding, the main one being this: the deep-seated desire for belonging that characterizes collective white settler subjectivity is necessarily a factor in how white women negotiate the solidarity encounter. In other words, part of being a settler involves a more-often-than-not subconscious yearning to live legitimately on stolen land. What I find most remarkable about this desire – a desire that attaches to liberal subjects in colonial contexts – is its manifestation in the solidarity encounter as a white desire to be "close" to Indigenous women. This is what I call the "desire for proximity." Accordingly, much of what I track in this book falls under the "problem with proximity." By this, I mean the fact that over-pursuing closeness through a multiplicity of ways and for a multiplicity of reasons – such as desires for acceptance, inclusion, forgiveness, healing, purpose, empowerment, or friendship – can potentially enable white women such as myself to disavow our complicity in colonial hierarchies. Working in tandem with the desire for proximity is the closely related white pursuit of exceptionalism, or the wish to be (or, more cynically, to be seen as) an exception to the rule – a "good settler" versus a "bad settler."

To describe the desire for proximity in both its latent and manifest forms, I coin two phrases: the "spectrum of proximity" and the "impulse to solidarity." Spectrum of proximity provides a way to group together the desires that I find connote, involve, or require proximity in one form or another, namely, the above-mentioned list of desires – for acceptance, inclusion, forgiveness, healing, purpose, empowerment, or friendship.[23] Impulse to solidarity refers to the latent or activated drive to satiate those desires through solidarity work. I argue that this impulse, which is in effect an impulse to pursue proximity through solidarity work, flows from a particular formulation of gendered colonial subjectivity. As I envisage it, the solidarity impulse relates to, but is distinct from, Barbara Heron's (2007, 6) "helping imperative" or the "desire for other people's development" that drives white/northern, middle-class women to do development work in the Global South. In contrast, the solidarity impulse happens "here" in Canada and can include what initially seem like contradictory drives: the white woman's desires to "help" and "be helped by" Indigenous Others. Expanding the point, the desire to help has an underside evoked with the phrase to be helped by. This underside contains an assortment of self-serving or, more accurately, self-making reasons why settlers in general and white women in particular might engage in solidarity with Indigenous Others. It is here, on the underside, where the desires for proximity defined above thrive best. In short, I argue that Indigenous women's embodied or metaphoric presence can help white women in the sense of facilitating our self-making projects.

It is important to emphasize that, in my view, it is the uninterrogated, unmitigated impulse to solidarity – not the impulse per se – that generates colonial tensions among women in solidarity encounters and undermines the effectiveness of political solidarity. Furthermore, I do not interpret the solidarity impulse as an all-encompassing concept that exhausts all possible forms of white women's engagement in solidarity work. Rather, think of it as a conceptual device that helps us identify the problems with proximity and some potential solutions, including ways to temper, disrupt, mitigate, check, forestall, pause, apprehend, or even stop the impulse.

I in no way mean to diminish the degree to which white women in solidarity encounters grapple with our collective privilege and foundationally tenuous or precarious status as settlers. As I mention above, some Indigenous participants emphasize that non-colonizing solidarity is already underway. Even as I signal the tenaciousness of white settler/liberal subjectivity and the quest for innocence at its core, I cite a cautious optimism among participants about facilitating and fostering non-colonizing solidarity.

One more point about this core finding warrants mention. The pervasiveness of spatial references in participant narratives prompted me to characterize both the problem (colonizing solidarity) and its solution (non-colonizing solidarity) in spatialized terms: when white settler women attempt to get too close to Indigenous women, we can cross boundaries or thresholds – figurative or literal – that we should not cross. In these instances, solidarity work risks being worse than ineffectual: it can reproduce white settler structural privilege. In the final chapter, I draw on participant insights to propose a framework for reconfiguring social relations in the solidarity encounter, a framework best encapsulated by the directive "step back, but not out," as put by an Indigenous participant. What happens when white settler women become aware of and curb the impulse to engage unthinkingly in solidarity? Half the battle, I suggest, is to recognize when our settler/liberal self-interest is about to take centre stage and compel us to come too close to Indigenous women, thereby diminishing the collective political project of solidarity.

On Indigenous–Non-Indigenous Alliances, Coalitions, and Solidarities

This book contributes to a growing cross-disciplinary scholarship on contemporary alliances, coalitions, and solidarities between Indigenous and non-Indigenous peoples on Turtle Island, and on Indigenous–settler relations more broadly.[24] I am especially indebted to the work of Indigenous studies and settler scholar Lynne Davis, whose edited collection *Alliances: Re/envisioning Indigenous–Non-Indigenous Relationships* (2010a) remains among the most comprehensive and wide-ranging texts on these subjects. In fact, Davis (2010b, 2) has long posed similar questions about solidarity's paradoxes, namely, how non-Indigenous people can "work in solidarity with Indigenous peoples without replicating the continuing colonial relations that characterize the broader frame of Indigenous/non-Indigenous relationships in Canada today." Gender and feminist studies scholar May Chazan (2020, 47–48) phrases the question slightly differently: "Can settler struggles for home and futurity become one critical 'site of uncomfortable change' in this project of decolonization?" I hope to enrich our collective answers to these questions and others. The broad consensus across this scholarship and in popular literature is that Indigenous–non-Indigenous relations in and beyond solidarity work need reconfiguring.[25] However, little material centres gender as an analytic or focuses intensely on intersubjectivity and the subject-making dynamics of solidarity work. This book attempts to do both.

Settler subjectivity is a vital if sometimes implied subtheme of this literature.[26] For example, settler anticolonial scholar Chris Hiller touches on a core theme of this book. In her study of twenty-two Euro-Canadian solidarity activists, Hiller (2017, 432) concludes that settlers grapple with their colonial complicity through upward (outward focused) and downward (inward focused) "competing spirals of reflection and action." My framework for non-colonizing solidarity points to the importance of balancing these spirals. In reflecting on his experiences of allyship with Indigenous peoples, geographer Adam Barker (2010, 326) warns settler allies that we cannot extract ourselves from colonial power dynamics just by "confront[ing] the colonial legacy within our own psyches." Here, Barker touches on the desire for transcendence that my findings suggest can underpin white women's negotiations of solidarity relations. Barker (2010, 328) cites other barriers to solidarity of relevance to my research, including the effects of settler-ally guilt arising out of egocentricity and settler abdication of our individual and collective responsibilities to take action. In a subsequent book, Barker and coauthor Emma Battell Lowman (Battell Lowman and Barker 2015, 99–105) describe how settler identity reproduces colonial structures and practices through "settler moves to comfort." They also describe how settler identity can, when unsettled, be a step toward dismantling colonialism (Battell Lowman and Barker 2015, 107). I build upon these threads of Battell Lowman's and Barker's work with empirical research into how settler moves to comfort manifest in white women's solidarity work and how we might mitigate them. Similarly, Corey Snelgrove, Rita Dhamoon, and Jeff Corntassel (2014) discuss various settler "moves to innocence," including recourse to a good–bad settler binary and declarations of settler privilege, which can facilitate a central aspect of settler subjectivity – the underlying desire to deny structural complicity in settler colonial systems. My qualitative study builds on their ideas by examining how such dynamics might unfold in a particular site: the solidarity encounter between Indigenous women and white women in the GTA.

Other themes relevant to this book, including settler self-reflexivity and transformation, permeate much of the literature. Like Barker, Paulette Regan (2010, 11) draws on her lived experience to consider the "pedagogical potential of truth-telling and reconciliation processes." As a former IRS claims manager who shares Taiaiake Alfred's critique of hegemonic reconciliation discourse, Regan (2010, 11) seeks to reframe reconciliation as a process wherein settlers would be induced to self-reflexively "unsettle" their internal settler selves and "deconstruct the foundational myth of the benevolent peacemaker – the bedrock of settler identity." Also invoking the would-be ally's need for transformation, Lynne Davis and Heather Yanique Shpuniarsky (2010) share a list of guiding principles for effective Indigenous–non-Indigenous alliances.[27] They describe coalitions as sites of pain for everyone but note how challenging it is for many non-Indigenous people "to look inward at their own roles within colonialization, and confront themselves" (Davis and Shpuniarsky 2010, 343). For Barker, Regan, and Davis and Shpuniarsky, settler and settler ally self-reflection is indispensable to solidarity projects. I agree with but also complicate this premise by suggesting that self-reflexivity can backfire and reproduce the white settler/liberal subject as dominant and the Indigenous subject as traumatized and in need of assistance (Million 2013). In this way, I chart the lingering gendered effects of the benevolent peacemaker myth on the settler-turned-ally and develop guidelines that include radical self-reflexivity as a necessary if fraught element for the subversion of this myth.

Like Davis and Shpuniarsky, scholar-activist Harsha Walia develops a list of basic principles related to solidarity. Walia's (2012, 30) list starts with the need for non-Indigenous people to acknowledge that we benefit from the illicit usurpation of Indigenous land and that we operate in "complicated ways, often as simultaneously oppressed and complicit" in colonial relations. Like Barker, Walia (2012, 28) warns against the paralysis of guilt that can ensue "when faced with this truth" and notes "the line between being too interventionist and being paralyzed." In "No More Silence, Toward a Pedagogy of Feminist Decolonizing Solidarity," I, together with Audrey Huntley (D'Arcangelis and Huntley 2012), echo Walia in citing the need for non-Indigenous people to balance their responsibility to ride toward decolonizing solidarity by not taking over the wheel. In this book, I complement Walia's macro view with a micro one, identifying a key challenge for white women: how to grapple with our colonial complicity without capitulating to white guilt or sending our settler desire for belonging into overdrive.

Critical whiteness scholars Barbara Heron (1999, 2007) and Emma Kowal (2011, 2015) are among the few scholars to complete empirical studies on whiteness and colonialism in relation to solidarity. As I mentioned, Heron's insights into the helping imperative jump-started my own thinking about the possibility of a similar impulse among white women in Canadian solidarity encounters. I also look to Kowal's (2011, 320) Australian-based ethnography on the "stigma of white privilege," a feeling engendered in some white people who take "responsibility for the effects of colonization on Indigenous people." I extend Kowal's work in a gendered reading of similarly aware white women in solidarity encounters. In the process, I raise the distinct and somewhat ironic possibility that a heightened awareness of one's settler status can provoke a crisis of belonging, which can set into motion or exacerbate the solidarity impulse.

Indigenous Women Take to Task "Whitestream" Feminism

As mentioned, the genesis of this research lies in my solidarity work with Indigenous women, which made me wonder why they expressed continual frustration, annoyance, even outrage toward white women's attitudes and behaviours in solidarity encounters – and how everyday interactions could reproduce structural colonial inequities. Likewise, Indigenous women's scholarship on their fraught encounters with whitestream feminist theory and practice have profoundly shaped my approach in this book.[28] Their critiques coalesce around three interrelated aspects of mainstream feminism that have hindered women's/feminist solidarity: a singular focus on gender and patriarchal oppression; an insufficient understanding and application of colonialism as an analytic; and the operation of a colonial impulse to "save" Indigenous women (Grande 2004; Maracle 1996, 2006; Monture-Angus 1995, 1999; Moreton-Robinson 2000).[29] While Indigenous scholars/activists acknowledge the pluralistic, heterogeneous, and dynamic nature of feminist theories and practices over time (see St. Denis 2007, 34), they target those mainstream feminist formulations that have privileged the issues of white, middle-class Western women. Scholars contend that as a result, certain academic and activist settings have overlooked or eclipsed Indigenous women's agency and concerns (see Green 2007c, 2017b). This book is my response to these and other Indigenous/feminist insights.[30]

Geonpul feminist scholar Aileen Moreton-Robinson (2000) is among those Indigenous scholars who have greatly influenced my approach to studying the solidarity encounter. In her pathbreaking book *Talkin' Up to the White Woman: Indigenous Women and Feminism,* she examines whiteness as a colonial instrument in contemporary Indigenous–non-Indigenous relations in Australia. She vehemently argues that white feminist academic privilege hinges on the structural invisibility of whiteness, which in turn allows white feminist academics to remain unaware of their complicity in racist, colonial processes. Her account of white feminist subjectivity aligns with other hard-hitting Indigenous critiques of whitestream feminism, including critiques of the liberal individualism lodged within its praxis.[31] Moreton-Robinson (2000, 147) argues that white Australian feminist academics epitomize this tendency to "perceive themselves as autonomous independent individuals, whose antiracist practice is orchestrated through an intellectual engagement based on objective rational thinking and behaviour." In other words, they can engage with race or colonialism without putting themselves in the picture and recognizing the embodied, lived aspects of their privilege. Moreton-Robinson's analysis deeply informs mine. I not only adapt her methodology to consider the ways in which white participants grapple with being settlers, but I also consider the problems that can ensue when white women unintentionally adopt an individualistic orientation toward the solidarity encounter.

Indigenous scholars also fault mainstream feminism's depoliticization of difference, which only reinforces the invisibility of Indigenous women. Moreton-Robinson (2000, xviii) finds that, despite claims to the contrary, a "deracialized but gendered universal subject" still buttresses white feminist claims about so-called difference. On a slightly different note, Sandy Grande (Quechua) (2004, 138) maintains that the linguistic turn in third-wave feminism can deflect attention away from colonial power inequities by evacuating feminist terrain of political struggle and populating it instead with "decentred subjects" more concerned with "struggle over language and representation." Both Moreton-Robinson and Grande are ultimately concerned with the disavowal and hence perpetuation of power inequities among women/feminists. The upshot, they argue, is a feminist praxis that remains overly concerned with the interests of white middle-class women of Euro-American descent (see also Johnson, Stevenson, and Greschner 1993; Stewart-Harawira 2007). My analysis points to instances when white women doing solidarity work appear to wield, knowingly or otherwise, tactics such as relativizing oppressions and thus risk prolonging a fraught relationship between Indigenous women and white women.

Unsurprisingly, Indigenous women have balked at the need to explain themselves in whitestream feminist terms, that is, to prioritize gender (and patriarchy) over other facets of their lives. Kanien'kehá:ka lawyer, educator, writer, and scholar Patricia Monture objects to defining herself "negatively," that is, in relation to whiteness by default (Turpel 1993, 187). Instead, Monture (1995) and many others describe race and gender as inextricably bound up in their sense of themselves as individuals and nations. Indeed, Indigenous feminist epistemologies posit an abiding connection between self, family, community, nation, and Creation (Anderson 2000; Cordova 2004; Simpson 2017; Waters 2004a). Cree scholar Winona Stevenson recounts her exasperation with (white) feminists who promote the notion of a common oppression among women, implying that colonial oppression creates a stronger bond with her male relatives than does gender oppression with non-Indigenous women (quoted in Johnson, Stevenson, and Greschner 1993, 167). These scholars strike at the heart of whitestream feminist praxis, which tends to privilege gender/patriarchy but downplay or even omit colonialism, and sometimes racism or classism, as an analytical category for conceptualizing women's oppression (Monture-Angus 1995; Ouellette 2002). This disregard indicates a broader failure among white feminists to interpret histories of gender relations beyond a European-based model on their own terms. The result is a misguided or inadequate understanding of the devastating impact of colonialism on those relations – often described with regard to the imposition of patriarchal gender norms and Christian values onto Indigenous nations and the dismantling of more equitable gender relations.[32] While Indigenous scholars debate the extent to which heteropatriarchy and sexism are colonial inventions, all agree that sex/gender discrimination is now an indisputable reality in Indigenous communities that must be redressed (Green 2007c; St. Denis 2007).[33] As a result, Indigenous women have framed political efforts to amend the Indian Act and to redress violence against Indigenous women as Indigenous struggles for sex and gender equality.[34]

I am mainly concerned in this book with the implications of mainstream feminism not applying an anticolonial lens. After all, Indigenous women and women of colour in particular have long critiqued mainstream antiviolence movements for their ethnocentric perspectives (Beads with Kuokkanen 2007; Maracle 1996; Monture-Angus 1995; Turpel 1993; Vickers 2002). Such movements have not understood why Indigenous women tie antipatriarchal struggles against sexual and gender violence to anticolonial struggles for self-determination. In fact, the necessity of integrating antipatriarchal and anticolonial struggles is now an axiom of Indigenous feminism (FIMI 2006; Green 2007a, 2017b; Jaimes Guerrero 1997; Kauanui 2017;

Kuokkanen 2012, 2019; Lawrence 2003; Maracle 2006; Mihesuah 2003; Million 2008; Monture-Angus 1995; Ouellette 2002; Sunseri 2000).[35] Simply put, when whitestream feminism is unable or refuses to link Indigenous women's empowerment to that of their communities, solidarity work can fall short. More relevant to my argument, white women/feminist praxis that lacks an anticolonial lens will occlude the complicity of white women in colonial processes (see Flowers 2015; Anderson 2000; Monture-Angus 1995; Moreton-Robinson 2000; Grande 2004; Lawrence and Dua 2005).

In their discussions of the ethnocentric, universalizing, and exclusionary elements of some feminisms, many Indigenous scholars express indebtedness to Black feminist thought and women of colour scholarship more broadly (Maracle 1996; Settee, cited in Rebick 2005; Simpson 2017; St. Denis 2007; Sunseri 2008; Turpel 1993). The theoretical advances of this vast literature also find echoes in this book.[36] For example, Black feminist scholarship on working across difference has indelibly shaped my assessment of solidarity relations. The ideas of Audre Lorde (2007, 123) saturate the fabric of my weave of solidarity's potential: "We sharpen self-definition by exposing the self in work and struggle together with those whom we define as different from ourselves, although sharing the same goals. For Black and white, old and young, lesbian and heterosexual women alike, this can mean new paths to our survival." I adhere to Lorde's belief in our potential to identify and achieve common goals through collective struggle. However, as Bernice Johnson Reagon (1983, 356) reminds us in a seminal piece on coalitions, despite their indispensability to the pursuit of social justice, coalitions are neither inherently easy nor safe, but threatening "to the core" for those involved. In other words, our very sense of self is often at stake – a central starting assumption of this book. bell hooks (2000) also acknowledges the exceedingly difficult but vital nature of working across difference. Adamant that neither women's common oppression or automatic sisterhood are givens, hooks firmly believes feminist political solidarity can – and must – be forged as a prerequisite for transforming society. For these visionary thinkers, what matters is how we conceive of and what we do with the undeniable differences between us: transformative potential is unleashed not through the formation of power-laden hierarchies out of differences but rather through the creative mingling of non-hierarchical differences (Lorde 2007). Likewise, for me, the real issue is how – not whether – white women should approach solidarity work with Indigenous peoples.

The concept of intersecting or interlocking oppressions also underpins my analysis (Combahee River Collective 1979; Crenshaw 1991; Hill

Collins 2000; hooks 2000; Smith 1983). As critical race feminist scholar Sherene Razack (1998, 14) explains, when women fail to understand oppressions as mutually constitutive, "we fail to realize that we cannot undo our own marginality without simultaneously undoing all the systems of oppression." In a coauthored publication of the same year, Mary Louise Fellows and Razack (1998) point to a major obstacle to understanding the interlocking nature of power: the "race to innocence" that results when women focus on their subordinate rather than structurally dominant position, an idea I apply when analyzing white exceptionalism as it relates to proximity desires. My logic in this book hinges on the practical directive embedded in understanding oppression and difference in these ways: rather than focus on cultural differences, dominant subjects (in this case, white women) would do well to focus on historically derived, structural power differences and how they are sustained through, for instance, white women's self-making projects (Razack 1998). As hooks (2000) points out, conceptualizing difference in cultural terms alone does not necessarily lead to identifying power differences or altering the material, exploitative consequences of "Othering."

Working effectively across difference requires all women, especially those with relative privilege, to attend to power relations between women. Accordingly, if I aim to analyze the effects of white settler colonialism on solidarity work, a close analysis of white women's negotiations of their structural privilege is in order. As Razack (1998, 21) writes, "Tracing complicity thus begins with a mapping of relations among women. We can then critically examine those constructs that homogenize our differences or package them as innate, decontextualized, and ahistorical." Returning to the story, I grounded my research in this insistence on mapping relations among women and understanding how oppressions interlock, in the hopes of developing a blueprint for making colonialism foundational to feminist praxis. In conjunction, Indigenous scholarship pushed me to ask *why* white women might find it hard to consistently adopt an anticolonial feminist lens. Might this difficulty stem from the historical involvement of white women in colonial/imperial projects? In other words, how has the evolution of a particular combination of gender, race, and class – the white settler woman subject – affected white women's self-perception as actors in contemporary solidarity encounters? I then had to fashion a theoretical approach that would allow me to examine the nuances of gendered colonial subjectivity – white women's proscribed roles in settler colonial contexts and everything that goes into how we negotiate them in the solidarity encounter.

Theorizing Gendered Colonial Subjectivity

Theoretically speaking, what does it mean to say that our very sense of self is at stake in solidarity encounters? Let me begin with a fundamental premise that dwells at the heart of this book: we cannot detach ourselves from or transcend the power structures around us; but we can, and do, shape and alter those structures. Moreover, because individuals and groups form in relation to other individuals and groups through discursive interactions, individual and collective subjectivities are interdependent (Boyd 2004). Hence, my repeated refrain throughout these pages that the seemingly individual desires, motivations, and behaviours of white women in solidarity encounters both mirror and shape our collective sense of what it means to be a white settler woman. When mindful of this two-way street, I suggest, we are better able to decentre our white settler selves in solidarity work and recognize our desire for belonging for what it is: largely a consequence of our structural position as members of a white settler collectivity.

I conceptualize subject positions as historically and discursively produced structural positions that reflect and consolidate power, endowing people with or stripping them of privilege, regardless of individual intentionality. Nonetheless, subject positions are impermanent states that we collectively construct over time through our attempts to "occupy" or "perform" them – leading to my next point. People exercise agency to "inhabit" (Mahmood 2011) the subject positions into which they are "interpellated" to varying degrees, at varying moments, and often contradictorily. This means there is room for manoeuvring. In short, I agree with Battell Lowman and Barker (2015, 16) when they claim, "individual choices and efforts building to collective action are required to create change." By rendering agency in this way, I hold the door open for white settler engagement in non-colonizing solidarity.

In this book, however, I take issue with a sharply contrasting assertion about subjectivity, what Leanne Betasamosake Simpson (2017, 154) describes as a "hyperindividualism that negates relationality." This is the sense of self that lurks in the shadows of solidarity work. As philosopher of education scholar Dwight Boyd (2004, 6) explains, this particular rendition of the liberal self has developed over the past five hundred years into a "tendency to focus on all forms of social interaction through the lens of the discrete individual" (read: pull yourself up by your bootstraps). In what amounts to a fictive, abstract, and idealized account of the self, human beings are endowed with four features – ontological uniqueness (as disembodied, discrete individuals), symmetrical positioning (as equals), intentional rational agency (reason), and the capacity for transcendence (of power structures) (Boyd 2004, 9–11). Operating under these rules limits our ability to fathom power hierarchies, let alone see ourselves as privileged members of a structurally dominant group such as white settlers (Boyd 2004). While I do note instances of white women's hyperindividualism in solidarity encounters, I also identify moments when we are prepared to perceive ourselves as members of a dominant collectivity. At the same time, the bricks and mortar of settler colonial logic (or, more accurately, illogic) can stymie even the best intentioned among us.

Fine-Tethered Friends: Whiteness, Colonialism, and the Liberal Subject

As I demonstrate in my analysis of the solidarity encounter, Patrick Wolfe's (2006) assertion that settler colonialism is a structure and not an event has direct implications for settler identity and behaviour. The dynamics go something like this: solidarity encounters are not one-offs or isolated events, but rather relationships occurring under the influence of the settler colonial state. Moreover, Canada's project to sustain its own permanence requires settlers to adopt a particular subject position or set of assumptions about themselves. As gender studies scholar and anthropologist Scott Morgensen (2011, 16) explains, settler colonialism enjoins settlers to engage in a particular act of self-making, that is, to "naturalize their presence on Native land as rightful, final occupants so that the question of conquest can appear to be 'settled'" (see also Veracini 2011). In short, we must convince ourselves, and one another, that we "belong" here. The matter appears far from settled, however. The inherent instability of a community/nation built on stolen Indigenous land cannot help but plague us, even provoking in some an identity crisis "born of [this] psychic and material need to emplace himself" (Razack 2011, 266). This is the desire for legitimacy/permanence referred to throughout this book, a desire that must be continuously mollified by denying colonial power hierarchies (Ahmed 2000). Through this disavowal, most settlers avert a crisis of belonging, even as it lies dormant. However, settler anxieties can surface for a variety of reasons, not least in the presence of Indigenous self-determination that poses "a threat to one's sense of self, of belonging and a hoped for ethical future," as Lisa Slater (2019, 22) says about Australian "good white people." Battell Lowman and Barker (2015, 95) draw a similar conclusion in their gripping analysis of settler subjectivity in Canada: "Seeing the indefensibility of colonialism, the dishonesty of defining national narratives, the threat of being illegitimate on the land" can shatter a settler's sense of belonging (see also Mackey 2016). Solidarity work may in fact do just that. By bringing colonial realities into sharp relief, it can cause the crisis to bubble up to the surface and reach a boiling point. While self-making through settler emplacement takes a variety of forms, in this book I chart some of the paths and fault lines of white women's self-making as it unfolds in the solidarity encounter.

I want to flag once again the distinction between settler desires for legitimacy or belonging, which are precarious by definition in settler colonial contexts, and the righteous desire to engage ethically with Indigenous peoples. Indeed, the coexistence, intermingling, and resulting clash of these desires – within and between subjects – is emblematic of the paradox of attempting solidarity in the colonial present and is at the very centre of this book. For this reason, I propose that understanding the white settler desire for belonging in its collective dimension could diminish its power and clear the path for ethical solidarity.

The women I spoke to offer evidence to suggest that truisms about gender, whiteness, colonialism, and Western individualism can combine to impede settler paths to ethical engagement with Indigenous peoples. Along these lines, a cross-disciplinary chorus of scholars argues that white settler/liberal subjectivity is essentially an amalgam.[37] For instance, postcolonial feminist scholar Meyda Yeğenoğlu (1998, 95) describes how ideas about progress, modernization, white supremacy, and universalism associated with the Enlightenment also acted as "legitimizing categories in the civilizing mission of colonial power." The Latin American Modernity/coloniality (M/C) group goes further, positing that Iberian colonial enterprises enabled post-Enlightenment modernity in the first place, thus ushering in the race and gender hierarchies that continue to underpin settler/liberal subjectivity.[38] In other words, the liberal subject comes into being in the colonial moment. I begin the next chapter by considering why this confluence of colonial and liberal subjectivity matters to the solidarity encounter. In fact, I suggest that white women are prone, though not inevitably, to adopt a settler/liberal outlook even prior to entering the encounter.

Saving Others to Save Themselves: Gendering the Subject
The next step was to gender white settler/liberal subjectivity, which required tracing the historical antecedents of white woman self-making. For this, I looked to Maracle's (1993, 126) characteristically direct and incisive analysis: "Nationalism and racism infused life into patriarchy and bent the

direction of [Euro-Canadian] feminism before it was ever fully conceived." In other words, middle- to upper-class white women in a majority-white women's movement sought "white male status," that is, inclusion into the broadly liberal, racist terms of the British Empire and, later, Canadian settler colonialism. They typically did this by embracing the role of saviour or helper to more oppressed women – whether at home or abroad. In Chapter 2 especially, I develop the concept of the solidarity impulse to consider the complicated effects of this history (see also "Proximity and Its Discontents" above). To summarize, this impulse refers to the white woman drive to satiate the desire for proximity to Indigenous women through solidarity work. Importantly, I argue that this impulse flows from a particular historical formulation of gendered colonial subjectivity, which I condense into the next five paragraphs.

This complex story has a multitude of diverse actors on both sides of the imperial/colonial divide, including some who straddled that divide.[39] Nonetheless, in post-Enlightenment colonial modernity, race conferred white women more power, however circumscribed, than that of their nonwhite counterparts. White women were to be the "mothers of the race" (Valverde 1992) – or working-class servants to those mothers – in British imperial pursuits. They were to model racialized thinking, "middle-class morality, nationalist sentiments, bourgeois sensibilities, normalized sexuality, and a carefully circumscribed 'milieu' in school and home" (Stoler 1995, 105). Especially apropos to this book, they were to espouse "the values of liberal rationality" (McClintock 1995, 168). In what would become Canada, many white women also played pivotal roles in securing empire and, later, nationhood.[40] For Leanne Betasamosake Simpson (2017, 97), figures such as Susanna Moodie represent the white settler woman who could harness race privilege over gender subordination to advance her status in a fledgling nation.[41]

Nevertheless, white protofeminists were in a bind, needing to negotiate their "double positioning" (Loomba 2005) as "the inferior sex in the superior race" (Burton 1994).[42] As feminist historian Inderpal Grewal (1996, 58) implies, it is no small irony that the same women who fought patriarchy upheld England's white supremacist, imperialist pursuits. Even the most progressive white woman would have capitulated to the "colonial realm and imperial habitus" of the day (Grewal 1996, 80).[43] In fact, the central strategy of liberation was to overcome one's subordinate gender status through embracing one's dominant racial status (Burton 1994; Grewal 1996; Lewis 1996; Loomba 2005; Valverde 1992; Ware 1992).[44]

In a word, their paradoxical positioning as marginalized by gender and privileged by race meant that Euro-Canadian white protofeminists were cast in a particular role in colonial modernity – as the saviours of purportedly more inferior women (Burton 1994). Indeed, white women were not automatically welcomed into the post-Enlightenment club. They entered modernity as universal, rights-bearing subjects by deeming themselves better than and thus equipped to help women elsewhere. This, according to Grewal (1996, 63), was the function of the British colonies; there, Englishwomen could prove their racial superiority and assume their place in what was "conceived of as a heterosexual and masculinist project." In short, they embraced the heteropatriarchal, racist terms of empire.

For these reasons, Euro-Canadian feminism and white women's "freedom" in colonial modernity have turned on a deep contradiction: our freedom at the expense of the "freedom and autonomy of native cultures" (Yeğenoğlu 1998, 96). Yeğenoğlu (1998, 103) explains the paradox of universalism, how white Western women learn to think of ourselves as autonomous individuals. Subscribing to a false freedom–unfreedom binary, we locate ourselves on the side of freedom – as paragons of womanly virtue, goodness, and benevolence – notwithstanding the oppressive material conditions of many white women's lives.[45] In this picture, we get to represent the universal category "woman" by relegating other women such as Indigenous women to the "particular."[46] Because the universalizing gesture is available to Western women precisely through the moment of colonial modernity, Yeğenoğlu, like Maracle (1993) before her, argues that mainstream Western feminism is colonial at its root.

To round out this discussion of gendered colonial subjectivity, I turn to Gayatri Spivak's (1985, 244–45) neat wrap-up of the ultimate prize in subject making for white settler/imperialist women at the time – individualistic personhood in "two registers: childbearing and soul-making. The first is domestic-society-through-sexual reproduction cathected as 'compassionate love'; the second is the imperialist project cathected as civil-society-through-social mission." In simpler terms, the white settler/imperialist woman is charged with double duty, that is, the reproduction of the white race in both literal (child-making) and figurative (soul-making) terms.

In light of this history, I considered what has become of this civilizing imperative in the solidarity encounter. Do white women still want access to a white, bourgeois men's club that still denies us entry? Does our position as the "inferior sex in the superior race" (Burton 1994) still trigger a desire to see ourselves as less oppressed than, superior to, and capable of "helping" Indigenous women? How might this desire simultaneously comingle with solidarity work and the desire for belonging? Chapter by chapter, I address these and other questions by mounting an argument about the complexities of the solidarity impulse – the gendered colonial drive to satiate our desires for proximity through solidarity work. Throughout, I highlight some of the ways in which white women are consciously – and conscientiously – reckoning with that subjectivity.

A Not-So-Trivial Pursuit: Proximity and the White Woman
To think about the actual practices of proximity – what white women might think, feel, and do to (re)position ourselves as modern settler/liberal subjects who "belong" – I turned to one of Sara Ahmed's earlier works, *Strange Encounters: Embodied Others in Post-coloniality*. Ahmed (2000, 12) defines colonial encounters as strange encounters that "involve, at one and the same time, social and spatial relations of distance and proximity." Most intriguingly for Ahmed, these encounters themselves set off a dynamic through which dominant groups come to think of themselves as superior to "strangers" (read: inferior Others). Ahmed (2000, 5) refers to this as stranger fetishism, the process by which dominant groups sever so-called strangers "from the social and material relations which overdetermine their existence" and simply know them as always already inferior. Dominant subjects forget the historical "processes of inclusion and exclusion, or incorporation and expulsion" that made them dominant in the first place (Ahmed 2000, 6). As a result, Others/strangers magically appear as different/inferior. This obfuscation of histories of structural (dis)advantage afford dominant subjects a sense of innocence.

This imaginary element – the dominant subject's capacity to remain wilfully ignorant of historical power relations – is what I find most revelatory for my purposes. Drawing on Ahmed, I theorize the solidarity encounter as a mode of proximity where there is a considerable, though never absolute, risk that stranger fetishism will kick in. When it does, I argue, stranger fetishism can obscure colonial relations and, along with them, white women's self-perceptions as members of a settler collectivity, leaving only atomistic liberal individuals in the wake. In fact, Ahmed's dominant subject is the classic settler/liberal subject of colonial modernity, brimming with fantasies of autonomy and transcendence. Like Dwight Boyd (2004), Aileen Moreton-Robinson (2000), and others, Ahmed debunks the ideal of the Western liberal subject personified by a white man with the rational capacity to know Others and move unrestricted through social or geographical spaces. Drawing on such approaches, I consider if and how settler self-making involves masking colonialism's "histories of determination" (Ahmed 2000, 31–32) – precisely what must happen for settler colonialism to become and remain naturalized (Morgensen 2011).

There is another aspect of stranger fetishism I find particularly useful, which is the phenomenon of "going strange, going native" (Ahmed 2000, 115). Importantly, the three main techniques of going strange, going native are "consuming, becoming and passing," which all involve proximity/closeness.[47] In Chapter 1, I "gender" Ahmed's account to consider how white women's desires for proximity can work in solidarity encounters to (re)produce gendered colonial subjectivity. I then examine how white women sometimes employ these and other techniques – including calls for friendship and acquiring knowledge of the Other – to reinstall settler dominance by (re)concealing settler colonial "histories of determination." Put another way, I underline ways in which white women sometimes mobilize proximity in attempts to transcend settler colonialism. In Chapter 2, I draw on Indigenous participant narratives to delineate the problem with proximity, namely, the invasive transgression of boundaries when that pursuit goes too far. In Chapter 3, I home in on the fantasy of "becoming other," where settlers seek to inhabit all things Indigenous – a fair summary of settler colonialism's essence. I also discuss the often convoluted paths settlers, and white women in particular, sometimes take – using Indigenous people as the vehicle – to reaffirm their sense of belonging on Indigenous land.

To summarize, white women are at risk of operationalizing white settler/liberal subjectivity's central dynamic – a deeply entrenched desire for legitimacy and belonging – through pursuing proximity to Indigenous women. Underpinning our pursuit are gendered assumptions about white women as the good helpers of Other women. Throughout this book, I discuss why this role can be extremely difficult to give up for many white women attempting solidarity work. Like most stories, however, this one is complicated. Thus, I consider the twists and turns of solidarity work or, more aptly, how white women negotiate our double positioning while in the solidarity encounter, which includes struggling with the solidarity impulse.

Reversing the Gaze: Encountering Methods

I start my course on Indigenous feminisms by warning students about the risk of focusing on "damage-centered studies, rescue research, and pain tourism," as put by education scholars Eve Tuck and K. Wayne Yang (2014, 812). In this book, I heed this warning by not focusing on Indigenous women's oppression but instead applying a central tenet of Indigenous feminism, which is to scrutinize colonial dynamics, in this case, those that infuse solidarity work, to keep colonial privilege in view (Arvin, Tuck, and Morrill 2013; Green 2017a). In other words, I have sought to engage in "reversing the gaze."[48]

While my years of human rights activism from the 1990s onward in the United States and Central America inform this book, it is a direct result of over a decade of scholar activism begun on February 14, 2006, when I attended NMS's first annual Strawberry Ceremony. I have been essentially "in the field" ever since, attending community events and various organizations' activities, collecting NMS-related documents, and keeping a personal journal. When it came time to conduct formal research, however, and in part to balance the trade-offs between insider and outsider status (D'Arcangelis 2015, 2018), I opted not to pursue NMS as a case study. Instead, I decided to examine the solidarity encounter per se and to interview women involved in the work with or without an organizational affiliation. I began my formal fieldwork, including participant observation, in fall 2008. From May to July 2011, I conducted in-depth interviews with thirteen self-identified Indigenous women and eleven self-identified white women who had done solidarity work in and around the GTA. Taking a narrative ethnographic approach, I drew judiciously on my life history, often as recounted in my journals, to consider what it might indicate about white women's collective subjectivity and investments in solidarity. I integrated these data by applying a feminist critical discourse analysis (Bacchi 2005; Gavey 1989).

As mentioned, this research has a specific geopolitical reference point – the GTA – and speaks best to the dynamics of Indigenous–non-Indigenous solidarity work in that context. My conclusions may, or may not, apply to other parts of Canada where colonial histories and present-day Indigenous–non-Indigenous demographics vary considerably. I share my analysis, and ask the reader to consider it, with these important differences in mind. Moreover, as qualitative research, I never meant the study to be representative of all women who engage in solidarity work. Rather, I present but a small window into what is a much broader phenomenon.

The Participants
I hold immense gratitude for the twenty-four women whose interviews provide the mainstay for this book. All participants were at least eighteen years old and had engaged in solidarity for six months or longer "around topics

including (but not limited to) violence against Indigenous women, Indigenous land reclamations, and environmental justice," as worded in my call for participants (CFP). The majority lived, worked, or attended university in the GTA, but three Indigenous women and two white women lived in nearby urban centres and had connections to individuals and solidarity networks in the GTA. While email and social media were useful for recruiting white participants (six of whom answered my CFP and were unknown to me prior to the research), I mobilized personal contacts to recruit nine of the thirteen Indigenous participants. Had it not been for my insider status in solidarity circles, this research would simply not have been possible.

My CFP described the project in general terms as "research on the limits and possibilities of political alliances or solidarity between Indigenous women and white women." I purposively brought to bear an ample and explicitly material definition of political solidarity to mean a broad array of practices in which people engage together to pursue a political goal.[49] These practices include common elicitations of political protest and mobilizations for social justice and the less visible practices of grassroots groups such as NMS, practices such as behind-the-scenes lobbying, group meetings, social events, email exchange, and the use of social-media platforms. I would be remiss not to add to the mix politicized art such as posters, billboards, art installations, or music videos. Some examples from my own experiences give a better sense of what I mean by the materiality of solidarity work.

I distinctly remember my very first, very snowy February 14 Strawberry Ceremony at Toronto Police Headquarters as a member of NMS. I was seven months pregnant and the designated police liaison; it was my job to mediate any encounters, tense or otherwise, with officers should the need arise. Most years after that, I handed out strawberries and water to the people in attendance. I took part in other more mundane activities such as shopping, cooking, and serving food at meetings. On occasion, I represented NMS at film screenings, distributed leaflets at non-NMS events, and raised money for various purposes, such as hosting the women of Walk 4 Justice.

Whenever possible, within the limits dictated by participant anonymity, I contextualize participants' statements about solidarity work in relation to these sorts of activities and settings. For the purposes of this book, I define political solidarity and the solidarity encounter in terms of "long-term commitment to structural change" (Arvin, Tuck, and Morrill 2012, 19; see also Flowers 2015; hooks 2000; Snelgrove, Dhamoon, and Corntassel 2014, 19, 24). As gleaned from their descriptions of solidarity work, I am confident that participants shared this baseline understanding of political solidarity.

At the time of the interviews, most participants had been involved in solidarity work for at least two years, and a high percentage – over half of the Indigenous participants and just under half of the white participants – had ten or more years of experience in political organizing around a myriad of issues. While I included women with or without a group affiliation, many had such affiliations. Taking all these factors into account, participants fell into three nondiscrete categories: (1) those who were members of (often multiple) social-justice groups, which included most participants; (2) those who regularly volunteered for or participated in a variety of political actions such as marches or vigils without necessarily any group affiliation, which included many participants; and (3) those whose exposure to solidarity work occurred in educational, paid employment, or artistic contexts, which described a minority of participants.

I relied exclusively on participants to self-identify as Indigenous or white women and note this general self-identification whenever I mention a particular participant. Because five participants, all Indigenous women – Zainab Amadahy (Cherokee, Seminole), Ruth Green (Kanien'kehá:ka), Lee Maracle (Stó:lō/Métis), Rebeka Tabobondung (Anishinaabe) and Wanda Whitebird (Mi'kmaq) – waived their right to anonymity, I refer to them by last name and also identify their Indigenous nation. I use first-name pseudonyms for the other nineteen participants, namely in alphabetical order, Ardra, Belinda, Danielle, Gabriela, Kellie, Lydia, Teresa, and Ursula (Indigenous participants); and Alicia, Carla, Chloe, Darcie, Dawn, Eve, Evelyn, Julia, Peggy, Rachel, and Sarah (white participants). While I did not exclude anyone who identified as mixed race, I did not use this identity marker in the CFP, mainly because of historical and ongoing settler state regulation of Indigenous identity and status where "mixed" can be misinterpreted by authorities and the (settler) public as "inauthentic" (Lawrence 2003; Morgensen 2011). That said, six of the thirteen Indigenous participants acknowledged mixed (Indigenous and European) ancestry even as they foregrounded their identity and experiences as Indigenous women. While only one of the eleven white participants mentioned having Indigenous ancestry, several discussed their mixed European ancestry. Admittedly, the absence of mixed as a possible identity in my CFP could have had the effect of discouraging some women from participating in the study.

In most ways, participants were *not* representative of the general population, except in terms of their ages, which ranged from twenty to sixty-five years. A disproportionately high percentage, roughly two-thirds, of both Indigenous women and white women had postsecondary education, which is likely because of my social circles as a PhD student and because of the high number of universities in the GTA. Additionally, conducting the study in an urban setting led to an overrepresentation of urban dwellers (though most Indigenous participants had ties with a nearby reserve or Indigenous community outside the province). Only two women (one from each group) self-identified as members of an LGBTQ2S+ community. Perhaps most importantly, the women constituted a self-selected group potentially predisposed to seeing the benefits of attempting solidarity between Indigenous peoples and (white) settler populations. This predilection, however, makes any critical views of solidarity relations all the more potent. As became evident in my analysis, participant narratives collectively reflected an extensive wealth of knowledge and a remarkable level of comfort and self-reflection in discussing the perils and promises of solidarity work. A number of participants were fluent and fluid in their use of activist and scholarly discourses. In this book, I attempt to do justice to this knowledge by tracking some of the more striking discursive patterns in their narratives.

Reading Proximity in the Solidarity Encounter
The intimate reach of this research has the potential to elicit strong reactions in readers. The first audience, of course, was the participants themselves. Following custom in qualitative research, I offered all women copies of their interview transcripts. Whereas only three requested the full transcripts of their respective interviews, a majority (fifteen women) wanted to review the passages in which I referenced their interviews using direct quotations. All participants also received a summary of the findings, which occasioned positive feedback overall. In fact, several women from both groups mentioned that the findings resonated for them. I had follow-up phone conversations, email exchanges, and face-to-face meetings with several people, five of whom had questions about my interpretation of their narratives. When warranted, I deleted or altered passages in response to their comments. While not always easy, these exchanges did more than sharpen my ideas: they were powerful reminders of the intensity of people's lived realities and of my responsibility as a researcher to recount these realities with integrity.

One of the most formidable methodological challenges I faced was how to ask about abstract concepts such as subjectivity or the negotiation of subject position. I learned what *not* to do through trial and error after encountering silence with certain questions. In the end, it was much more useful to ask people about four overarching themes: what led them to do solidarity work; what were the tensions, challenges, or power dynamics of that work;

what if any steps had they or others taken to foster non-colonizing solidarity; and what ways had solidarity work transformed them either individually or collectively. I modelled my methodology on Aileen Moreton-Robinson's (2000, xxii–xxiii) study of feminist praxis in Australia, which compares and contrasts "the self-presentation and representation of the subject positions 'middle-class white woman' and 'Indigenous woman' … [to] provide a context for different bodies of knowledge to meet and disrupt each other." Putting participant self-presentations alongside their representations of others' involvement in solidarity work gave me a sense of the solidarity encounter's intersubjective dynamics. I then analyzed discursive themes across questions, which allowed certain solidarity dynamics to emerge that might have otherwise eluded scrutiny.

In fact, I did not anticipate the central theme of this book: white women's desires for proximity to Indigenous women. None of the interview questions mentioned proximity nor was the term per se raised in discussion. As I discuss in Chapters 1 and 2, proximity as a theme surfaced only when I juxtaposed the two sets of narratives: Indigenous women's representations of white women and white women's self-presentations. In effect, I found myself interpreting Indigenous descriptions of the solidarity encounter's challenges side by side with white women's self-ascribed reasons for engaging in the work. The bulk of my analysis involved unearthing what this juxtaposition reveals: a sometimes unacknowledged and often problematic aspect of gendered colonial subjectivity in solidarity work, which is white women's desires for and pursuit of proximity to Indigenous Others.

Before I launch into my analysis, I am compelled to issue three caveats. First, my goal has never been to make claims about individuals but rather to identify discursive patterns across participant narratives that indicate something about subject formation within broader relations of power, or what anthropologist Saba Mahmood (2011, 33) describes as "the historically contingent arrangements of power through which the normative subject is produced." My focus is the collective subject formation processes that constitute individual white women and the discourses available to them, for instance, autonomous liberal personhood. As Moreton-Robinson (2000, xxii) explains, dominant subject positions are "implicated in relations of ruling" and "represented in discourse through and beyond the activity and experience of individual subjects." For the record, my study of how white settler women think about ourselves and negotiate our positionalities is not about "the personal preferences and proclivities of the individual" (Mahmood 2011, 33). Instead, I consider what participants' expressed motivations for entering into solidarity work indicate about collective white settler woman subjectivity and the power relations at play. However, even as I point to the white desire to retain liberal-subject status as a key force in solidarity encounters, I am not suggesting a false homogeneity for white women, or Indigenous women for that matter. While I may highlight the collective, discursive construction of subject positions, I leave room for individual agency, that is, self-making as an ongoing process of grappling that occurs within certain discursive constraints.

The second caveat is about the possibility of oversimplifying participant narratives and overamplifying the white desire for proximity to Indigenous Others. I identified at least three other discourses related to women's motivations for entering into solidarity: responsibility and accountability; shared political analysis and social-justice inclinations; and practical or strategic motivations. To discuss proximity as a pattern across white participant narratives, I artificially disentangled our complex investments and motivations for engaging in solidarity work. Rarely do we describe or live our motivations in discrete terms; each participant described a multitude of often intertwined reasons for doing solidarity work. My analysis of the solidarity impulse focuses on the proximity-related dimensions of white women's involvement in solidarity.

My third and final caveat concerns one of my presuppositions about allyship prior to the research. I was operating with the common understanding of ally as "a member of an oppressor group who works to end a form of oppression which gives her or him privilege" (Bishop 2002, 152). However, I began to wonder about the unforeseen limitations or flaws in this definition. Might it prop up a patronizing one-way flow of solidarity as something bestowed to the "less privileged," thereby sustaining the very hierarchical relations it means to challenge? Does it preclude people outside of dominant groups, including Indigenous women, from being allies in struggle (Sullivan-Clarke 2020)? An exchange midway through one of my early interviews, with an Indigenous participant, sparked these concerns. When asked to define "ally," she inquired back, "As a white person or as a Native person?" Her response left me temporarily flabbergasted and, frankly, panicked. Had I been conceptualizing allyship in unidirectional terms the whole time? The subsequent reaction of another Indigenous participant struck me equally forcibly. Allyship was again the theme. I casually commented, "It's kind of interesting that we don't have a word to contrast with ally." She hesitated and said, "That's because allies are, I thought, equal – so there shouldn't be anything to contrast with ally." Only if you see solidarity work as charity, she clarified, would there be a contrasting concept: "The poor person, the injured, the grievance seeker, the person who has been aggrieved, the wounded, the victim, the helper versus the victim in the most classic patronizing way of doing solidarity." My self-doubt intensified: Had I already assigned white women the role of helper and Indigenous women the role of beneficiary?

Jolted into awareness of one of my deeply held orientations toward solidarity work, I modified my methods. From then on, I asked two questions – one about the role of Indigenous women as allies and another about the role of white women as allies – to disrupt presumptions about a one-sided flow of solidarity from white woman ally (as subject) to Indigenous woman (as object). I also began considering what if anything my belief indicated about a normative logic at work in the discourse of allyship, a sort of default modality for other white women. Does this logic cloak and therefore re-entrench the kinds of hierarchies solidarity is supposed to dismantle? This line of reasoning solidified a focal point of my research: If white women already think of themselves as autonomous/liberal subjects, how might that matter to the encounter? Does colonial "helping" behaviour itself flow from a liberal notion of the self? In other words, do common understandings of allyship presuppose an autonomous subject (the white settler woman) capable of assisting a downtrodden Other (Indigenous woman)? These are the kinds of questions that led to theorizing the solidarity impulse – a drive characterized by two concurring, seemingly contradictory desires on the part of white woman to "help" Indigenous women and "be helped by" solidarity work.

Map of Chapters

My theory of the solidarity encounter unfolds in five chapters. Throughout, I concentrate on the problems with proximity, or those sticking points that result when white women uncritically follow the colonial playbook. That is, when we inconsistently apply an anticolonial framework in solidarity work, certain outcomes are more likely, namely, the invasive behaviours and paternalistic attitudes derived from our historical role of "helper." In this way, I want to disrupt white settler/liberal business as usual and prepare ground "for the production of a new kind of [white settler woman] subject" (Razack 1998, 5) capable of extending non-colonizing solidarity.[50]

In Chapter 1, I develop one of the fundamental concepts of the book, the spectrum of proximity. The idea here is that white women doing solidarity work sometimes go to great lengths, conscious or otherwise, to pursue proximity to Indigenous women so they can continue to see themselves as autonomous/liberal subjects. In Chapter 2, I feature Indigenous participant narratives to reveal the problem with proximity, or the invasive dimensions of this pursuit, and solidify my main argument: the white woman's pursuit of proximity to Indigenous women is destructive when it transgresses boundaries – material, intersubjective, or epistemic – and leads to colonizing forms of solidarity, as defined by Indigenous women. I also tease apart the site-specific complexities of intersubjective dynamics in solidarity encounters, coining the phrase impulse to solidarity to refer to the operation of gendered colonial subjectivity. The sequence of Chapters 1 and 2 reflects my methodological process over time. Only after months of poring over interview transcripts was I struck by how consistently Indigenous women found some white women's behaviours and reasons for engaging in solidarity work to be problematic – even invasive. By presenting my spectrum of proximity first, I provide the framing needed to contextualize Indigenous women's commentaries, giving them the final word, as it were.

In Chapter 3, I continue my exposé of the problem with proximity by homing in on an element of the proximity spectrum – an attraction to or appreciation of Indigenous culture, tradition, or spirituality. By tracking the complex discursive moves from appreciation to appropriation in the interests of white settler self-making and Canadian nation building, this chapter sheds light on the deeply embedded collective practices and dynamics that constitute white settler/liberal subjectivity. In Chapter 4, I focus on the ways in which race, specifically whiteness, coupled with gender can mark gendered colonial subjectivity in the form of white guilt and moves to exceptionalism. I also consider the likelihood that a deep-seated desire for innocence underpins white guilt (when it emerges) as well as the fraught role of self-reflexivity in negotiating that desire.

In Chapter 5, I most directly attend to the practical implications of theorizing the solidarity encounter in the way that I do – as a place run rife with solidarity impulses. Drawing on participant insights, I propose a framework for non-colonizing solidarity that includes measures for rewriting colonial scripts, for disrupting or minimizing the reproduction of pernicious forms of gendered colonial subjectivity in solidarity work. It features a continual succession of self-reflexive double turns (Ahmed 2004) toward and away from the white settler back to the colonial structures – sociopolitical, religious, economic – requiring dismantlement (D'Arcangelis 2018). Intentionally avoiding overly prescriptive strategies, and in the methodological spirit of decolonial scholars Walter Mignolo and Catherine Walsh (2018), I aim to think *with* other white women and our Indigenous allies to develop context-specific non-colonizing solidarity practices. I hope this final chapter in particular spurs further reflection about and inspires a multitude of such practices.

1

The Spectrum of Proximity
White Women, Solidarity, and Settler/Liberal Self-Making

Dusk had settled, and empty chairs dotted the mostly vacated room of the Native Women's Resource Centre in Toronto. Tasked to clean up after a documentary film screening about violence against Indigenous women, I unintentionally eavesdropped on a conversation between two Indigenous women organizers of the event and a white woman I had once met in passing.

"Thank you for making me feel welcomed," the white woman said as she left.

After some mutual eye rolling, I talked with the Indigenous women about what had just happened. Although I might have been confused, they were not. They made it clear that she was another white woman who wanted to feel welcome in what she saw as an Indigenous space. For these Indigenous women, this exchange was not an isolated incident but typical of the kinds of solidarity encounters they have with some white women. I felt a swooning sense of self-righteousness, what I later heeded as a sign of my own desire to be exceptional, to be (seen as) a good settler who knows better than to make such statements.

~

What does this exchange – and my reaction to it – indicate about contemporary solidarity encounters? How does a white settler desire to feel welcome or belong on Indigenous land matter to these encounters?

Positioned for Encounter

As a key component of white settler/liberal subjectivity, the desire to belong mostly lies dormant, leaving intact the individual and collective identities of many white settlers. At some level, however, settlers remain haunted by a desire for legitimacy on stolen land that, by definition, is never permanently satisfied (Morgensen 2011). Plus, because white settler/liberal subjectivity seems largely unaware of itself, white people are apt to register the collective desire for belonging as simply "personal" or individualistic. White women in solidarity encounters are no exception; we enter the work (sometimes unknowingly) troubled by this same longing. What's more, my research suggests that solidarity encounters themselves – through providing white women with occasions for a sustained look at our colonial complicity – can provoke a crisis in and exacerbate the desire for legitimacy that marks us as settlers. In such instances, pursuing proximity to Indigenous women might ease this discomfort.

Thus, I begin by backing up ... to the moment when liberal individualism enters the scene. I do this to consider the ways in which Western individualism appears to mark the white woman subject and the possible consequences that has for anticolonial political struggle. I then scour white participant "fantasies of becoming" (Ahmed 2000), the sometimes fantastical stories we tell ourselves about who we are and how we got that way, for glimmerings of proximity desires. Interspersing white participant narrations of the solidarity encounter with my own, I paint a picture of how white women in these encounters, knowingly or otherwise, can deploy proximity in our self-making projects to achieve a sense of belonging on stolen Indigenous land.

As noted in the previous chapter, this book's main theme – white desires involving proximity – emerged out of participant perspectives on why women engaged in solidarity work and on the major tensions involved, and, less so, on how they were transformed in the process.[1] You will recall that my definition of political solidarity includes an array of practices undertaken by people working together toward a political end. While participants confirmed that their solidarity experiences fit these criteria, many clarified that they frequently use other terms – such as "relationships," "alliances," "collaborations," or, simply, "work" – instead of or in addition to "solidarity" to describe their involvement in political activism. When quoting participants, I use their preferred phrase(s).

At first glance, the reasons why Indigenous women and white women became politically active or engaged in solidarity do not appear much different. For instance, most participants were motivated to pursue social justice and, though fewer, several Indigenous women and white women talked about the existential importance of living and working together for all peoples. A closer look revealed a rather consequential divergence, however. Indigenous women tended to position themselves explicitly as members of a collectivity whose foray into political activism or solidarity stemmed from their responsibility to ensure the survival of that collectivity. However, white women tended to position themselves (ourselves), implicitly or otherwise, as individuals whose involvement in political activism or solidarity was a matter of personal choice.

None of this would surprise Aileen Moreton-Robinson, who argues that where we "sit" in relation to power structures informs what we (can) do and believe. As Moreton-Robinson (2000, 147) explains, "Having a place in the centre of white culture confers privilege and the capacity to be able to make choices about one's identity that is not accorded those positioned in the margins." She specifically addresses how white women's subject position affords them a certain wilful ignorance (the choice to not see themselves as members of a dominantly positioned collectivity), noting that this option stems from and enables a sense of liberal individualism. For Moreton-Robinson (2000, 12), in many instances colonial hierarchies trump other elements of difference, including class, to overdetermine Indigenous–non-Indigenous relations. To put it bluntly, odds are that white women are unlikely to reflect critically on our colonial complicity – especially before entering solidarity encounters. In a study of white pre-service teachers' performances of Canadian national identity, education scholar Carol Schick (1998, 172) also comments on the regulatory forces forestalling white attention to collective privilege, pointing to the "elaborately circuitous routes ... [that] keep subjects from saying anything that would cause them to confront directly their own complicity and racial privilege." The upshot? We would not expect sustained awareness among white women of their membership in a white settler collectivity.

My research both corroborates and complicates this conclusion. Clearly, it is hard for white women to persistently imagine ourselves as members of a collectivity and thereby to stay with our complicity in colonialism, notwithstanding our best efforts to do so. That said, white participants reported varying levels of awareness of their positionality and expended, in some cases, a great deal of energy to negotiate their dominant status. However, despite or perhaps because of this cognizance, white participants overall, myself included, can become haunted by our settler status and swayed toward positioning ourselves as individuals who could conceivably stand outside of colonialism. Indeed, as Emma Battell Lowman and Adam Barker (2015) imply, a heightened awareness of one's settler status brings into sharp relief the unattainability of belonging in a settler colonial context and, I argue, risks kicking the impulse to solidarity into hyperdrive.

White Settler Women and (the Language of) Privilege or Choice

One can get a sense of the divergence in Indigenous and non-Indigenous approaches to political activism in the narrative of Teresa, one of the thirteen Indigenous participants. We met on a chilly afternoon on her front porch, warmed by blankets, hot tea, and the treats I brought. With over twenty years of organizing experience, Teresa had lots to share. When asked if Indigenous women have a role to play as allies in the struggles of other women, she contrasted her communal orientation to political struggle as an Indigenous woman with what she understands as a Western propensity toward individualism:

> I think that with the birth of Protestantism and capitalism and that sense of individual gain, a lot of Western women have isolated themselves from community struggles. And it's become more of an "I" thing. [A] student ... asked me how I would define success, and it's not a personal thing, really, at all. Success for me is sovereignty for our nations and other nations, the freedom to have access to their own ideology in academic institutions, freedom to access information, clean drinking water, proper housing. On an international [level] would be ideal. First, we have to struggle for that for our own communities but at the same time try and draw those parallels of international struggles.

Indigenous narratives such as Teresa's suggest that there is indeed a default modality for white women entering solidarity encounters – liberal individualism. However, do white participant depictions of their political activism or solidarity work confirm or challenge this idea?

Tellingly, but perhaps unsurprisingly, when discussing their activist paths, not a single white participant described her involvement in solidarity work as a matter of collective survival. Also in contrast to Indigenous participants, white participants rarely talked of having found themselves propelled into solidarity work with little option. Instead, some white women described having the choice or the privilege of engaging in the work, without necessarily identifying their underlying responsibility to make that "choice" in the first place. Tucked away in an empty university classroom corner, Alicia and I talked about our circuitous paths to solidarity. At one point, Alicia compared her entry into Indigenous political solidarity with the activism of second-wave white feminists:

> Maybe ... it's a matter of me being spoiled that I have the luxury of time to be able to care about these things. Because I think that's a criticism of feminism is that it was spearheaded by white middle-class women who had the privilege to go out and fight for something. They weren't struggling with a baby on each arm and scrubbing a toilet at the same time and didn't have other constraints that would stop them ... They were educated; they had relative affluence, and so they had this privilege. In a sense, I see it for me as – maybe it's a privilege that I have the opportunity to care about an issue.

In this passage, and in the context of our overall exchange, Alicia clearly sees herself as a white woman exercising her relative privilege – but not necessarily structurally derived responsibility – in choosing to "care about" Indigenous women's issues. At the same time, the tone hovers perilously close to that of "helping" less fortunate Others, who may still be "struggling with a baby on each arm and scrubbing a toilet at the same time" in contrast to their white middle-class counterparts.[2]

Why does it matter how we conceptualize our decisions? What is the possible fallout? I venture this answer: The white woman who understands her privilege, and choices afforded by that privilege, in individualistic rather than structural terms is more apt to see Other women, including Indigenous women, as underprivileged rather than structurally oppressed and is perhaps more likely to adopt a saviour mentality as opposed to an anticolonial critique.

Mi'kmaq Elder Wanda Whitebird validated concerns that the discourse of privilege and personal or individual choice (as opposed to structural privilege and collective responsibility) can coax white women into a politics of saving. Whitebird lives in Toronto and is a member of the Paq'tnkek First Nation in Nova Scotia. She is a self-described "ceremonial practitioner in the Traditional ways of First Nations people. I embrace the philosophy of harm reduction or, as I like to call it, love for our people wherever they are on their journey healing from the genocide that colonialism has impacted on our people." During our interview, Whitebird drew on decades of experience ranging from frontline work in community agencies to grassroots organizing in groups such as No More Silence (NMS). We met on a marvellously sunny day along Toronto's harbourfront, full of squawking pigeons and sun-screen–drenched tourists. When discussing the vital role of Indigenous women as allies in other women's struggles, Whitebird recalled a white woman who may not have thought the matter through. In Whitebird's assessment, "I think she'd be surprised that [Indigenous people] live on the Queen's Quay [in downtown Toronto]. I think that she thinks that we're people who don't say anything, and we're all victims and we need saving." It is not a stretch to conclude that white women who think in terms of Indigenous victimization as opposed to collective struggle are less likely to recognize the structural dimension of their privilege.

Eve was another white participant who correlated personal choice and solidarity with little inference to structural privilege or responsibility. We chatted in her kitchen, which overlooked a typical (tiny) Toronto backyard. Eve's candour, a trait she shared with many participants, put me at ease. For her, alliances or coalitions did not constitute examples of political solidarity absent the element of choice. Eve contrasted her experience of solidarity-like relations with Indigenous women in the present with her solidarity experiences in the past:

> It could be [that I'm doing solidarity work now]. I just don't call it that, and I feel different about it because it was something that I have to do, as opposed to "I chose to do." That for me feels like a pretty fundamental difference … So it's not like I don't enjoy it; it's not like I'm not learning from it or I don't want to be there, but it was not something that we created together. It was something that I was brought into, in a way.

> I think, just like in any activist organizing, I think you should have the choice of who you want to work in solidarity with. In a coalition, it's much more difficult, but I would just make sure that I would have a choice in that. I think that's really important. I would also make sure that there is a basis of unity, or common understanding, or basis of solidarity around the fundamental reason why you're together, regardless to what that reason is.

Eve held that we should always be able to choose with whom to work in solidarity and presumably make that choice based on political conviction. In fact, NMS as a group takes this same position (D'Arcangelis and Huntley 2012).

However, more striking is what Eve left unexamined, and what Indigenous participant narratives did not – the structural privilege that enables choice on individualistic terms (Moreton-Robinson 2000). In fact, choice featured in both Alicia's and Eve's solidarity work in ways that differed from Indigenous women's descriptions of solidarity. In the latter, solidarity can be a default outcome or requisite aspect of political activism – whether because, as one Indigenous participant noted with ironic humour, there are "always white people involved, they always get in" (Belinda), or because Indigenous people out of necessity seek white allies for viable political action. Even so, white participants wrestle explicitly with their collective privilege in other ways.

Keeping the Personal Political: Grappling with Collective Privilege
To be certain, it is as individuals that both Indigenous women and white women decide to engage in solidarity work, if under distinct structural constraints. The difference, I argue, lies in the degree to which and how we invoke our membership in a broader collectivity. Admittedly, white participants varied in this regard. There were those like Alicia and Eve who explicitly cited a sense of individual privilege or personal choice as a motivating factor for engagement in solidarity. A few others implied personal responsibility as a motivating factor. Other narratives remained opaque. Yet only a minority of white participants explicitly cited their settler position – and by extension, structural privilege – as the main factor that propelled them to do solidarity work. These participants also tended to be overtly attentive to colonialism, which suggests a correlation between an anticolonial politic and a sense of one's responsibility or accountability as a member of a white settler collectivity. Even so, as I make evident in this and upcoming chapters, the discursive act of locating one's self in power relations is an ongoing and fraught process. Put another way, it is exceedingly difficult to keep structural privilege in view without taking things personally, as several Indigenous women emphasized, or without engaging in the kind of self-referential thinking that reproduces white settler/liberal subjectivity.

To appraise the challenge for white women of keeping the personal political in solidarity encounters, I turn first to the white participant narratives that most directly confront what it means to be a white settler woman in those encounters. Peggy's is among them.

Apart from the muffled voices of a few other customers and the occasional whirring of an expresso machine, Peggy and I sat undisturbed in your average local café. A veteran activist with over three decades of Indigenous solidarity work around a range of issues, from cultural resistance to land reclamations, Peggy's trajectory reminded me of my own; she, too, had an experience abroad in her twenties that profoundly altered her perception of her country of birth and prompted her political involvement with Indigenous women. As she recalled:

> It just made me look at Canada in a different ... see Canada much more clearly. And that just felt like ... Colonialism with Indigenous people is Canada's original sin. It's just like where it starts from ... But I do see North American colonialism against Indigenous people as kind of the foundation for a lot of other oppression. And for a certain structure of the state that has to be changed.

Moreover, Peggy has long acknowledged her settler status, together with that of her ancestors: "My ethnic background is predominately British Isles – Scots-Irish, English, Welsh. There's a little bit of Dutch, but it's mainly English. But my father's family, at any rate, arrived in North America in the 1600s, at least some branches of it. Some branches of my family have been here for a long time, thirteen generations."

Carla, who in her mid-twenties already had several years of activist experience under her belt, similarly related her lineage and settler status to her solidarity work with Indigenous women:

> I think that people who benefit from the privileges from a history of colonialism and ongoing colonialism owe it to themselves and the general population to try and make things better. And part of making things better is being in solidarity with people and trying to make radical change ... My mom's side ... is fourth-generation Canadian; on my dad's, I'm closer to seventh or eighth. And I do know he had relatives who came with the Hudson's Bay Company a couple hundred years ago. So dealing with Native issues for me is in direct relation with me knowing my background, my ancestry, my family's lineage.

Then there is Evelyn, who thought it imperative to educate herself extensively on Canada's colonial history before doing solidarity work. After our time expired in the library room booked for our interview, Evelyn and I relocated to a nearby, very, very, noisy, café. She remarked on the current state of Canadian colonial affairs:

> I'm living in a society ... my existence is predicated on oppressing other people, oppressing all sorts of people, globally as well as locally ... And,

there's lies; politicians are lying. It's an omission; it's lying by omission, not telling the whole story and not redressing past wrongs ... [Politicians are] playing an interesting game ... I think they're still trying to wipe Indigenous people out. The reason that the Truth and Reconciliation thing took so long is because they wanted more of the generations to die off, so they didn't have to make retribution, financial or otherwise.

Evelyn took pains to call herself a settler whenever doing solidarity work, especially online:

I always identify myself, particularly online, as a settler so that people know exactly where I'm coming from. I think that's a term that most people are aware of now. And it situates me in people's minds ... It lets people know that I know that I'm a newcomer, you know, that no matter if I'm third-generation Canadian, I'm a newcomer. I don't necessarily belong here. And I'm gonna, I'll accept that. I don't know how to redress that issue, but ...

Peggy, Carla, and Evelyn all explicitly situated themselves and their family histories in relation to the colonial project and, more or less explicitly, tied their decision to engage in solidarity work to this understanding of colonial realities, past and present.

However, the matter of how white women register their privilege is also important. The thing is, not all settlers can easily invoke personal narratives that involve multiple generations of "settlerhood," which raises the question, Could this sort of reckoning retain too much of a personal dimension? How much should settlers tie their responsibility and accountability to their personal family history versus their structural position (or both)? These questions beget others, including one I leave for Chapter 4: How do settlers with (or without) family histories contend with white settler guilt and the self-serving engagements in solidarity it can engender?

Like Carla, Julia located herself as a white woman who benefitted from the colonial dispossession of Indigenous peoples. A grey sky cast shadows, enlivening the metallic surfaces of the diner where we talked – mostly about Julia's time in a group comprised predominately of white women and Indigenous women, with a few men, both Indigenous and non-Indigenous:

My interest in that group was really around, as a white person, how do I benefit from that colonial experience of [Indigenous] people and how do I perpetuate that and how is it that I'm responsible to make some positive change in that regard? As white people, how do we continue to perpetuate that colonialism now? It's our responsibility to educate ourselves on that and to educate others. It's not the responsibility of the Indigenous folks to educate us. They've done enough of that.

As Patrick Wolfe (2006) would have it, Julia sees colonialism as an ongoing structure that generates a responsibility in the current political moment, among other things, to educate herself and other white people. When asked about the role of white women as allies in Indigenous women's struggles, she was just as forthright: "I think, first and foremost, it's that piece of understanding my unearned privilege ... I sit on this land. I sit as somebody who can walk in and not be criticized." Julia's narrative is among the few that most freely, explicitly, and repeatedly grapple with the participant's membership in a white settler collectivity.

However, it also speaks to the complex layers of gendered colonial subjectivity, particularly the plausibility of the ironic twist I consider in detail in the next chapter: increasing awareness of one's privilege can intensify the desire to equalize power relations through recourse to white settler/liberal ideas. Moreover, certain passages in Julia's narrative, and those of other white participants, read as attempts to present oneself as an exceptional white ally. As a preview to that argument, I can say that the effectiveness of acknowledging one's status as a white woman is dampened by the simultaneous claim of being exceptional, for example, as more colonially aware than most white people or uniquely situated to liaise between white and Indigenous peoples.

Sarah, another white participant, graciously hosted me at her home, where she was on maternity leave. Sitting there stirred up memories of my own daughter's infancy. Besides parenthood, we shared the experience of solidarity work around the issue of MMIWG2S people. Coincidentally, Sarah's narrative contains the most explicit mentions of colonial land theft:

> The land that we live on now is not our land. I really believe that that land was stolen, and there are all sorts of agreements that weren't honoured. So now we're living on stolen land, so when people come to this country from other countries, they're also living on land that is not theirs ... At the same time, these are people who are experiencing racism and violence in their own way, but are they ... can you say that they're participating in the colonization? I don't know. That's what's so interesting to me about the way that people can embody power and be victimized at the same time ... can both wield power and be powerless.

Having the wherewithal to name the elephant in the room – the unresolved matter of stolen land – is a strong move in the right direction toward considering one's structural privilege. At the same time, Sarah's narrative points to another risk I have seen play out in solidarity circles. Whether intentional or otherwise, the effect is the same, which is deflecting attention away from white settler structural privilege by switching to the contested topic of who counts as a settler. This can readily shift the conversation to the status of people of colour, and of immigrants and refugees, especially those racialized as nonwhite, in relation to Indigenous peoples.

Another potential source of distraction might surprise you. While many Indigenous participants encourage settlers to connect emotionally to solidarity work, such connections can divert white women's attention away from their structural privilege. Remember, Indigenous and white participant motivations for doing solidarity work overlap. Virtually every participant mentioned directly or indirectly the pursuit of social justice as the main reason for their political engagement. Moreover, participants in both groups expressed anger, passion, and a desire to act. However, a more complicated story emerges when we account for how different groups can wield emotion to different political effect. Over half of white participant narratives contained intertwined references to emotion and notions of caring often proceeded by a stated urgency to act. Interestingly, Barbara Heron's (2007, 39) study participants also expressed a desire "to go and *do* something," suggesting that such sentiments indicate a lot about the complex layers of white women's collective investments in solidarity work. To be more specific, passages that reference emotion clarify what can happen when we understand colonial complicity as simply personal: one's position in a structurally dominant collectivity can recede from view, and analytical critique and warranted outrage can easily slide into the desire to help.

The following passages exemplify the impassioned tenor of many white participant narratives. In an astonishing parallel to my own story involving NMS, Alicia recalled being "totally floored" on finding out about the high rates of violence against Indigenous women:

> I thought, "How could I have never learned this before now? How could this be that it's such a pervasive problem according to this pamphlet, yet I've never learned about this, no one's spoken about it?" I've realized that there was a huge issue in my backyard, in my own country, and I had no awareness of it ... It was almost like my own ego, huge ego: "How can I possibly

not know about this? I know about things. I'm aware. I'm with it. I get the whole social justice scene." I read [the pamphlet], and I was shocked.

Julia likewise became abruptly conscious of Indigenous issues, but back in Grade 3, when children from a nearby Indigenous reserve were bused into her school: "Suddenly, they were blamed for everything that had ever gone wrong." She was even "smacked" after commenting to a teacher about the unfairness she saw. Noting that this was a pivotal moment in her life, Julia added, "I've always been somebody who questions things and didn't take things for just whatever was sitting on the surface. Antiracism and that sort of thing is a big part of who I am as a person." Darcie echoed Alicia's and Julia's passion – and my own – in explaining what drew her to solidarity work with Indigenous women. In an otherwise unadorned, artificially lit space, Darcie sat patiently across a table full of my stuff. She radiated positivity, which I appreciated under the circumstances. It was my second interview in the project:

> I think that that's what solidarity means to me. It's having a real desire to try and better the world ... I don't really know if there's one factor that really drives me [to work in solidarity with Indigenous women]. I just know I get really upset or I respond very passionately to the lack of awareness among most of the Canadian population, most of settler society, of what I see as a fundamental injustice, and I just think that needs to be addressed if we're ever going to move forward as a society.

Sarah shared her equally emotional response to the situation of Indigenous women in Canada:

> So already racialized peoples in this country are subject to brutal racism and violence, but with Indigenous women, there's this added genocide: the colonization that is still continuing to happen – not "sort of," it is. When I'm looking at and thinking about that in my country there are children that don't have access to water – that's genocide, that's continuing. That's a whole other level to me. It's something that I feel, when I look at injustice, that seems to be the greatest injustice of all, and it makes me angry.

Notably, woven through Sarah's emotional response was a highly developed anticolonial critique.

Anticolonial aspects aside, the unintended effects of commonplace emotive explanations of what might draw one to Indigenous solidarity deserve more scrutiny. First, I agree that the passionate desire to redress social injustice "can and should be read as conscious resistance to social injustice" (Heron 2007, 41). Second, the white participants quoted above made great strides in understanding the "relationship between knowledges, social responsibility and collective struggle which one would expect to find in antiracist pedagogy" (Moreton-Robinson 2000, 131) and anticolonial praxis, I would add. However, personal outrage can keep the white woman in the realm of the personal, individualizing her engagement in solidarity work. Ruth Green clarified this idea. A Kanien'kehá:ka woman with Celtic ancestry on her father's side, she described herself as "an activist and social worker turned academic and educator. I am dedicated to disrupting education systems through both indigenization and decolonization and focus my work on raising good people so that they rise." Green called on white women to engage emotionally but not to conflate that with being emotional:

> It's different to be emotionally engaged than to be emotional. Does that make sense? Like, when [white] people hear about the residential school system for the first time, the "Indians" have to caretake the emotions again. When people hear about the missing and murdered, for us it's like, "Yeah, five hundred of my sisters are missing or murdered. What the fuck's wrong? Whatever. Let's move on. Forward ahead!" We have to stop and turn around and comfort the ... Oh, my god! I'm sick of having to hand the tissues.

As Green suggests, the problem arises when personal outrage overshadows the white woman's political analysis and allows her self-making interests to take centre stage.

Just as angry as Sarah or Darcie in her explanation of why she works to raise awareness about MMIWG2S people, Whitebird focused on the Indigenous women "who died [and who] need not be forgotten." She emphasized that she was involved in solidarity work out of concern for the Indigenous women "being exploited in this country [who] need to be heard." As Heron (2007) explores in relation to development work, even when social justice is a motivating factor, the white subject does not necessarily develop or sustain an anticolonial critique or avoid typically colonial behaviours (see also Flowers 2015). Social-justice motivations do not guarantee effective (non-colonizing) solidarity but can instead serve white women's desire to reproduce themselves as innocent, self-determining, or charitable. The myriad ways in which the personal featured in white participant narratives flags a risk that I suggest is endemic to solidarity encounters – the slip into an individualistic mode of investment that leads to solidarity tensions – as we shall see.

The challenges of grappling with white settler collective/structural privilege, or as I like to say, keeping the personal political, are perhaps most recognizable in two other white participant narratives. Before our interview, Dawn found me amid a haphazardly arranged collection of wrought-iron tables and chairs, outside in a park under a dazzling blue sky. I appreciated her upbeat energy and outspokenness. Dawn's description of the collective Canadian responsibility vis-à-vis violence against women in general and against Indigenous women in particular provided a starker example of the complexities – and contradictions – of gendered colonial subjectivity:

> We're doing a very bad job [of preventing violence against women], and you might say that the failure to address things at an early stage then escalates into a murder. So when you look at the Aboriginal women issue, that's sort of like the worst of the worst. But you know what? Overall, it's not so hot. It gets back to your issue of partnerships. So whose problem is that? It would be ours, because it's the effectiveness of an essential institution [police and justice systems] in democracy; it's the effectiveness of your security and protection, and how well is that working. So it's not their problem. It's our problem.

In this passage, Dawn accepts the problem of violence against Indigenous women, along with violence against all women, as the collective responsibility of settler Canadians and commits to doing her part to ensure Canadian democracy for all. In the next breath, however, she questions how helpful it is to use "colonialism" as a term of political struggle. When I asked if she had witnessed any dynamics in the solidarity encounter that she would define as colonial, she replied,

> I guess any time one assumes, which I think we all do, that our perspective is more informed than the other guy's, that's a form of colonialism ... My sense of colonialism is that if you read history, people are continually whacking people ... There is no race or group that has ownership of that thing. It embeds the "them" and "us" thing and it undermines really what you need when you talk about partnerships. Your partners can happen anywhere. This happened when I was very involved with women's issues a long time ago. At that time, the women didn't want the men involved ... If you are focused on an outcome, you find your partnerships wherever they are, and trust yourself to be able to identify them. [The term colonialism] has a lot of baggage to it. It's them and us, and "All those guys did it to us, and we have to watch those guys." And you do watch those guys. Why not? Watch them,

but some of them are the ones who can be your allies. Any good warrior always figures out where your allies are.

In my estimation, Dawn's point about finding allies where you least expect them is sound advice.

However, her rejection of colonialism as a useful analytic gave me pause and appears to validate Indigenous critiques about whitestream feminism. When Dawn implied that invoking colonialism can impede partnerships, her preferred term for solidarity, I thought immediately about false equivalences, the idea that different concepts or items are comparable.³ In her analysis of third-wave feminist texts, Rebecca Clark Mane (2012, 81) describes how false equivalencies about forms of oppression function to reproduce white privilege: "Through the deprivation of history, a syntax of equivalences is enabled: all differences and marginalizations become theoretically equivalent and thus interchangeable." Echoing the perspectives of Indigenous scholars such as Aileen Moreton-Robinson (2000) and Sandy Grande (2004), Clark Mane insists drawing false equivalencies about diverse women's oppression is tantamount to not accounting for power differences.⁴ Dawn's narrative appears to judge as temporally and thematically comparable what I would categorize as two distinct sets of social and political relations. This action, as discussed in detail below, can serve to conceal the specific "histories of determination" (Ahmed 2000) that constitute Indigenous–settler relations in Canada.

First, however, it is worth discussing one more narrative. After my long journey on three different modes of public transportation, Chloe kindly ferried me to our designated meeting place – a building that housed various nonprofit and social-justice groups. Like the other participants, Chloe graciously shared her story, disclosing several life-changing events in the process. During the interview, she emphasized her opinion that white women should benefit from the solidarity encounter:

> You're asking the white woman to do that and say, ["I did this wrong, and I did that wrong"]; that has no value to her. You've got to give her something for herself. And that's not doing it. So, she comes and talks to you, and she talks to a Native woman. She is maybe able to help or suggest or even to listen to the Native woman, sit down and talk. Suddenly, her life becomes ... she starts telling her stories. And it's really all about telling your stories. And that gives her value. It lessens *her* load, and she has more energy to do work with you too. Sometimes this nonsense about guilt (I hope we're not getting to that) ... and who's the bad guys and who's not the bad guys. We've all been

bad guys at one time; we've all been good guys at another time ... Let's tell our stories, listen to each other, and get on with what we have to do together to make it better. I just don't see any point in [guilt] ... You're going to tell some people who are nasty to Indians in Canada whose ancestors came from some place where they were starving to death in Europe ... There's no value in doing that type of thing. It's good to listen to everybody's story though. Because you learn where they're coming from and where you're coming from.

As I read it, Chloe's narrative contains a striking refusal to acknowledge the complicity of white women in colonial processes and thus the ongoing reality of white settler structural privilege. In generalizing that no single group has a monopoly on being "bad" or "good," Chloe, like Dawn, may well be employing a logic of false equivalencies that downplays the specificities of historical and contemporary settler colonial relations in Canada. To the same effect, and reminiscent of Sarah's focus on disenfranchised non-Indigenous groups, Chloe turns to the oppressive histories that might have prompted some groups to emigrate from their homelands to Canada. Finally, Chloe's insistence that "you've got to give [the white woman] something for herself" provides a perfect segue into a deeper analysis of the self-making dimensions of solidarity work. In other words, in pursuing proximity to Indigenous women for "self-serving" reasons, white women can potentially eclipse collective political struggle.

While Dawn's and Chloe's were minority responses in their sometimes blatant dismissal of the relevance of colonial relations to contemporary solidarity encounters, their sentiments align with other white women's more subtle attempts to relativize histories and power differences through recourse to proximity. The alignment occurs along the same fault line, namely, between the white collectivity that recedes from view and the critical white individuals who take its place. In the rest of the chapter, I lay a blueprint for mapping the complex ways in which solidarity encounters can aid and abet the self-making goals of white settler women.

Proximity and the (Un)making of the Gendered Colonial Subject

It is one thing to assert that the white settler woman's pursuit of figurative or literal closeness to Indigenous women can be problematic. It is quite another to describe what that involves. What does it mean to say that white women avail of proximity discourses for their/our self-making needs? What are the dynamics at play? How might the solidarity encounter, like development or missionary work, become a space where white women reaffirm our place in modernity as universal subjects, as Gayatri Spivak (1985) or Meyda Yeğenoğlu (1998) might put it? How do some white women self-servingly engage in solidarity work as liberal subjects or "autonomous independent individuals" (Moreton-Robinson 2000) (who perceive themselves as) capable of transcending race and colonial power relations? To begin to answer these questions, I offer the spectrum of proximity, beginning with an anecdote from my own life.

Telling (About) Autobiographical Moments: On Desiring Proximity

Out of many memorable exchanges I experienced during the interviews, one stands out. I was with Ardra, one of the Indigenous participants. As we chatted into the early evening, our conversation turned to the parameters of white women's roles as allies. Sitting cross-legged on her apartment's living room floor, captivated by the vibrant colours in the room, I listened as she speculated about white women's reasons for engaging in solidarity with Indigenous women:

> I just questioned whether it was actually more of an opportunist reason, meaning that the white allies are in the group more because they want to work with Native women than because they really want to work on these issues. So if there's no more Native women, then they're not getting what they really came to the group for, and so it's motivated by that rather than a commitment to what we say we are doing.

Ardra's observation stunned me into silence and deep reflection. Her insights and our ensuing conversation ignited a chain reaction in my thinking, which conjured up an earlier interview I'd had with a white participant, Darcie:

> There's only one Indigenous woman in [the program]. I know we had ... an Aboriginal history class, and there were no Aboriginal people in it. I don't know, it's an interesting phenomenon that there's seven white people learning from an Aboriginal woman ... but she's the only one who can speak from that experience. So, I mean, it could be a good thing because it shows some white people are interested in learning about it; but then it's also, like, it feels like maybe there's something missing there.

What or, perhaps more to the point, who could have been missing? Avoiding the temptation to presume what Darcie meant, I can tell you what I took from the words. In that instant, I felt an unmistakable, disconcerting sense of identification. After the interview was done, I thought of various times in my life, before and during my involvement with NMS, when I had felt "something missing" in an encounter that I hoped would consist of face-to-face interactions with Indigenous women (or men). I had never stopped to ponder what might have been at stake for me in such moments.

Given her focus on classroom settings in the Canadian context, Carol Schick's (1998, 186) reading of white desire for proximity to Indigenous people is especially relevant for analyzing such scenarios: "Desiring the other [for white people] is a way of disassociating from the revulsion of genocide and colonization and feeling good about themselves in the process. Sometimes the desire is for Natives themselves to be available in cross-cultural classes – embodied and present – as cultural guides and Native informants to describe their experiences of the everydayness of being the other."

Had I throughout my life sought the company of Indigenous people for similar reasons? In a journal excerpt from September 26, 2011, I consider the possibility that my solidarity work had been motivated by the prospect of "feeling good about" myself. I reflect on finally feeling accepted as a "good settler ally" by an Indigenous woman with whom I had worked for years:

> There's something nice about this "new-found fame," but also something discomfiting. Is this what I've been seeking? Is this why I've been involved in solidarity work? I remember years ago seeing a white woman on a panel speaking articulately about being a settler. I had quietly, internally vowed to attempt to walk this path. Have I for years been trying to arrive at the point of the good ally? Was that the end of the road for me, as opposed to Indigenous sovereignty or an end to violence against Indigenous women?

This reflection alone would suggest that something more "personal" besides the political issues at hand was in the balance for me. I suspect that even now I retain the hope of distancing myself from colonial processes and logics. I also continually seek more understanding of how my desire might manifest itself: Have I attempted, or do I attempt, however unwittingly, to accomplish this feat by seeking proximity to Indigenous women? Relatedly, do I reproduce hierarchical Indigenous–settler differences by placing Indigenous women on a pedestal of sorts? What I do know is that solidarity work remains for me in part an individualistic self-making journey despite, or perhaps because of, my efforts to come to grips with my structural colonial privilege. I have never been able to permanently assuage the desire to be the good settler ally.

Although white women may experience our desires for proximity as personal, both Schick (1998) and Emma LaRocque (2010) suggest that these desires should be more accurately understood as part of the historical development of a collective white settler subjectivity. Schick (1998, 184), for example, considers white preservice teacher investments in attaining closeness to Indigenous bodies as "a modern day version of [the] colonialist presumption [wherein] the purpose of Native bodies remains in their service to dominant populations." LaRocque (2010) sheds light on what early settlers expected from or presumed about such bodies, hinting that some settlers still look for a contemporary version of the "noble savage." Consider these words uttered in 1899 by Charles Mair, secretary to the Halfbreed Scrip Commission for northern Alberta:

> There presented itself a body of respectable-looking men, as well dressed and evidently quite as independent in their feelings as any like number of average pioneers in the East ... One was prepared, in this wild region of forest, to behold some savage types of men; indeed, I *craved* to renew the vanished scenes of old. But alas! One beheld, instead, men with well-washed unpainted faces, and combed and common hair; men in suits of ordinary store-clothes, and even some with "boiled" if not laundered shirts. One felt disappointed, even defrauded. (LaRocque 2010, 129)

Mair's desire to reaffirm the noble savage stereotype is striking and, in contrast with the impulse to solidarity, decidedly *not* well intentioned by twenty-first-century standards. Nevertheless, when putting Ardra's and LaRocque's insights into conversation, two things astound me: the white settler desire for proximity that spills out across temporal, spatial, and political spectrums, and my opaque thoughts about the matter. I would not have thought twice about Darcie's comment – or my emotive response to it – if not for Ardra's observation. Only afterwards could I both understand these as incidences of my own desire for proximity and, perhaps most importantly, reframe that desire as part of the historical development of a collective gendered colonial subjectivity.

Structuring Desire: The Spectrum of Proximity
My spectrum of proximity takes inspiration from Sara Ahmed's (2000, 12) theory of colonial encounters as strange encounters that "involve, at one and the same time, social and spatial relations of distance and proximity."

If Ahmed uses "distance" to refer to power hierarchies between dominant identities and "native subjects" then, somewhat counterintuitively, proximity reinforces these power hierarchies rather than undoing them. Especially relevant for my purposes in this book, present-day strange encounters provide a window into historical inequalities even as they keep the latter intact. Seneca scholar Mishuana Goeman substantiates this point. She powerfully recollects how colonial spatialities reproduced inequality over time in the spatial schema of her childhood: "At play here was more than the material location or even more than the present material social relations; instead evident here was the idea of Indians as criminals already, in a long history of colonial/Native relationships" (Goeman 2013, 9). In this example, "common sense" would have us forget that the cliché "Indians as criminals" is undeniably a fabrication of history. For Ahmed, this "forgetfulness" results from stranger fetishism, the mechanism that fans the flames of a fantasy on the part of dominant groups that power relations either do not exist or can be equalized or transcended.

When I imagine the solidarity encounter as a "contemporary mode of proximity" in which stranger fetishism conceals historically derived power inequalities (Ahmed 2000, 13), my beef is not with "the stranger" or subjugated Other but rather with the "I" or dominant subject. For this task, the fantastical element of stranger fetishism is singularly useful. When the Other becomes the object of dominant desires, Ahmed (2000, 133) tells us, dominant subjects seek proximity to the Other through discursive techniques such as "consuming, becoming and passing," which in turn cement the effects of stranger fetishism. Through these self-making tricks, dominant subjects forget anew how the "I" and "the stranger" are historically produced and continually remade – in this case, through settler colonial relations. Dominant subjects assume early on that Others are "knowable, seeable and hence be-able" (Ahmed 2000, 133) to them. Not only do these techniques facilitate knowing the Other; they promise the "I" self-discovery and transformation. In other words, the Other becomes a vessel for Western settler/liberal self-making. My analysis fleshes out how these techniques seem to work in solidarity encounters – presenting in combination and/or involving formulations of proximity such as calls for friendship or collaboration.

I spent months tucked into my carrel in the recesses of Robarts Library at the University of Toronto, participant narratives my main companions. Gradually, a variety of phrases, passages, and situations absorbed my attention, many of which I would later organize under the banner of "proximity." Building on the work of Ahmed (2000) and others, I developed a container concept – the spectrum of proximity – that could accommodate the phenomena I was analyzing. The spectrum contains an array of entwined desires, associated discourses, and dynamics that meet two criteria: first, they connote, involve, or require proximity in one form or another; and second, they potentially facilitate white settler/liberal self-making in subtle or blatant ways. In this manner, I link proximity desires to the broader project of white settler self-making.

I conceive the spectrum as a heuristic device, as opposed to an expression of some pre-given, fixed reality. I list its contents here according to the desire in question, in order from most- to least-occurring in participant narratives to give a sense of proportion. While a generalized white settler desire for belonging underpins the whole spectrum (the opening scene of this chapter being a perfect example), proximity desires took many forms and came up in both implicit and explicit ways in participant responses to any number of questions. The most prominent element of the array, in fact, is an explicit desire to be included or welcomed into an Indigenous community or to be accepted by an Indigenous person, which can incorporate a desire for forgiveness. The second most common element is the desire to be healed or taken care of. The third involves desiring self-empowerment, worth, or purpose. The fourth desire features an attraction to or appreciation of Indigenous culture, tradition, or spirituality (sometimes coupled with a critique of Western society). Last, but not least, is the desire to learn or be challenged.

Turning again briefly to method, participant narrations of the solidarity encounter in its many facets are the spine of this book. This proximity schematic flows most directly from my reading of what white participants told me about their reasons for engaging in solidarity with Indigenous women. It reflects my interpretation of the ways in which proximity desires infuse white participant expressions of their own motivations, or the motivations of others, for doing the work. While some factors were more primary than others for a particular person, each participant shared a complex bundle of reasons for doing solidarity work – bundles that would need to be kept intact to get a sense of a given person's subjectivity. To reissue a caveat from the Introduction, my intention is not to make claims about a particular person's investments in solidarity but rather to identify discursive patterns across participant narratives following the methodologies of Schick (1998) and Heron (2007). In a word, I aim for a composite sketch of the white woman subject and her approach to solidarity. Therefore, my spectrum artificially isolates different aspects of proximity for analytical purposes. In fact, the proximity discourses and behaviours I describe are often copresent or coconstitutive in any one narrative. For example, a participant might link the desire to be included in an Indigenous community with the desire to gain a sense of purpose in one's life. Likewise, a desire for acceptance can imbue an attraction to Indigenous culture, tradition, or spirituality. Notably, while the desire for acceptance might not be an initial motivator, it could become operative after a white woman begins to engage in solidarity.

Other dynamics and desires animate the proximity spectrum, most prominently, the white settler sense of entitlement to access Indigenous spaces or contexts in which Indigenous peoples predominate in number and presumably influence. Likewise, common across much of the spectrum is the expectation of self-improvement via engagement with the Other (Ahmed 2000). In accord with Ahmed's (2000, 119) assertion that "contemporary Western culture is imbued with fantasies of becoming," in what follows, I identify some of the main narratives of becoming or self-making that permeate white participant narratives. In the process, I home in on what might ultimately be at stake: white settler women's self-transformation and transcendence.

Narratives of Becoming: A Matter of Self-Worth

What do white women's narratives of becoming in the context of solidarity encounters look like, and what might they indicate about our desires for proximity in these encounters? The following exchange from my interview with Alicia paints an overall picture of my take on proximity discourse in action. The exchange not only illustrates the multiple, interconnecting layers of proximity desires, and their perceived benefits, that saturate many white narratives but also the ways in which white women grapple with our dominant position to varying degrees:

> CAROL LYNNE: What brings you to do this work? I'm wondering what responsibilities you feel as a non-Native person, uh, woman in particular, to be doing this work?
>
> ALICIA: As I mentioned before, obviously people get something out of the work they're doing or else they probably wouldn't be doing it. Whether they're aware of it or not is another story. I like being in the community; I like being in the culture; I feel at home ... I think a sense of community is an important part of mental health and wellness, and maybe among the general population of regular Western/Canadian

people I don't necessarily feel that there's a community of people. So there's a sense of community there that has drawn me in, that I feel a part of. I feel aligned with, as I said, the beliefs and values and the spirituality of it almost as if I had, I was like a spiritual person in a past life or something, you know? ... I've spoken with lots of spiritual leaders and Elders who've said to me, I'm thinking of one woman in particular who's a healer who said to me, "I think that you were a Native woman in a past life." You can take that for whatever you think that is ... Or maybe she meant metaphorically that "there's something in you spiritually that is driven or aligned" ... I don't think we always know why we are the way we are. Like, of all my siblings, why am I the only one who's into any activism work, who has a ton of gay friends, who has lived abroad? ... I feel a bit like a citizen of the world. I don't feel very aligned with being Canadian. I think I may have been when I was younger, just without, because I didn't really know any different or any better. I don't feel entirely Western in my mind either because I've been exposed to different cultures and people.

Alicia's response conveys a heightened awareness of her positionality as a white settler and of how she has pursued proximity to Indigenous women (and men) through both activism and (we later learn) academic research. Recall that social justice is central to Alicia's initial involvement in solidarity work – she was outraged on learning about the disproportionably high levels of violence directed against Indigenous women and girls. (Later in the interview, she noted that, along the way, Indigenous women have continually encouraged her to remain involved.) In relation to self-making, she was forthcoming about a host of other reasons that sustained her interest in solidarity.

In fact, the above excerpt encompasses many dimensions of my proximity spectrum, including a desire to be accepted by an Indigenous community, given the supposed lack of community among "regular Western/Canadian people"; an attraction to and identification with Indigenous "beliefs and values and the spirituality"; and a desire for self-improvement (by embracing other ways of knowing or being). Additionally, Alicia cast herself as different from her siblings and most Canadians, a move potentially indicative of the distinct but related desire to acquire exceptional or good settler status. Finally, there is what goes unsaid and what white individuals such as myself might presume – our unrestricted right to access Indigenous spaces. Critical whiteness scholar Shannon Sullivan (2006, 16) refers to this sense of entitlement as "white ontological expansiveness," or the tendency for white people "to act and think as if all spaces – whether geographical, psychical, linguistic, economic, spiritual, bodily or otherwise – are or should be available for them to move in and out of as they wish." Alicia's passage raises key questions about whether some white women in solidarity work assume this right of access.

At the same time, situating this passage in the context of Alicia's entire narrative allows for a more sympathetic account of the gendered colonial subject – a subject who often struggles with her historical position as a white settler and, in this book's terms, her desires for belonging and proximity. For instance, Alicia expressed an awareness of why doing solidarity for personal or self-interested reasons might be problematic. Citing a "laundry list" of colonial laws and practices that Indigenous peoples have endured, she recommended empathy:

> You kind of have to empathize with where [Indigenous people] are coming from ... I know I sound hypocritical because I just said I was carrying around that baggage, but to some extent you can't take things personally all the time. If you really get the [historical] context of what the work is, then you really shouldn't take things personally. If you really take things personally all the time, then maybe you're still too caught up in the self, the ego self.

Alicia's assessment that the white tendency to "take things personally" is problematic aligns with what several Indigenous participants advise white women allies *not* to do, as I discuss in the final chapter. In addition, Alicia registered an awareness of white ontological expansiveness, expressing profound, ongoing reservations about her right to access Indigenous contexts: "I have all these doubts that I second guess my work in the area as a white woman." Rather than dissuade her, these doubts have led her to think more carefully about how to be an ally: "The only way I've made peace with it so far is to say that I see myself as someone who is here to help. It's not someone setting the agenda. I'm here as a tool with certain skills and resources. 'Please use me if I can be of service.'" Importantly, she understands "help" to mean not dictating the terms of the encounter.

Having engaged in solidarity as part of her graduate research, Alicia was also aware of the historical associations between research and European imperialism and colonialism (Smith 1999) and lingering suspicions about non-Indigenous researchers:

> I worked with ... [an] Aboriginal woman, and she was wonderful to me. Open arms, "great-that-you're-interested-in-this-let's-get-to-work" kind of thing. I've

> had mixed reviews as a white woman coming in to work in this community, and I understand why. There's a legacy of a lot of negative behaviours by white researchers, et cetera, coming in and trying to do the work. Some people were not okay with me being there. I'd say the majority of my story has been pretty positive. I think for the most part people have said, "Thank you for giving a shit. You didn't have to. A lot of people don't who are non-Native. But you seem to, so thanks for caring to some degree." There were some people who were very suspicious of my motives and what I was doing and that kind of thing. With [this Indigenous woman] I didn't just get the master's, I got involved.

In "giving a shit," Alicia answers Indigenous calls for settlers to care about and take up issues of colonial inequity. Moreover, and much to her credit, she repeatedly questions her role and effectiveness as a white woman working in Indigenous communities.

Alicia was not alone in voicing self-reflexive misgivings about her gendered role as a white ally, including whether she was even entitled to do the work. Evelyn, who considered herself relatively new to solidarity work, admitted that she was "still trying to find [her] place." Even so, as she learned while attending Toronto's annual Indigenous Solidarity Week, she was adamant that her role in the decolonization process was *not* one of spokesperson. As she explained, "I've never been a good spokesperson, not even for myself half the time. I just know I want to be on that side, and not the side I've been given or privileged to have been born into. That sounds weird, kind of odd. I'm not negating who I am. I haven't figured that one out fully yet." What initially stands out to me – especially in statements like "I just know I want to be on that side" – is a seeming straightforward liberal desire to renounce privilege by transforming the self. The plot thickened, however, when Evelyn responded to my question about the possibility of white women engaging in non-colonizing solidarity:

> I'm still trying to figure that out. Is there a purpose for me to be aligned with Indigenous women? Whether I do have anything to offer, it's probably minimal. Because I don't have the education behind me. I don't have prospects ahead of me that, you know ... I have very minimal ... I can do a few things at work ... But I don't have any leverage, so in that way I'm not of much use to anybody. But that's like saying my life is useless. I think there's a minimal amount that I can offer. And that's what I'm willing to give.

Often speaking with a humble, self-effacing tone, Evelyn did not presume or exaggerate her capacity as an individual to effect change. What I find interesting, though, is how Evelyn's answer to a general question about non-colonizing solidarity reveals a search for self-worth and purpose – both of which feature prominently in my proximity spectrum. In this sense, and most pointedly when she contemplated the reason or "purpose for [her] to be aligned with Indigenous women," solidarity work *does* seem bound up in Evelyn's narrative of becoming,

It may come as a surprise to know that during the interview itself, I did not find Evelyn's words in any way extraordinary, which relates to one of this book's central findings: certain white settler behaviours that Indigenous women perceive as self-serving, and ultimately detrimental to political solidarity, often go unnoticed by white women like me. Instead, we typically present and, if I am any indication, typically read such scenarios as plain and straightforward accounts of empowerment through solidarity work. Take the following excerpts from three white participant narratives, starting with Evelyn's. She recalled being bestowed respect as an older woman in a "non-hierarchical" Indigenous context:

> It's the first time that as an older woman where my grey hair is showing gave me some level of respect without even garnering that respect. I got to eat first. By virtue of being a woman, I got some respect. That harkens back to where feminism kind of failed ... If not everybody was onboard with [feminist ideology], it didn't work because you're the only one thinking you were important. If the rest of your coworkers, female or male, didn't think it was important, it didn't matter whether you were a feminist or not. In this [Indigenous] group, in these teachings, there's a sense of "everyone's important, every voice needs to be heard," the non-hierarchical aspect of it, "everyone's valuable."

Alicia similarly cited respect for women and a "nonoppositional" blending of spirituality and political activism as attractive features of the Indigenous cultures with which she is familiar. Evoking yet another element of my proximity spectrum, Chloe affirmed that solidarity work not only gave her life value, it also enabled her to heal from difficult experiences:

> It helped me get over the anger I had felt from my treatment as a separated woman in Canada. It helped in the healing I had to do; it helped by doing things and meeting people who not only valued my help and understood it, but who basically appreciated it ... and to a certain extent my life was of value then. And everybody wants to feel that their life is of some value.

Taken together, these statements begin to paint a picture of how gender factors into solidarity work and, in the process, of the composite figure of "the white woman ally subject."[5]

Chloe, Evelyn, and Alicia were all attracted to the same feature of solidarity work: the value and respect they would potentially receive as women in Indigenous spaces. From her vantage point as an Indigenous woman, Teresa assured me that she believed "people who want to join in solidarity are also attempting to fill the gaps in their own community. There's a gap in respect of women, and so they wanted to join our communities somewhat in order to learn how to fill that gap with respect." At least one explanation springs to mind: solidarity encounters can provide an avenue for white women, consciously or otherwise, to tap into one side of our historical double positioning. In other words, we can use the encounter to redress our subordinated status as women while letting our dominant status as white settlers go (temporarily) unnoticed.

A palpable sense of what we might call female self-improvement infuses these particular white participant narratives. This is especially clear when Alicia described having acquired "an element of purpose" through her work with Indigenous women (and at times men):

> I feel in a sense that I've been enlightened a little bit to some of the issues. I think that's an important area to be in. I think we're all looking for something to drive us in our lives, to feel passionate about, something that we feel is important. This is something I feel is important and gives me an element of purpose in my life.

To summarize, these passages demonstrate one of the ways in which proximity in solidarity encounters can serve white women's settler/liberal aspirations: it recovers or enhances our sense of value, importance, and purpose. It bears noting that the desire for self-worth in these cases dovetails with the fourth element of my proximity spectrum: an attraction to or appreciation of Indigenous culture, tradition, or spirituality, to which I dedicate Chapter 3.

Gender, Self-Discovery, and Transformation in Solidarity Work

In my thought horizon, the proximity spectrum forms part of a larger constellation of self-making processes that can involve fantasies of self-discovery, transformation, and transcendence in the sense of overcoming power relations. Ahmed (2000, 123) explains these dynamics clearly in her analysis of the film *Dances with Wolves*, whose main character, Dunbar, seeks to overcome his white settler outsider status in relation to Sioux on the American frontier. To achieve belonging, he strives to transcend his "difference" from the "Indians" by transforming into a settler–Indigenous hybrid. Note the fantastical logic of stranger fetishism at play:

> The way in which this narrative of becoming Indian most clearly involves fantasy is in the very assumption that the structural relations of "antagonism" between Indians and white men can be simply overcome through the act of getting closer. [Dunbar's] agency is central to this fantasy of overcoming; *not only can he make but he can unmake the border between self and other, between natives and strangers.* (Ahmed 2000, 124)

In what follows, I adapt Ahmed's account of colonial masculinity to think about a comparable fantasy of overcoming in white participant narratives and hence in the solidarity encounter.

We already have a sense of how settler narratives of becoming, and associated proximity dynamics, can take gender-specific forms. A big part of what Chloe, Evelyn, and Alicia gained from their solidarity work – an increased sense of their value and respect as women – was a consequence of their status as white women. Alicia's narrative provides further clues as to how gender norms can influence the kind of settler, and settler ally, we might become. Recall Alicia's expressed desire for community, something that Dunbar in fact shares: "The shift from confrontation to becoming emerges through his desire for company; his desire for access to the multiplicity that he lacks" (Ahmed 2000, 121). Like Dunbar, Alicia recounted being drawn to solidarity work by "a sense of community" she feels is lacking in Western society. Alicia shows herself to be different from Dunbar, however, in her inclination to "help":

> I was also giving a class presentation about the higher rates of violence against women that I had taken from that literature, and one of my classmates was an Aboriginal woman and didn't like what I was saying. She stood up and complained how high the rates were, how I was pathologizing Aboriginal women. I started to cry because I felt so ... bad that my intention was to help. And the fact that another woman was telling me that I was wrong, that I was pathologizing, that I wasn't helping was just so deflating for me because I wanted to help so much. And to find out I had hurt someone in some way.

Alicia's reaction implies that colonial contexts position white women as helpers in a way that they do not position white men. In other words, vestiges of our historical position as the "helpers" of less fortunate Others appear to hold sway in today's solidarity encounters.

However, Alicia tests assumptions about what white women helping in solidarity work might look like. Later in the interview, she shared a mesmerizing account of how being involved in Indigenous community research enabled her growth, self-discovery, and transformation:

> It was totally different from any other academic forum I had been in. Everything was done in a circle formation, and we did a really long check-in. Everyone cried, people sang and did drumming. I started to realize that this work wasn't just about yet another white woman swooping in and wanting to help; this was also a good opportunity for me as a person to expand my ways of knowing and my ways of being for the better, that I had lived a life that was relatively cognitive in nature up until then just as a virtue of the culture that we're in. Yet here was a group of people who were being emotionally expressive ... who were shedding a tear about whatever was moving them at the moment ... who had a spiritual connection. These other dimensions opened up to me that I hadn't really been exposed to prior to that ... Here I was in a space where there was drumming and singing and smudging, and people were speaking differently about things, and they were thinking differently about things. I was very intrigued as the little scientist, but I was very moved emotionally by this new sort of forum to be in.

Alicia's description of her eye- and soul-opening experience resembles my own. In the following journal passage circa 2008, I recall my time with the United Nations Mission in Guatemala (MINUGUA) in the 1990s. I reflect on my vivid memory of a hike with two Indigenous men:

> At that moment, something shifted in me; I was struck by the power of the land beneath me, its living essence, its spirit, indeed its sadness at having borne witness to so many years of anguish and trauma. There was no explaining the slaughter of hundreds of Indigenous people, forever etched into the memory of the land beneath my feet ... Having been an avid hiker since my youth, through this particular interaction with two Q'ekchi' men I was able to rekindle in myself a respect for the sacred, the sacredness of "Mother Earth." At the same time, this and other experiences served to demystify for me the image of the "noble savage," a figure who I had learned

to imagine, by virtue of having dutifully consumed Western ideology, as the quintessential inferior "other."

In employing discourses of the sacred, I paint a picture similar to Alicia's: my interaction with two Q'ekchi' men transformed me spiritually, and later politically. While not a solidarity encounter with Indigenous women in Canada, my tale of transformation merits inclusion for its striking parallels with Alicia's story; in both, it would seem that our structural positions as white woman settler and *extranjera blanca* (white woman foreigner), respectively, overdetermined our "strange encounters" with Indigenous Others. Moreover, in both cases, the ostensible helper *gets* helped, the focus of the next chapter.

Notably, Alicia and I both conceptualized our transformations as an opening up of the underdeveloped emotional/spiritual side of our personas. In doing so, do we begin to resemble Dunbar from *Dances with Wolves* in the sense that our self-discoveries are "mediated as a discovery of the truth about the Indians" (Ahmed 2000, 123)? After all, as Ahmed (2000, 123) suggests, proximity to Indigenous Others is precisely the thing that appears to facilitate self-discovery: the Indigenous characters "remain at the service of a white, masculine story of (self)-discovery. Rather than being annihilated as a threat, they become reincorporated to provide what is lacking in him self [sic]." Dunbar's transformation, Ahmed (2000, 123) continues, is really "the story of the ability to transform [the settler self]." It is the story of the desiring white man who, feeling lack, finds appeal in "becoming other." Ours, however, is a white, feminine story of (self)-discovery. After pondering Alicia's interview and my journal in their entireties, I would say the difference lies in how white women frequently maintain residual doubts about our transformations. Does this make us more or perhaps differently haunted settler subjects than our male counterparts?

To begin to answer this question, I turn to the last line of Alicia's passage where she mentioned being "very intrigued as a little scientist." Following Ahmed (2000, 120), I wonder if this seemingly sudden shift in perspective is a move toward liberal rationality and the "'distancing' perspective of the masculine, colonising gaze." Alicia's comment jogged my memory of a conversation with Dawn. Early in the interview, Dawn spoke about the impact of her sister (also not Indigenous) on her own social-justice leanings: "My sister had a difficult life. I don't think she worked the [Vancouver] Downtown Eastside [DTES], but she definitely got involved with shady characters. She wasn't an alcoholic, she wasn't a drug user, but she hung out with people like that because she felt that that's as good as it got for her." At this point, Dawn emphasized her sister's "difficult life" while differentiating – we might say distancing – her sister's circumstances from those of others in the DTES. Moreover, because Indigenous women make up a disproportionate part of the DTES, Dawn's statement inadvertently risks reinforcing colonial stereotypes that continue to devalue Indigenous women's lives. Fast forward to where Dawn explained her interest in the issue of MMIWG2S people:

> One is, it has a face for me, and that face, really, is my sister. That's sort of all women in a sense, who are seeking to make it in the world, and there's just a lot of pitfalls out there waiting for us in many, many ways. So there's that. Then there's another aspect, which I love ... It's fun to pick an issue, for me, that is stuck and say, "How do we unstick this?" ... It's a challenge to say, "How do we move this sucker?" ... It's like, "Oh my god." It's an edge for me.

On the one hand, by subsuming "all women" and the "pitfalls" they face under one category, Dawn risks promoting a false equivalency a second time. On the other, Dawn's reference to loving a challenge – another element of my proximity spectrum – keeps Indigenous women at a distance in much the same way as Alicia's "little scientist" remark. Both women's statements invoke the liberal subject's rational capacity for discernment.

Aileen Moreton-Robinson's (2000) study of white feminist academics sheds light on why this parallel in Alicia's and Dawn's narratives is likely not coincidental. According to Moreton-Robinson (2000, 142), these women keep their distance from racism by acting like liberal subjects: "The [white feminist academic's] intellectual engagement with racism inspires her and enhances her personal development. However, racism here too is treated as something public and external to the subject position middle-class white woman; it is something that one gets involved in by choice." In other words, white feminist academics treat racism as something that does not apply to them. Paradoxically, they think of themselves as new and improved, more effective feminists for having intellectually engaged racism. That is, they undergo personal development/transformation *without* feeling implicated in power relations. Liberal subjectivity makes this possible. In Dwight Boyd's (2004, 10) terms, white feminist academics position themselves outside of power relations by acting like ontologically unique individuals exercising the "muscles of rational choice and intentionality." As I discuss in the first half of this chapter, white women are predisposed to viewing our immersion in political struggle/solidarity as a matter of "choice." Put differently, we are likely to view our immersion in antiracist or anticolonial efforts through the liberal lens of personal choice and not through the lens of structural privilege and a corresponding responsibility as members of a white settler collectivity. To recall Ahmed (2000), proximity keeps strangers at a distance (imagined as inferior) while it simultaneously enhances dominant subjects (imagined as superior). However, is there a gendered specificity to distancing?

Alicia's, Dawn's, and my distancing efforts are arguably rooted in what Meyda Yeğenoğlu (1998, 107) describes as white settler/imperialist women's "simulation of sovereign masculine discourse." Unable to gain emancipation in the metropole, relatively well-off white women – fatefully positioned as both dominant and subordinate – turned to the colonies where they could perform like men, especially in relation to "more oppressed" women. In short, by aligning themselves with patriarchal empire, they became modern subjects with universal pretensions. Does white women's double positioning explain the only partial transferability of Ahmed's (2000) theory of white settler masculinity to solidarity encounters? More to the point, do we still model ourselves after the white men in our midst, baking gendered doubt into our very marrow?

In other white participant narratives of becoming, discernable links between the desires and dynamics of proximity/distancing, self-discovery/self-transformation, and gender are less conclusive. For example, Peggy defined her subject status as "in-between" due to having spent extended periods working with Indigenous women (and, more recently, men):

> PEGGY: In political organizing, we can get these ideas that are useful. But, if you just construct them as binaries and there's nothing in-between – and I've been in-between a lot of the time, all the time.
> CAROL LYNNE: Can you give an example?
> PEGGY: I was not trying to be Native [in the dream]. I was not doing any of that, but the spirit world spoke to *me*; according to [an Indigenous friend] that was what happened ... I've been so deeply influenced after all these years of working with Indigenous people in various ways that I can't say I only work from a Western perspective. And yet I can't say that I write from a Native perspective. But what is it? And it's not just appropriation; it's also engaging really deeply and fully and respecting Indigenous concepts, teachings. We don't really have a word for that yet, or we don't have an acknowledgment of who *we* [white people] become when we're changed through this process.

Peggy's narrative – and subjectivity – is laden with complexity.

Throughout the interview, she was clear about the political nature of her solidarity encounters. She was also concerned about misappropriating Indigenous concepts and teachings. At the same time, after "working with Indigenous people in various ways" over the years, Peggy described herself in terms of hybridity, reminiscent of Dunbar. She talked of having gained access to an Indigenous perspective through her solidarity encounters and becoming profoundly changed as a result. Unlike Dunbar, however, she did not assume that her mere agency or "ability to move" in Indigenous spaces could easily re/make or "unmake the border between self and other, between natives and strangers" (Ahmed 2000, 123–24). On the contrary, Peggy grappled with understanding what settler transformation without appropriation would look like or be called. Above all, Peggy's hard-earned knowledge suggests the importance of questioning our assumptions about transformation, given the slippery slope of settler colonial desire. To what extent do we retain the hope of escaping structural power relations through self-transformation? Rather than pass judgment, about Peggy or any other white participant, I want to highlight the variability between and within white participant "narratives of becoming" and the intersubjective negotiations to which they point. In recurrent conversations, in fact, I was admonished by Lee Maracle (Stó:lō/Métis) about the dangers of imputing meaning to someone's statements outside of the words they had uttered. In accordance with Maracle's interpretation of such moves as invasive, I have tried to raise questions rather than provide definitive answers. All told, the narratives examined so far drive home a point worth repeating: many white women in the solidarity encounter *do* think about our dominant position in a white settler collectivity, albeit to varying degrees and to different effect.

"To Become without Becoming": Transcendence and White Settler Belonging

Chloe, as you may recall, expressed enormous gratitude for what solidarity work had done for her. I am equally indebted to her for sharing intimate details of her life. This openness expanded my thinking into white women's shifting positions on the proximity spectrum and in relation to its dynamics, especially transformation. As I interpret it, Chloe's narrative of becoming is particularly suggestive of how the desire to transform the settler self through the Indigenous Other can manifest as a desire for proximity. To make better sense of Chloe's story, it is worth reviewing Ahmed's (2000,

122) interpretation of *Dances with Wolves*. Recall that a particular dynamic structures Dunbar's narrative: "[His] story of becoming involves not just a destructuring of white masculinity, but its restructuring in relation to the other, who ceases to be a stranger, but instead becomes one's 'native self.'" I glimpse traces of such fantastical elements in Chloe's "tale of becoming." Allow me to explain.

About a third into the interview, Chloe made repeated mention of her "Native self." In fact, she moved to her current geographic location in part to be closer to her distant "Native roots," which is why she considers herself an insider of sorts: "I'm not an outsider working with [Indigenous women]." For Chloe, her status alters the nature of her solidarity work: "I'm one who got by all the doors, through all the doors. I'm a little ahead of [Indigenous women] in progression, in the good things of life. I'm trying to help. Again, it's something that we're trying to help people who we, where we're related to them, there's blood ties, get ahead too. It's not a social service."

If we apply a gendered version of Ahmed's theory, we find that a "particular self–other dynamic" does, indeed, structure her narrative – in this case, a de- and restructuring of white femininity. At first glance, we find a white woman becoming a helper of Indigenous women through proximity. However, in claiming "blood ties" to an Indigenous community, Chloe redefines herself "in relation to the other, who ceases to be a stranger, but instead becomes one's 'native self'" (Ahmed 2000, 122). When I pressed her to elaborate, Chloe explained that she thought of her work with Indigenous women as neither solidarity nor charity but as a process of reconnection with extended members of her family. She also conveyed her desire to change what she considered her estranged status to that Indigenous community:

> I feel that it's more a family feeling than solidarity. I feel that they are relatives ... We're not going [to the upcoming celebration in a nearby Indigenous community] to stay with strangers; we're going there to see distant relatives. [Solidarity] is not the feeling I have toward Native people because I'm aware that there's this link, family link.

Invoking only to reject the concept of strangers, Chloe claimed the status of Indigenous Other, taking her out of the political and into the personal realm. In the process, she appeared to perform a blend of Ahmed's (2000, 115) "three key modalities of 'going strange, going native': consuming, becoming and passing." What to make of her final thought, "I'm a little ahead of them in progression, in the good things of life"? Even as Indigenous–non-Indigenous hierarchies are blurred and then levelled, not unlike what we saw in Alicia's and Dawn's narratives, statements such as this function to retain that binary and Chloe's superior position within it. Not incidentally, Chloe's statement also accords with the liberal idea of progress.

I am perhaps most fascinated by the way in which Chloe sees herself as occupying two subject positions simultaneously – Indigenous woman and white settler woman. A thought flashes: Is this more fallout from white women's historical double positioning as oppressor (by race) and oppressed (by gender)? Is it another moment of encounter where we identify with our subordinate gender status but leave our structural power as white settlers undisturbed? Passing is a useful concept for thinking through how white women can accomplish this feat. As Ahmed (2000, 132) describes it, dominant subjects can use passing simultaneously to disavow and retain their dominant status: "In assuming the place of the other rather than simply being the other, the difference [between self and other] is perpetually reaffirmed ... Passing is here the fantasy of an ability (or a technique) 'to become without becoming.'" Chloe can have her proverbial cake and eat it too; she can "become" an Indigenous woman while remaining a settler. We might say that in claiming Indigenous ancestry, Chloe risks glossing over the social antagonisms of colonial history or, to quote Ahmed (2000, 128), "the processes whereby [Other] subjects come to be seen as 'having' a prior and fixed identity." The next question is equally tricky: How does believing in one's capacity "to become without becoming" convince white women (and men) that historical power inequities have been levelled?

I look to the consuming modality of going strange, going native to offer an answer, however tentative and incomplete. Drawing on bell hooks's (1992) work into the racialized dynamics of intersubjective relations, Kim Anderson (2000, 106–7) discusses her experience of being Othered as a Cree-Métis woman: "Sometimes people glow all over you about your heritage; others want to use you as some kind of showpiece. It is a sexualized identity, which, in my case, has, for example, resulted in the humiliating experience of being called 'my little Indian' as a measure of affection." For Anderson (2000, 107), "this syndrome" is encapsulated by hooks's seminal notion of "eating the Other," a process whose central logic involves the desire for proximity: "People with a desire for 'eating the Other' do not see themselves operating within a racist framework; rather, they think they are progressive in their desire to make contact. hooks suggests that relations of this nature may further be used to assuage guilt and 'take the form of a defiant gesture where one denies accountability and historical connection.'" There are strong parallels between eating the Other and going strange, going native. In both, proximity becomes a vehicle for concealing historical relations of domination and subordination and for re-establishing the autonomy and innocence of dominant subjects. Anderson (2000, 107) identifies the two common denominators: first, "a desire to cross some kind of frontier [and] to be transformed by the experiences"; and second, the hope that getting closer "is proof that we have all transcended the racism [including its colonial forms] that plagues the Americas." As for a gendered reading of these dynamics, it is fair to say that white women would be far more inclined than white men to, as Anderson (2000, 108) says, "befriend an Indian" and then help her, rather than to sexualize and/or dominate her through physical force.[6]

As implied above, I identify deeply with Peggy's story, which is likely why I find it so powerful. For me, Peggy's rich history of solidarity work compellingly illustrates the challenges of traversing the bumpy road of solidarity relations. Her narrative corroborates the assertion not only that collective white settler/liberal subjectivity exists, propped up by a collective desire for belonging, but also that proximity via solidarity can become the vehicle for satiating that desire. More vitally still, Peggy's story speaks to white women's struggles to come to terms with our historically rooted desire to belong.

Continuing our talk about how to decolonize settler transformation, Peggy reflected on her own desire to be accepted into an Indigenous community:

> I will never be ... I don't think in my lifetime I will ever be completely accepted within an Indigenous community, not fully. And yet that could be my only community, if I moved in, lived there, whatever ... I understand. But that's the complexity of belonging and not belonging, being part of, not being part of. And I think we all have a yearning – certainly, I find it in myself – for unity, for being one, for resolving the differences, for being fully accepted. And it's hard to accept the limitations on that. And yet they're real.

As noted earlier, Peggy had a social-justice bent and deep understanding of her structural position as a settler, and that understanding deeply influenced her solidarity work. At the same time, she described the profound personal stakes – a sense of belonging – that for her stood alongside the political stakes of an anticolonial project. As to whether most white settlers in solidarity work feel similarly, she answered with exceptional candour:

> I really don't know. I shouldn't say that's what all people feel. I don't know ... But certainly, I know a lot of white activists have that desire [to be part of

an Indigenous community]. And I think it's partly wanting to belong here on this continent; wanting to feel like you can be here legitimately, ethically, fully. And that also you can be proud of who you are, what your heritage is, and what your ancestors did. I'd like to feel that.

This passage suggests that the desire to belong – "legitimately, ethically, fully," in Peggy's words – so often experienced as being personal by settler activists, is actually a collective phenomenon. In Ahmed's (2000) vision, a complete sense of belonging would constitute the ultimate in self-transformation for the settler subject. That said, in invoking a desire for ethical relations with Indigenous peoples, Peggy's narrative helps to disentangle an arguably radical and progressive desire from an untenable desire for legitimacy as a white settler. In fact, I wager that the intermingling, coexistence, and clash of such desires is emblematic of the paradox of attempting solidarity in a colonial present. Peggy's narrative raises the added question of whether awareness of the inextricable links between individual and collective subjectivity might help thwart the impulse to solidarity – a point I revisit.

Here is my follow-up question to Peggy about seeking legitimacy and belonging and the exchange that followed:

CAROL LYNNE: Do you think you'll always have that need to be accepted, to not be one of those "bad settlers"?

PEGGY: Yes, of course! The way that you want to be part of [Indigenous struggles]. And you just want to be part of that excitement and positive change and creativity. But then it's not quite yours. Or you think, "Oh this culture. I like this about this culture, or I like that about the culture. It's so much better in this or that way than my culture." It's really easy to feel this way. And if these people are your friends – some of these people are my best friends, and yet I can never fully join them in certain things. That's painful.

In this statement, Peggy once again confronts the seemingly intractable white settler desire to belong. In the process, she mentioned cultural difference, which in turn caused me to wonder: Would an excessive focus on cultural difference, in lieu of colonial hierarchies, inadvertently keep the liberal subject's pursuit of proximity in motion and colonial power relations intact?

~

In charting the course of gendered colonial subjectivity – everything that goes into how white women negotiate our prescribed roles in settler colonial contexts – as it meanders through the solidarity encounter, I became sure of at least one thing: the story is complex. Without trying to be theoretically evasive, I say this to highlight the back and forth in many white participant narratives between focusing on the personal versus focusing on the political and retreating again into liberal individualism. Even as white women struggle to come to terms with our settler status, a desire for belonging insinuates itself into our negotiations of solidarity work and often manifests as an individualistic desire/pursuit of proximity to Indigenous women. (Recall my telltale autobiographical moment.) This despite what Anderson (2000), LaRocque (2010), Schick (1998), and others, as we shall see, say about the collective/political dimension of proximity desires. Despite our best efforts to fathom our structural privilege, whether we label it as such, at one point or another in our solidarity trajectories, most white participants exhibit behaviours or attitudes characteristic of the gendered colonial subject.

This tension is precisely what caused me to speculate that the solidarity encounter itself – through providing an occasion for a sustained look at settler colonial complicity – provokes or exacerbates a crisis in our white settler desire for legitimacy. Drawing on the work of Sara Ahmed (2000, 13), I theorize the solidarity encounter overall as a "contemporary mode of proximity" where the risk is considerable, though never absolute, that stranger fetishism will kick in. When it does, I argue, the effect is an obscuring of colonial relations and, along with them, white women's self-understanding as members of a settler collectivity, leaving only atomistic, transcendent individuals in its wake. This theorizing lays the groundwork for charting how the pursuit of proximity to Indigenous women can become the vehicle to satiate the white settler desire for belonging – and why this can be detrimental to solidarity encounters.

Imagine the white settler woman subject poised to enter the world of solidarity. I had this image in mind when I began evaluating whether white participant narratives exhibit the liberal underpinnings of gendered colonial subjectivity. My analysis reveals a divergence in participant modalities of entering into political activism or solidarity. Whereas Indigenous women tend to view political activism/solidarity as a collective responsibility to ensure their nations' survival, white women take a more individualistic approach. This propensity conforms to the liberal individualism through which we become (and, in some cases, thrive). Further analysis bears this out; a considerable number of white participants were predisposed to position ourselves as individuals who had personally chosen to enter into solidarity relations rather than as members of a white settler collectivity obliged to do so. In thinking through notions of choice versus responsibility in relation to white women's reasons for engaging in political solidarity, I homed in on the trickiness of responding emotionally to colonial inequities. As Green astutely brings into focus, personal outrage, while warranted, can lodge white women firmly in the realm of individualistic self-making, distracting us from collective political goals. This set the stage for tracking what becomes of the white settler woman subject – her desires, attitudes, behaviours – once she's in the thick of the solidarity encounter.

This is not, however, the straightforward story of your average liberal subject. It is complicated by the many moments of recognition that pepper white participant narratives. Most of us do acknowledge and wrestle with our structural privilege, if inconsistently and to varying intensities. Alicia's and Peggy's narratives are particularly instructive examples – proof that gendered colonial subjectivity is not invincible or inevitable but rather inherently fraught and contested by white women themselves. In fact, a minority of white participants identify settler responsibility as the primary reason for engaging in solidarity work. Even such overt leanings can coincide with more individualistic understandings of the subject, however. In a word, the numerous ways in which the personal features in white narratives – such as pronouncements about ancestral colonial histories – reveal the endemic risk for white women of slipping into the individualistic, self-making mode of investment that can lead to solidarity tensions.

How is the solidarity encounter a potential means for white women to maintain our default liberal status? To answer this question, I considered what it looks like when solidarity functions as a space of reaffirmation for white women. In other words, I described how it is that white women's self-making processes can bind with solidarity work and involve (sometimes too much) proximity in the process. The spectrum of proximity concept consolidates an otherwise scattered array of desires, discourses, and dynamics that connote, involve, or require proximity in one form or another. While a generalized, often implicit desire for belonging suffuses the entire spectrum, it encompasses five broad categories: (1) the explicit desire to be accepted by an Indigenous person or included/welcomed into an Indigenous community; (2) the desire to be healed or taken care of; (3) the desire for self-empowerment, worth, or purpose; (4) an attraction to or appreciation of Indigenous culture, tradition, or spirituality; and (5) the desire to learn or be challenged. In a close reading of selected white participant narratives of becoming (Ahmed 2000), I identified instances of seeking spiritual connection, self-worth, empowerment, and transformation more broadly – sometimes, but not always, in noticeably gendered forms. In outlining these forms, I gender Ahmed's account of colonial masculinity to note a "fantasy of overcoming" rooted in white women's historical double positioning as both oppressor and oppressed. As these instances demonstrate, white women can pursue proximity through a variety of techniques – consuming, becoming, passing, and friendship among them – whose operation I flesh out in proceeding chapters.

Of course, I could not know when a particular white participant was consuming, becoming, or passing as an Indigenous Other in order to attain white settler belonging and/or ease white settler guilt.[7] Knowing for certain, in fact, has never been the point. As Aileen Moreton-Robinson (2000) reminds us, individual intentions are not necessarily relevant since structural dominance endows us with certain power and privileges regardless. What I did detect overall is an assemblage of proximity desires dotting these narratives in subtle and blatant ways. I also saw desire and deliberation in concert, which is to say that participant narratives address issues of settler colonial status and power, if in different ways and to varying extents. In the next three chapters, I continue to analyze how white women can self-servingly mobilize proximity in our attempts to maintain a sense of belonging on Indigenous land.

2

Transgressing Cherished Spaces

Indigenous Women on the Impulse to Solidarity

> I have a formal request that white women don't touch me or cry on me after shows. It drains my energy to comfort you. Keep the feeling in your heart and go home and research and ruminate and do something constructive with it.
>
> – TANYA TAGAQ

> There's a space between us that's the cherished thing. In my language, this is the home of the breath that we share. Both our breath is here ... Our common breath. The sound we make here is going to go around the world. It'll take a hundred years. It'll come right back to this spot. That's sacred ... This is what we cherish. So when you come too close and take up this space, then the cherished thing is gone.
>
> – LEE MARACLE

On June 3, 2020, renowned Inuk singer, songwriter, and activist Tanya Tagaq posted a Twitter message for white women everywhere: respect Indigenous women's boundaries. What I call the problem with proximity, and what Tagaq so clearly expresses, was not always self-evident to me. Even to this day, I find myself asking, "If the solidarity encounter is a 'mode of proximity,' doesn't that mean that solidarity actually *requires* proximity?" Then I remember the words of prominent Stó:lō/Métis writer, scholar, and activist Lee Maracle, one of the thirteen Indigenous participants in my research. Maracle's poetic observations remind me of solidarity's nuances and complexities. A certain proximity between people, groups, and even ideas is, indeed, necessary for the creation of a common breath, to use Maracle's metaphor. However, a problem ensues when white women try to get too close in their solidarity engagements – or music concerts, in Tagaq's case. The result, as Maracle explained, is a transgression: "When you come too close and take up this space, then the cherished thing is gone." Put differently, white settler women's behaviours in solidarity contexts (and beyond) are colonizing when they are invasive in either metaphorical or literal terms. These transgressions reflect and resolidify a colonizing relationship between Indigenous women and white women. All of this is to say that, more important than proximity per se are the kinds of spaces created by solidarity encounters as well as the dynamics of those spaces (i.e., how white women might seek closeness) in particular sociopolitical contexts. Proximity as a framework is valuable precisely because it allows us to think about the spaces and dynamics that continually (re)shape solidarity relationships over time. In this chapter, I draw mainly on Indigenous depictions of solidarity encounters to develop a more fulsome account of the problem with proximity.

To be sure, the majority of Indigenous participants qualified their harsh assessments of white women's solidarity work. They were quick to say, for example, that not all white women display egregiously problematic behaviours all or even most of the time. Nonetheless, several Indigenous participants pointed to the inevitable presence of at least one white woman whose "needy do-gooder" behaviour was deemed inappropriate or unproductive at best and invasive or damaging at worst. Such depictions of white settler "neediness" support my broader argument in two ways: by confirming that white desires for proximity to Indigenous Others are, indeed, operative in solidarity encounters, and by gesturing toward the role of settler/liberal subjectivity in how white women negotiate those encounters. In this way, Indigenous narratives lend both texture and heft to my spectrum of proximity. They testify to the risky business of solidarity encounters: at every turn, the white settler woman's objective in these encounters can too easily veer away from the anticolonial one of dismantling colonial structures toward the (seemingly) personal one of settler self-making. In a word, Indigenous insights into white neediness make clear the links between the helping behaviours, self-making processes, and proximity pursuits of white settler women.

At the same time, Indigenous women's takes on white neediness suggest the importance of thinking deeply about what has become of the colonial roots of Western feminism in contemporary solidarity relations. I attempt to do just that by reading white women's present-day helping behaviours with an eye to prototypical helping behaviours of yesteryear. Enter the impulse to solidarity, a companion concept to the spectrum of proximity. The impulse to solidarity refers to the white woman subject's latent, activated, or actualized drive to satiate her desires for proximity (and therefore belonging) through the solidarity encounter. As I define it, the solidarity impulse fuses the seemingly contradictory white desires to help and to be helped by the Indigenous Other. This is helping with a twist; white women stand to gain from the encounter as much as they stand to contribute to it. The phrase "to be helped by," then, marks the underside of the more familiar idea of helping, thus accounting for the assortment of self-serving or, more accurately, self-making reasons why white women might decide to engage, or stay engaged, in solidarity work with Indigenous women. Clearly, white women are not always or only involved in solidarity work for self-serving reasons. Rather, I want to think about whether and how solidarity encounters might inadvertently set into motion helping with a twist, which leads me to remark on how the solidarity impulse dovetails with and differs from the similarly fraught helping imperative theorized by Barbara Heron (2007).

Methodology Matters

Fundamentally, this book is my response to Indigenous women's critiques of whitestream feminism. In heeding the advice of one of whitestream feminism's staunchest critics, my analysis is informed by "an Indigenous critical gaze," anything less being tantamount to "methodological erasure" (Moreton-Robinson 2000, xxiii–xxiv). In other words, I feature Indigenous women's voices to shine the theoretical spotlight on white settler women's collective subjectivity. In practical terms, an Indigenous critical gaze affords us a better chance of unlocking the more inscrutable aspects of white women's negotiations of the solidarity encounter. As Aileen Moreton-Robinson (2000, xxiii) writes, "Indigenous women's life writings unmask the complicity of white women in gendered racial oppression." Moreton-Robinson is not alone in her approach; other Indigenous, feminist, and anticolonial scholars urge researchers "to make visible, center, and privilege those knowledges that have been placed in the margins because they represented threats to power" (Cannella and Manuelito 2008, 56; see also Arvin, Tuck, and Morrill 2013). Moreover, as many critical race scholars have since pointed out, those endowed with white privilege are not readily inclined to acknowledge it.

If white folks are not experts on their privilege, then who is? In her study of the predominately white world of Ontario midwifery, education scholar Sheryl

Nestel (2006, 9) centres racialized women's voices, given that "official norms of antidiscrimination and multiculturalism guarantee that whites do not normally admit to discriminatory practices." For her, researchers learn the most about discriminatory systems by speaking with people on the receiving end of those systems' effects. Chandra Mohanty (2003, 231) applies a similar logic in her work on transnational feminist solidarity, which relies on "analytically inclusive methodologies" that would "read up the ladder of privilege" to expose the workings of power.[1] In this chapter particularly, but throughout the book more generally, I count Indigenous women as the experts on white settler colonial privilege, given they are among those who most keenly feel its effects.

I draw on Indigenous participant thoughts about the same three broad themes addressed in Chapter 1: definitions of political activism/solidarity; motivations for engaging in political activism/solidarity; and understandings of solidarity tensions/challenges. To retrace the storyline, I must admit that my analytical strategy, which seems the obvious choice in retrospect, was in truth unplanned and evolved over several months. During that time, I was struck repeatedly by a general disconnect between Indigenous and white women's respective descriptions of solidarity encounters. Where Indigenous women saw tension or invasiveness, white women saw motivation and interest. I was struck by how white women overall did not perceive their investments in solidarity work as problematic let alone colonial. Only then did it occur to me to correlate Indigenous women's descriptions of solidarity tensions with white women's descriptions of what led them to the encounter in the first place. Therefore, while Chapter 1 provides an overview of proximity discourses as presented in white women's narratives, this chapter features Indigenous women's theorizations of some of the same discourses as colonial. I purposively present my ideas in this order (as they evolved) to drive home the point that, for me, and perhaps others like me, the problem with proximity is not readily apparent and takes repeated effort to comprehend – and apprehend! Anticipating an overly pessimistic interpretation of this chapter – and, indeed, my broader research – I would like to remind readers about Indigenous participant calls for and appreciation of white women allies.

Apathy Is What Got Us Killed: The Value and Limits of Caring in Solidarity Work

While my objective is not to vilify white women engaged in solidarity work, I do want to theorize the complexities and messiness of intersubjective relations in the solidarity encounter. This goal necessarily involves a critical stance and discussing some of the more "negative" aspects of Indigenous–white relations in settler colonial contexts. As Emma LaRocque (2010, 6) concedes, "Can we ever move past colonization, especially when it remains as an active toxin in the lives of Aboriginal peoples? Is it not better to try to understand its workings than to deny its existence or to judge its analysis as being necessarily 'negative'?" I aim to decipher some of the subtler ways in which colonization remains an active toxin in the solidarity encounter.

I detected similar sentiments in several Indigenous participant narratives. Attentive to the endemic problems of solidarity spaces, these women nestled their critiques within clear demands for non-Indigenous support of Indigenous self-determination. Despite solidarity's challenges, they not only ask white women to engage in it, but also laud our efforts in that regard. Take my conversation with Maracle, who was a member of the Stó:lō nation born in Vancouver but who had spent the last thirty years in Toronto.[2] She had an extensive history of political involvement with white women but noted that more recent interactions had been through events rather than participation in a specific group.[3] She was, she told me, more inclined to follow Indigenous youth and play less of a protagonist role in political activism altogether. All told, Maracle was optimistic when I posed this question:

> CAROL LYNNE: Is it possible to work together in a non-colonizing way at this moment?
>
> MARACLE: I think a lot of work being done together is non-colonizing. I'm not saying that it's not without its contentiousness ... [or] that there's never any colonizing behaviours in that context. But most of us get together to do something that is non-colonizing, like the solidarity with Aboriginal women on the West Coast. I think if you do nothing, that's a colonizing behaviour. I think if you participate, that's a non-colonizing behaviour. Even if you try to speak for us, it's still a non-colonizing behaviour with an appropriation spin on it, which can be a bit problematic. But the behaviour itself, of going out and stopping some kind of injustice, is a non-colonizing behaviour in this [colonizing] country.

While aware of solidarity's limitations, Maracle stressed the importance of *attempting* political projects that bring Indigenous and non-Indigenous people together. At the same time, Maracle called for being realistic about what solidarity can accomplish: "We cannot eradicate [colonialism] in a solidarity action.

What we can do is accomplish a task and come together as human beings, and establish relationship. And anything that gets in the way of that relationship has to be moved." Her message highlights the simple fact that non-colonizing solidarity will not develop if people do not take up solidarity in any way.

Other Indigenous participants, including Lydia, did not dismiss the motivation to help that seems intrinsic to some white women's decisions to enter solidarity work. Prepared with a variety of sweet and savoury snacks, I met Lydia at her home. Settled at the kitchen table, we talked about her decades of political involvement, which she modestly described as simply "the work that I do." She continued, "I don't think I necessarily consider myself an activist. I'm just doing what's in front of me, doing what I encounter. Certainly, I'm starting to see that label and wondering if that's a label I want, but I don't know if I would say that, so much as I'm just trying to live my life." Midway through our interview, Lydia's answer to a question about white guilt in solidarity encounters took me off guard:

> LYDIA: I've more encountered the "I need to help" kind of syndrome, but they're helping without critically reflecting on how their actions may be hurting.
> CAROL LYNNE: I know I've sort of asked this, but where do you think that helping syndrome comes from?
> LYDIA: I don't know that it's always guilt that [white women] are feeling, that's an assumption. I think it's just compassion, empathy, and need. I don't think it's a dirty thing or a bad thing. I think it's a beautiful thing. I think it's terrible when people try to spin it into a bad thing. I mean, isn't that just something we innately do, is want to nurture and care for one another?
> CAROL LYNNE: But you're saying it can have bad consequences if it's done in the wrong way?
> LYDIA: Yeah, if white women haven't critically reflected on how their helping may actually hurt. It's kind of like a psychologist, when you think about it. They have to be really critically reflective about their own issues and make sure they're not projecting them onto the patient ... You really have to do your own work if you're interested in genuinely helping.

As it turned out, Lydia was less concerned with guilt than with the "I need to help" syndrome, which she embraced as a potentially "beautiful thing." In fact, she was critical of those who would "spin it into a bad thing." In the end, though, Lydia took a practical approach: the work of solidarity has both positive and negative potential. As for what a white woman's "own work" might entail, I save that discussion for the final chapter.

Teresa joined Lydia in pinpointing the desire to nurture. Introduced in Chapter 1, Teresa identified primarily as Cree with some European ancestry. Her foray into politics was through academia. Again, like Lydia, she believed some women, whether Indigenous or non-Indigenous, join movements out of political passion and a sense of urgency around the collective need to act:

> It doesn't matter whether you're a white woman, but I think it's got more to do with spirit and heart, and the reason why you want to join in solidarity toward a movement is because you feel passionate about the cause ... As women, we're all matriarchal, so we all have this nurturing sense about us, whether we're mothers or not. We want to take care of things. We feel community's important ... There's this sense of urgency that we need do something for the sake of humanity and the protection of Earth.

Teresa explicitly named the imperative of a broad, collective struggle, which drives, according to her, Indigenous and white women alike. Setting aside any issues of sex/gender essentialism arguably arising in Lydia's and Teresa's narratives, I want to highlight a different, and very significant, undercurrent of both – Indigenous women hold simultaneously positive and critical views of white women's decisions "to join in solidarity."

In addition, Teresa tied "this sense of urgency" to act to a lack of complacency: "I think a white woman who comes to the table in an attempt to work in solidarity toward an Indigenous issue is not complacent, and that's why they're there." Paralleling Teresa, Maracle interpreted a white woman's commitment to solidarity as a tangible sign of caring about Indigenous women, a point evident in her broader remark about solidarity and transformation:

> I think always when people work together ... [transformation] can be really limited or quite profound depending on the nature of the work together. I think the [white] women who are working with bringing attention to the murdered Aboriginal women, I think that transformation's quite profound, because you're fundamentally saying, "We care about these women." It requires that you care. So the people who are not caring are saying "It's appropriation," or "It's this," or "It's that"; they have a lot of reasons for not going, but the main one is they're very scared to care. If you care about us, then it changes things. And I've talked with a lot of those women on those

little marches ... They're deeply caring people ... I think *that* change is the most important change ... Because apathy is what got us killed. Apathy is a killer. So the caring is more important than anything to me.

What some think of as a healthy fear of appropriation by white women, and perhaps a justifiable reason for not doing solidarity work, Maracle considers no less than a pretext for settler inaction.

Yet another Indigenous participant invoked the notion of care. I joined Belinda, one of my first interviewees, in a dusty, drab room at the University of Toronto but our conversation was anything but! As a Cree woman with an expansive definition of political solidarity or activism and extensive involvement in facilitating antiracist workshops, among other things, Belinda defined political solidarity as a "coming together for a common goal and working toward that goal." When asked to describe white allyship, Belinda directed the question back to me:

I guess, really, you care, that's why you're there, right? You want to do something even if you don't know what it is you should be doing, but you want to engage somehow. You are open and willing to learn how to be a helper, and you don't necessarily have to have all the answers. You don't have to be the expert; just your presence makes a big difference ... And just to show that people do care ... [about] what's happening to a group of [Indigenous] women that maybe don't show they care in the same way, but just can't afford that time, maybe not being able to come to all these meetings.

In this instance, Belinda was referring to solidarity around the issue of MMIWG2S people. For her, white women have a responsibility to engage with this issue, especially in light of the socioeconomic and other structural barriers that constrain many Indigenous women's political activism. (Ardra, an Indigenous participant introduced in Chapter 1, likewise mentioned "the crisis management and business that most Indigenous lives are filled with.") While unambiguous in her position that white women should care about violence against Indigenous women, Belinda also set parameters around that involvement: white women should be present as peers, not experts, and demonstrate a willingness to learn *how* to help. In other words, Indigenous leadership should be front and centre to mitigate the possibility of ally domination in the solidarity encounter, another point I elaborate on in the final chapter.

Although it is somewhat muted in the above passages, there was a strong critique among the Indigenous women I spoke with that white women's decisions to help or care are risk-laden. Recall Ruth Green's (Kanien'kehá:ka) warning in Chapter 1 about the dangers of conflating emotional engagement with being emotional. For that matter, Lydia also offered a qualified stance on the white woman's desire to help Indigenous women. The problem, as I see it, lies in how "being emotional," to borrow Green's phrase, can keep the white woman stuck in the realm of the personal, individualizing her engagement in solidarity work and steering her away from the collective political goal of dismantling colonial structures. Put more directly, our actions fall prey to the flipside of the proverbial coin – what I label the "to be helped by syndrome," to riff off Lydia's analogy. In the rest of this chapter – and, indeed, this book – I attempt to elucidate the particulars of this risk – essentially, the setting into motion of gendered colonial subjectivity or, more particularly, its quest for legitimacy and belonging. More specifically, by reading Indigenous women's perceptions of and experiences with white neediness through the lens of the white desire for proximity, I make visible the constitutive underside of white women's desire to help – the desire to be helped by Indigenous women in our self-making.

Scholars of international development, Gada Mahrouse (2009a) among them, offer transferable insights into the complexities of dominantly positioned subjects' desires to help Others.[4] In her critical appraisal of white/Western citizen-journalists who travel to conflict areas in the Global South, Mahrouse echoes Indigenous participant voices in two ways: first, by maintaining that the political exigencies of our times warrant the inclination to help; and second, by advising journalists to examine this inclination carefully and continuously. Mahrouse (2009a, 670) "refutes the simplistic resolution that people with Western privilege must not participate in such practices" even as she illustrates how racialized hierarchies are reproduced through the "witnessing, documenting and reporting practices" of these citizen-journalists.

Barbara Heron (2007, 6) also contributes to conversations about the ethical dilemmas of international development work with her analysis of the helping imperative, defined as the "desire for other people's development" that drives white/northern middle-class women to do development work in the Global South. Tracing the historical contours of this imperative, Heron notes four colonial continuities or ideas that persevere in the minds of many such development workers: planetary consciousness, self-affirmation through racialized comparisons, a sense of obligation and entitlement to do development work, and a fascination with Others.[5] Most significantly, white/Western women's desires to help become a vehicle for ensuring their goodness, that is, the fulfillment of "a moral imperative in processes of white feminist identity formation" (Heron 2007, 16). I build on the ideas of Mahrouse, Heron, and others to theorize the complexities of intersubjective dynamics specific to the solidarity encounter between Indigenous women and white women in Canada – dynamics that coalesce in the impulse to solidarity.

The Problem with Proximity: Transgressing Cherished Spaces

To reiterate, most if not all of the Indigenous women I spoke to took the position that non-Indigenous solidarity is necessary, important, and possible. What's more, they reported that extreme cases of blatant colonial attitudes or behaviours, while they exist, are not the norm. Nonetheless, several Indigenous participants noticed ever-present patterns of self-serving desires among some white women that they typically described in terms of neediness. According to Moreton-Robinson (2000, 19), Indigenous women in Australia have observed white academic feminists to be similarly "impersonal, individualistic and egocentric with interests to protect." To explain the links between neediness, proximity, and gendered colonial subjectivity, I examine what Indigenous critiques of white women's comportment indicate about the problem with proximity and white settler/liberal subjectivity more broadly.

Above all, Indigenous narratives lay bare the potentially detrimental effects on political solidarity of the white woman's pursuit of proximity to Indigenous women. In remarking on white women's needy attitudes and behaviours, their narratives identify the desire for proximity that appears to mediate much of white settler subject formation, painting an unmistakable picture of its pitfalls and complications. Maracle's unforgettable words featured in this chapter's epigraph cut to the quick. When asked to explain what makes for colonizing behaviour, she summed up the cost of white women's unchecked desires for proximity to Indigenous women:

> MARACLE: Well, [there's colonizing] when there's invasion involved and the other person has to push back to get a space.
> CAROL LYNNE: Whether that's in a solidarity encounter or ...
> MARACLE: Exactly, or anywhere else. So there's a space between us that's the cherished thing. In my language, this is the home of the breath that we share. Both our breath is here. Not just my breath, not just your breath, but our common breath. The sound we make here is going

to go around the world. It'll take a hundred years. It'll come right back to this spot. That's sacred. You can't get more sacred than that. So this is what we cherish. So when you come too close and take up this space, then the cherished thing is gone. So [solidarity] requires noninvasive behaviours.

Maracle encapsulates a simple yet profound message that emerged from Indigenous participant narratives: white women's behaviours in solidarity contexts (and beyond) are colonizing when they are invasive in either metaphorical or literal terms. Maracle's use of Stó:lō understandings of the breath and the sacred tie into broader Indigenous ontological principles, such as what Mishuana Goeman (2008, 298) calls "the intergenerational philosophy of the breath ... [that] connects all living entities to each other as relatives." Similarly, Opaskwayak Cree philosopher Shawn Wilson conveys a pertinent message of connection in describing the spaces between us, including between people, or between people and concepts, as sacred: "When bridging that space," we are "entering the sacred."[6] Viewed from within these paradigms, our intersubjective performances in the shared, mutually constructed space of the solidarity encounter matter. A first step in figuring out how white women can strive for ethical relations in solidarity work is to dive deep into Indigenous women's assessments of the problem.

Needing Goodness: White Settler Women, Self-Interest, and the Desire for Proximity

Certainly, needy do-gooder was among the less flattering phrases Indigenous participants used when analyzing white women's negotiations of solidarity encounters. According to several Indigenous participants, this type of woman is an unfailing fixture of these encounters. For my purposes, the figure of the needy do-gooder warrants scrutiny for one reason: her personal reasons for engaging in solidarity work can overshadow or displace her political reasons for doing so. As Lydia put it, "If you think about it, there are probably going to be some non-Indigenous women who feel compelled out of guilt and sympathy and empathy [to engage in solidarity]. I think that's great, as long as you're not a leech about it. As long as you don't suck out of us, whatever that is."

I read Lydia's comments in relation to the vicissitudes of gendered colonial subjectivity and proximity dynamics. In this light, they point to a threshold similar to the one introduced by Green as the difference between "emotionally involved" and "emotional." For Lydia, the difference was between sympathy, empathy, or even guilt versus leech-like behaviour, the latter a form of self-making at the expense of the Indigenous Other. In other words, we can also conceptualize the problem with proximity as one of crossing a threshold.

As Indigenous participants asserted, white women sometimes enter solidarity spaces to pursue their own agenda, however defined, at the expense of Indigenous political goals. Another excerpt from Lydia's narrative hints at the full range of ways, from blatant to subtle, that a white woman might pursue her personal/self-making interests. When asked about what causes tension in solidarity encounters, Lydia listed a slew of behaviours that she found indicative of white women's more individualistic reasons for being involved in solidarity work:

> White women not being able to handle it, and they run to the patriarchy, or they have their own agenda, and so they know that there's too many layers of lateral violence to deal with women, so they go to the men, so they push a patriarchal agenda. Again, they're not standing in solidarity. They're not being collaborators. They're not genuinely being allies. They're not standing behind us and saying, "What do you want us to do? And we're willing to deal with all the oppression that you have ... We know you're going to be angry toward us. We know you're going to even possibly be racist toward us, but we're going to stand behind you instead of running away from what you're going to do to us to a patriarch" ... That's, I think, my most crucial analysis of what white women are doing to us. It's because they're not coming to us to be true allies and collaborators. They're coming to us to see what they can get ... Academic gain, economic gain, political gain. A lot of them have their own issues, and they feel like they need to be Indigenous people's saviours. A lot of them, I think, are spiritually disenfranchised, so they run to Indigenous people to get their spiritual enfranchisement ... I find they're impinging on us, and we don't have the resources to help them with their issues ... They shouldn't be coming to us for help. But that's no better than academics who come to us for a topic.

Notably, Lydia's comprehensive portrayal of the self-interested white woman ally in solidarity work – in pursuit of academic, economic, political, and spiritual gain – calls to mind my spectrum of proximity and the associated risks of crossing a line: "I find they're impinging on us, and we don't have the resources to help with their issues." Moreover, in noting that white women sometimes "run to the patriarchy" and "push a patriarchal agenda," Lydia explained the encounter in explicitly gendered terms. Lydia's observations also suggest that privileging the political stakes of solidarity work (over the personal) would make white women better able to withstand personal criticism and stay engaged, a point I discuss further in Chapter 5.

Three other Indigenous participants – Danielle, Kellie, and Gabriela – explicitly invoked the figure of the needy do-gooder as the personification of misguided white settler investments in solidarity work. After a tour of her office, I sat down for tea, cookies, and conversation with Danielle, an Indigenous woman with decades of experience in the antiviolence and Indigenous rights movements. We spent much of the time discussing this fundamental question: "How do you think colonial attitudes manifest themselves today, especially in the solidarity work that you've done?" Danielle answered in two parts. First, she cited the general population's tendency to embrace the myth of Canadian benevolence (Mackey 2002; Regan 2010) in a state of wilful ignorance (Moreton-Robinson 2000). With infectious energy, Danielle insisted, "Everybody just makes this assumption that things are on the up and up, that Canada's rooted in this real just ... that there's equity in Canada and that discrimination and racism don't exist. 'Not us Canadians! We're generous and we're peaceful, we're kind and we all say thank you and we're sorry.'" Shifting the focus to solidarity encounters, she added, "I guess the other piece is that there's some pretty needy individuals who are mixed up in the social-justice movement who need attention, who need to identify, who need all of these things."[7] Danielle's point distilled is this: "[They] need to have a cause; they need to do good; they need the attention; they need the power; they need the control." Once I accustomed myself to Danielle's upfront manner, I processed her description of the average needy do-gooder as usually, but not exclusively, a white woman who exudes arrogance. I found myself wondering to what extent this figure, like Heron's (2007, 34) development worker, embodies the need "to construct a sense of self in moral terms." I also couldn't shake the spellbinding possibility of my resemblance to this figure.

My interview with Kellie yielded insights into a related aspect of gendered colonial subjectivity. Kellie is an Indigenous woman from beyond Turtle Island who lives in Toronto; her political activism runs the gamut from antipoverty to anticolonial work. We decided to meet in an unassuming coffee shop not far from my apartment. Noise factor aside, the place was nice and the food tasty. About a half hour into our discussion, I heard echoes of Danielle's assessment of needy do-gooder egoism when Kellie described a case of solidarity gone wrong. I prompted the story by asking her if she had ever witnessed the appropriation of Indigenous ceremonies or cultures in solidarity spaces:

> [The two Native men] were saying, "Do you know how disrespectful this looks?" And [the white woman] was like, "But I've got every right to own this because this is the feather that I have and I'm studying in the shaman school, and you've got no right to criticize me and my ability to be a shaman." [They went on,] "But you understand that you're trying to make this a welcoming solidarity space, but the first thing a Native person sees is that? They're going to want nothing to do with you ... You don't even deserve to own this [feather]" ... The worst part is ... maybe if she was like, "I'm sorry, I didn't know." She just didn't care ... It was her damn right as a white person to do whatever [she] wanted.

As Kellie described it, the situation revolved around a self-ascribed white woman self-ascribed ally spurred on by a sense of entitlement, which left Kellie incredulous: "She's claiming she's in solidarity. Like, the word 'solidarity,' she's claiming that was a solidarity space!"

Once again, I thought of Heron's (2007) development worker. Listening to Kellie, I caught glimpses of the colonial attitude Heron describes as planetary consciousness (a prelude to the link between individual and collective subjectivity discussed at length in the next chapter). Heron (2007, 34) writes, "Both as individuals and as national subjects, white middle-class Canadians and other Northerners continue to construct through the prism of a planetary consciousness a sense of self in moral terms that expresses the entitlement and obligation bourgeois subjects feel to 'help' Others." Heron's analysis, alongside the commentaries of Danielle and Kellie, reveals more about the entwining of the desires to help and to be helped by. This composite figure can feel both entitled and obliged to engage in activities to establish her moral rectitude.

This brings me to a trapping of white settler/liberal subjectivity more broadly – a sudden, exaggerated belief, brimming with paternalistic undertones, in one's capacity to effect immediate change. To clarify, I adhere to the idea that individuals can make a difference and must therefore act responsibly, recognizing the potential impact, whether minimal or sizable, of their actions in the world. However, both Danielle and Kellie were concerned about the arrogance of this posture, which can beset white women, and likely white men and gender-diverse folks – especially those learning about colonial realities for the first time – and slide them into helping behaviour. To be clear, there was little indication of such a brazen approach in the white narratives I heard. As I establish in Chapter 1, many white participants remained troubled or uncertain about their entitlement to do solidarity work, which I suspect means that entitlement in contemporary solidarity encounters is quite nuanced in expression, a point I take up further in Chapter 4.

On par with Lydia's sentiment about leech-like behaviour, Gabriela used equally strong language and spatialized imagery to describe the debilitating effects on solidarity encounters of the white woman subject's need to do/be good. Gabriela is a publicly engaged scholar, writer, and artist with years of solidarity work under her belt, including her recent involvement in a mixed (Indigenous–non-Indigenous) solidarity coalition of mostly women, with a sprinkling of men.[8]

Thoroughly enveloped by the intensity of the moment, I sat in Gabriela's small corner office as she talked about how she came to be in the group. She recalled a particularly disturbing incident with a white woman from the coalition. At one point, Gabriela conveyed the gravity of the situation by motioning *stop* with her arm outstretched:

> GABRIELA: I'm not explaining it very well, but there's a lot of tension around how to [address bad behaviour], and there are people who are not Indigenous people who I experience – and other people too, I know – who are really needy and want to engage with you in a way that [*she motions "stop"*] you want to really move away rather than toward ... well, kind of like a succubus, the ones who are kind of ...
> CAROL LYNNE: A succubus?
> GABRIELA: Yes, a succubus. You know what a succubus is? It sucks ...
> CAROL LYNNE: The blood?
> GABRIELA: The blood out.

While admitting that "other people" besides white people can be "really needy," Gabriela experienced white needy do-gooder behaviour on a whole other level – as predatory, akin to interacting with a succubus, interpreted here in vampiric rather than seductive terms. In this way, Gabriela vividly imagined a central feature of this behaviour as described by Indigenous participants: a desire for and pursuit of proximity that morphs into invasiveness, whether metaphoric (e.g., draining Indigenous women's psychic or emotional energies) or embodied (e.g., coming too close and/or occupying too much physical space).

Picking up where we left off in our conversation about colonizing behaviours, I asked Maracle if white women must acknowledge our settler status to engage in non-colonizing solidarity. In her response, she spoke further about the settler desire for proximity that can interfere with solidarity efforts, this time absent an explicit gender analytic:

> The Oka Crisis required a higher level of engagement, and nobody I worked closely with saw themselves as anything but a settler in that moment, because it required that kind of deeper understanding of what the relationship was, a deeper understanding of what we were doing, a higher level of commitment.[9] All of that sort of looking inside and looking outside, and understanding history, and understanding what the future ... all of this ... But to do a project that's got an anticolonial outcome, you don't have to have a view of yourself as a settler. But I will tell you that you will run into difficulty working with Aboriginal people unless you're clear about that. Because I think the expectation is that they'll get *close* to us. People who don't have an understanding of the colonial relation want to be *close* to us. That's been my experience. And that doesn't happen, and then they'll be disappointed [emphasis added].

In this statement, Maracle touches on the key theme of this chapter in at least three ways. First, she identifies an expectation that infuses the solidarity work of some white people – the belief that "they'll get close to us" – especially those who are unreflective about the magnitude of settler colonial history. In short, she not only detects the white settler desire for proximity, which I argue takes specifically gendered forms, but also corroborates the importance of an anticolonial analysis for keeping the personal political. Second, she registers the disappointment of those who do not achieve closeness, a scenario that holds true in my own solidarity experiences. Third, in insisting that a "deeper understanding" of the colonial relationship is necessary to sustain a "higher level of engagement," Maracle raises the intriguing idea that white settler investments in solidarity can happen along a continuum, a thread I pick up again in Chapter 4.

Overall, white participants did not readily relate solidarity tensions to white neediness. Julia was a notable exception. Her reply to a question about cultural appropriation spoke volumes:

> CAROL LYNNE: Were there other examples of what you would see as appropriation?

> *JULIA:* I think, just in general, for white folks going to different events and wearing the garb and that kind of ... really blatant, obvious examples of appropriation. But for a good chunk of it, it's just to be seen for some of these folks, just to be seen as "I get it, I'm a do-gooder" piece ... For some people that was, I think, a push to be seen as being a member of a [Indigenous solidarity] group.

Julia's response conjures up images of my proximity spectrum, founded on a generalized white settler desire for acceptance by Indigenous people (as in, "a push to be seen"). In addition, like Kellie when she described the white woman who went to "shaman school," Julia connects white settler neediness to cultural appropriation – this time, across genders. In the process, she clarifies how the desire for appropriation can fit the white settler needy do-gooder profile.

The Burden of Care and White Settler Takeovers

Indigenous participants narrated experiences that corresponded to other elements of my proximity spectrum, including the desires for healing and empowerment, which appeared to manifest most readily as demands for Indigenous caretaking. According to Indigenous participants, these caretaking demands are a major limitation in the solidarity encounter but one that they or, perhaps more accurately, white women can and do overcome, if temporarily and in rare instances (for example, when Indigenous women do not have to explain indigeneity or, by extension, whiteness). To pre-empt any misunderstandings, my concern is not whether Indigenous women are up to the task of caretaking (or educating, as I discuss in the next section). To make this the concern risks assessing the Indigenous subject as damaged, inferior, or in need of saving. Rather, the issue is that Indigenous women identify these caretaking demands as invasive and therefore as an impediment to solidarity efforts. Through the lens of proximity, these are, in effect, demands for Indigenous women to cede space or take a back seat to white women in meetings or events. Moreover, these demands are instances of white women's self-making and thus reflections of gendered colonial subjectivity, that is, negotiating the solidarity encounter as an autonomous individual rather than as a person embedded in a settler collectivity.

Some Indigenous narratives of solidarity experiences are about mixed gender spaces. As such, they provide valuable insights into white settler desire across genders. Take the following case of a "hijacking" described by

Kellie in spatialized terms as crossing a boundary. This time the protagonist was a white settler man:

> The meeting was over, essentially. He hijacked it with his own pain ... That's where I think it becomes, not cultural appropriation, but there's a boundary that's been crossed which, you haven't been invited over. Because suddenly it wasn't about the meeting, it wasn't about that one [Indigenous] woman sharing her pain or why she felt the word "genocide" was important and her story and her collective cultural story she was telling. Once again a white man has hijacked the whole space. "Now, again, we have to stop what we're doing in our own healing to make sure you're okay. Even though you're our oppressors, we have to make sure you're okay?" ... What a waste of energy that is.

For Kellie, this was a familiar story: a white settler attempting to take over, knowingly or otherwise, a space dedicated to Indigenous collective sociopolitical concerns accessed, in this case, through Indigenous storytelling. In effect, the white settler called on the Indigenous people in the room to set aside their own needs, whatever they may be, to assume a caretaking role.

Three more excerpts from Indigenous narratives tell similar tales of the white settler desire to be cared for:

> GREEN: You know what really pisses me off about [white/settler guilt]?
> CAROL LYNNE: No. What?
> GREEN: It's that settler people and white people, white people specifically, get to cry about [colonization]. Why the fuck do they get to cry about it and I don't?

> I expressed some emotion; [the white woman] became reactionary and made an emotional decision ... I really think that happens a lot. The thing that's really unfair in that situation is I have a lot of reason to be emotional about what's happening. There's a whole community of people that I'm trying to care for. You don't have that experience and neither does that other person. And it's not just emotion, it's spiritual knowledge. That's how spirit emerges, through emotion. So, I guess what I'm supposed to do, Carol Lynne, is to moderate my emotions about what colonization has done because it's offensive to a lot of people, but I feel like I'm extra burdened. (Lydia)
>
> Well, in one of those workshops, like the [one on] decolonization, a white woman might stand up and say ... I remember vaguely something like

this happening, where she'd be, like, "I just feel so bad." And then she would start crying, "But it's not really my fault because I was born into this." Then there's a caretaking aspect, where ... "Yeah, no, it's not your fault. It's okay," you know [that] kind of thing. So that's been an issue. Then having to tiptoe around really naming things or calling people out because we don't want to hurt people's feelings. (Ursula)

In the first excerpt, Green remarks candidly on the white guilt that might underpin the settler desire to receive care. Then come Lydia's and Ursula's equally frank perspectives on the repercussions of such desires. All three described being "impinged" upon, to use Lydia's word, by the desires or needs and corresponding self-making processes of white settler subjects – both women and men – at the expense of the political agenda on the table. Gender is nonetheless a factor in that Indigenous *women* are the targeted caregivers. To boot, the onus is on them not only to control their emotive responses (e.g., sadness or anger) to Indigenous dispossession, but also to comfort the emotive reactions of white settlers to the same.

In relation to the (however subconscious) presumption that Indigenous women are there to perform the role of healer or caretaker, Zainab Amadahy drew parallels to a long-standing critique by women of colour in North American feminist circles. Amadahy is a long-time researcher, organizational development consultant, author, and educator based in Toronto who identified as African American, Cherokee, Seminole, and Polynesian with some European heritage. She shared this insight during dinner at a popular Indian restaurant on Yonge Street in downtown Toronto, where the dimly-lit room buzzed with air conditioning. While recognizing that white settlers will need support in some form at some point to engage effectively as allies, Amadahy was emphatic that Indigenous women are not responsible for extending that support:

Take your supports where you can find them. I know you need healing, but I'm not going to heal you. I'm not here for that. It's kind of like that whole question African Americans used to say, "I don't want to be your antiracist teacher." So it's kind of like, "I don't want to be your healer. Deal with that. I understand you have to go through it ... Come to me when you're ready to deal with it." That's how I feel about it.

In other words, Amadahy wanted to establish a different precedent, one where white women do not automatically assume Indigenous women will heal them or provide emotional comfort in solidarity settings. This would include, as Amadahy's analogy suggests, any related white expectations about Indigenous women's roles as teachers.

The Burden of Proof and White Supremacist Thinking
Without a doubt, many white women do seek out information about settler colonialism. They take it upon themselves to learn about how white women both benefit from and perpetuate it, to paraphrase Julia. Along the same lines as Amadahy, Julia acknowledged, "It's not the responsibility of the Indigenous folks to educate us. They've done enough of that." However, as a small though vocal chorus of Indigenous voices proclaimed, Julia's approach is not representative of every white woman's approach. In these Indigenous women's experiences, white settlers have not only repeatedly asked them to teach about Indigenous struggles but also presumed the information would be in white settler terms. This (rather contradictory) expectation affects Indigenous peoples globally, as Janet Conway (2010) notes in her study of the World Social Forum; smaller-scale, rural-based movements especially are often unintelligible as political traditions to white/Western audiences unless they can articulate their practices in hegemonic modern/Western terms. Green explained the challenge this way:

> So much of my world, I find, is that. We're not listened to until we can put ourselves in the ideas of the colonizer. That happens no matter where we are, be it solidarity, be it ... Very rarely have I found that my experience as an Aboriginal person can stand as just that unless it's equated to something the settler can understand.

Basically, Green and Conway both reject the demand that Indigenous peoples speak in terms palatable to white settler/Western interlocutors in order to be judged by those interlocutors as having valid concerns.

Following these thinkers, we can link the demand for epistemic palatability, shall we say, to colonial subjectivity more broadly. Gada Mahrouse (2009a, 667) does just that when noting a judgmental tendency among white/Western citizen-journalists in non-Western contexts:

> Their determination to obtain the truth, however well-intentioned, resulted in an "investigative tenor" ... insofar as they often doubted what they were being told and felt the need to discern the authenticity of the personal

stories they heard. Most helpful for the purposes of understanding this dynamic is Said's (1978) observation that racialized binaries "naturally" set up the Westerner not only as a spectator, but also as a judge of the Others' behaviour (109). In this sense, the activists' presence is imbued with a racialized function of surveillance and a measure of accountability.

Despite being the one seeking knowledge, the Western citizen-journalist adopts a doubtful, investigative tenor and positions herself as capable of judging (knowing) the Others' truths.

Conway, Green, and Mahrouse are not alone in alluding to a paradox in white settler subjectivity that nonetheless adheres to colonial logic: the dominant (white settler) subject's need to learn from the Other often coexists with an unrelenting desire to reconstitute oneself as the one who knows in contrast to that so-called unknowing Other. As you may recall from the last chapter, Sara Ahmed (2000) reconciles this seeming inconsistency by theorizing strange encounters as colonial encounters. In reference to the creation of ethnographies, she quips: "If the stranger [or Other] is admitted as possibly knowing differently, then the document and the 'who' would lose the easy identification that allows the stranger to be figurable as the 'what'" (Ahmed 2000, 73–74). In other words, if white settlers/Westerners were to trust and listen to Others, we would be forced to stare historical inequalities in the face, rendering us no longer able to fetishize Others as inferior by nature. Thus, Ahmed sheds light on why the Other must remain unknowing, even in ironic exchanges where that Other is nominally seen in an instructive capacity: to ensure that colonialism's "histories of determination" stay masked.

Echoing Green, Mahrouse, and Ahmed, Amadahy gestured toward how the need to retain the ethnocentric parameters of white settler knowledge production (that is, to remain the one who "knows") connects to the practice of tokenizing Indigenous peoples:

> I think that there's been a difference for the most part ... in working with people of colour, because I think people of colour kind of understand the position that I'm in and the nuances and the complexities and the contradictions of the position that I'm in [as Indigenous to Turtle Island, but not Ontario]. That's a generalization, because it's not true with everybody. With whites, I kind of felt like they were looking at me through a set of lenses that said "Indian." So if they needed a token, or a representative, or an interpreter, or a door-opener, I was the go-to person for a very long time

for many, many people because they didn't know any other Indians, or they didn't like the other Indians that they knew, or they didn't think that the other Indians that they knew were competent, or could function in their world and could understand their analysis or share their analysis.

While noting that settlers of colour can also succumb to tokenizing beliefs and behaviours, Amadahy found white settlers, regardless of gender, more likely to engage in solidarity in ways that reinforce a white settler worldview, which includes stereotypes about Indigenous peoples.

Rebeka Tabobondung, an Anishinaabekwe (Ojibwe woman) from Wasauksing First Nation with Dutch ancestry, complemented Amadahy's assessment. Seated at a big stool in Tabobondung's open concept living room, I was more than a little in awe of this community documentary filmmaker, poet, and Indigenous knowledge researcher and editor of *MUSKRAT* magazine. I calmed my nerves enough to listen intently as Tabobondung spoke about the extensive temporal and contextual reach of white-supremacist thinking. She associated this thinking with "Westerness" and the marring of Indigenous–non-Indigenous relations. Noting the depth of decolonization work awaiting white settlers, Tabobondung stated, "I really oversimplify things sometimes, but it's such a deep level of white-supremacist thinking that their reality is the only reality that could possibly exist in the universe ... Everyone goes through their own process [of decolonization] where they're in denial for a bit." Reminding me of Green, Tabobondung cited repeated displays of white settler guilt as typical:

> [White settler guilt] impacts [the solidarity encounter] because if somebody who's non-Native reveals an aspect of their guilt too much – I mean, you could do it once, and we can all help and talk through things – if you continue to have the same mental block, where the Indigenous person has already explained to you once why they might feel this way, or why it should be done this way ... then I think that will stop further conversation. The Indigenous person's not willing to invest even more time because it's your issue ... When I say *you*, I mean non-Indigenous or white women. You need to have your own journey ... It's like white people, they want you to prove to them something, prove to them the impacts of colonization.

Here, Tabobondung spells out a seemingly incessant feature of "white-supremacist thinking," which is the white subject's tendency to doubt the veracity of Indigenous claims about ongoing colonial dispossession, violence, and discrimination directed toward Indigenous nations. Tabobondung pays equal attention to Indigenous capacities to counter the potentially disruptive impacts of white guilt, doubt, and supremacy – by (re)establishing boundaries. Simply put, when a white person refuses to take cues from an Indigenous person, Tabobondung insists, "I think that will stop further conversation. The Indigenous person's not willing to invest even more time, because it's your issue." Not incidentally, by focusing on Indigenous agency, Tabobondung also pushes back against mainstream feminist frameworks that do "not allow for the theorisation of Indigenous women as socially situated subjects of knowledge" (Moreton-Robinson 2000, 91). Tabobondung's message, together with those of Amadahy and Green, suggests that another step toward non-colonizing solidarity would be for white women (and white people of other genders) to recognize certain demands, including placing the burden of proof on Indigenous women/peoples, for what they are: examples of white-supremacist thinking.

Teresa – who, as I mention above, appreciated the passion that drives any woman to social-justice work – went further. When asked about her definition of a colonial dynamic, Teresa tied white-supremacist thinking even more directly to a host of seemingly individualistic desires that can accompany white women into the solidarity encounter:

> Whenever there is a [colonial dynamic], it comes from that ... learned place: the need to be the authority when they're not the authority, or the need to be heard and to be recognized when, usually, you're the only one who is heard and recognized. Well, now's the time to be a bit complacent in that need ... Yeah, it's always, always coming from that place. The other stages of colonization that Burgess talks about are surface accommodation and tokenism. I think that happens a lot in circles. There's only a token understanding of what's going on. Indigenous women are only accommodated on the surface, but when it comes to Indigenous women delineating any type of structure of solidarity, it's not easily understood by a Western woman, because the structure is *so* completely opposite. Like the structure of the medicine wheel versus the patriarchal, capitalist structure of the pyramid. It's a process of thought that needs to be undone in order for solidarity to really work well.

In Teresa's experience, white women in solidarity encounters caught up in a Western colonial mentality often attempt to draw attention to themselves. In citing "the need to be the authority," she also reminds us of the range of characteristics embodied in the composite figure of the needy do-gooder: the need to do good, perhaps by "saving" Others, coupled with the need for attention, power, authority, or control. Such inferences to the arrogance and ethnocentrism of some white settlers were consistent across the Indigenous participants' narratives.

When talking about white-supremacist thinking, it seems paradoxical to couple the white settler desire to learn from Others with the need to assert one's status as superior and/or knowledgeable. On top of being paradoxical, the connection between the two desires is confusing and not always easily discernable. Barbara Heron's (2007, 34) work on colonial continuities helps explain the relationship between what seem like incompatible tendencies, including "the interrelated pulls of dread and desire, and fear of and fascination with racialized difference which has marked white engagement with the other from the era of empire." As Heron (2007, 34) explains further, there really is no contradiction, seeing as these "interrelated pulls" ultimately serve the same goal, which is maintaining an us–them hierarchy: "The desire to know the other takes various forms: romanticizing, identifying with (being 'at one with'), caring for, saving, being seduced by, and being transformed through this relationship. Nevertheless, binary relations remain unchanged throughout: it is a question of 'them' being known by 'us,' and being assessed by and understood through 'our' standards."[10] Heron's analysis of "the desire to know the other" conjures up several aspects of my solidarity spectrum, including the desire for transformation at its base. By adding "learning from" to Heron's list, I suggest that my desire as a white woman to receive instruction from Indigenous women entwines deeply with the desire to "know" them – filtered through the lens of white standards – that arises out of my dominant structural position as a settler. In other words, the white settler sense of superiority and desire to learn from/know the Other are parts of the same whole.

This constitutive link – between white-supremacist thinking and white settler desires to learn from and know the Other – cropped up in my fieldwork. I was at a public event organized primarily by Indigenous women. Little time remained when the MC invited one final question from the audience. A white woman immediately took the floor and proceeded to ask a question tangentially related to the event's topic. After getting an initial response from the panel that left her unsatisfied, she asked a follow-up question, whereupon the MC intervened and gave the final word to an Indigenous woman. In my recollection of the event, the tension in the room was palpable and left me wondering about Indigenous women's reactions to the white woman's words, which included a self-declaration of her status as ally.[11] When asked about the event, which she, too, had attended, Wanda Whitebird (Mi'kmaq) made three points about the colonial nature of the exchange. First, she noted that the white woman asserted her own agenda (asking a question not central to the topic) as well as her will to be heard: "We were down to the last five minutes. [Her] question should take twenty minutes to answer ... and it had nothing to do with the film." As if speaking directly to the woman, Whitebird continued, "We weren't here to educate you on our issues. We're here to get support on our issues." She then emphasized, "That's a woman who wanted to be heard." Second, in Whitebird's assessment, the white woman made a judgment veiled as a question, which was in turn laced with the desire to instruct in the proper ways of being – a behaviour Whitebird associated with the historical, and gendered, missionary impulse:

> I guess it's that she was trying to change us. Or she was trying to blame us. So blame us for being on the highway, blaming the women for being raped and murdered ... We were savages. We didn't know any better. So when [the missionaries] got here, they had to change us. We don't know any better. We don't know what we're doing, so you need to change it ... "So you can do it my way, because I know what I'm doing, and it's better than you, and it's what we're going to do."

Lastly, Whitebird took issue with the white woman's self-ascription as an ally to Indigenous women, explaining that an ally is "somebody that I don't have to educate every day of the week about who I am. They just understand and get it and respect that. That I'm not always defending myself or who I am and why I think the way that I think." For Whitebird, as for Tabobondung and Green, the white woman's need to learn from Indigenous women is often – although, importantly, not always – accompanied by the desire for confirmation of her own knowledge/superiority, an affirmation of her liberal/colonial self. Whitebird's comment suggests that, notwithstanding the importance of knowledge, learning about indigeneity should not be the focus of solidarity work, a point to which I return in the next chapter.

Several Indigenous participants openly acknowledged the immensity of the challenge white women face in negotiating our structural privilege. Take Lydia, for example:

> You can have the intellectual understanding or the critical capacity to understand what it is to be a good ally, but at the level of practice you're not

manifesting it ... I think embodied knowledge is hard to change, even if you have a critical awareness of it, because what you are beneath the surface is so much greater than what you are intellectually. It's gigantic.

Here, Lydia notes the difficulty of developing and applying an analytical understanding of allyship or alliances. While Indigenous women recognize, for example, the potentially paralyzing effects of white settler guilt, they ask that white women find the appropriate venues, people, and occasions for meeting these (seemingly) personal needs. In recalling a particular white settler man's display of guilt, Ardra distinguished between appropriate and inappropriate times and spaces for white people to express guilt and seek help in dealing with it: "For me, it's also about time and place. I guess that would have been a repeat of the colonial story if he had done that in an inappropriate setting, say at a public event, and he had taken up a bunch of space and dominated the discussion."

My question in this book is about what lies "beneath the surface," to quote Lydia. Extending Lydia's and Ardra's comments, I suggest the importance of conceptualizing these types of personal needs as expressions of collective white settler subjectivity. In fact, in the majority of cases, neither Indigenous nor white participants connected the conduct of individual white women to collective white settler subjectivity. This oversight, I argue, can inadvertently reduce or misconstrue the problem with proximity to its symptoms (e.g., as an issue of helping, healing, or inappropriate/appropriate settler behaviour) rather than causes, namely, the broader project of white settler legitimacy or belonging.

Teresa was among those Indigenous participants who went furthest in assessing scenarios like these in relation to collective white settler subjectivity: "It's kind of like [white] women come into the circles in order to find a prescription for their own guilt, which we recognized and I don't think they recognize." In other words, white women often seem to lack an awareness of the self-serving/self-making reasons that may propel them to seek solidarity encounters. In one of our postinterview communications, Teresa added that despite understanding that white women may well need "to process what *you're* feeling and what *you're* going through," she was increasingly tired of situations where Indigenous women were saddled with, in my terms, the burden of care or the burden of proof. In her words, "I find [Indigenous women] struggle too much to be able to take on another's burden and sickness, and when I lived in Toronto, I tried assisting non-Indigenous women, and I just became too burned out." What we should be doing, said Teresa, is "giving precedence to the Indigenous cause" around which people are organizing. In the final chapter, I elaborate on how white women might approach solidarity in ways that would more effectively do just that.

Helping with a Twist: The Impulse to Solidarity

It is tempting to say that helping is not what it used to be! After all, Indigenous and white participant narratives attest to the fact that white women in solidarity encounters rarely exhibit the unfettered paternalistic helping behaviour associated with days gone by. However, if Barbara Heron (2007) is right, helping behaviour has always had a tinge of something else. In what follows, I draw on her work to account for expressions of white settler neediness in solidarity work as observed by Indigenous participants, expressions that exceed the desire to do good by including other, often intertwined, wants such as the desire to be cared for or taught by Indigenous women. In this way, I visit the constitutive underside of the desire to help – white women's desires to be helped by Indigenous women – a relational phenomenon vividly signified by the composite figure of the needy do-gooder. Concisely put, my point is this: in some instances, the white settler woman needs to help or "do good" for self-making reasons, reasons, as I argue throughout this book, broadly derivative of the need to feel a sense of legitimate belonging on Indigenous land.

In studying the subjectivity of Western/northern women development workers in the Global South, Heron (2007) calls into question the prevailing notion that development is inherently positive. Instead, she exposes the gendered colonial self-making processes often at its core: "The operation of colonial continuities can also be detected in constructions of gender, which position middle-class white women as simultaneously subjects and non-subjects who may enhance their hold on bourgeois subjectivity through the performance of 'goodness'" (Heron 2007, 7). The operative word here is "goodness." Heron is alluding to, of course, the white settler/imperialist woman of the British Empire, a precursor of today's Western/northern development worker. In other words, displaying our moral rectitude by performing goodness via helping is what white/Western women have been "socially mandated to do" (Heron 2007, 44). Put differently, helping has been the preferred strategy of white women for establishing ourselves as worthy of inclusion in modernity as universal subjects (Spivak 1985; Yeğenoğlu 1998). In referring to this social mandate as the helping imperative that drives some if not most Western/northern women development workers in the Global South, Heron (2007, 2) infers a correlation between the desires to help and to be helped by:

> Development work still is, as it has been from its inception, axiomatically assumed to be altruistic. It is touted as a "life-changing" experience for *us,* and its constitutive effect on Canadian and other Northern development workers' identities is considered indisputably laudable. The enduringness of these understandings about what it is to do development work is an effect of discourse circulating in Canada about the "Third World"/"developing countries," "development," and what "we" are doing to "them" over "there."

In the above passage, Heron maintains that this particular coupling – of the desires to give and get help, as it were – has played a persistent part for some time in the lives and consciousness of helpers of the "less fortunate." Heron's observations about white/Western development workers' desires for affirming and yet life-changing experiences "there," in the Global South, invite us to think about the specific dynamics and desires that may propel solidarity work "here," in Canada.

To that end, I offer the concept of the impulse to solidarity. As I define it, this impulse incorporates Heron's ideas about altruistic development work and its effects on white women's selves – but as these effects unfold here in Canada through solidarity work in a white settler colonial context and not only or necessarily there in the Global South. Importantly, the solidarity impulse of my imagining springs from a normative version of gendered colonial subjectivity. As outlined in preceding chapters, this version of what it means to be a white settler woman has evolved over time and depends on liberal, racialized assumptions about white people as rational, autonomous/ self-determining, and transcendent. The historical result? White women positioned as the superior helpers of Other women who are ostensibly more oppressed than we are. With this backdrop, the solidarity impulse refers not only to the drive to satisfy our desire for belonging on Indigenous land through helping in solidarity encounters but also to the manifestation of that drive through and as proximity. That is to say, the impulse to solidarity often manifests as white women's efforts to get close to Indigenous women. The issue is not so much that this impulse reflects a certain collective white settler investment in solidarity work, which I believe it does. The more significant point is this: white women's self-making projects, when propelled by and through our desire for proximity, can generate tensions in solidarity work. We need only review Indigenous women's insights into the problem when white neediness manifests in invasive ways, that is, when the pursuit of proximity leads white women to "come too close and take up" the sacred space that is "our common breath" (Maracle).

While Heron's (2007) helping imperative and the solidarity impulse both involve the desires to help and to be helped by Others, the solidarity impulse arguably turns on a distinctive constellation of intersubjective dynamics, especially when it comes to why people engage in the work. Before turning to key divergences, however, I want to highlight another remarkable parallel between white/Western development workers and white women in solidarity encounters. An equally important similarity between the helping imperative and the solidarity impulse is satiating the desire for "something different" through proximity. Heron (2007, 51) describes this desire as it pertains to the helping imperative: "Longing for relationships with the Other and experiences of Otherness are implicit in participants' acknowledgement of wanting adventure, the experience of living in another culture, of 'something different.'" Heron (2007, 51) concludes that white people or Westerners go outside of Canada to gratify their longing for adventures in Otherness:

> The encounter with the Other that is sought – that seems to count – can only be obtained by going to the spaces of the Other. The same Othered people on our home ground do not satisfy our need for these engagements with difference ... To some extent this is a craving for a fictional space, but it cannot be separated from a longing for a fictional/fantasy Other.

Here is where I respectfully depart from Heron's overall sound analysis. Contrary to what Heron argues, the solidarity encounter under examination, occurring "on home ground," does appear to "satisfy our need for these engagements with difference." In this sense, "here" is not so different from "there." I am really raising the question, To what extent is a here–there logic operating within the boundaries of what is now called Canada? Do "we" (white women in particular) think about the spaces in which Indigenous peoples predominate as "there" and not "here"? There seems to be a comparable here–there logic duplicated in some Indigenous–non-Indigenous solidarity work, as I discuss at more length in Chapter 3. Even as it occurs here in Canada, not in the Global South, the solidarity encounter arguably provides a site for the construction by white settlers of a fictional space filled with fictional/fantasy Others and, I would add, fictional white selves. In this way, I offer a revision to Heron's theory about where white people/Westerners seek out engagements with difference.

Yet, there is a way in which the here–there distinction, as Heron (2007) defines it between the Global North and Global South, does apply to our respective research sites, although perhaps not in the way she might imagine. Hear me out. White settler allies "here" are obliged to reckon with our illegitimate status as settlers in a way that Heron's development workers "there" are not. Why would this be so? In short, I propose that geography matters when it comes to the particular constellation of intersubjective dynamics of the solidarity encounter. The crucial fact that this encounter occurs here on contested Indigenous land, as opposed to there in the Global South, makes all the difference. Something deeper is at stake for the white settler woman ally, namely, achieving a sense of belonging "legitimately, ethically, fully" (Peggy) on "Canadian" soil. If I am on to something, we can think of the solidarity impulse as bound up in this desire to belong – and not just to be (seen as) moral and good – to varying degrees, depending on the white woman in question.

Moreover, it is perhaps not remiss to say that participating in solidarity work could exacerbate the desire for belonging that arguably underpins white settler/liberal subjectivity. Confrontation with one's complicity in colonial inequalities, a logical by-product of many if not all solidarity encounters, may well amplify the white settler's deep-seated desire for legitimacy in proportion. In this case, white women are apt to experience a heightened sense of our precarious status as settlers, which could lead to an intensification, at least at first, of proximity desires. We might well find ourselves negotiating two competing desires: the desire to belong here on Indigenous lands, on the one hand, and the desire to pursue non-colonizing (or decolonized) Indigenous–non-Indigenous solidarity relations, on the other. The result is a fraught subjectivity in which the impulse to solidarity, and associated desires for proximity, can take hold.

Along these lines, the same Indigenous woman who ignited my thinking about proximity, Ardra, noted that the desire for proximity can be most intense among "more radical" solidarity activists: "The people who see it as a good thing to be liked by Native women, who see that as giving them more cred, those are usually more radical people than people who are helping in a paternalizing ... Those [less radical] people don't really want to be friends with Indians; they want to be seen as helping Indians, right?" Here, Ardra suggests that the "more radical" the white person, the more likely they are to seek friendship with Indigenous women, which corresponds to a primary element of my proximity spectrum, the explicit desire to be accepted by an Indigenous person or included/welcomed into an Indigenous community. In this way, Ardra's comments forecast discussions in the next two chapters about the slippery slopes of cultural/spiritual appreciation and friendship, respectively. In addition, they make explicit an idea that is intrinsic to my understanding of the proximity spectrum and solidarity impulse: white women's proximity desires and pursuits are highly variable in degree and kind and potentially inconsequential, depending on how we handle them.

Ardra's insights spark the possibility of one final dissimilarity between Heron's helping imperative and the solidarity impulse that requires theorization. Whereas the former could be said to denote the archetypal colonial desire to help or save the Other, the solidarity impulse connotes something different or perhaps additional – the inclination among some if not most white women to disassociate from stereotypical forms of helping behaviour. Certainly, the discourse of solidarity evokes a goal of securing non-hierarchical, non-colonizing, and decolonized relations between Indigenous women and white women. Both anecdotally and in this research, I have found that most white women actively attempt to avoid being (seen as) saviours. Along these lines, many white participants were open about the more personal, seemingly individualistic aspects of why they engaged in solidarity, even if they did not always recognize the risks involved in pursuing these needs and desires. Moreover, as made evident in the previous chapter, many white participants grappled one way or another with their structural position as settlers and questioned their role as allies – even if these struggles did not necessarily disrupt a unidirectional outlook on solidarity as something bestowed to those less privileged, as I touch on in the Introduction. However, could these very tendencies – to eschew classic helping behaviour; to self-reflexively trouble one's role as an ally and one's reasons for doing the work in the first place – backfire to reproduce the hierarchical relations solidarity intends to dislodge? Would this approach to solidarity work cause the impulse to solidarity to gain steam? More specifically, do some white women attempt, if unknowingly, to transcend their structural position by claiming exceptional – that is, good or innocent – settler ally status? In short, could the discourse of solidarity, as opposed to the language of helping, inadvertently mask any colonial conduct that exists on the part of white women in the solidarity encounter? As a concept that speaks to the specificity of intersubjective dynamics in the solidarity encounter, I offer the impulse to solidarity as a starting framework for thinking through these questions and more.

~

Perhaps Maracle says it best: "I think if you do nothing, that's a colonizing behaviour. I think if you participate, that's a non-colonizing behaviour." I close the chapter as I opened it, reminding readers that the Indigenous women with whom I spoke generally appreciated white women as allies in struggle. Indeed, many expressed compassion for the challenges white women undoubtedly face in negotiating our structural position and corresponding privilege. Overall, their narratives did not vilify white women's inclinations to care or to help but instead clarified how that inclination can go astray, good intentions notwithstanding.

While not portraying Indigenous–settler relations within the solidarity context in entirely negative terms, Indigenous participants did experience certain white practices and attitudes as invasive and as sources of tension that compromised the effectiveness of political solidarity. Indigenous participants had a lot to say, as it turns out, about the contemporary vestiges of the historically derived whitestream feminist urge to help Other, purportedly more oppressed, women. Their perspectives, I argue, reveal the constitutive other side of the desire to help – which is the desire to be helped by, perhaps best personified by the composite figure of the needy do-gooder. Abidingly attentive to power relations, Indigenous participants pointed to the subtle and not so subtle ways that white women's desire to help can involve pursuing proximity to Indigenous women in invasive ways that preserve settler structural dominance. While noting that instances of extreme neediness are not the norm and that needy behaviours run a gamut, Indigenous participants nonetheless highlighted the invariable presence of a needy do-gooder in most solidarity settings. By making the analytical connection between "needing" and "doing good" (i.e., needing to do good), Indigenous narratives point squarely to the self-making imperatives bound up in the white settler woman ally's desire to help, imperatives I argue are tied to the collective white settler need to belong on Indigenous land. Put differently, Indigenous narratives identify the desire for proximity that mediates white settler/liberal subject formation and place the problem with proximity in stark relief: white women's attitudes and behaviours in solidarity contexts (and beyond) are colonizing when they are invasive in either metaphorical or literal terms. The problem, in other words, is getting *too* close.

In this way, their narratives substantiate not only my fundamental claim about the problem with proximity but also the idea that proximity desires exist across a spectrum. For example, Indigenous women cited instances of white women's (and even some white men's) desires to be healed by and/or to learn from Indigenous women. These examples fall under my proximity umbrella precisely because they can lead to invasive, parasitic behaviour through the depletion of resources (time, energy, physical space) that Indigenous folks would otherwise direct on their own terms. In short, when read through the lens of proximity, Indigenous narratives clearly point to a constitutive underside of the white woman's desire to help Indigenous women, which is the desire to be helped by Indigenous women.

Putting these insights into conversation with Heron's (2007) analysis of development work, I offer a conceptual framework for analyzing what propels white women's solidarity work here in Canada as opposed to white/Western women's development work there in the Global South. By thinking in terms of an impulse to solidarity, I suggest, we can account for the kind of helping with a twist that occurs in white settler colonial contexts such as Canada. In a word, the solidarity impulse refers to the bundle of latent or actualized desires on the part of white women to engage in solidarity with Indigenous women in ways that often involve proximity. These desires, as I theorize them, turn on a similar yet unique constellation of dynamics as compared to Heron's (2007) helping imperative. For starters, partaking in solidarity encounters in Canada seems to satisfy the white "longing for relationships with the Other and experiences of Otherness" that Heron (2007, 51) claims white people/Westerners only look for abroad. The unique dynamics of solidarity work, in fact, reside exactly in this encounter with colonial difference. Because solidarity encounters occur here on contested Indigenous land, I suggest that something deeper is at stake for white women – the need to attain belonging or legitimacy as a settler subject.

The solidarity impulse as a conceptual springboard sparked my thinking about how and why place matters when it comes to the particulars of solidarity and allyship. In this spirit, I offer a host of questions for our collective consideration: Do solidarity encounters exacerbate the desire for belonging that arguably underpins white settler/liberal subjectivity? Are proximity desires most intense among "more radical" solidarity activists? Might the discourse of solidarity, just like (or even more so than) the language of helping, inadvertently mask the colonial conduct of white women in the solidarity encounter? Might it prevent us from recognizing when we threaten to "get too close" to Indigenous women in the pursuit of our (seemingly) personal needs? In sum, does thinking about solidarity in the way that many of us currently do, reflect – and reinforce – an individualistic approach to the work, preventing us from understanding the complex connections between individual and collective subjectivities? The value of the solidarity impulse as a concept, I suggest, lies in its potential to answer these questions and raise others.

It is worth re-emphasizing that white participants were open about their personal reasons for engaging in solidarity, even if they did not always recognize the risks involved. I, too, am increasingly aware of the self-serving reasons that drove me to solidarity work and keep me here, even if I remain fuzzy on the problem, as my autobiographic musings suggest I might be. In fact, some Indigenous participants did not always recognize why a white woman's decision to help or care about Indigenous women was risk-laden. In this chapter, I explain this risk as one of setting into motion the solidarity impulse. Allow me again to stipulate, however, that the concern is not white desires for proximity or the solidarity impulse per se. The problem with proximity occurs when the white woman ally's objectives veer away from the political one of dismantling colonial structures toward the (seemingly) personal one of settler self-making – causing her to invade the cherished spaces between us (Maracle). In the next chapter, I reflect further on why this might be so by focusing on just how deeply our personal or individualistic reasons for attempting solidarity are embedded in the collective (national) imagination. Put another way, I ascertain the links between the personal and political.

3

Risky Romanticization
Cultural Difference, National Belonging, and Indigenous Resistance

In my experience, most white women engaged in Indigenous solidarity work know that cultural appropriation is problematic, even if we cannot quite explain why. Nevertheless, we may find ourselves on the slippery slope from appreciation to appropriation, which explains the existence of the fourth element of the spectrum of proximity: an attraction to Indigenous culture, tradition, or spirituality. Admittedly, blatant manifestations of appropriation were present in a small minority of the white participants' narratives. But given our proneness to experiencing proximity desires as benign personal matters, perhaps white women could use more practice registering this particular dimension of the problem with proximity. Moreover, the dynamics of appropriation warrant attention precisely because they reveal the collective dimension of white settler/liberal subjectivity in its gendered forms. In this chapter, I zero in on the appropriation of Indigenous "cultural values" in the interests of white settler self-making and Canadian national belonging. My main contribution is tracing a four-step discursive pattern that hinges on "Western lack" (defined as something – an ethic, value, belief – thought to be missing in mainstream society) that played out in a vocal minority of white narratives. By outlining this pattern, I hope to demystify how admiration of an often nonspecified indigeneity can all too easily slip into an appropriative/invasive mode.

It would be astonishing if the Indigenous and white participant narratives did not converge in some respects. After all, they operate within the shared discursive field of settler colonialism. Yet, it may still come as a surprise that some Indigenous narratives also appeared to idealize indigeneity and vilify "Westerness," to use Anishinaabe participant Rebeka Tabobondung's wording from Chapter 2. As Indigenous scholars remind us, however, appearances can be misleading. Indigenous peoples have long been under pressure to demonstrate their "authenticity" in order to achieve collective political aspirations (Lawrence 2003). Read in this light, Indigenous allusions to cultural difference and Western lack are part of a broader pattern of Indigenous resistance to ongoing colonialism (LaRocque 2010).

As a settler, I sit uncomfortably with this seeming convergence to consider the risk posed by a framework of cultural difference for conceptualizing Indigenous–non-Indigenous relations. Such a lens is not necessarily attentive to power imbalances (Razack 2004).[1] I suggest that a focus on Indigenous cultural difference, regardless of provenance, can deflect attention away from a structural critique of settler colonialism and therefore benefit collective white settler subjectivity. Put in terms of the proximity spectrum, indigeneity is more likely to be homogenized, romanticized, and appropriated – and solidarity boundaries transgressed – when cultural difference becomes the main paradigm through which Indigenous–non-Indigenous relations are understood. To set the stage for my analysis, I review the idea of precarity.

Appropriation, Precarity, and Settler Colonial Subjectivity

In the previous chapter, I share my strong suspicion that solidarity encounters count as viable spaces for satisfying the white settler need for engagements with difference (Heron 2007, 51). The concept of settler precarity goes a long way in supporting that supposition, as outlined in the Introduction. To summarize, the yearning to belong on Indigenous land, aptly referred to as the desire for emplacement (Razack 2011), is a distinguishing feature of white settler/liberal subjectivity. According to Scott Morgensen (2011, 17), settlers as a collective strive to "both supplant *and* incorporate indigeneity to attain settler subjectivity." That is, settlers enlist appropriation of indigeneity as a technique for yielding a collective sense of belonging. Morgensen (2011, 17) explains the convoluted logic this entails:

> The very demand upon settlers to replace Natives simultaneously incites white settler desires to be intimate with the Native authenticity that their modernity presumably replaces. Indigeneity's civilizational replacement

thus is complementary to the settler pursuit of primitivism. Impersonating indigeneity and believing in colonial modernity are noncontradictory acts, given that settlers preserve Native authenticity as a history they must possess in order to transcend.

In other words, settlers seek intimacy with (read: proximity to) habitually romanticized renditions of Indigenous peoples and cultures in order to impersonate, replace, and transcend them – all in an assertion of settler superiority. A by-product of this move, but no less a feature of white settler/liberal subjectivity, is a lingering, often dormant sense of precariousness with which all settler subjects, including white women in solidarity encounters, must contend.

Morgensen (2011, 16) reminds us of what Indigenous peoples have never forgotten: at its core, appropriation is a method of dispossession that naturalizes white settler colonialism, a process that occurs "whenever conquest or displacement of Native peoples is ignored or appears as necessary or complete, and whenever subjects are defined by settler desires to possess Native land, history or culture." While Morgensen refers to the United States, others, including geographer Bruce Erickson (2011), note a parallel appropriative logic in Canada. Erickson analyzes the textbook example of Grey Owl, né Archibald Belaney, whose performances of "Indian surrogacy" are legendary.[2] With respect to such cases, Sherene Razack (2011, 270) concludes, "Playing primitive ... is an integral part of modern identity; settlers must take the place of the Indian, however fantastic a story or violent a dispossession this requires." The prize? Nothing less than settler emplacement – the sense that one rightfully belongs here (on Indigenous land) – which turns on the dominant subjects' fantasies of becoming, overcoming, and transcendence (Ahmed 2000).

Cultural critic Renée Bergland (2000) illuminates how playing primitive may well foster a collective sense of national belonging among white settlers alongside residual doubt about that belonging. Focusing on the US context, Bergland links modern Western subjectivity to a colonial geography where Euro-Americans "become" Indigenous – through consuming or eating the Other in Ahmed's (2000) and hooks' (1992) terms – to justify taking Indigenous land and resources. For Bergland, this "haunted rationalism" is born of precarity and particular to modern Western subjectivity. Bergland finds evidence of haunted rationalism in the omnipresence of Native Americans in US literature as ghosts, arguing that this "discursive technique of removal" parallels white settler appropriation of "Indian" identities and makes way for the dispossession of their lands and resources. Bergland (2000, 5) writes, "As Indians are made to vanish into the psychic spaces of the American citizen, the psychic space within each citizen is itself transformed into American territory, and each citizen comes to contain an America, to be *homo Americanus*." So it is that non-Natives become Native, and Native Americans are "transformed into ghosts [who] cannot be buried or evaded, and the spectre of their forced disappearance haunts the American nation and the American imagination" (Bergland 2000, 5). Notably, Erickson (2011) also ties settler internalization of the spectral to the material dispossession of Indigenous peoples in Canada.

As a theoretical tool, haunted rationalism offers a useful way to think about the collective aspects of white settler/liberal subjectivity, in particular the ongoing identity crisis that appears to mark white settlers of all genders. Haunted by Indigenous peoples who refuse to vanish from Indigenous lands, white settlers are left with a "compulsion to perform the colonial fantasy" (Razack 2011, 266, 1), which pivots around "the disavowal of conquest, genocide, slavery, and the exploitation of the labour of peoples of colour."[3] Assuming that this compulsion factors into solidarity encounters, the question is not whether but how white women negotiate the desire for emplacement and the colonial relation at the core of modern Western subjectivity.

It is worth re-emphasizing the hierarchy of the colonial relation: Indigenous Others do not gain equal footing when internalized by settler subjects. As Colin Calloway (2008), Emma LaRocque (2010), and others assiduously point out, prevailing ideas about "civilized" and "savage" peoples facilitated (and were strengthened by) the folding of modern Western subjectivity into a colonizer–colonized binary: "they" were uncivilized and deserved to be colonized by "us."[4] As Bergland implies, Euro-Americans retain a sense of superiority, troubled to be sure, vis-à-vis "our" internalized Indigenous Others. This is the deep-rooted white-supremacist mode of thought noted by Tabobondung and reminiscent of Chloe's self-description as "a little ahead of [Indigenous women] in progression, in the good things of life," cited in Chapter 1. Declarations like Chloe's can unintentionally tap into white-supremacist thinking, defined by Tabobondung as the "myth that colonization was inevitable because Indigenous people were just hunter-gatherer primitive groups and Europeans had evolved further along, [that] Indigenous people's lives were 'nasty, brutish and short' [and that colonization] was an evolution of humanity." Tabobondung powerfully sums up the mindset that characterizes white settler personhood, rationalizes white settler emplacement, and naturalizes white settler colonialism.

The goal now is to assess if and how hierarchal thinking and settler precarity infuse white participant narratives and the intersubjective stories they tell. As elsewhere, I flag those moments when white participants appeared to wrestle the most with our precarious role as settlers.

Picking up the (S)lack: Proximity, Appropriation, and Nation Building in Canada

My interviews coincided with Conservative prime minister Stephen Harper's time in office, which, at least for Evelyn, complicated the patriotic feelings of some white participants:

> I've never been very national-minded, but I do think that Canada is one of the greatest countries in the world. I don't really want to travel anywhere else. I've been a lot of places in Canada, going to different places when I was a kid. I just think that there's such a wealth here that we've lost. I mean, our government is completely destroying our country, completely dismantling it. I might have been blind to things as a child and a teenager, but now I'm more aware. It's probably been happening all that time, but it's on a massive scale. I'd like to stop it.

Evelyn's statement speaks to the complexity, ambivalence, and fraught nature of settler self-making. During our conversation, Evelyn was simultaneously critical and proud of Canada as "one of the greatest countries of the world." Later in the conversation, she clarified that "wealth here that we've lost" referred largely to a more sustainable environmental ethos that she associated with indigeneity. Darcie, the white participant who prompted some of my initial thinking on proximity desires, expressed a similar ambivalence when I asked if solidarity work had affected her attitude toward Canada or being Canadian:

> I think, growing up, you hear this, I would say, very one-sided view of Canada, not that Canada isn't a great place to live. You hear from newcomers, too, you know – it's peaceful, you don't have to worry, we're very privileged to grow up here, to live here. I'm always aware of that, but at the same time, there is a population at whose expense we're having this great upbringing and this very privileged life. So, my view has kind of changed from being, from when I was younger seeing Canada in a completely positive light, and you're instilled with the national anthem and all those patriotic

things ... I'm obviously very thankful to live here because I can't really think of anywhere else that I would have the life that I do, but at the same time acknowledging that there are problems. This country isn't perfect; there's a lot of things that need to be improved and that it's okay to be critical of it. That's necessary if we're ever going to improve things.

Like Evelyn, Darcie vacillated between praise and putdown in her no longer "one-sided view of Canada." She expressed gratitude for "this very privileged life" while being aware of the costs borne by the Indigenous population. How to explain this contradictory embrace of Canada? Are white women such as Evelyn and Darcie made uneasy or haunted (Bergland 2000) by the knowledge that being Canadian rests on the dispossession of Indigenous peoples?

As discussed in Chapter 2, for several Indigenous participants, white women's desire to do good sometimes attached itself to self-serving desires, including the need to be healed through exposure to Indigenous culture or spirituality. In contrast, the corresponding thread in white women's narratives was more apt to be positive, expressed as an appreciation of or even identification with Indigenous culture, spirituality, or values. The problem, however, is that appreciation becomes appropriation when it facilitates the white woman's uncritical sense of belonging on Indigenous land, thus further cementing the colonial relation. Admittedly, this form of the white desire for proximity was subtle in most of the participants' narratives. However, the more blatant examples point to a so-far-undertheorized factor in the solidarity impulse: Western lack, the idea that something is missing in Western society at the individual or collective level.

A quick review of the genealogy of the idea of Western lack allows us to understand what the discourse can accomplish when followed by white settler praise of Indigenous values. LaRocque (2010) traces white societies' juxtaposition of Indigenous utopias and Western dystopias back to the European primitivist tradition ushered in by thinkers from the Renaissance to the Romantic period. Looking for a "new social order," these Europeans found one in the figure of the "noble savage" and his world, a vision largely devoid of actual Indigenous peoples. As LaRocque (2010, 127–28) writes, "The European idea of the noble savage was abstract; it was meant as a tool for social criticism. The ennobling of the Indian was almost accidental, and Native peoples as human beings were largely inconsequential to European (and later White American) concerns."[5] Similarly, in studying the prestige garnered by Belaney, Erickson (2011, 27) cites the antimodernist movement's nostalgic belief in the freedom to be had in "Indian masquerading" and the "elevation of a primitive way of life."

Other scholars note the continuation of white settler nostalgia into the contemporary moment. For example, Anna J. Willow (2009, 39) charges mainstream non-Indigenous environmentalists with "recasting the noble Indian" in the search for sustainability: "If Western society is viewed as hopelessly corrupted by consumerist greed and competitive individuality, for instance, Native society becomes a symbol of contrasting tendencies, including ecological enlightenment and communal harmony."[6] In my analysis, I explore how settler accolades of Indigenous values can function as "a tool for social criticism" (LaRocque 2010) in four steps that unleash part of the problem with proximity.

Making Sense of Western Lack

The colonial logic that can underpin such seemingly contradictory stances toward Canada was readily discernable in only a small number of white participant narratives. In these cases, references to Western lack were often the first of a four-step discursive pattern that I would describe as follows: (1) articulating a critique of Western society; (2) contrasting Western society with Indigenous society; (3) outlining the deficiencies of the former and the wisdom of the latter; and, finally, (4) adopting/appropriating Indigenous identity or culture as a way to make up for the lack.

As it happens, Western lack is a distinctive component of the impulse to solidarity and very much not of Heron's helping imperative. In fact, Heron (2007, 3) found that white/Western women development workers in Africa tended to the contrary: they exercised agency "by erasing the agency of local peoples who are Othered in these processes, and by presenting 'our' (read white, middle-class Northern) knowledge, values, and ways of doing things as preferable and right." In my study, a vocal minority of white participants did the opposite. Rather than holding up white, middle-class virtues, they criticized certain beliefs and behaviours they associated with mainstream Canadian society. In both cases, however, a notion of "absolute difference" appeared to operate, which is essential to white settler impersonations of Indigenous people (Erickson 2011) and to maintaining the hierarchical colonial relation. Starting with Steps 1–3, I look at how the discursive pattern of Western lack can reproduce a framework of absolute difference.

As far as white participants go, Alicia was among the harshest critics of Western society. With an excoriating undertone, she explained:

> I don't think, growing up in Western culture, that [humility is] a value that's really imparted. I think it's the opposite: Be the first to the finish line.

Be the first to put your hand up. Be the first to get an A on everything. Compete, compete, compete, for everything. Sell yourself. Say why you're great ... That's part of that capitalist competitiveness of white, Western culture in Canada, I think. I learned from Aboriginal cultures and from Elders to be quiet, to be humble, to listen ... to be open to other ideas; to not enforce your values or shove your ideas down their throat. Do not insist on being right.

Steps 1–3 are readily discernible in Alicia's narrative, which pits putatively Western cultural traits/values such as competition, consumerism, and lack of humility against Indigenous cultural traits/values such as attentiveness and humbleness. You may recall an earlier passage in which Alicia employed the discourse of lack even more directly: "Among the general population of regular Western/Canadian people, I don't necessarily feel that there's a community of people."

Evelyn similarly contrasted Indigenous culture and white culture in her depiction of North American society as "completely dysfunctional." Evelyn's reference to dysfunction is most telling when viewed alongside a candid iteration of her desire to be accepted by Indigenous activists. As part of a postinterview email follow-up, I asked Evelyn to clarify what she meant by "the awkwardness and sense of loss" she felt at "not being a part of something." Here is part of her response:

This [desire for acceptance] is not so much about inclusion in a Native community, but rather for an identifiable role or status in relation to Indigenous struggles, which has multiple meanings – it's really an internal struggle for me. I am getting to feel more comfortable, gaining some niches. But when I attend a speaker's night ... I'm not an academic; [Indigenous women's] marches, I'm not "working" in any Indigenous agency, educational institute, community centre. I have no status, so to speak of; I'm a learner/observer, mostly. The loss refers to how I feel separate from my own culture (white, Canadian, mainstream) or the Canadian mindset/values of consumerism, et cetera. The Canadian public does not take the destruction of land seriously enough. It does not recognize the struggle most women still have being safe and respected. Murder of Native women/the environment is a nonissue to most people. The loss also refers to my envious joy of the Anishinaabe bringing back their culture of inclusiveness of animals, land, creation in their daily lives; in my community, this has no place. I could go on and on.

I certainly identify with the sentiments Evelyn shares in this passage, which harken back to the narratives of becoming I discuss in Chapter 1. I, too, have searched for "an identifiable role or status in relation to Indigenous struggle." In fact, a precarious sense of self/belonging seems to characterize both our approaches to solidarity. In Evelyn's case, the search for a definable role in Indigenous struggle enmeshes with feelings of "envious joy of the Anishinaabe bringing back their culture of inclusiveness." Through repeated allusions to what she lacks (evident in the use of "no status," ironically, a term linked to Indigenous and immigrant struggles), Evelyn positions herself as vulnerable and deficient. In this way, her message bears the stamp of neediness that, according to Indigenous women, not only marks some white women in solidarity encounters but also steers them dangerously close to appropriating indigeneity in the name of belonging.

At the same time, Evelyn was clearly wrestling with her structural position as a settler. More remarkably, Evelyn's internal struggle ensued because she positioned herself as an outsider in relation to two spheres posited as largely separate. Her inability to belong or feel emplaced was contingent upon what she saw as her tenuous relationship to both contexts. If we filter Evelyn's dilemma (and my own dilemma, or even Alicia's, analyzed in Chapter 1) through Erickson's (2011) lens of absolute difference, we might see a white settler who enjoys modern standing while relegating the "Indian" to an inferior, primitive status, forever marked as "vanishing." Admittedly, however, in contrasting Indigenous and Western cultures, Evelyn did not invoke the myth of the vanishing Indian. In fact, she saw Anishinaabe culture as undergoing a process of revitalization. Nonetheless, her statement points to Indigenous cultural difference and her desire to access it rather than to the impact of colonial structures on Indigenous social and political systems. The risk I want to highlight here is that framing difference only or mostly in cultural terms can uphold a modern–primitive binary, regardless of the issuer's intentions.

A final example better illustrates how white critiques of Western society can conjure up absolute difference between Indigenous and non-Indigenous cultures and how such discursive patterns can unfold in seemingly benign ways. Halfway into our interview, before her remarks about the term colonial (see Chapter 1), I asked Dawn to describe any power dynamics she had encountered in her partnerships with Indigenous women. In answer, she denounced the tendency of "outsiders" to minimize the importance of "core" Indigenous teachings "as quaint and a nice thing." Dawn then called on "all of us Canadians" to deal with the fact that "we are profoundly imbalanced":

When you dig into the First Nations, there is, in all of the spiritual teachings, a recognition of the balance between masculine and feminine and male/female. One is not lesser than the other. In fact, if you hear some of the stories of Six Nations women in particular, the grandmothers, the Elders, they had the final say in a lot of things. One of the possibilities in addressing the issue [of violence against Indigenous women] and respecting and honouring Indigenous culture is that we, all of us Canadians, can start connecting with that as well; so not only recognizing it in this but actually understanding that we are profoundly imbalanced. If you look at Indigenous spiritual practices, [mainstream Canadian society] is not just beating up human women; we're destroying Grandmother Earth. We are destroying the feminine on almost every level ... To think that we can just overpower, have everything our way ... take what we want with impunity.

In this statement, Dawn's heartfelt esteem for Indigenous spiritual and cultural teachings is abundantly clear. It also adheres to the theory that Western lack can be a critical linchpin of some white women's solidarity work. More specifically, Dawn reinforces what has become, in activist circles and beyond, a commonly issued distinction between Indigenous and non-Indigenous societies: an imbalanced, overly rational, masculinized, and violence-prone Canadian culture versus a harmonious, spiritual, feminized, and respectful Indigenous culture. However, it is also worth considering if Dawn's statement comes dangerously close to crossing a line by recognizing the colonial tendency to "take ... with impunity" while arguably condoning more of such behaviour by advising that "all of us Canadians" should go beyond "respecting and honouring" to "connecting" to the Indigenous culture of her renderings. As argued below and consequent with the colonial logic discussed above, the process of claiming legitimate national subject status ("all of us Canadians") hinges on the white subject's ability to simultaneously romanticize and internalize indigeneity, which itself hinges on the positing of two separate spheres.

The gendered aspects of both Evelyn's and Dawn's statements merit closer attention. Not just any Indigenous teaching appeals to Dawn; she admires the "recognition of the balance between masculine and feminine and male/female," a topic that came up repeatedly in several participants' narratives (see Chapter 1). Likewise, Evelyn laments that mainstream Canadian society "does not recognize the struggle most women still have being safe and respected." Dawn and Evelyn also repeat the concerns of many Indigenous scholars, including Erin M. Konsmo (Métis/Cree) and A.M.K. Pacheco

(Kanaka Maoli) (2016), Rauna Kuokkanen (Sámi) (2019), and Leanne Betasamosake Simpson (2017) in linking violence against Indigenous women and environmental violence. This is all to say that these narratives offer another glimpse into how gender can inflect white settler approaches to solidarity.

In addition, we might read the "present absence" of whiteness in Dawn's allusion to "all of us Canadians."[7] In *Rethinking the Great White North*, geographers Audrey Kobayashi, Laura Cameron, and Andrew Baldwin (2011, 6) describe Canadian national belonging as spatialized and racialized. Canadianness, they argue, is a social construction wherein "whiteness in all its historical-geographic variability is fundamentally concerned with spatializing racial difference in ways that allow for its spatial practices to pass unquestioned." For these scholars, naturalized "national discourses find spatial expression" in a multitude of ways and spaces, including in relation to "the urban, the rural, landscape, place" (2011, 7). Adding "solidarity encounter" to this list, we can trace how condemning Western lack and praising indigeneity can rather convolutedly facilitate white settler claims to Canadian belonging.

Settler Gain, Indigenous Loss: Appreciation to Appropriation to National Belonging

How can white settler celebrations of indigeneity morph into the disavowal of colonial power disparities? In other words, how does one get – or better yet, avoid getting – to Step 4 along the circuitous path to white Canadian national belonging? The move, I argue, involves white settlers identifying what they find lacking in themselves and/or dominant society. Sara Ahmed's (2000) breakdown of the white, masculinized protagonist in *Dances with Wolves* is again enlightening. Dunbar's makeover is modelled on an exact image, "the Indian as more in tune with nature, as more in tune with each other ... [Dunbar's] fascination with the Indians and the fascination with the wolf inhabit a similar terrain; the wolf and the Indian come to 'stand for' what is lacking in the white man's face, the desire, movement and closeness of nature itself" (Ahmed 2000, 122–23). In his imagination, Dunbar can achieve intimacy with "nature itself" by getting close to wolves and "Indians." Here, we see the potentially pivotal role of lack in setting off the white pursuit of proximity to Indigenous Others.

I propose that Dunbar's "fascination with the Indians" can take gendered forms. Recall Dawn's rationale for respecting and honouring Indigenous culture – to correct an imbalance that has led to violence against all women, and Indigenous women disproportionately: "We're not just beating up human women; we're destroying Grandmother Earth. We are destroying the feminine on almost every level." We might say that Dawn's interpretation of Western lack has everything to do with one side of her historically gendered and racialized double positioning – the subordination of women. That is, Dawn's interest in Indigenous culture binds with a desire to reinstate respect for "the feminine." What's more, there seem to be false equivalencies (Clark Mane 2012) on the horizon: in suddenly switching focus to "beating up [all] human women" and "destroying Grandmother Earth," Dawn's statement risks eliding the specificities of violence against Indigenous women, if accidentally. Even subtle moves in this direction can re-entrench whitestream feminist antiviolence strategies that do not account for gendered colonial violence – the very practices Indigenous feminists have criticized for decades. In its entirety, the passage arguably glosses over Dawn's original focus – violence against Indigenous women.[8]

Evelyn also focused on Western spiritual deficiencies, in direct relation to mainstream environmental groups, which, she argued, incorporate a spiritual dimension shallowly (if at all). She shared her perspective in answering a question about whether support work (her preferred term for solidarity) can provide a space for personal or collective transformation, as she defines it:

> Certainly, there's an element of transformation happening for me. I'm now free to ... it's kind of odd because Native spirituality has ... I've always felt that nature was special – flora, fauna, our kind of connection to it. But there's no room for that in Western culture, except for in the environmental movement, and it doesn't go beyond protecting species and ancient seeds and the land. It doesn't go beyond that; it doesn't animate nature into something that is part of us. That's allowed me a little bit more freedom in my comfort in feeling connected [to Indigenous people].

As in Dunbar's case, certain things permitted the "element of transformation" that Evelyn experiences: her solidarity work with Indigenous women (and sometimes men), and her predisposition to a spiritual relationship with the land. While both Evelyn and Dunbar admire Indigenous peoples' relationships to nature, Evelyn's narrative of becoming differs in at least two substantive ways – ways that I propose are reflective of gendered colonial subjectivity. For one thing, her fascination is with flora and fauna, not with wolves. For another, Evelyn's interest in nature extends to Indigenous spirituality, which does not hold much appeal for Dunbar. In fact, taken together, Dawn's and Evelyn's "fascination with the Indians" appears to flow from the white woman's gendered role of helping with a twist, that is, the desire to help return balance – gender, ecological, and spiritual – to Western society and, by extension, themselves.

Crucially, the positive transformations of Dunbar, Evelyn, and mainstream Canadian society all depend on "a very precise imaging of the Indian as more in touch with nature" (Ahmed 2000, 122), or what Anna Willow (2009) calls the "ecological Indian." Moreover, drawn to Indigenous peoples' presumably more balanced, harmonious existence, the fact of their white settler structural advantage notwithstanding, Evelyn, Dawn, and Alicia all invoke Western disadvantage or lack at the individual or collective levels. This shedding of advantage, arguably part of what constitutes the move from fascination to disavowal, is precisely what interests me.

The crux of the matter lies in a particular way of "playing Indian" (Deloria 1998), which deploys indigeneity as "a tool for social criticism" (LaRocque 2010). Morgensen (2011, 5–6) explains it like this: "White Americans associate marginality and resistance with the Indians as an internal antagonist to settler society, which then lets them impersonate indigeneity when they launch social critiques that reconcile them to settler society." That is to say, settlers can adopt indigeneity as a way to oppose a certain aspect of their society. Playing Indian for protest purposes puts the discourse of Western lack in a less benign light, suggesting a slippery slope between identifying with "Indians" to identifying as "Indians." Adapting Renée Bergland's phrase (2000, 5), we might put it this way: transforming one's psychic interior to *homo Canadianus* allows the white settler subject to secure a sense of legitimacy and belonging. We could also think of these as cases of identificatory mobility, which settler scholars Margery Fee and Lynette Russell (2007, 188) define as the tendency of "self-acknowledged antiracist white people to think themselves emphatically 'Other,' and thus [to be] able to identify with the disempowered and marginalized without ever having to try and understand their [white] difference."[9] Morgensen's (2011) analysis of gay rights activist Judy Grahn is a perfect example. By likening her exile as a queer person with the colonial dispossession of Indigenous peoples, Grahn achieves a sense of "indigenized emplacement." While we cannot know if Dawn, Evelyn, or Alicia were playing Indian in this way, we cannot discount the possibility.

Two more dimensions of the dynamic warrant mention: nostalgia and salvific benefit. Using both concepts, Carol Schick (1998, 185) helps us begin to explain how moving from Step 3 (outlining Western lack) to Step 4 (adopting/appropriating Indigenous identity or culture to make up for the lack) subtly re-creates the colonial relation (Calloway 2008; LaRocque 2010):

> Whereas the contemporary version of colonialism would disavow the overt desire for dominant/subordinate roles ... In the present day, the [Indigenous] other is required for the production of nostalgic and salvific benefit to the [settler] subjects. Renato Rosaldo (1989) calls the [settler] subjects' desire "imperialist nostalgia" in which they regret and mourn the passing of that which their culture has helped to destroy. In spite of the imperialist connections in which this nostalgia is rooted, subjects' expressions of this desire are offered as something positive.

In other words, figurative proximity to Indigenous Others affords the settler a chance to appear virtuous (and innocent) in their appreciation of Indigenous culture.[10] As we know, however, settler self-making is nothing if not fraught; many white participants were aware of the colonial histories that begat their structural privilege, and the majority of their narratives do not conform to a neat logic of imperialist nostalgia. While they might lament the devastating impact of ongoing colonialism on Indigenous communities and traditions, most white participants departed from the myth of the vanishing Indian in noting a resurgence in Indigenous cultural practices.

Salvific benefits tell a more straightforward story. As Mahrouse (2011, 376) explains in her study of socially responsible tourism, Western tourists benefit from focusing on "the non-material wealth of the locals and the idea that 'we' westerners stand to learn from 'them.'" For Mahrouse, this is an example of the "discourses of reversal and equation" tourists deploy to make peace with their role in and responsibility for global inequities. I conjecture that analogous dynamics are at work in solidarity encounters, perhaps explaining why some white women might praise the "social, emotional, and spiritual wealth" (Mahrouse 2011, 382) of Indigenous nations without remarking on the material realities of these nations' subordination.

Take Alicia's interpretation of the film *Avatar* relative to her own life and outlook on the difference between being a saviour versus being a helper. On its face, this passage seems transparent:

> [Being a helper] is not being a saviour. It's interesting because I remember after *Avatar* came out, there was a lot of criticism. "Here's another group of Aboriginals being saved by this white guy." Ultimately, it was the Indigenous

people who saved the white guy ... My take on it? The Indigenous people were the ones who defended themselves. They actually rescued the white guy from his shitty culture that had him after greed and money and things like that. Maybe that's the same case with me. "I'm not here to rescue you." Aboriginal people have rescued me from a life of consumerism, competition, greed, self-centredness. Other people reach spiritual enlightenment through Buddhism, I learned through Aboriginal Elders, things like respect.

On the one hand, Alicia makes an important differentiation here, one made by Indigenous women themselves, who applaud white women for approaching solidarity work as helpers of Indigenous women on Indigenous terms. On the other, Alicia's sentiments seem to align with the self-making desires on the underside of the solidarity impulse, that is, with the white woman's desire to be helped by Indigenous women. As Alicia claims, "Aboriginal people rescued me from a life of consumerism, competition, greed, self-centredness." Moreover, part of Alicia's passage could qualify as a "discourse of reversal and equation" (Mahrouse 2011, 376). Put simply, Alicia may go too far in her justifiable critique of saving behaviour. By highlighting how she has been "rescued" (i.e., accrued salvific benefit) through working with Indigenous communities, Alicia unwittingly sidelines the fact that Indigenous sociopolitical structures have buckled under the weight of settler colonial dispossession.

Viewed through these lenses, Dawn's and Evelyn's narratives also suggest that reconciling one's privilege can correlate with appropriating Indigenous culture for self-making purposes: the settler's need to emplace herself is facilitated by proximity to the Other (e.g., what "they" can teach "us") and accomplished with reversal and equation. In such instances, narratives of Western lack become precursors to appropriation and comprise one strand in a complex web of narratives of becoming.

To review the argument up to this point, when participants lambaste Western society – for its lack of spirituality, community, and concern about violence against (Indigenous) women, and its environmental destruction – they also valorize Indigenous alternative ones, implying that we can access these alternatives to make up for Western lack at both the individual and collective levels. These discursive manoeuvres imply a constitutive link between two levels of lack. Alicia, Dawn, and Evelyn seemed compelled to make the following two parallel sets of connections: first, tying what they lack as individuals to what "white Western culture in Canada" (Alicia) lacks as a whole; and second, tying how they can benefit individually to how Canadian society can benefit collectively by embracing Indigenous culture. Here exposed is the indelible, typically unrecognized link between the desire to reconstitute the individual *I* and the collective *we*.

The colonial logic so brilliantly crystallized in the combined works of Bergland (2000) and Morgensen (2011) is helpful here. Because modern Western/Enlightenment subjects remain forever haunted by the existence of real Indigenous peoples, they must continuously work to legitimize their presence by becoming part Native: "Settler colonialism is naturalized not only in Native people's seeming 'disappearance' from a modern, settled landscape but also in indigeneity's recurrent appearance within and *as* settler subjectivity. Whether erasing or performing indigeneity, omitting or celebrating it, settlers practice settlement by turning Native land and culture into an inheritance granting them knowledge and ownership of *themselves*" (Morgensen 2011, 18). Extending Morgensen's point, celebrating indigeneity can be part of the problem, especially when these celebrations coexist with discourses of Western lack. Moreover, when individuated stories accumulate in collective narratives of national belonging, white settler erasures, performances, omissions, or celebrations of indigeneity become the acceptable norm.

The solidarity encounter of my research was not immune to these dynamics. Although rare, explicit instances of Canadian nation building did occur in the white participants' narratives. I end this discussion with two particularly striking examples. When asked to comment on how solidarity work might have transformed individual people or entire groups, Dawn openly invoked Canadian nationalism when citing one memorable occasion that changed her. She described participating in an Indigenous ceremony to honour a long-time Indigenous woman activist:

> I can see and experience some of the culture and see what an opportunity it is for Canada when they begin honouring that culture, the contribution that that can make ... I really think that [Indigenous culture] is one, like I said, of the treasures that Canada has. It thinks that it has just got mineral resources and stuff. No, no, no. It has got an incredibly rich spiritual core that if it connects with, some other things, like harmony and balance with the environment, will start falling into place, the honouring of women in general. It's all part of the same piece. We will become a stronger nation.

Dawn's appreciation of Indigenous ceremony can be interpreted as "something positive," to recall Schick (1998), a sign of her knowledge of Canadian colonial history. We could similarly interpret Alicia's implicit reference to the superiority of non-Western (i.e., Indigenous) ways: "There's a different way to be living on this planet: to be more in tune with themselves, to be more in tune with nature, to understand colonization, to try some decolonizing work, to get back to our roots, to know what a community means." What to make of Alicia's suggestion that "we" get back to "our" roots? Is this appropriation? If so, does Dawn perform an equally appropriative move when she claims "Native culture" as Canada's treasure, its rich spiritual core? To recall Moreton-Robinson (2000), settler intention is often beyond the point; our words bubble forth from a toxic colonial cauldron of meanings. So, too, do Dawn's and Alicia's statements suggest the ease with which settlers (even, or perhaps especially, through celebratory means) can "turn Native land and culture into an inheritance granting them knowledge and ownership of *themselves*" (Morgensen 2011, 18). Perhaps most problematically, by placing an inordinate emphasis on culture, such narratives steer us away from more difficult conversations about the colonial structures that have dismissed the value of Indigenous cultures in the first place.

Chloe's narrative shed additional light on the potential problems with white settler admiration of Indigenous peoples in the solidarity encounter and beyond:

> Eventually you get back to the core thing, and I think if you get back to that, most Canadians realize their great respect for Native tradition, and it goes back to our feeling ... the first settlers in Canada like Champlain, he respected the Native people. Why? Because they had a classless society. They had a way of doing things: they produced healthier children, nobody starved to death, they were courageous, they were hard working. He admired the people that they met when they first got off the boat. I think some of that is still within our heritage. I'm hoping it's all across Canada. I think it is.

Chloe was confident that most Canadians shared her respect for Indigenous peoples and traditions. The fact that this sentiment might have come directly from John Ralston Saul's *A Fair Country* suggests how representative it is of a certain strand of Canadian national discourse.[11] Saul (2008, 3) rests his argument, apparent in the book's opening sentence – "We are a métis civilization" – on a characterization of Canadian society comparable to that of Chloe's: "When I dig around in the roots of how we imagine ourselves, how we govern, how we live together in communities – how we treat one another ... what I find is deeply Aboriginal. Whatever our family tree may look like, our intuitions and common sense as a civilization are more Aboriginal than European or African or Asian." According to David MacDonald (2013, 61), Saul is arguing that Canada "is actually based on a long history of Aboriginal–settler partnerships, which created forms of 'métissage' – political and social cultures that amalgamate many ways of knowing and being. The key to a successful future, Saul holds, is for Canadians to rediscover and celebrate this shared past."

While not disputing the importance of acknowledging the contributions of Indigenous peoples to Canadian society, I want to highlight Saul's seamless slippage into *we*, the third-person plural (a move also made in Alicia's narrative). On the one hand, Saul could be lauded and considered virtuous (Schick 1998) for his knowledge of colonialism and Indigenous social and political processes; on the other, his main claim is arguably doing the work of reversal and equation (Mahrouse 2011) for nostalgic and salvific benefit (Schick 1998). MacDonald (2013, 62) homes in on a core problem with nostalgia – its links to a historical revisionism that whitewashes Canada's colonial history and invalidates Indigenous historiography and contemporary political struggle. Emma LaRocque (2010, 15–16) also stipulates the need for a detailed study of the CIV/SAV (civilized–savage) doctrine at the heart of the colonial enterprise. Otherwise, she insists, there can be no respectful recognition of the multifaceted contributions of real, as opposed to spectral, Indigenous peoples to Canadian society. Commenting directly on Saul's core premise, she urges, "It is incumbent on us all to understand [CIV/SAV's] twisty workings in our cultural productions. There is no 'metis civilization' for Canada otherwise."

Danielle was one of the most outspoken Indigenous participants on the matter of white needy do-gooders. Her reading of Canada's mainstream pulse also countered those of Chloe and Saul. Citing high levels of ignorance and arrogance on the part of most Canadians, she questioned the legitimacy of the Canadian state itself:

> [Settlers are], like, "Just because we say it's so, it's so." I find that with the government. I find that with the whole foundation of Canada, that for three hundred years, they've been saying this, so then it must be true. For three hundred years, it's been this lie in place, so ... it must be true, when we [as Indigenous peoples] know the truth because we have an oral tradition, and we keep telling the story over and over and over.

In fact, as Danielle shared, she had committed much time and energy to combatting this three-hundred-year-old lie about Canada's foundations by "telling the truth" in as many public "speaks" as possible. Following Danielle and MacDonald, one might ask how the material realities of Indigenous peoples in Canada – such as unresolved specific and comprehensive land claims – figure (or not) into equations such as Saul's or Chloe's. What appears to unite statements like those issued by Dawn, Chloe, and Saul is a resolute belief in the following assumptions: contemporary Canadian society owes much to its Indigenous inhabitants; all Canadians should honour this legacy; and, as such, we can/should rightfully claim it as our own.

A picture of the twists and turns of Canadian nationalism is incomplete without considering how Indigenous and white participant narratives converge in critiquing Western social norms, values, and practices and in praising Indigenous ones.

Indigenous Women and Collective Survival

In her seminal work *When the Other Is Me: Native Resistance Discourse, 1850–1990*, Emma LaRocque (2010, 3) reminds us of the "contested ground upon which we, the Canadian colonizer-colonialist and Native colonized have built our troubled discourse." I interpret this to mean that I must read white and Indigenous participants' deployments of Western moral deficiency and Indigenous moral virtuousness differently. Several Indigenous women joined their white counterparts in deprecating aspects of Western societies while extolling aspects of Indigenous societies. Women from both groups depicted Indigenous cultures as generally tolerant, inclusive, respectful, and thoughtful in contrast to Western tendencies toward intolerance, exclusion, intrusiveness, and impatience. However, these seemingly shared depictions, LaRocque (2010, 130) implies, are not commensurate: "Native people have had to punctuate cultural differences to counter the portrayal of themselves as uncultured, unregulated savages. In this defending and repositioning, we have, inevitably perhaps, utopianized our culture(s)." Following LaRocque, I read Indigenous self-presentations of cultural difference through the lens of resistance in the face of ongoing colonial dispossession. While this may look like a move toward assessing Indigenous subjectivities, it is not. I temporarily shift focus to better understand white settler subject making.

In Chapter 1, I discussed the tendency of white participants to position ourselves as individuals (as opposed to members of a settler collectivity) who chose solidarity work, even as tacit desires for proximity may have fuelled this choice. I also noted that, despite our differing modalities of political activism/solidarity, equal numbers of Indigenous and white participants defined activism in broad terms beyond the narrow confines of protest politics and described coming to political activism through a variety of avenues, including the academy or the arts. Approximately half of both groups eschewed the activist label, albeit with distinct rationales. However, it is worth revisiting two salient dissimilarities. First, Indigenous narratives contain little indication of the desire for proximity (to white women, in this case) that suffuses white narratives. Second, and more strikingly, Indigenous participants' notions of political subjectivity comprise a unique weave of political activism, individual/collective survival, and communal responsibility, as we shall see.

Politically Positioned: Indigenous Women and Collective Survival
Indigenous feminist scholars, including Rauna Kuokkanen (2007, 2012, 2019), Aileen Moreton-Robinson (2000), Makere Stewart-Harawira (2007), and Lina Sunseri (Kanien'kehá:ka) (2000), demand that Indigenous self-determination struggles be defined as feminist struggles. Their approach rejects the false binary that pits Indigenous women's "individual rights" against Indigenous "collective rights." It also signifies a departure from liberal values and opens the gate for community-focused political activism in which "female, male, tribal, and racial oppression" are inextricably linked and "gender is inexorably tied to [Indigenous women's] race and tribe" (Mihesuah 2003, 162; see also Irwin 2007; Trask 1999). For Indigenous and equity studies scholar Bonita Lawrence (Mi'kmaq), despite the risks of further entrenching settler views of Indigenous women as tradition-bound, Indigenous women cannot afford to contest such views on liberal, individualistic terms, which would only increase threats to community survival (cited in Thorpe 2005). The ultimate stakes for Indigenous political struggles are high, as Robyn Bourgeois (mixed-race nehiyaw iskwew) reminded me all those years ago in front of Robarts Library at the University of Toronto: "This is the only land we [Indigenous peoples] can call home."[12]

In symmetrical fashion, Indigenous participants identified inseparably as Indigenous women and explained their political engagement as an embrace of this identity, the respect it is accorded, and the communal responsibility it involves. They described themselves as principled actors dedicated to solidarity work for strategic reasons. As a result, their narratives reflect widely circulating discourses about Indigenous women's traditional roles as caretakers at the centre of a range of collectivities – from families to communities, nations, future generations, and Creation (Anderson 2016;

Lawrence and Anderson 2003; Miller and Chuchryk 1996; Monture and McGuire 2009). At the same time, Indigenous feminist scholars warn against an uncritical embrace of this role, which can feed into romanticized, essentialized, and homogenized notions of womanhood and indigeneity or, worst still, uphold patriarchal traditions (Anderson 2010; Green 2007a, 2017b; Pyle 2020; Simpson 2017; Starblanket 2017; Wilson 2018). As Kim Anderson (2010, 88) stipulates, "If we want to embrace essential elements of womanhood that have been problematic for Western feminists, (such as motherhood and the maternal body), then we have to make sure that these concepts don't get stuck in literal or patriarchal interpretations."[13] Given my concern with white women's self-making, however, I want to think through how white women like me can read Indigenous approaches to solidarity to avoid Step 4, that is, romanticizing and appropriating "authentic" Indigenous cultural differences/values for our own sense of belonging.

Indigenous participants strongly conveyed the message that to be Indigenous is to be political regardless of one's political inclinations or lack thereof. In other words, the Indigenous woman subject is an inherently political subject. Teresa was succinct: "I think we're born as Indigenous women into political positioning whether we like it or not." She depicted political engagement as an almost unbidden result of being "born as Indigenous women." Corroborating Teresa's point, Seminole philosopher Anne Waters (2004c, 167) argues, "American Indians [in the United States] are political beings, as all tribes share in the struggle against the continuing genocide perpetrated against our people and our nations." Therefore, I consider Indigenous participant narratives in light of a political struggle born of necessity.

In the following passages, Belinda and Lydia define activism in survivalist terms, that is, as sustained political efforts of Indigenous peoples as peoples to resist centuries of colonial onslaught:

> But when I think back on it, you know, I realize that everything is political. I mean just staying alive as a Native woman is political; just deciding that you are going to live and be well and go to university and write is political. Deciding that you are not going to end up in jail and be on welfare and lose all your kids, you know, that's political in the sense that I'm not going to be crushed and fall under all the crap that gets thrown at you all the time ... [It's about] taking your own power, deciding to live in a good way. (Belinda)
>
> I think some people would label me an activist. Some people would say I'm a warrior. In my bio, I don't use the title [activist] because I don't think I've made a conscious [decision that] I'm going to become involved in

activism. I'm just trying to uncover the layers. That's more what I'm doing. I think if that's what people call activism, that's okay, but I think that might be an inadequate label. It's more I'm trying to survive and do what I need to do. Maybe I'm being a good role model versus an activist. (Lydia)

Both statements echo LaRocque's (2010, 23) characterization of survival as political resistance: "A simple assertion of one's (Native) humanity is a form of resistance, given the magnitude of dehumanization over a span of 500 years ... In this sense, every politically aware Native teacher, scholar, writer, artist, filmmaker, poet, or activist is ultimately a producer of resistance material." As the above-cited passages bear out, politically aware Indigenous people of diverse genders have been compelled to produce resistance material by the colonial circumstances that engulf us all, though in distinct ways. As Moreton-Robinson (2000) spells out, Indigenous women's structurally subordinate position requires them to be astute political actors in their everyday lives. For several of the Indigenous women in this study, this position figured prominently in decisions to take political action, however defined. While white women and Indigenous women both chose political engagement, the latter connected that decision to their politically charged subject position as members of a dispossessed and marginalized collectivity.

Such was the case with Lydia, Danielle, and Ruth Green (Kanien'kehá:ka). Here is Green's response to my question about whether she considered herself part of an activist community:

I would say I'm upholding my responsibilities as an Aboriginal woman to this land. If that's what you call activism, so be it, but I'm not really going to label myself that. I'm going to ensure that I uphold Guswenta, the Two Row Wampum ... If that's activism, well, then it's activism; but for me, it's just being who I am. It's the responsibility.

What she deems her "responsibilities as an Aboriginal woman to this land" require her to undertake what others might label political activism.

Following suit, Lydia upheld Indigenous women's responsibilities to their communities as a component of her steadfast commitment to the cause:

When any Indigenous woman takes on something, she has communities, a reserve community, whether the whole nation, behind her. Like Sharon McIvor, she has a whole nation of Indigenous women that she's caring for, same as Jeannette Corbiere Lavell. When a white woman comes in and makes a decision, she doesn't have those responsibilities. People like Sharon and Jeannette and Sandra [Lovelace],[14] when they take on their ... even women in the reserve communities trying to establish, let's say, a shelter or a food bank, they have a community of people that they're caring for. White women don't have that. Sure, white women may have kids at home, but they don't have a whole country of oppressed people that they're caring for, and so they have a privilege that Indigenous women don't have. They don't have the same pressure. I think that's the biggest thing ... they seem to not understand that this is not just activism.

Here, Lydia sharply contrasts her situation with white women in Canada, who from her perspective "don't have a whole country of oppressed people" to be responsible for. For her, political responsibility derives from her status as an Indigenous woman. Her analysis validates the fact that structures of power position and constrain us in distinct ways with respect to political engagement and, by extension, solidarity work.

Danielle also traced her political activism back to her positionality as an Indigenous woman even as she extended that responsibility to foster social change to all people. In explaining why she did political activism/solidarity work, she consistently linked political mobilization to "our [Native and non-Native] principal duty and responsibility to all of Creation":

As I stood there, I thought about how I was lining up with the earth and the moon and the sun and stirring the ashes and saying, "I can do this. I know I can handle this." Because what it's about is ensuring that the cycles of life continue. And what it's about is respecting all of Creation. And what it's about is doing our principal duty and responsibility to all of Creation, and that's to be kind and to care ... What we're experiencing today is a pretty mean and nasty come-around – when we're dealing with earthquakes and fires and floods. We're the ones that bombed the shit out of Tora Bora [in Afghanistan]. We're the ones that made war. We're the ones that are starving our people. We're the ones that are letting Aboriginal people live in conditions that are rated seventy-fourth in the world while we enjoy conditions that are eighth ... So I like to put in that bigger perspective of why I do the work. I do the work so that when I go across that sky and I take my place back up there with my ancestors, and I got to face my grandma, and I get to see my Great-Grandmother Moon, I don't want her to be ashamed of me.

She continued:

> Fifty-four percent of our [Indigenous] population is under the age of twenty-seven. I say to people, "What does that look like in fifty years – my lifetime – what does that look like?" For me, I choose to think that it looks like a pretty rosy picture. It's not so rosy if we don't do anything. It's real damn rosy, though, if we meet the needs of those kids, if we stand them up and give them what they need, and we feed them properly, and we connect them to their role and their responsibility and their duty. That's a huge army. That's a huge army for peace and kindness and tolerance and understanding and all those things that we know we have to get to if we think we're going to end violence against women.

Broad in its parameters, Danielle's definition of activism has her seeing her duty as an Indigenous woman in collective terms, that is, in relation to her ancestors (Great-Grandmother Moon) and future generations. Importantly, Danielle's message about how "to end violence against women" evokes Dawn's statement (above on the same topic) in which she (a white woman) suggests all Canadians should respect and honour Indigenous culture as a way to mitigate the destruction of "Grandmother Earth" and "the feminine on almost every level."

Consistent with viewing the Indigenous woman subject as inescapably political, many Indigenous participants highlighted their dedication to collective political struggle as the primary motivating factor in their decisions to do solidarity work (as opposed to the more self-serving, individualistic needs they ascribed to many white women). Accordingly, their engagement in solidarity did not cause, but rather resulted from, their political activism, which they claim is not the case for all white women. In short, neither achieving solidarity per se nor getting close to white women is the main goal of Indigenous women's political work; solidarity is a means to a political end.

Moreover, some Indigenous women described ending up in solidarity encounters without having chosen to be in them.[15] Take Wanda Whitebird (Mi'kmaq) – a seasoned, self-ascribed activist who had only recently and purposely worked in a mixed Indigenous–white group:

> I don't know if it's a conscious decision [to work in solidarity]. I didn't step out of the world to do it. My world is basically most of the time filled with Aboriginal people. To be honest with you, I don't use the term "solidarity" and all those other kinds of things. That wasn't something that we used,

> except for in the Leonard Peltier movement ... I mean, I've been involved in different protests and those kinds of things, and it's never been an issue whether [people] have been white or not white. The issue was what was the matter. I think this is the first time I've been involved in a [mixed Indigenous–non-Indigenous] group. And it was really good for me to be a part of that. I've seen some things that I probably needed to see in my life.

In hesitating to call her decision to work with white women a conscious one, Whitebird minimizes the centrality of solidarity in her political work; in her experience, "the issue" is what has mattered to most Indigenous people in her orbit. The issue for Whitebird in this instance is the disproportionate numbers of MMIWG2S people.[16] Lee Maracle (Stó:lō/Métis) endorsed a similar stance with added nuance: "I like the Indigenous sensibility about, we're on a journey of exploration, that we're trying to understand each other in the process of doing this work, and that the more important thing is the work, but we are struggling to understand each other." In other words, while positive cross-cultural intersubjective relations are important, they are secondary to the greater goal or "more important thing," which is the work itself.

This is not to say that the Indigenous women with whom I spoke did not ever seek solidarity or see it as vitally necessary. Danielle was emphatic about the need to "create allies, informed allies, who aren't working out of ignorance, who have the proper information and the truth ... That's why I go and do any talk that I'm invited to do ... because what I'm doing is creating allies and I'm informing people." Likewise, as an organizer, Tabobondung sought non-Indigenous allies for specific projects. She offered this account of one such coalition:

> There was an urgency to [the activism] because this was specific legislation that we did not want put in place and so we were calling on a coalition. So, it was great that non-Native people joined the coalition, but it turned out that many needed so much educating, you spent all your time educating people, and they're at various levels of their education. And then you hear the white guilt that comes out of them, and then you realize, "I don't want to invest so much time into this."[17]

In sum, to the extent that they seek solidarity with white women, these Indigenous participants generally do so for a specific cause or project. Additionally, in contrast to white participant narratives of their solidarity trajectories (Chapter 1) and Indigenous participants' readings of white women in solidarity work (Chapter 2), Indigenous participant narratives do not contain obvious allusions to any desire for proximity to white women.

When pressed on the question of choice in relation to solidarity work with white women, Whitebird clarified that "for me [this last time], it was a conscious decision; but a lot of times, you're absolutely right, it's not. I don't have a choice. It's already in place, and they're already there." Whitebird then made the subtle distinction between acknowledging the need for white women allies and expressly desiring them. While seeing allies as essential in political struggle (she noted the alternative as "standing at Parliament Hill by myself with a sign"), Whitebird admitted, "I would still say I don't want to work with white women … It would depend on what it's going to be that we're doing or the white woman who wants to be involved with us." Zainab Amadahy (Cherokee, Seminole), also with decades of activist experience, much of which involved solidarity encounters with white women, shared Whitebird's view:

> It takes a lot out of me. I used the word "retraumatized" before, and I'm not kidding about that … I walked into a room at one point where I was one of two Native women in the room, and everybody else there was white. I felt like I was surprising people when I spoke or made suggestions about things because I just had this sense people had low expectations of my ability to think, to organize, and I just felt like every time I made a suggestion, people were like, "Wow, she's got a brain," kind of thing. I just got sick of it … So it's not my priority. If white people are there, and they're supportive and stuff, it's fine. If they're included, it's fine. It's not like I avoid them, but my priority, in terms of relationship-building, would be with racialized people.[18]

Amadahy ends by describing her engagement in solidarity with white people as "just hard work." My conversations with Whitebird and Amadahy validated two impressions I had up to that point in the research: many Indigenous women view solidarity as a means to an end, and while recognizing the need for allies, they do not always want them or want to actively recruit them. If we are to make sense of the discursive convergences between Indigenous and white participant narratives to which I now turn, it is crucial to keep in mind the divergent meanings of political activism that animate both.

Indigenous "Romanticization" as Reaffirmation and Resistance

Indigenous resistance discourse, as LaRocque (2010, 210) emphasizes throughout her book, is inescapably "shadowed by the savage, both the noble and ignoble," meaning that in its attempts to counter the colonial dehumanization of Indigenous peoples, resistance discourse is "textured with [that] idealization and internalization." I find LaRocque's thesis useful for interpreting certain interactions in the solidarity encounter, for instance, when Indigenous participants took explicit steps to depict themselves and their communities as deeply human(e).

Several Indigenous participants joined their white counterparts by embedding critiques of Western values within positive appraisals of themselves, their communities, and their nations. For example, Whitebird and Maracle contrasted an Indigenous affinity to listen and to deliberate with a Western tendency to interrupt, argue, and be impulsive when communicating. Whitebird recalled one white woman's unsuccessful attempts to control the agenda for a meeting: "She wants to control everything, which means a list of questions. And the list of questions came from her perspective, not the people's perspective. That's another thing about us: we think about everything behind us and ahead of us when we speak. Non-Native people don't think like that. White people don't think like that." In agreement, Maracle named colonialism and patriarchy as the underlying culprits of what she called invasive or colonizing behavioural practices:

> This would never happen in a Stó:lō community. Someone wouldn't cut you off before you finished your thinking, and they would actually think about what you said, especially if they disagreed. They would really play with what you said. And they would say something like, "I'm going to get back to you on that," because it doesn't need to get solved today. What needs to happen is you have to give weight to that person's words ... When someone is doing this argumentative thing and cutting me off, I don't get to be me, so it's very annoying. So some differences actually rob your ability to be yourself, and the person doesn't realize it, but the differences are the invasive behavioural practices that come from a colonial and patriarchal society. I don't think that everyone that's non-Native or non-colonized have analyzed that enough and ... looked at the cultural practices that arise out of that. Because those aren't just differences, you see. They're colonizing behaviours.

In this statement, Maracle stresses a point she repeated during our time together, which is the ability to discern between differences of opinion that will (and, in her assessment, should always) exist and power differences that impinge on selfhood or the "ability to be yourself." She also validates one of this book's main points – seemingly individual behaviours emanate from interlocking oppressive structures such as patriarchy and colonialism.

In lockstep with Maracle, Danielle also implicated patriarchy, this time in the fostering of a racist divisiveness in Western society:

> I think it comes down to a European mentality and kind of patriarchal way of thinking – that everybody believes that we have these colours on us. We see that circle, the four colours of man, as one. It's not our analysis, it's not our way of looking at things, that you're white and I'm brown, and somebody else is yellow and someone else is orange and somebody's got pink polka dots. That's not our way. We look at each other as human beings. We look at each other as Onkwehon:we, carriers of water here on land ... That was really what we saw when Christopher Columbus came bopping across. They looked at him as a human being and extended their friendship and their kindness, because that's our duty and our responsibility, to work together with all of Creation. That's the oldest law. That law supersedes Canadian law. I think that's what they tried to wipe out, that real protocol and the medicine and the strength that comes from working together and accepting each other and tolerating each other as individuals.

Like Maracle, Danielle here points to the importance of embracing (non-invasive) differences instead of creating hierarchies of difference and/or demanding sameness, as Maracle might add.

Belinda accessed a similar discourse of tolerance in her description of Indigenous ways of relating:

> Native people, they don't close the door on anybody. They don't say, "You can't come here because you're not this or too that." Well, maybe they do in some situations, like with traditional ceremony; there are certain rules. But I mean in organizing groups, they don't leave anybody out, especially when there is food when someone's hungry ... And they tend to tolerate a lot more than white people do because they realize that some people just don't know any better and maybe they'll learn. And, you know, kindness is the most human thing you can do ... It was one of those things that made us so vulnerable, that kindness and openness and generosity, that made them exploit us.

In these statements, Danielle and Belinda associate divisiveness and exclusion with Western ways of being, and unity, cooperation, inclusivity, and respect with indigeneity. Both argue, in fact, that it was because of Indigenous societies' capacity to do, in Belinda's words, "the most human thing you can do," that colonizers targeted them for exploitation. Teresa, quoted above on the inherently political nature of being an Indigenous woman, maintained that the same predisposition toward inclusivity can render Indigenous communities vulnerable in the contemporary solidarity encounter: "I think that it's really important in working in solidarity that we do a profile of the people that come into our circles ... I think our communities are a bit *too* welcoming to people who come in. There might be violence issues, abuse issues, addiction issues." Danielle concurred with Teresa, as is evident in her description of a "needy" ally's behaviour:

> She just needs to be listened to and heard and have attention because she's lonely and living alone, and her family never comes to see her. And here are these Indians, always so kind and so caring and welcoming and tolerant. "Put up with me and give me attention and don't correct me when I'm offensive and monopolizing the meeting and talking and talking so no one else gets to express anything. I'm just talking for the sake of talking." Meanwhile, [she] should have had respect for that Elder. Don't waste his energy, because he doesn't have a finite supply, and neither do I. I'm happy to do the work. I'll work hard, but I won't waste my time. I don't have time to waste.

Kindness, tolerance, the generosity of spirit with which Indigenous peoples greeted Europeans – as much as these attributes may be in part idealizations of Indigenous cultures and subjectivities, they are also strong reaffirmations of the humanity of Indigenous peoples. As such, they demonstrate the wisdom of LaRocque's (2010, 120) call to historicize and contextualize the "idealizations" that are "woven throughout [Native] deconstructive argumentations."

Interestingly, Indigenous spirituality, which is often the target of non-Indigenous romanticization, was not a significant reference point for Indigenous participants in this research, at least not in the same way it was for several of the white participants. There are at least three plausible explanations for this. First, I did not ask participants directly about their religious or spiritual beliefs, as this was not the focus of my research; consequently, Indigenous participants may have thought these beliefs irrelevant to the topics under discussion. Second, spirituality and religion are not necessarily significant factors in the lives or solidarity practices of Indigenous women. To assume otherwise would be to essentialize and/or tokenize Indigenous women and leave little room for atheism or secular beliefs on their part. This was among the issues that forced our collective hand at No More Silence (NMS): as it turned out, "An Indigenous former NMS member who did not identify strongly with Indigenous spiritual traditions expressed discomfort with having to be an 'expert' on Indigeneity" (D'Arcangelis and Huntley 2012, 49). Finally, because Indigenous participants were speaking to a white woman, they might have been hesitant to discuss certain beliefs with me (recall Belinda's comment regarding restrictions sometimes placed on non-Indigenous access to certain ceremonies).

In fact, most of the Indigenous participants who brought up the issue of spirituality did so vis-à-vis white women's spiritual/religious beliefs. For example, Tabobondung advised white women to learn about their own ancestry and traditions as a safeguard against cultural appropriation:

> Everyone has to do their own work. I think that's that subtlety, when people are like, "Teach me, show me." You have to do it yourself, too, look at your own life. How are you impacted by colonization, your family? The dynamics between you and your own mom, your parents, the roots of your ancestry. Who are you? Once you figure that out ... not figure it out but explore that before you just go to something else. Explore it. Because that's who you are. Then we can share aspects of our spirituality and philosophies with each other.

With an implicit allusion to white women's desire for healing and the appropriation of Indigenous religious beliefs or practices that can ensue, Tabobondung identifies a measure white women can take to mitigate appropriation, something I discuss further in the concluding chapter.

Indigenous participants occasionally brought up the topic of religion/spirituality in other ways. For instance, Kellie, whose story of white settler hijacking is in the previous chapter, described the benefits she gained from Indigenous political activism. Not unlike how Evelyn described her personal transformation as a white woman through solidarity work, Kellie remarked:

> It's been really great because it's allowed me to become more in touch with my spiritual roots. Because I find with mainstream white culture, there's not a spiritual element to their activism. I think that leads to all the burnout that we see, and anger and aggression, and people just going to a demonstration

and yelling at the police because they're pissed and they're angry ... You know, the smart thing to do is to be the intellectual activist who's agnostic and who's very rational, linear-minded, right? ... Activist culture for First Nations is very different than when it comes to mainstream white culture, even when it comes to the heroes. Definitely, my life has improved, not just in activism, but in general, being more open to allowing spirituality to be part of my activism and see how they belong together. It's unnatural to separate them ... not to say that spirituality cures everything, but it definitely keeps you on your centre.

While Kellie's sentiments may resemble those found in some white participant narratives – including my account in Chapter 1 of being transformed in Guatemala – Mahrouse's (2011) warnings about discourses of reversal and equation suggest the danger of assuming any such equivalency. Rather, what Kellie's comments underline for me is the cultural and spiritual disenfranchisement wrought by colonial oppression. Finally, I read Kellie's statement for what it exposes about the contradictions of white settler/liberal subjectivity. In identifying the "anger and aggression" among (presumably white) agnostic intellectual activists, eruptions seemingly at odds with the "rational, linear-minded" thinking expected of white settler/liberal subjects, Kellie signals the need to reconsider hierarchical, dichotomous notions of thought versus emotion.

Deconstructing the "Indigenous Woman Subject"

Alongside their resounding commitments to the survival and welfare of their nations, Indigenous participant narratives open up nuanced perspectives on the figure of the Indigenous woman subject working selflessly on behalf of her community. More to the point, they deconstruct romanticized and essentialized depictions of Indigenous peoples as inclusive and respectful and Indigenous women as caregivers singularly concerned with their nations' well-being. For example, Danielle's sarcasm, evident in comments about a white woman's attraction to "these Indians, always so kind and so caring and welcoming and tolerant," is an acknowledgment of the caricatured nature of this depiction – especially in the minds of those she calls needy allies. Adding to this view, Maracle reminds us that we all swim in the same colonial waters and that Indigenous people are not exempt from exhibiting "bad" behaviours:

> The thing is, you can't compensate for [the massive structural inequity between Indigenous and non-Indigenous populations]. And some [white]

people try to by being overly generous and all that sort of stuff. Letting Aboriginal people behave badly is another example. So that's not going to help ... We all have colonial patterns of behaviour. Europeans generally have a bigger sense of entitlement, are generally more invasive, and all that, but it doesn't mean that we don't find the reverse to be the case too. Sometimes white people are more humble than they need to be, and sometimes Native people are more arrogant than they should be. So, we have to take care of it all. We have to be on the lookout for some basic sense of decency and understanding.

According to Maracle, white people sometimes enable Indigenous people to behave badly because of our white desire to compensate for the massive structural inequity that defines settler colonialism, a desire I attend to in more detail in the next chapter. Moreover, even though she may distinguish Indigenous and Western societal organizing principles, Maracle would likely reject the existence of a rigid dichotomy between the two (Waters 2004b).

Maracle's view of solidarity also debunks simplistic visions of the Indigenous woman as an unindividuated altruist dedicated solely to her Indigenous community or nation. Maracle accomplishes this by acknowledging the personal advantages/aspects of solidarity work:

You have to figure out how to get the job done without your various cultural and personal differences getting in the way too. So really doing work with someone outside of family makes you a broader and more accepting person. So I try to do things with other people besides family for that reason, because it's going to help me grow as a human being. In the end, I'll be a better grandmother, a better friend, a better sister, a better aunt ... I'll be happier spiritually; I'll have more connections; I'll be more loved. I think that all of these efforts we make ... so I think it's way more than solidarity for me.

Maracle highlights the individual growth and spiritual happiness that can come from doing solidarity work, albeit benefits she views as bound up with the primary goal of solidarity encounters for many Indigenous women – "to get the job done." Maracle's approach to solidarity also invokes an underlying tenet of Indigenous philosophies – the indivisible interconnectedness of the "I" and the "we" – as explained by philosopher Viola Faye Cordova (Apache) (2004). Said another way, this ontological approach holds that individual and collective subjectivities are inextricably coconstituted, for better or worse, I might add. Therefore, individual autonomy must be respected and individual gifts enhanced to ensure the benefit of the collective (Anderson 2016; Simpson 2017). Leanne Betasamosake Simpson (2011, 43) makes a similar point about the individual–collective dynamic when discussing Mississauga Nishnaabeg resurgence: "The performance of our 'theories' and thought is how we collectivize meaning. This is important because our collective truths as a nation and as a culture are continuously generated from those individual truths we carry around inside ourselves. Our collective truths exist in a nest of individual diversity." In short, the collective should not eclipse the individual; instead, individual diversity (that is, individuality, not individualism) comprises and finds meaning in the collective.

Cordova's (2004) work is part of a burgeoning literature on Indigenous social and political thought that explores Indigenous epistemological and ontological precepts sometimes, though not always, in comparison and contrast with Western philosophical belief systems.[19] In her treatise on Native womanhood, Kim Anderson (2016) touches on many of the same points made by Indigenous participants, particularly about Indigenous women's traditional responsibilities to their nations. In the concluding conversation with Bonita Lawrence, Anderson (2016, 240) also discusses the risks of romanticizing Indigenous women or burdening them with too much responsibility. Lawrence then takes issue with ideas circulating among "urban traditionalists" about Indigenous women's responsibility in some activist settings:

> I worry about this urban traditionalism, and when I hear this constant emphasis on the responsibilities of women, it bugs me. How many responsibilities are most Native women already saddled with? Especially single mothers with the lowest income and the largest families. Native women know more about responsibility than any other group in this whole society! [*laughs*] And yet all the urban teachings keep going on about the "roles and responsibilities" of Native women in ways that I think are about creating this image of womanhood which gives us pride in our nations. And this is problematic.

Lawrence's statement is part of a broader conversation among Indigenous women (often, but not always, within Indigenous feminist discussions) about the merits and pitfalls of "tradition," particularly as related to Indigenous women's roles in Indigenous self-determination struggles.[20] Early on in her interview with Anderson (2016, 232), Lawrence gestures at how Indigenous feminists are redefining Indigenous philosophical traditions in empowering ways – reconfiguring the tenet of interconnectedness between the "I" and the "we" to delineate a respectful relationship between Indigenous women and their nations:

> I'd gotten an impression from the first Elder I worked with that following traditional ways simply meant giving of ourselves endlessly for the needs of our people ... I like how [Kim Anderson] challenge[s] this way of thinking – especially that analogy about how the European approach has been to treat Mother Earth like something to use up – and that this was how women have been treated as well. I like the idea that caring for ourselves is part of caring for the earth – but not in a "new age" sense – in a sense that we are an important resource which needs to be called upon respectfully.

Complementing Lawrence's point, Simpson (2011, 60) explains the importance of decolonizing "our conceptualization of gender as a starting point" for discussions of Indigenous resurgence, nation building, and self-determination, adding that "for Nishnaabeg people there was fluidity around gender in terms of roles and responsibilities" (see also Simpson 2017). My point is that Indigenous participant allusions to their identity and responsibilities as Indigenous women have historical reference points and theoretical foundations and are the subject of ongoing debates about Indigenous tradition as it relates to Indigenous women in particular – and must be interpreted in this light.

Indigenous participants' self-presentations are complex in other ways. While understanding that inclusivity and interconnectedness are features of many Indigenous philosophical traditions, Indigenous participants recognized the potentially negative repercussions of such values for Indigenous women's political struggles. Amadahy noted that the culturally sanctioned move toward inclusivity can be counterproductive when it comes to anti-violence organizing. Her point emerged in our discussion about a conference call that took place (and in which I participated) to organize the annual February 14 events to honour MMIWG2S people across Turtle Island. Invoking inclusivity as an Indigenous value, some organizers wanted the events to broaden their focus to include all women. I broached the subject with Amadahy to make sense of what had been my intensely negative reaction to the idea at the time. As I told Amadahy, in retrospect, I could read this reaction for what it was: a sign of my investment in being (seen as) an exceptional/good white ally (for more on exceptionalism, see Chapter 4). In short, the idea of broadening the focus to all women was threatening to me, or more accurately, to my desire for proximity to Indigenous women, the possibility of which seemed to be evaporating with every minute of the conference call. My reflections on the topic prompted Amadahy to talk about a unique tension facing Indigenous women who organize around the issue of colonial violence against Indigenous women:

> It still bothers me that that type of thing [opening up the struggle to honour women from all nations who have been victims/survivors of violence] happens, because [violence against Indigenous women] is a very specific struggle, and you lose the specifics ... Indigenous women, yes, they are victimized by violence, and so are white women and so are Black women, but we're victimized in very particular ways, and that means the solutions are different. And if we lose that, and we just say, "We're all victims of violence, and let's just try and work on it with the same strategies and the same groups" ... It still kind of irritates me when it comes out of that place, but I understand that, again, from the mindset that people have ... if you're aware of the interconnectedness and you have to acknowledge and understand that we want to stop all violence against all women, because it doesn't matter if it's happening to me in my community or not ... if it's happening to any woman, it affects me.

Amadahy's concerns bring us back to the nefarious workings of false equivalencies (Clark Mane 2012) that can downplay the specificities of the settler colonial violence experienced by Indigenous women as well as the anti-Black racist violence experienced by Black women.

Since then, I have seen the matter of how to frame activism around violence against Indigenous women come up repeatedly in different settings. I suggest that this is indicative of the broader issue facing Indigenous peoples of when (and when not) to stress Indigenous specificity in political struggles. Indigenous participants seem to recognize the need to strike a balance between following traditional values (especially in abstracted and decontextualized ways) and veering away from them to ensure that, for example, appeals to Indigenous inclusivity do not overshadow the specificity of colonial violence against Indigenous women.

Several years later, I had a similar conversation with a Toronto-based Indigenous activist about the language organizers use to frame the disappearances and murders of women in Vancouver's Downtown Eastside

(DTES), a disproportionate number of whom are Indigenous. Notably, as the lead organizers of the February 14 Memorial March, Indigenous women apply Indigenous ceremonial protocols. However, the language of the Women's Memorial March Organizing Committee honours all women who have gone missing or been murdered in the DTES. I cite this as an example of how it is possible to acknowledge specificity while also being inclusive.

The Allure of the "Authentic Indian"
Indigenous peoples and white settlers both become as individuals and as collectivities in the same colonial context, although under markedly different sociopolitical constraints. High on the list of these constraints is the need to satisfy widely held non-Indigenous expectations of Indigenous authenticity. When actual Indigenous people fail to meet what Lawrence (2003, 23) calls "the white need for certainty about Indian difference," the result is consternation at best and hostility at worst. Under these conditions, Indigenous peoples must confront daily the mainstream's fascination with "the imaginary Indian" (Francis 1992) defined by a host of racialized and gendered stereotypes (Anderson and Robertson 2011). As LaRocque (2010, 135) explains, the paradox is that Indigenous peoples are "wrapped in stereotypes and yet ... expected not only to produce 'authentic' material ... but even to look authentically different." Indigenous artists and intellectuals especially are placed in this "untenable situation" and called upon to reproduce fetishized notions of Indigenous difference. Moreover, as Leanne Betasamosake Simpson (2017, 49) eloquently explains, in today's neoliberal settler colonial context, Indigenous radical resurgence movements are conveniently misapprehended to mean "a resurgence of story, song, dance, art, language, and culture [that] is compatible with the reconciliation discourse, the healing industry, or other depoliticized recovery-based narratives."[21] In the dominant national imaginary, an apolitical discourse of cultural difference, which also imbues state policies of multiculturalism, dilutes the radical essence of Indigenous resurgence.

Indigenous women may face a comparably untenable situation in the solidarity encounter if they are expected (or expect themselves) to act the part. Whitebird used offhanded humour and irony in noting that Native status is now in vogue in some solidarity circles, suggesting her disdain for anyone, non-Indigenous or Indigenous, who would contribute to this fetishizing of indigeneity in the current sociopolitical environment: "I have a bumper sticker that says, 'I was Native longer than it's been cool.'" On a related note,

Amadahy admitted with remarkable honesty to having "enjoyed my celebrity status ... in white activist circles":

> There was a time when I really quite enjoyed my celebrity [status] in white activist circles ... I really enjoyed being the go-to person ... being in a position of telling people off and saying, "Your politics need work," and that kind of stuff. I've been manipulative ... My story isn't unusual in the sense that I'm a person who was raised outside of the Native community, outside of Native culture, who's trying to relearn that and reclaim it ... So it's really nice to be actually seen as someone who has skills and wisdom and is put on that leadership pedestal; whereas in my community, it was very clear that people appreciated me, like I say, for the skills that I had, but they knew the learning curve I was on. There are roles that I could never have taken on within the community that I could take on outside of the community. So I think that was a part of it.

To some extent, solidarity work for Amadahy offered a way to bolster her self-worth. However, as Amadahy makes clear, her story is part of the colonial story, just as white women's stories are. The tactic she employed in response to colonial dispossession and cultural loss – donning the role of the authentic Indigenous go-to person – is just that, a tactic born of necessity. Yet, more pertinent to my objective of theorizing white women's negotiations of the solidarity encounter is the fact that white solidarity activists eagerly slotted Amadahy into that role.

Danielle remarked on the related phenomenon of the "celebrity Elder," often though not always an Indigenous man well known in non-Indigenous contexts who relishes being in the public spotlight to represent his Indigenous community. Like Amadahy, Danielle implicated the uncritical reverence of settler activists who enable such celebrity Elders:

> So then, if [a non-Indigenous activist] were going to call on somebody to do a ceremony, you would ask the Aboriginal people, "What Elder do you want to come and do the ceremony?" And they'll all say, "This [person], because he's traditional and he speaks the language and he knows the ceremony." And if you ask the [non-Indigenous] activist community who they want to do the ceremony, they'll say this guy who they've seen all the time, who has the media attention ... So the one that's doing the real work on the ground is left out in the dark, in the cold, and here's this guy who's willing to be on the camera all the time and willing to monopolize everything and willing

to talk and talk and talk, whether or not he's got anything to say at all. He's just got the attention ... I've seen this more than once, where you have that celebrity Elder, whoever's on TV all the time, and you see all these white people sitting around their feet. They're working with the eagle feathers and they're putting the medicines together, and when it comes to taking the smudge around, it's them: "I'll do it! I'll do it! Auntie, Auntie, I'll do it!" So then they're taking the feather, and it's like this big show ... and you can just see the feather going, and they're like, "He big Elder told me it's gotta go this way, so then it's gotta go this way."

Importantly for Danielle, the celebrity Elder does not necessarily have extensive ties to their community – ties that, if anything, would be stronger indicators of Indigenous "authenticity."

As an Indigenous woman from beyond Turtle Island who therefore considered herself an ally to Indigenous struggles in Canada, Kellie described a similar scenario:

They were looking for a Native speaker, and all they saw on the horizon was [so and so] doing his posturing and stuff. I had to take them aside and say, "You know, there's other First Nations speakers in Toronto who are equally or more competent than [him] to speak on the issues." But they're not the ones pounding their chests and standing at the front ... But they're more reserved, or they're too busy doing their work, so they don't have time to be pounding their chest on TV.

For both Kellie and Danielle, the "ones pounding their chests" are usually, but not necessarily, Indigenous men.

Ursula described herself as an Indigenous woman with light-skinned privilege. We met in a stuffy though pleasant enough computer room on a university campus. In answering my question about what differences matter most to solidarity work, Ursula took me in an unexpected direction, highlighting the political pitfalls for BIPOC activists especially when they focus inordinately on colonially imposed differences:

In my ["mixed" Indigenous–non-Indigenous] activist circles, all we think about is our differences. I think we should think more about our commonalities, because we get stuck on our differences sometimes, even among Native peoples: "Are you on reserve, are you off-reserve, are you Status, are you non-Status, are you real, are you authentic, are you dark, are you light?"

... What makes you more Indian than not?" This is colonial. All those questions are colonial. I mean, [it's] important to consider ... our privileges, but they're created by the colonial system, if you think about it. Status and non-Status, light and dark, whatever. I think, more importantly, what nations? And how do we respect our differences in a way that will encourage stronger solidarity? Because [focusing on differences] is such a block ... We have to break it down and then move on, because if we're all there, committed to doing this one thing, say a fundraiser, let's just do it, instead of getting stuck.

Here, Ursula is especially critical of the colonially induced conundrum of having to prove one's authentic Indigenous status. In making her point, Ursula also provides a glimpse of the internal challenges and complexities of Indigenous political struggle.

In a candid moment reminiscent of the one I had with Amadahy, Belinda divulged her desire to occupy a "special place" as an Indigenous person in solidarity circles. In contrast with most Indigenous women in the study, Belinda talked about seeking primarily white-dominated spaces for her political and professional work:

The [solidarity] work that I did there was mostly white women and men, white people. You know you're always the odd Indian ... I guess I'm used to being the minority. I don't know what that's about really, but I'm sure there's a reason. Well, I think I have a lot of distrust of my own people. That may be the reason I am not doing as much solidarity work with them. Or could it be that I don't see them as having something to offer me? Possibly I feel above them. I don't know for sure, but this seems to be a recurring theme in my life. I am isolated either by consciously choosing to be on my own and away from other Native women or ... am I more comfortable being the minority, being "the Native person" might have its special place?

In contemplating the "distrust of [her] own people" that she may have harboured over the years, Belinda directs us to another unsolicited consequence of the settler colonial focus on difference: Indigenous peoples' internalization of negative colonial stereotypes along with the shame and self-rejection that often accompany that internalization (LaRocque 2010, 121). At the same time, however, throughout our conversation Belinda exuded the resilience echoed in the writings of Indigenous scholars such as Simpson (2011, 13–14), who describes coming to grips with the "legacy of colonial abuse, the unspoken shame" that Indigenous peoples collectively carry:

> It is a shame rooted in the humiliation that colonialism has heaped on our peoples for hundreds of years and is now carried within our bodies, minds and our hearts ... This colonial shame felt like not only a tremendous burden to carry, it also felt displaced ... I began to realize that shame can only take hold when we are disconnected from the stories of resistance within our own families and communities. I place that shame as an insidious and infectious part of the cognitive imperialism that was aimed at convincing us that we are a weak and defeated people, and that there was no point in resisting or resurging.

Like LaRocque, Simpson shares stories of resistance/resurgence with future generations. In relation to my objective of theorizing white women's negotiations of the solidarity encounter, my takeaway is this: we would do well to interpret Indigenous participant affirmations of Indigenous cultural values, and Indigenous women's caregiving responsibilities, as radical resurgence (Simpson 2017) and, as such, incommensurable to white women's invocations of the same.

~

I have often wondered about the meaning and allure of "going strange/going native" (Ahmed 2000). In this chapter, I offer one explanation of its enduring appeal for some non-Indigenous people living in settler colonial contexts. To do so, I analyzed participant narratives for what they indicate about the intricate paths white settlers can take to foster a sense of national belonging. Peeling back the layer of any national imaginary is difficult, not least because of the commonsense status it comes to enjoy over time. Still, I contend that discourses of Western lack help do just that, especially when they meld with the fourth element of my proximity spectrum – an attraction to or appreciation of Indigenous culture, tradition, or spirituality.

As demonstrated by a few white participant narratives, often warranted and seemingly benign references to Western societal failings can set colonial logic in motion. More specifically, I identify a discursive pattern that unfolds in four steps with Western lack as its linchpin: in these instances, a white settler woman (1) names a problem with Western society; (2) contrasts Western culture with Indigenous culture; (3) outlines the deficiencies of the former and the wisdom of the latter; and (4) adopts/appropriates Indigenous identity or culture as her own. This four-step explanatory model is precisely that – one model for tracing the often-convoluted paths from appreciation to appropriation that white settlers risk traversing when we uncritically pursue our attraction to – or, in the language of this book, desire for proximity to – Indigenous cultural differences, variously defined. Drawing on scholarly insights into settler colonial subjectivity, I explored how that pursuit can culminate in a number of dynamics such as impersonating idealized versions of indigeneity to launch critiques of settler society (Deloria 1998; Morgensen 2011; LaRocque 2010), identificatory mobility (Fee and Russell 2007), nostalgic and salvific benefit (Schick 1998), and discourses of reversal and equation, false equivalences, and disavowal (Clark Mane 2012; Battell Lowman and Barker 2015; Mahrouse 2011; Razack 2002). When run through the colonial mill, white settler critiques of what they or their society lack become strategies for the remaking of white settler subjects, or perhaps more accurately, our sense of national belonging at both the individual and collective level. That is to say, white settlers may find ourselves turning to Indigenous cultures to fill the so-called voids of Western society. I also bring attention to the gendered aspects of these dynamics: notions of Indigenous gender egalitarianism would likely be of particular appeal to white women.

Picking up a thread from the previous chapter, I explain this four-step discursive chain as signalling another difference between the impulse to solidarity and the helping imperative (Heron 2007): the former turns on allusions to the ethical shortcomings of Western society and the superiority of Indigenous cultural values, whereas the latter works in reverse. This distinction vindicates the paramount importance of social, political, and geographic context. It matters that solidarity encounters happen "here" and not "there," in a space beyond Canada's national borders. As a result, white women in solidarity work cannot fully escape the dictates of collective white settler/liberal subjectivity, namely, desires for emplacement, a lingering sense of precarity, and, at least for some, the tendency to "play Indian" or engage in similar techniques to yield the perception of belonging on Indigenous land.

While blatant manifestations of this feature of the proximity spectrum were rare in participant narratives, the white settler attraction to Indigenous culture, tradition, or spirituality deserves our attention for at least two reasons: first, the striking clarity of the examples that do exist; and second, their resonance with Indigenous narratives that access the same discourse of Western lack. In fact, in juxtaposing these narratives, I identify the potential limitations of a framework of cultural difference for non-colonizing forms of solidarity and, more broadly, for denaturalizing settler colonialism as the overarching organizing principle of society.

Despite notable divergences in their respective modalities of political activism/solidarity, a number of Indigenous and white participants appeared to be invested in dislodging Western social norms and practices while upholding Indigenous alternatives. This shared focus on cultural difference, I argue, is not necessarily a good or even benign thing but rather a potential breeding ground for white settler/liberal subjectivity. Based on what we know so far about that subjectivity, an inordinate focus on cultural difference could very well occlude a focus on colonial power differences. This eventuality prompted me to wonder if Indigenous references to cultural difference could inadvertently feed into the white tendency to romanticize indigeneity and thus complicate white women's efforts to disrupt the solidarity impulse. This is what I mean by the potentially limiting framework of cultural difference.

At the same time, when invoked by Indigenous peoples, "Indigenous difference" can become a tool of resistance and resurgence that reveals hierarchical power relations. Moreover, applying an Indigenous feminist lens enables seeing beyond the parallels – common generalizations about cultural differences such as Western competitiveness, hierarchy, and unsustainable consumerist practices versus Indigenous cooperation, egalitarianism, and sustainability – to the dissimilar ways in which white and Indigenous participants are likely to understand and deploy these discourses. Overall, white participants placed equal emphasis on attacking Western cultural values and praising Indigenous ones, whereas Indigenous participants gave more weight to appraisals of Indigenous values as superior. As LaRocque (2011) and Simpson (2017) suggest, this variance in emphasis reflects the fact that Indigenous cultural resurgence is always already political, that is, linked to Indigenous self-determination.

To be sure, Indigenous participant narratives testify to the difficult task Indigenous women, communities, and nations face in negotiating the questions of identity, representation, and power that derive from their structural position as "the colonized." Indeed, Indigenous feminists for some time have been raising and addressing questions about romanticized notions of Indigenous tradition that perpetuate (often colonially imposed) patriarchal notions of Indigenous womanhood and Indigenous self-determination (Anderson 2016; Kuokkanen 2019; Starblanket 2017; Sunseri 2000).[22] Moreover, Indigenous participants were aware that stereotypes are apt to affect their performance in the solidarity encounter. Nevertheless, several spoke about the subject position "Indigenous woman" as inherently political and about political activism as a matter of individual/collective survival. For me, the lesson for white women solidarity practitioners comes down to understanding the political dimensions of much Indigenous cultural resurgence, of appreciating Indigenous women's invocations of indigeneity as a strategy to resist colonial oppression. Perhaps doing so would make white women (and others) in the solidarity encounter (and beyond) less likely to essentialize, fetishize, and appropriate Indigenous cultural difference and more likely to further the anticolonial project of redressing power differences.[23]

This chapter raises unsettling questions about Indigenous peoples and white settlers alike as potential enforcers of a limited framework of cultural difference. Some will find my approach inappropriate, offensive, or even colonial. I risk such reactions to attempt three things: first, to underscore the importance of contextualizing Indigenous narratives in settler colonial contexts; second, to note the ironic prospect that similar discourses about indigeneity can bolster both Indigenous and white settler nation-building processes (a topic that warrants further study); and third, to demonstrate that identity-making processes at the micro/individual and macro/collective levels are always intertwined, intersubjective enterprises. In what comes next, I focus on the third theme by turning to the whiteness of white settler/liberal subjectivity.

4

Claiming Exceptionalism as the Rule

"Good/White Settler Allies" and the Politics of Declaration

> There were a few [white] folks that were able to – at least on the surface – bridge the gap, but from my perspective, it almost came across to me as appropriation of culture, which wasn't what I was interested in. I was looking for a place to be challenged myself, to have my implicit isms – racisms, whatever – challenged, and to do some work that I believe in, to do some good work ... I'm not shopping for culture. That made me uncomfortable, and it made me uncomfortable in that I don't want to be seen as somebody who's trying on a culture and trying on different things. I was there to learn and to be part of a group that would challenge our society that we sit in.
> – JULIA

When we met, Julia recalled with admirable candour and conviction why she, a white woman, had joined a local Indigenous–non-Indigenous solidarity group: for the "political social activism" and "education piece, and really dissecting colonialism in the now." In the above passage, she alludes to a rift in the group that ensued shortly after its inception. One camp consisted of like-minded people who shared her activist and educational goals, the other, of people "looking more for – I don't know how to word it – a sense of community, I think. A sense of connection to both Indigenous and non-Indigenous people." While the camps did not break down exactly along

Indigenous–non-Indigenous lines, Julia was mainly concerned about the white women in the latter who appeared to be "shopping for culture."

Even if my aim were to do so, I cannot easily slot Julia into the proximity spectrum. She was decidedly *not* drawn to solidarity work out of a desire to feel welcomed by an Indigenous community or to have exposure to Indigenous culture – both prominent elements of the spectrum. If anything, Julia wanted a challenge, the fifth element in the spectrum; even so, the challenge for her was as much (if not more) collective than it was individual. Above all, Julia took exception to being categorized as someone whose engagement in solidarity was founded in cultural appropriation.

Why open with this passage? I did so not out of any interest in the veracity of Julia's claims about settler moves to appropriation, however much these claims bolster my argument. I want to assess how and why white women like Julia make "claims of exceptionalism" to differentiate themselves from other white women in the solidarity encounter. In other words, I am interested in how and why we might position ourselves as exceptional good white settler activists. Unlike the pursuit of proximity whose apparent focus is the Indigenous Other, moves to exceptionalism involve white people contrasting their activist exploits – and by extension, themselves – with other non-Indigenous Canadians, often other activists.

If Emma Battell Lowman and Adam Barker (2015, 100–1) are correct, seeking exception is a common enough reaction among settlers confronted by the illegitimacy of our claims to land and national belonging. And if, as I suggest, the solidarity encounter can induce a more acute awareness of settler precarity, then moves to exceptionalism are likely a regular feature of the impulse to solidarity. Seeking exception, then, is one more way in which white women in the solidarity encounter, in proximity to Indigenous women, negotiate our structural dominance.

In short, I contend that claiming exceptionalism is yet another expression of the collective white settler desire for emplacement (Razack 2011) or, in less pejorative and more nuanced terms, the desire to live "legitimately, ethically, fully" on Indigenous land, as Peggy so powerfully put it. I also look at how claims to exceptionalism link to that thorniest of matters, white settler guilt, and to one of the underlying elements of my proximity spectrum – the desire for acceptance or forgiveness. Similar to the way I approach matters of cultural appropriation, I do not make determinations about whether white settler guilt is at play in a particular instance. Rather, drawing on a range of feminist, critical race, and critical whiteness scholars, I focus on tracking the claims themselves.

What most struck me when reading white participant narratives is the good–bad settler binary that is implicitly established when we position ourselves as exceptions to a norm. As an expression of the desire for belonging, moves to exceptionalism do not rely on a straightforward disavowal of settler colonialism but rather on a constant reckoning of one's complicity therein. They are more like attempts to quell settler colonial anxiety than to negate settler identity and privilege entirely. Nonetheless, making such claims is facilitated by an individualistic approach to solidarity work: it is easier for the white woman (who thinks of herself as) entering solidarity as an autonomous individual, rather than as a member of a white settler collectivity, to sustain the fantasy of overcoming, however temporarily, colonial power relations. A self-determining individual could conceivably be or become exceptional, whereas a member of a collectivity cannot – at least not without fundamental structural change. To what extent can self-reflexivity help us out of these binds? I end the chapter with ruminations on the fraught promise of self-reflexivity for tempering this and other facets of the impulse to solidarity.

The Rule of Exception: Gender, Whiteness, and Morality

Somewhat ironically, white claims of exceptionalism appear to be anything but. What is it about whiteness that lends itself to such claims? It would seem that a belief in white morality, goodness, and innocence is a defining feature of white subjectivity in general. According to Melanie Bush (2011, 17), white people in the United States remain steadfast in the "sincere fiction" of their goodness even as they "hold beliefs and support positions that presume an assumption of white superiority." Writing about the Canadian context, Sherene Razack (2002, 2) centres on the correlated phenomenon of white innocence – a "quintessential feature of white settler mythologies" that manifests as "the disavowal of conquest, genocide, slavery, and the exploitation of the labour of peoples of colour." Barbara Heron (2007, 136, 6, 128) discusses the various "strategies of containment" white bourgeois women employ to convince themselves and others that their international development work is both "unproblematically 'good'" and an indication of their "moral" nature. In fact, one of their strategies is to make claims to exceptionality, that is, to differentiate what they do – so-called alternative development – from harmful development practices.

In relation to the solidarity encounter, claims of exceptionalism become part of fostering the illusion that white women can transcend colonial inequities. The influential work of feminist scholars Mary Louise Fellows and Sherene Razack helps explain why. Fellows and Razack (1998, 339) coined the phrase "race to innocence" to describe how hierarchical relations among women are often sustained in feminist political solidarity work. As they explain it, a race to innocence ensues when "women challenged about their domination respond by calling attention to their own subordination," implying that because they are subordinate, they cannot "be implicated in the subordination of others." Put another way, striving for exceptionalism in solidarity work is another way for white women to embrace the subordinate aspect of their "double positioning" (Loomba 2005) within settler colonial relations to claim innocence. Aileen Moreton-Robinson (2000, 143) has identified a similar dynamic among white feminist academics in Australia. Rather than acknowledging that white race privilege is "inscribed on white bodies," they claim a "personal relationship with racism ... through a moral position that allows one to put distance between oneself and other members of the dominant group who are evil and racist." These white feminist academics claim virtuousness by equating white race privilege with instances of individualized racial hatred. For Moreton-Robinson, to claim exceptionalism is to distance oneself from other dominant group members – a fantasy sustained by a liberal model of subjectivity that enables the disavowal of the embodied, collective, and systemic nature of white privilege.

White Australian anthropologist Emma Kowal (2011, 2015) addresses the nuances of a somewhat distinct dynamic among self-styled progressive White antiracists working with remote Indigenous populations in Australia – a focus that strongly resonates with my own. Willing to take responsibility for their role in colonization and acutely aware of their racial positioning, these progressive subjects come to experience their whiteness as a stigma and are prompted to employ discursive strategies of stigma management. To avoid being cast as "missionary, mercenary or misfit," they most often attempt to minimize their agency by describing themselves as "merely" behind-the-scenes helpers. The ultimate fantasy is "to divest themselves of power altogether (if only discursively)" by casting themselves as "children" who stand to learn from the "experts" – Indigenous people (Kowal 2011, 325). Even more in line with my main argument, Kowal (2011, 320) sees white stigma as being produced by the Indigenous–settler encounter, that is, proximity: "[White stigma] only takes effect when these White people are engaged in Indigenous issues, usually in the context of paid employment, but also through activism, education and personal encounters ... Only upon entering post-colonial spaces such as the Institute or remote communities does the stigma of Whiteness come into play." I apply Kowal's theory to argue that the solidarity encounter certainly qualifies as a space that can generate white stigma.

The supposition that white stigma or guilt infuses, if sometimes in amorphous ways, white settler desires for goodness and hence exceptionalism would not surprise Eve Tuck and K. Wayne Yang (2012, 10). For these scholars, settler guilt is relentless and haunting, as are attempts to alleviate it: "Settler moves to innocence are those strategies or positionings that attempt to relieve the settler of feelings of guilt or responsibility without giving up land or power or privilege, without having to change much at all." Going further, feminist postcolonial scholars Reina Lewis and Sara Mills (2003, 7–8) draw attention to the whiteness of white guilt – a historically derived, unproductive collective response to nineteenth-century colonial exploits:

"White guilt" developed from an awareness that Western powers ... had subjugated a large portion of the world and exploited these territories and their populations for material gain, and that white people had benefited directly and indirectly from that exploitation ... The link between past exploitation and present affluence, and indeed the deeds of past colonialists and oneself, is one which white people have found difficult to deal with in constructive ways.

According to Lewis and Mills, as well as Tuck and Yang, white people in colonial contexts are predisposed to feel guilt. This suggests that white settler guilt, while usually thought of as a personal feeling, is part of a historically constituted collective white settler subjectivity (Ahmed 2014). In this sense, settler guilt is one logical outcome of the lingering precarity of white settler/liberal subjectivity, and it would be surprising if it did not fuel white women's claims of exceptionalism in the solidarity encounter to some degree.

White Settler Guilt and the Desire for Forgiveness in Solidarity Work
As it turns out, Indigenous and white participants alike observed white settler guilt to be among the most powerful motivators for settler engagement in solidarity, although few theorized it as having a causal relationship with claims of exceptionalism. Ardra, the Indigenous participant whose insights into proximity proved invaluable to my thinking, implicitly linked

the two in her portrait of the needy do-gooder with a penchant for appropriation. Like Lewis and Mills (2003), she noted a propensity for guilt among white feminists in Western countries, including Germany and Canada, and its effect on solidarity:

> [Solidarity work] can just be a place for people to appropriate, romanticize, and project their wishes on others. I think what [Bonita Lawrence] is talking about is how people will use Indigenous struggles in particular as this utopia, this idea of this place to project their deepest desires ... especially white feminists in Germany who just eat that stuff up. But then they go pay for a sweat lodge. Then they want their Indian name. They want [indigeneity] to give them something. They want it to give them healing. They want it to make them better people. I kind of had that suspicion about people in [the group] sometimes ... Like this desire to work with Native women is about wanting to be better people and be seen as better people: "I'm a better person because ... I'm being validated by these Native women as a good ally," you know? "That makes me feel better about myself and alleviates my white guilt," and that ends up not being very transformative at all ... if that person doesn't ever question or become aware of that dynamic happening to them – *if* that's what is happening.

With incisive clarity, Ardra describes how the desire of some white women to be good allies, much like the desire of progressive White antiracists to dissolve their white stigma (Kowal 2011, 2015), can both materialize in and be satiated through the proximity of the solidarity encounter. What's more, Ardra explains the allure of solidarity for some white women in terms of the absolution of white guilt, that is, forgiveness. (No small wonder that I include forgiveness in my proximity spectrum!) In these instances, solidarity encounters become opportunities for white women to receive validation for their status as the good settler ally or comparatively better person. Yet Ardra leaves open the possibility that guilt may not be what is happening in all cases.

Teresa also tied solidarity work to guilt and the corresponding self-making needs of white women who, it seemed to her, failed to make this association: "I understand that Western women have a sense of needing to do [solidarity work] for themselves as well ... It's kind of like women come into the circles in order to find a prescription for their own guilt, which we recognize, and I don't think they recognize." Both Ardra and Teresa questioned white women's powers of discernment when it comes to recognizing white guilt.

Similarly, Wanda Whitebird (Mi'kmaq) said that on those occasions when she perceives guilt to be the main motivator for white women's solidarity work, "It just bugs the hell out of me." Like Lewis and Mills (2003), Whitebird sees guilt as an ineffectual political tool and unproductive response to colonial inequity:

> They're there because they think they understand that we've been done wrong and they want to change it, right then and there. They can't change it. They can't change history. You can come with all the guilt you like, but you can't change that. What you can do is, like I said, stand with us as an ally. That's how you can change it. Don't come to try to appease your own guilt. So you're feeling bad about, "Oh, I read about how you were put on reserves, and my ancestors did that" ... The only thing we can do is go forward. One of the things is to accept that it's happened and change it.

Here, Whitebird also astutely identified the unfettered liberal subject lurking behind the scenes – the "I" who wants to and conceives of herself as able to "change it, right then and there." For Whitebird, this guilt often arises out of the non-Indigenous person's newfound "understanding that [Indigenous people] have been done wrong" by one's ancestors.

While careful not to speculate about the role guilt plays for any given settler, Lee Maracle (Stó:lō/Métis) viewed it as arising out of a combination of religious influence and non-Indigenous people's recognition, at some level, of the illegitimate conquest of Indigenous land. As she declared, "I think that the guilt in this country is from having acquired a continent from the people that don't have access to it." By ascribing guilt to settler awareness of colonial land theft, Maracle joins Tuck and Yang (2012) and Lewis and Mills (2003) in suggesting a fundamental way in which settler colonialism overdetermines white settler–Indigenous relations across genders and sociopolitical contexts.

Carla was the very first person – and white woman – I interviewed. She was attentive to the role white guilt can play in solidarity encounters. It was early evening, and we sat comfortably cross-legged on my tiny living room rug. Carla alluded to a white desire to be "let off the hook." She suspects it is attributable to guilt: "I think some [white] people do solidarity the wrong way, like they think they're doing solidarity, but they don't really know what they're doing, and they think very problematic things: 'I want to work on Native issues; therefore, I'm scot-free.'" For critical whiteness studies scholar Barbara Applebaum (2010), the relative ease with which some white people proclaim blamelessness results from three mutually reinforcing discourses of whiteness: believing in white moral agency, believing in the white capacity for transcendence of structural injustices, and conflating direct culpability with complicity/responsibility. Applebaum (2010, 7) explains that because this conflation underlines individual "causality, knowledge, control, choice and/or intention ... well-intentioned white people are able to effortlessly let themselves off the hook since they can honestly claim they did not intend to perform anything wrong, and they were ignorant of or had no control over the wrongful outcome." As Moreton-Robinson (2000) and Boyd (2004) would agree, such liberal understandings of the subject simply do not countenance that these collective "whitely ways of being" (Applebaum 2010) perpetuate structural injustice.

For those operating under the assumption that only direct culpability makes one complicit/responsible, perhaps it is more an express lack of guilt that allows the person to claim innocence. As an Indigenous woman, Gabriela witnessed this phenomenon among white activists of all genders and called for the same detangling of direct culpability and responsibility as Applebaum (2010). Gabriela responded with ironic humour when asked about the existence of white guilt among settler allies:

GABRIELA: I can say that I know a couple of people, but that's it.
CAROL LYNNE: Okay, what do you mean by that? Do you want more people to feel guilty?
GABRIELA: Absolutely [*laughs*]! Not Jewish guilt or something ... Catholic guilt isn't what we want either. But it's realizing that you've got to get beyond the guilt, too, in the sense of moving beyond that, because you don't want to be stuck in it. But it's recognizing that you're part of the problem, even if you're not a bad person, you know what I mean, or somebody who's racist. A bad person is racist. So I think there are a whole bunch of people – non-Aboriginal people – who either tell you to just get over it, "This is where we are now, and you don't have such a bad deal, we're not doing that anymore," or you have people who want to be in [the group], but they don't really see themselves as being part of the problem.

Gabriela's and Carla's analyses converge. They both identified the predisposition of white settler allies to claim innocence, either by not seeing themselves as part of the problem or by thinking of themselves as being "scot-free." They also both cited the possibility of thwarting that tendency by foregrounding the structural privilege of all white settlers, even "good" white settler allies.

Other white narratives speak to the range of reactions that white settler guilt can elicit – from complete withdrawal or paralysis, to feeling awkward or self-silenced, to an overzealous impetus to take action. After admitting to having felt guilt, when asked how this had affected her activism, Alicia noted her variable responses: "It has probably made me a little bit more shy to reach out all the time. It has also forced me to be more engaging than I would have otherwise been, because I'm trying to make up for something." Notable here is not precisely what "that something" is or could be, but rather that guilt matters in the first place: Alicia felt compelled by guilt to be "more shy" or "more engaging," the latter arguably indicative of a move to proximity.

While also noting that she was vulnerable to feeling guilty, Julia said she is nonetheless alarmed when people assume white guilt always operates in solidarity work. Julia and I had the following exchange after she described being "raked over the coals" by an Indigenous woman for asking about the correct terminology to refer to Indigenous peoples. After this incident, the group atmosphere changed for Julia, and she no longer felt comfortable posing such questions:

CAROL LYNNE: What impact do you think white guilt has had on the solidarity encounter?

JULIA: I think the biggest piece is that, for me, trying to push the envelope a little bit, asking the tough questions, being vulnerable to ask that question, and then the response was so abrupt. So that when you go, that white guilt really kind of becomes a filter for the questions that you're going to ask, the critique that you might give, and that sort of thing. I think that comes into play, yet being very conscious of that's not what I want this to be. That will have a life of its own, but that's not what I want this to be about.

CAROL LYNNE: You don't want it to be about assuaging your white guilt?

JULIA: No, what I don't want is for that guilt to *be* a filter ... I don't know that it's necessarily that you feel white guilt, but it was like, "God, if I ask that question, is it going to look like white guilt? Is it going to look like that's where it's coming from? Or will it be taken for what it truly is: me asking a question, wanting to be better, to do better and to learn?" Not that it's anybody's responsibility to teach me. I'm taking responsibility for that. I'm trying to figure out this piece, and I want to – with you, in solidarity – tease that out. What *is* that?

On the one hand, this exchange makes clear that we cannot reduce white women's motivations for engaging in solidarity to the existence of guilt or the desire for its alleviation. On the other, Julia's concerns suggest that white settler guilt, whether real or perceived, has profound and pervasive effects on intersubjective dynamics in the solidarity encounter. Moreover, we can infer from participant remarks about what happens when guilt does rear its head that it is also a key ingredient of claims to exceptionalism.

The Art and Politics of Exception

Aside from what drives white settler claims of exceptionalism is the matter of their implementation – the art and politics of exception, shall we say. To illuminate what comprises these claims and how they work, I turn to Sara Ahmed's (2004) theorizing of the politics of antiracist declarations. Simply put, an individual or institution engages in these politics when they acknowledge their own wrongdoing or "bad practice." The twist is that this "'admission' itself becomes seen as good practice" (Ahmed 2004, para. 11). Ahmed notes six categories of such "nonperformative" declarations of whiteness, classified as such because they do nothing to change antiracist structures. By conflating saying and doing, the declarative speech mode allows for "a fantasy of transcendence in which 'what' is transcended is the very thing 'admitted to' in the declaration" (Ahmed 2004, para. 54). These seemingly inconsequential personal statements function in decidedly political ways to perpetuate a collective fantasy of transcendence on the part of dominantly positioned individuals. Ahmed's approach to the politics of antiracist declarations helps us to think precisely about how white subjects enact their sincere fictions (Bush 2011) and white moral agency (Applebaum 2010): white people can cloak our claims of exceptionalism in admissions of guilt, for example. Ahmed implicates the discipline of critical whiteness studies in these politics by noting the birth of the "anxious white subject" who openly acknowledges and frets about her white privilege.[1] As Corey Snelgrove advises, however, it would be a mistake to equate antiracist declarations with statements such as "I am a settler," which can be, but are not necessarily, moves to innocence (in Snelgrove, Dhamoon, and Corntassel 2014, 15). What I find valuable is the mechanism Ahmed describes.

As it happens, Ahmed (2004) herself applies the theory to a settler colonial context. When the Australian government invited non-Indigenous (white) Australians to acknowledge the forced removal of Indigenous children from Indigenous communities, the result was nonperformative declarations of shame at the national level. In this instance, shame permits collective absolution for past wrongs; it "becomes the ground for a narrative of national recovery ... The transference of bad feeling to the subject in this admission of shame is only temporary, as the 'transference' itself becomes evidence of the restoration of an identity of which we can be proud" (Ahmed 2004, para. 23). As Barbara Heron (2007) might put it, admitting shame becomes a containment strategy. Cleansed and inoculated against further "bad feeling," settlers regain individual legitimacy and collectively remake the national body politic. Put another way, nonperformative declarations become mechanisms of stranger fetishism that help conceal the history of structural inequalities in the present (Ahmed 2000). Building on Ahmed and Maracle, Barbara Applebaum (2010, 19) points to the religious overtones of what she calls "confessions of whiteness," shedding further light on the "complex and thorny" ways that white people deny complicity in structures of inequality.

Philosopher Claire A. Lockard (2016, 19) provides a robust explanation of the ineffectiveness of "the racist confession" by combining the insights of Ahmed (2004) on nonperformative declarations, Shannon Sullivan (2006, 2014) on white privilege as an unconscious habit, and Michel Foucault (1978) on the role of confession in Western modernity. Lockard (2016, 15) argues that white people's admissions of white privilege/racism are compelling precisely because they offer the promise of redemption: "[White people] believe, in other words, that confession changes and purifies our core selves." Refining Ahmed's terminology, Lockard calls these admissions "unhappy performatives" or "unhappy confessions." As an example, Lockard (2016, 11) cites an antiracist rally on a university campus that became an occasion for white students "to attempt to show their solidarity by talking at length about their privilege and racism rather than using their privileged voices" in other ways. Lockard notes growing expectations in a variety of social movement spaces – to which I would add the solidarity encounter – that dominantly positioned people will confess to their privilege.

Feminist scholar and activist Viviane K. Namaste troubles one such increasingly common practice – identifying one's pronouns, especially by cisgender activists. Namaste (2015, 136) identifies a critical dimension of the problem, which is that "activist confessions of privilege focus on interpersonal conduct, but avoid examining systems of oppression." In relation to whiteness, this dynamic establishes people of colour as the ones who can release white activists from that privilege (Namaste 2015, 135; see also Lockard 2016, 17). The prime risk, according to Namaste (2015, 136), is that those caught up in this self-reflective, confessional mode "think they are engaging in the real work of social change, [but] they actually miss the mark." When confessions stand in for political practice, they assume the role of nonperformative speech acts and keep structural privilege intact. The theories of Ahmed, Lockard, and Namaste expose the pattern at work: in admitting one's racist or colonialist flaws, a white person can claim exceptional status as the enlightened (read: "woke") white racist/settler. As a reminder, I am not interested in the veracity of any unhappy confessions I might find in white participant narratives; rather, I am interested in what these claims facilitate, if anything, about white woman self-making in the solidarity encounter.

Claims to exceptionalism can be veiled or, as Carol Schick suggests, more transparent. Schick (1998, 174) describes white preservice teachers' "positive" claims of exceptional cultural awareness as "credibility claims or warrants which participants call upon to construct for themselves a sympathetic, positive identity ... By these claims, subjects show that they are agents in the production of their own identity – and not objects, not one of 'them.'" Apart from shedding light on the purpose of credibility claims, Schick also implies something about collective subjectivity: the claims used by individual white teachers to differentiate themselves from less knowledgeable ones reveal something about white teachers as a group.

Bear with me for thoughts on one last tool in the arsenal of white exceptionalism – friendship. In referencing the colonial antecedents of US white antiracist subjectivity, critical whiteness scholar Audrey Thompson names the potential of friendship to be both a manifestation of white desires for proximity to Others and a strategy of white exceptionalism. Thompson (2003, 7–8) writes, "Custer himself declared that the white man was 'the Indian's best friend.' But we mean it differently, not *that* way. We mean that we are supporters of people of color, that we understand about white racism and that we are against it. We are not that sort of white; we are good whites." Simply put, to have or seek friendships with people of colour can be a way for white people to claim exceptional/antiracist status, sidestepping their complicity in racism and reproducing a good–bad white settler dichotomy in the process. While white resistance and settler resistance to acknowledging structural racism and colonialism, respectively, are not collapsible, they are hard to disentangle in a white settler colonial context. White settler moves to innocence would involve the disavowal of both.

Thus, in relation to the solidarity encounter, friendship becomes another strategy of exceptionalism that blends the pursuit of proximity, self-reflexivity, and the desire to achieve good settler status all into one. In what follows, I analyze what I consider instances of exceptionalism in the self-making processes of white participant narratives. I explore how these instances expose an aspect of gendered colonial subjectivity particular to that encounter: the desire to be (seen as) an exceptional or good antiracist/anticolonial activist who stands apart from other less progressive white activists. In this way, I argue, claims of exceptionalism can reflect and enable the broader white settler/liberal desire to transcend structural power relations.

Making Friends

While relatively rare in white participant narratives, friendship as a strategy of exceptionalism in the solidarity encounter requires consideration for three reasons. First, anecdotally, I have repeatedly heard it said that friendship is a prerequisite for political solidarity work. Second, it has a powerful attraction for those who use it. Third, as noted previously, Ardra identified friendship as a favoured approach of "progressive" white activists for seeking the acceptance of an Indigenous community. In line with Ardra and much like Thompson (2003), Ahmed (2000) counts friendship and love as among the discourses white settlers use to achieve proximity to Others and to release themselves from the violence inherent in relations of unequal power. As Ahmed (2000, 124–25) insightfully expresses, "The possibility of [friendship and] love is tied to a liberal vision of the white self as always open to others ... Not only do such multicultural fantasies of becoming involve releasing the Western subject from responsibility for the past, but they also confirm his agency, his ability to be transformed by the proximity of strangers." I am by no means suggesting that friendship is always a gateway to exceptionalism. However, as Ahmed persuasively argues, it can be a vehicle for white people to feel good and transcendent.

First introduced in Chapter 1, Darcie was a white participant whose solidarity involvement occurred primarily in a university context. Like others, Darcie discussed these experiences in transformative terms. Despite or, as the logic of exceptionalism would dictate, because of her substantial knowledge of colonization acquired in various contexts such as Indigenous studies courses, Darcie could think of no examples of power relations in solidarity work that involved her personally. Unlike other participants such as Alicia, who described negative receptions by some Indigenous women, Darcie described only positive experiences:

> When I first got involved [with the Indigenous students' group], I wanted to learn; so I went there ... feeling like an outsider and sort of being apprehensive about that, but then realizing that if you go in with a good mind, an open mind and an open heart, and you're sincere, people respond to that very well, and you can become a part of that community ... I think just having the ability to listen and exchange ideas when that needs to happen ... If I wanted to get involved in the Indigenous community, I'm not Indigenous, I don't have that background, so I need to learn to try and understand. Because you can read books about what's happening and what needs to be done, but until you actually talk to people from those communities, then you actually find out ... It's sort of like going to the source to try and figure out what is best.

Later in the interview, Darcie explicitly tied friendship, along with knowledge of and acceptance by Indigenous communities, to engaging in effective, meaningful solidarity:

> I think it's hard for people to be involved in work around Indigenous people without really getting involved in the community. You can do it, but for me, I don't feel that that's right. I wouldn't be comfortable doing that. That's why I've always tried to make friendships and get to know people and get involved in [Indigenous interest] groups when they're available. So, that was kind of frustrating this year to try and encourage [non-Indigenous] people to come out, especially people who are doing work around Aboriginal people. It's like, "You should come be part of this group," not just for their own ... but also to support the group. Because if we can expand and get more members, then it will increase visibility on campus – all those sorts of things. Plus, all the people who are participating will learn things.

When Darcie urges non-Indigenous people to do solidarity work, she cautions us against thinking about solidarity solely in terms of self-making. In this way, she identifies the importance of doing solidarity work for political reasons, that is, to raise the visibility of Indigenous struggles. However, Darcie also echoes a piece of advice commonly issued in solidarity circles about the importance of relationships. While I agree that a restructuring of Indigenous–non-Indigenous relations is necessary, my goal in this book is to flag some of the risks and tensions involved in determining the parameters of this relationship. What I find most significant here – apart from Darcie's emphasis on establishing friendships, getting involved in

Indigenous communities, and learning from the experience, exercises in proximity to be sure – is Darcie's attempt to establish herself as exceptional in this regard. Moreover, her narrative of becoming appears to presume the right to access and learn from Indigenous communities, which evokes the fifth element of my proximity spectrum. All told, Darcie's narrative supports my observations about the multiple, sometimes contradictory approaches white women take in negotiating the rough and rocky terrain of solidarity encounters.

In the interest of full transparency, when I look at Darcie, I see myself. I recognize the allure of friendship in my own story. Thompson's (2003, 10) work is useful here: "Indeed, [US white academics] often take it for granted that our studied antiracism is the standard to which other whites should be held; at the same time, however, we may anxiously try to prove our antiracist credentials by positioning ourselves in unproblematic solidarity with scholars of color." There have been countless times as an academic or activist that I have tried to display my "studied" anticolonialism or my ability to make friends with Indigenous people (or, for that matter, people of colour). I even try to temper my class lectures about solidarity work with admonitions about not making it all about the white settler. Nevertheless, I remain an anxious subject (Ahmed 2004) saddled with a relentless desire for reconciliation (Tuck and Yang 2012) and intent on proving my good settler status.

Darcie was not alone. Alicia admitted that friendship held a lot of attraction for her in solidarity encounters with Indigenous women and men:

> I definitely appreciated when I was at the ... language camp, and they referred to us as [Indigenous people] and friends of [Indigenous people]. It made me feel that sense of solidarity. That there was a place for me, not as [an Indigenous] person, but as a friend – someone they saw as aligned, someone in solidarity, someone who was not hurting them ... I felt like there was a place for me in that construction of this kind of work. That really felt nice.

For Alicia, part of what is at stake is evidently personal, namely, a sense of belonging vis-à-vis the Indigenous people in the encounter. Perhaps less obvious is the collectively derived desire of white women to secure exceptional good settler status. Alicia's subsequent answer to a question about decolonization is clarifying in this regard:

> I think [decolonization] is part of the experience of participating in community events, doing spiritual events, learning the language, learning

about other cultures, not just Indigenous cultures here. I went [abroad] and met some Indigenous peoples there ... You totally reorient to a different worldview that's not rooted in West-is-best and Eurocentric values ... It's like learning to walk in more worlds. I feel comfortable walking into a Native community event. I understand the protocol, the cultural constructs. Likewise, I'm comfortable being around white people. I understand. I grew up with a lot of Black friends; I'm comfortable going to my Black friends' homes for family events and the dynamics of their families too.

For Alicia, decolonization requires cultural immersion, which, by definition, reflects a desire for proximity to Indigenous Others. Moreover, in recounting the steps she has taken to decolonize, Alicia emphasizes her remarkable skill in making friends with any strangers, in particular her ability to traverse multiple worlds. I cannot state definitively whether Darcie or Alicia assumed that friendship neutralizes Indigenous–white power relations between women and that they were thus beyond colonial reproach. What I can highlight is the near conflation of (individual) friendship and (group) solidarity in these narratives as well as in my own experiences. Importantly, Darcie, Alicia, and I all claim expertise in the art of friendship in our bids to exceptionalism.

We could look at the friendship dynamic a bit differently, however. Critical whiteness scholar Robyn Wiegman's (1999, 119) theory of white disaffiliation posits that liberal white people in the postsegregationist United States define themselves in opposition to acts of white supremacy considered more egregious.[2] This would suggest that white women such as myself, Darcie, or Alicia are not trying to lose (by which I mean deny) our white settler privilege as much as we are trying to gain a sense of exceptional status as progressive white women engaging in "unproblematic solidarity" (Thompson 2003). Interestingly, Darcie extended the invitation of exceptionalism to other settler allies, who, she said, can also successfully engender friendship and solidarity by interacting "sincerely" with a "good mind, an open mind, and an open heart."

With typical astuteness, Peggy thoughtfully weighed in on the limitations of friendship as a force for overcoming colonial power relations.[3] This is consistent with how Peggy wrestled with her structural privilege as a white woman in solidarity encounters and beyond. She described developing profound, lasting relationships with Indigenous women through political activism, a point she stressed when asked how her solidarity work with Indigenous women has changed over time: "I [now] have deeper, more trusting relationships with [Indigenous women]. They're complex, deep rich relationships that aren't just working as allies; they're friendships. We love each other. That's what it comes down to. That's taken time to build." However, for Peggy, friendship neither negates Indigenous–non-Indigenous hierarchies nor guarantees belonging. Recall her affirmative response in Chapter 1 to my question, "Do you think you'll always have that need to be accepted, to not be one of those 'bad settlers'"? Below, she explains that friendship does not and, perhaps, cannot extinguish this feeling:

> And you just want to be part of that excitement and positive change and creativity. But then it's not quite yours. Or you think, "Oh this culture, I like this about this culture, or I like that about the culture; it's so much better in this or that way than my culture." It's really easy to feel this way. And if these people are your friends? Some of these people are my best friends, and yet I can never fully join them in certain things. That's painful.

Here, Peggy acknowledges the deep-seated desire of settlers to belong fully in an Indigenous context: she does not want to be a bad settler. She also acknowledges an inability to give up that desire: the longing to shed bad settler status continues because as a settler she can "never fully join" her Indigenous women friends. In these ways, Peggy's narrative reflects an understanding of settler status as a collective structural positioning that white people cannot overcome.

Peggy's narrative also suggests the need to disentangle two desires that can coexist, clash, or be conflated: the tenable desire to engage ethically with Indigenous peoples, on the one hand, and the unsustainable white settler desire for legitimacy/belonging on Indigenous land, on the other. I would like to facilitate the former by understanding the latter. If settler legitimacy under current settler colonial conditions is impossible, then, by definition, no settler can be a good settler. If so, what is the effect of discourse – glaringly evident in my question to Peggy – that links good settler status to belonging and, by extension, bad settler status to not belonging? Further, does lamenting the impossibility of belonging have the inadvertent effect of upholding a good–bad settler dichotomy and fuelling the solidarity impulse? Does it imply that if settlers were able to "fully join" their Indigenous friends that they would no longer be bad settlers? In short, can a fantasy of transcendence prevail among settlers insofar as a good–bad settler binary remains intact? In what follows, I consider examples of exceptionalism discourse that uphold the good–bad settler dichotomy and, thus, I argue, the white settler/liberal fantasy of transcendence.

Making Declarations

Claims of exceptionalism in white participant narratives tend to come in two forms that are often interlinked: claiming to have superior knowledge of colonialism past and present compared to that of the "average Canadian," and, even more pronounced, claiming to be more progressive relative to other non-Indigenous activist allies in the solidarity arena. It bears repeating that I am not interested in the veracity of these claims, which may in fact be true, but rather in how such claims potentially function in white settler women's negotiations of the solidarity encounter – as a mechanism for transcending structural privilege. Even as a sense of self-righteousness or entitlement to be in solidarity spaces sometimes underpins these claims and actions, they often coexist alongside a sense of responsibility to engage in the work. In fact, most examples of what I call exceptionalism discourse rest within the white participants' responses to questions about their responsibility to do solidarity work as well as their settler privilege and use of the term settler as a collective identity. More specifically, I asked all twenty-four participants how necessary it was for white women to acknowledge, to themselves and others, their status as settlers and their complicity in colonialism in order to engage in non-colonizing solidarity. At the time, it never dawned on me that I might have formulated the question this way out of a desire to secure my own exceptional status; after all, duly schooled in the art of confession (Namaste 2015), I have regularly followed convention by outwardly naming my whiteness, along with other normatively defined identities.

Even before taking on this research, I had witnessed the tendency among white settler activists to consider ourselves superior to the average Canadian when it comes to, for example, our knowledge of settler colonial history. Participant narratives only confirmed this observation. An excerpt from Alicia's interview is particularly instructive on this point. When I asked her if she felt a responsibility as a non-Indigenous woman to do solidarity work, she replied:

> With respect to what's my place within this work, I had a bit of an epiphany once. This last winter, I was struggling with my place in this work, and as a white woman, and would I continue this kind of work ... Should it kind of be left to Indigenous folks to sort out where they want to go? Am I kind of interfering? ... I was at this nature camp. I was doing what they call a night walk through a forest ... When I was in that forest, I kind of had this moment where I felt like I had just as much right to care about these important

issues relating to Indigenous cultures – globalization, Westernization, environmentalism ... I have just as much right as a child of this world to care about these things, and it doesn't matter that I'm white. And that there is a role for me to play, even if it's just helping other white people learn, get out of their bubble, get out of their Western construct, their narrow construct of "I need to get a job, get a car, buy a boat, go to the cottage." There's more to life. There's a different way to be living on this planet, to be more in tune with themselves, to be more in tune with nature, to understand colonization, to try some decolonizing work, to get back to our roots, to know what a community means ... I feel I've been given this gift of awareness from the Aboriginal cultures or communities that I've been a part of, and maybe there's a role for me in sharing that same awareness with other non-Native people who continue to be Westernized and colonized in their way of thinking.

This passage along with others in Alicia's narrative demonstrates the complexities and contradictions of gendered colonial subjectivity.

Alicia was rightly concerned about globalization, Westernization, and environmental sustainability as issues that affect all peoples and notes a responsibility to "help other white people learn," something long called for by marginalized communities. She was also mindful of "interfering" and questions her "place in this work and as a white woman." In these ways, she seemed riddled with doubt and settler anxiety. Perhaps this was why she answers a question about her responsibility as a non-Indigenous woman to engage in solidarity with commentary on her right to do so. Might this response indicate a desire to mollify her doubts, or her perception of my doubts, about our "place in this work"?

This interpretation is plausible when we consider, as Barbara Heron (2007, 45–46) does in the case of white/northern women development workers stationed in the Global South, that discourses of responsibilities, rights, and entitlements are closely linked for many: "Not only do participants feel morally obliged to intervene ... but we take for granted that we can go to, live in, and be active in other people's countries – and lives – *if we choose* to do development work." Even as Alicia's approach to solidarity was fraught with doubt, her claim of having the "right as a child of this world to care about these things" connoted this sense of entitlement. It is further clarifying to contextualize her claim of entitlement within the broader narrative of becoming that frames her solidarity work (see Chapter 1). Overall, she presented herself less as a white woman who has developed an anticolonial analysis and more as a privileged individual who has been bestowed the "gift of awareness" (an achievement of proximity). When we conceive of ourselves on such individualistic terms it becomes much easier to position ourselves as exceptional, in Alicia's case as uniquely poised to bridge the Indigenous–settler gap and to teach other settlers about the perils of "their Western construct." Having confessed how ignorant she felt in the not-so-distant past about Indigenous issues, Alicia now distances herself from that past and the public at large, whose lack of awareness remains a source of anger to her. To her credit, Alicia's appeal to exceptionalism was genuinely transparent in that it made explicit what nonperformative antiracist utterances (Ahmed 2004) often leave unsaid – claims of having overcome ignorance.

When asked the same question about what responsibilities come with being a white woman in Canada, Rachel gave a strikingly similar response. She cited her elevated levels of awareness and understanding of Indigenous issues relative to most of her friends and alluded to the educator role she has assumed, which includes inviting them to "interesting events":

> In a way, I'm almost an interesting bridge for you. I'm guessing you have talked to a lot of people with a strong sense of responsibility. Or at least they have chosen to commit a part of their life to work or alliance in that way. When I look at myself, I am unusual within the context with the friends I have from a variety of contexts. They would perceive me as more socially and politically engaged than themselves. "You work, do good work, work with a soul. We work in marketing, publishing, law, business" ... It's interesting because I don't think that 99 percent of the people that I know in this world think that they have any responsibility to do with the context of Canada's colonial history. I know people who would say, "You know what, Native people need to get over it." I know people who would say that. I know people who would say, "I'm an immigrant to Canada. Native people don't know or care what I went through." In a really distorted way, that's like a settler. I don't even know how paradoxical and complicated that statement is. I think, in all of those contexts, I'm one of the voices of "that's an interesting event, maybe we should hear about this Indigenous speaker from Burkina Faso about what traditional knowledge is." I'd go with a few friends, and we'd have an interesting experience.

Like Alicia, Rachel positioned herself as exceptional in relation to "99 percent" of her circle when it comes to feeling responsible for redressing Canada's colonial history and present. Only now, years later, do I recognize another layer of Rachel's response, which is the risk I discuss at length in the previous chapter: coaxing friends into caring about Indigenous issues by exposing them to cultural difference may lead us away from thinking about structural oppression.

When a question was too abstract and failed to elicit a response – as happened when I asked participants to "locate themselves" in relation to Canada's colonial history – I decided not to mince words and to simply ask, "Do you call yourself a settler?" This was (and perhaps still is) a hot-button topic that elicited the most demonstrable moves to exceptionalism, ranging from slight to dramatic in degree. When asked if she identifies as a settler, Peggy answered:

> I would say yes, I'm a descendant of settlers and a member of that culture. I would say, at this point, I don't see myself only as a settler through my activism. Definitely still embedded and implicated, but I'm trying to create an alternative, as opposed to someone who's unconsciously a settler, who has made no effort to change the dynamic.

In this statement and others, Peggy presents a nuanced understanding of her positionality as a settler. While she recognizes and resists the risk of claiming transcendence (she acknowledges being "definitely still embedded and implicated"), she also seeks to differentiate herself from "someone who is unconsciously a settler who has made no effort to change the dynamic." Whether Peggy is different is not the point; what I want to underscore is the frequency across white participant narratives of making such claims. To recall Carol Schick (1998, 174), "By these [credibility] claims, subjects show that they are agents in the production of their own identity – and not objects, not one of 'them,'" *them* in this case referring to the average settler.

Darcie's reflections on her relationship to Canadian settler colonialism combined Peggy's awareness of her structural privilege and Alicia's commitment to "help white people learn." By the end of her reflection, the latter element was on full display:

> That's a good question. Well, obviously, I've benefitted from settler colonialism, and I'm aware of that, so I think that maybe places me on the fringes of that? I don't know. Because, you know, a lot of people aren't aware or don't want to be aware of the ways they've, everything that they've gained from that system, because a lot of negative things have happened, and it brings up these feelings of guilt, and nobody really wants to feel guilty. But I think

that doing the work that I do and just trying to be the person who I am and working toward alliances with not just Indigenous people, but other people as well, and trying to bridge that if I can. I try to educate my family and friends about those sorts of issues. So, I'm hoping to try and be a positive influence or a force for good.

To reiterate, the white woman's desire to be "a force for good," as Heron (2007) might also stress, is abundantly evident in Darcie's narrative. Moreover, her statement contains several recognizable patterns of exceptionalism discourse so far. First, like Alicia, Rachel, and Peggy, Darcie cites her awareness of settler colonialism as the factor that distinguishes her from "a lot of people" and that possibly places her "on the fringes of" colonial power. Darcie also claims to be exceptional in not having succumbed to "feelings of guilt." Second, she described herself as "trying to bridge" Indigenous–white settler difference (while adding a third category, "other people"). Like Alicia and Rachel, she described the instructional roles she has taken on in "trying to educate my family and friends about those sorts of issues." At the same time, Darcie harboured doubts about having moved to the so-called fringes of settler colonialism. In this way, Darcie, like Peggy, exposes the fallibility of exceptionalism discourse as a white settler strategy to overcome or transcend one's complicity in colonial relations, a fantasy sustained only if one embraces a "hyperindividualism that negates relationality" (Simpson 2017, 154).

Let's revisit Darcie's attempts at exceptionalism, this time to evaluate if they adhere to what, according to Ahmed (2004, para. 16), is the nonperformative declarative logic of whiteness studies: "The argument that we must see whiteness because whiteness is unseen can convert into a declaration of not being subject to whiteness or even a white subject ('if I see whiteness, then I am not white, as whites don't see their whiteness')." I wonder if a comparable fantasy of transcendence operates when settlers acknowledge the benefits we have enjoyed because of colonialism ("if I see how I have benefitted from colonialism, then I am not a bad settler, as bad settlers don't see that"). Do Darcie's statements reveal an aspiration to move outside of settler colonial privilege at the precise point when it comes into view (Ahmed 2004, para. 16)? As Ahmed suggests, given the slippery nature of privilege, white people are unlikely to spot fantasies of transcendence in our speech, let alone psyche.

Eve, however, a white participant whose views on "choice" appear in Chapter 1, addressed the contradictions of conceding privilege in this way.

In our exchange about the use of settler in activist versus social-service contexts, she hit the proverbial nail on the head:

> EVE: I feel like that language really comes out of activist communities ... I think it's quite common language that doesn't necessarily have a negative ... well, I guess it does still have a negative connotation to it. But not negative in a bad way. Do you know what I mean?
> CAROL LYNNE: Yes. You're *supposed* to acknowledge your settler complicity?
> EVE: Exactly. So it's kind of bad that you're a settler, but it's good that you acknowledge it. Whereas I think that in [a] more social-service context, [Indigenous people] don't want to piss off the white people who are their funders, right?

As became apparent in our ensuing conversation, Eve and I agreed on at least two points. First, there is a general expectation that as white settlers we will declare our status in solidarity encounters. Second, a certain "street cred" or enhanced status as progressive settler activist ally (if only among other such activists) flows from these declarations. Ahmed (2004, para. 20) explores the paradoxical effects of such an achievement with relation to racism: "The paradoxes of admitting to one's own racism are clear: saying 'we are racist' becomes a claim to have overcome the conditions (unseen racism) that require the speech act in the first place." Eve and I both noted a similar nonperformative logic operating in solidarity encounters between women and in mixed-gender groups, which suggests that the practice is not gender-specific but takes gendered forms. (For example, given our historical socialization to help Others, it is probable that white women would emphasize our capacity to educate when making claims of exceptionalism, as did Alicia and Darcie.) In short, having learned in our respective settings to declare our dominant status – be it white, settler, middle-class, or combinations thereof – Eve and I understood quite well the moral importance attached to such declarative practices.

As someone who lived in Toronto but hailed from another part of North America, long-time activist Zainab Amadahy (Cherokee, Seminole) purposively claimed settler status even as she ascribed limited power and meaning to such statements. Here, she zeroes in on the limitations of such declarations while not completely dismissing their importance:

> ZAINAB: I think it's what you do with that acknowledgment that matters to me. I acknowledge it too. I'm a settler here too. This is not my

land. I'm benefitting from the genocide as well. It's what you do with it that matters. And I'm not interested. I don't really care. I'm tired of people saying, "I'm a settler" and doing the whole ...

CAROL LYNNE: Confession thing?

ZAINAB: Yeah. I don't care about that. Tell me what you're prepared to do to fix things.

Amadahy touches on the insights of Ahmed (2004), Lockard (2016), and Namaste (2015) in suggesting that such declarations are frequently, though not inherently or inevitably, best classified as confessions that leave a disconnect between speech and action in their wake.

Additionally, Eve and I registered competing declarations of allyship (and, by extrapolation, desires for transcendence) among white women activists in the solidarity encounter. In fact, Indigenous and white participants alike noted a widespread propensity toward competition in activist circles. These observations accord with Emma Kowal's (2011, 321) finding that white antiracist strategies to manage white stigma include "criticising other Whites, including other White antiracists." Along these lines, Ruth Green (Kanien'kehá:ka) sometimes found, particularly among white women scholar-activists, "that solidarity work is a competition of 'I am so much better an activist than you.'" When asked why allies compete, Green answered without hesitation: "Oh, it's about the guilt. If I can be a better activist, obviously, I'm not doing as bad stuff." This answer, common to participants across the board, backs up the idea that white stigma/settler guilt is central to white settler/liberal subjectivity, as well as Ahmed's (2004) theory about what white people often "do" with/about "bad feeling" – make declarations!

As a long-time social-justice activist working with Indigenous communities, Peggy had also witnessed a proclivity for competition among white settler activists. Here, she speaks to the layered nature of settler declarations, including her own, to establish that "I'm not one of them":

PEGGY: You can't take off your whiteness, your privilege, the benefits you've inherited – it's stuck to you. You're fooling yourself if you think you can leave it behind. I think a lot of people think that when they first become activists, that there's this denial, this appropriation of a Native identity, because it's painful. You'd much rather be able to identify with the oppressed. [There's] a certain self-righteousness that you can't have as one of the oppressors ... You can see it in some activists in the way they really denounce and shun other non-Indigenous people that don't have quite the same politics.

CAROL LYNNE: Could you give me an example of that?

PEGGY: It doesn't just happen in this context, in any sort of activist politics. People consider themselves the vanguard. The best analysis. The most radical. Everyone else is a sell-out just reinforcing the colonial agenda. Personally, I don't like that binary thinking; I don't think it's accurate. I think that there are many ways to be an activist, to contribute to decolonization. It can be really small, it can be quiet, it can be loud, it can be visible. I'm wary of people who are extremely judgmental in that way. It's one thing to say, "I don't agree with what they're doing," but there's a degree of put down and condemnation. I think it's part of the same dynamic that "I'm not one of them."

CAROL LYNNE: You're denying the fact that you can't take off that colonial imprint?

PEGGY: Yeah, you will discover at one point that you still have it.

Here, Peggy begins by noting "a certain self-righteousness" that comes with identifying with "the oppressed," a self-righteousness she has seen across activist contexts. Such "identificatory mobility" (Fee and Russell 2007) enables settler allies to feel superior to other activists who they judge to be, in Peggy's words, "a sell-out just reinforcing the colonial agenda." Moreover, the settler activist who thinks of herself as part of "the vanguard" with the "best analysis" and "most radical" politics bears an uncanny resemblance to the "learned white" person who has studied whiteness and is therefore superior to "others, whether those others are 'unlearned whites' or learning or unlearned non-white others" (Ahmed 2004, para. 40). Peggy combines Ahmed's work on "learned whites" and Audrey Thompson's (2003) on "studied antiracism" to reveal the "learned settler" who can shed or at least mitigate their colonial status and power through becoming the one who knows. Peggy's insights also demonstrate how discourses of exceptionalism such as claiming the vanguard can coexist with proximity desires, including the "appropriation of a Native identity."

According to Amadahy, competition between white activists can reach a fevered pitch. She recounted, "[White] supporters often compete with each other to impress each other as well as Native people about how much they know, how involved they've been, who they know in Native struggles." She illustrated the potential fallout with a story of what took place during a political action in downtown Toronto involving Indigenous groups from outside the city. In the following passage, she refers to representatives of white solidarity groups, also based outside of the city, as "white interpreters":

> So here we had urban Native people wanting to talk directly with the [rural-based Native] activists ... who had to go through these white interpreters. So the white interpreters were always kind of competing with each other: "Well, I spoke to the Elder ... and she said this." "Well, I'm sorry, but I spoke to someone in [another place], and they said that." So the whole conversation was kind of like that. It was very "my Indian says this" and "my Indian says that," this kind of stuff. Yeah, they like to compete with each other about who they know, how much they know, how long they've been doing this, how respectful are their relationships, and whether "their Indians" are taking more leadership than "your Indians." It's like, holy fuck.

As Amadahy recalled, in their self-appointed role as intermediaries between rural Indigenous communities and urban-based Indigenous activists, these white interpreters essentially claimed ownership over Indigenous individuals and communities. Amadahy provides a stark reminder of the insidious ways in which, despite our good intentions, non-Indigenous people who see themselves as supporters of Indigenous political struggles can reproduce colonial dynamics.

Unlike in most examples I cite, men (by which I mean any male-identified person) were predominate in number among Amadahy's white interpreters, which raises questions about the gender dimension of white settler ally competition. Does competition manifest differently in mixed-gender groups, particularly in its public display? Is patriarchy a factor? While I did not ask participants about this, based on a No More Silence (NMS) scenario, I would answer yes to both questions. Since its inception, NMS has been open only to women and gender-diverse people. Men of all nations are welcome to stand in solidarity at the February 14 vigil but do not do crowd control or, barring exceptional circumstances, speak until the postvigil feast (for which Indigenous men prepare the food). When the topic of men's roles surfaced in 2011, NMS members reconfirmed the underlying aim of our position – to guard against patriarchal tendencies. As Whitebird explained, "A lot of times, though, for the man it becomes about taking control. And this [day] should be about our time to honour the women. This is a time for women to get their message out. Men should respect that and not interfere." Based on NMS's experience and Zainab's description of a mixed-gender group of settlers, I suspect that the patriarchal tendency to (attempt to) dominate would be in full, if not fuller, display in a mixed-gender group of settler activists.

Other participants zoomed in on the nonperformative aspects of activist rivalries when expressed as public declarations of allyship. Take Carla's analysis of what some white allies seek to accomplish through certain self-congratulatory declarations:

> CARLA: "As an ally" means never allowing yourself to say that you're off the hook, that you can't do and appropriate things because you're an ally, and knowing that it's a constant process your whole life, that it's something you have to consistently self-reflect on and be conscious of your actions ... So, for instance, there's a guy I know who is white, who would always see himself as a good ally to people of colour groups. And he was in a relationship with one of my friends who was a woman of colour and at one point said to me: "You know my girlfriend is a woman of colour; I'm off the hook – I can't be racist." I think that can be really damaging to say to someone who wants to think that because of an association you are sort of guilt-free. It eases your conscience.
>
> CAROL LYNNE: What is the danger of having an eased conscience?
>
> CARLA: Well, you know racism and all forms of social discrimination can replicate themselves in intimate relationships, in friendships, in activist circles, so I think it negates that. I think it says, "I am a lefty; therefore, I am absolved of any harm." You could actually still be doing things that are quite harmful and actually use it as a shield to say, like, "You can't attack me. I am not racist because ..."

The scenario described by Carla is instructive for at least two reasons. First, it is a reminder that discourses of friendship and love can be tools for achieving proximity to Others and proving one's exceptionalism. Second, it exposes the "lefty" who seeks to ease his conscience as one of Ahmed's (2004, para. 34) anxious white subjects: "I suspect that bad feelings of racism (hatred, fear, pain) are projected onto the bodies of unhappy racist whites, which allows progressive whites to be happy with themselves in the face of continued racism toward non-white others." Any way you slice it, such moves to exceptionalism reflect and sustain white settler fantasies of "autonomous independent individualism" (Moreton-Robinson 2000), preventing activist allies from sitting with the discomfort of their structural complicity in settler colonial affairs (see Boudreau Morris 2017, on cultivating relationships of discomfort).

In explaining what solidarity means for her, Eve built on Carla's critique of using public declarations or self-congratulatory language in one's quest to be (seen as) a good settler ally:

> I think solidarity and allyships are really similar in a sense. It's language that has to be given to you, not that you can take. I think I would never call myself an ally of a particular community unless the community has called me an ally ... Because most of my work now ... is around sex work politics, I see a lot of people calling themselves sex work allies, and they're not. They're really, really, not. It's the thing that the community has to give you that language in order for you to be able to claim it.

For Eve, the act of declaring oneself an ally involves a certain level of appropriation. Though not as extreme as the pitched battles over "my Indian" described by Amadahy, unilateral claims of allyship nonetheless are examples of the white activist ally taking what they have not yet been given. As an Indigenous woman from elsewhere in the Americas, Ursula agreed:

> I consider myself Indigenous, but I'm not from this territory, so I also work in solidarity, and I'm an ally as well to the Haudenosaunee people and Anishinaabe people of this territory. I also think that you need to be careful when talking about allies. A lot of people can say "I'm an ally," but I think you need to be named as an ally by the Native community themselves, not just call yourself an ally willy-nilly. So that's like an honoured title.

Listening to Ursula, I recalled Whitebird's conclusion about the hollowness of one white woman's declaration of allyship made at the end of a public film screening: "By the tone, by the question, she's not an ally ... because she doesn't understand what that means, and she has her own agenda, obviously." Unilateral self-ascriptions do not lay claim to Indigenous individuals or communities to the same degree as the competitive posturing of Amadahy's white interpreters, but they are still expressions of colonial subjectivity. As such, they are nuanced manifestations of both the settler/liberal subject's sense of entitlement to engage in solidarity and the pursuit of proximity that serves, as Whitebird says, white settler activists' own agendas.

Beyond Claiming (As) a Path to Exceptionalism

My analysis so far suggests that white women activists sometimes traverse great lengths and circuitous paths to prove our exceptional ally status. I have relied mostly on participant observations of other people, which implies that we rarely disclose our own desires or competitive moves for that status. This raises a host of questions, including whether limiting one's comments to the actions of other settler activists itself constitutes a move to exceptionalism and/or a lack of self-reflexivity. While rare, there were times when white participants reflected on the spectre of exceptionalism in their own lives. In my assessment, these instances divulge even more about the nuanced functioning of the politics of declaration in solidarity encounters and of the good–bad settler dichotomy in particular.

Recall Julia, quoted at the start of this chapter. She was worried about being perceived as shopping for Indigenous culture. In the following exchange, she reflects on why she had not previously used the term solidarity to describe her work with Indigenous women.

> CAROL LYNNE: You answered the call for participants, and it said "solidarity" in the title, so why don't you use the term?
>
> JULIA: I don't know.
>
> CAROL LYNNE: Does it have negative connotations for you?
>
> JULIA: No, it's really a benign ...
>
> CAROL LYNNE: So, if it's not solidarity for you, what is it?
>
> JULIA: Oh, it is. If I were to think about it, it absolutely is. It's just not if I refer to ... I guess maybe now that I'm talking about it and I'm saying it out loud, I think it seems if I used the word, whether it be within my own social circles or if I'm talking to Indigenous folks, "Aren't you a good little white lady, working in solidarity. Isn't that good for you." That's not what it is for me. I don't need to make a public declaration.
>
> CAROL LYNNE: What's wrong with a public declaration of solidarity for you? What is it?
>
> JULIA: I don't want it to be seen as self-serving for me. I am really okay with a public declaration around antiracism work and political activism and that sort of thing, for the cause and for the reason that I'm there. I don't need to be congratulated for that. So I guess maybe when I say "working in solidarity," then it becomes about me.
>
> CAROL LYNNE: Have you seen that happen?

JULIA: Yes ... That's a big piece for [the researcher], is that [they're] seen as working in solidarity. But I think, for me, a lot of what [they do] is ... I don't ever want to be seen as an expert on Indigenous culture. I'm not Indigenous. I've lived a white life. I worry that, for some white folks, they see themselves as experts on Indigenous experiences and life and culture. I'm the expert in my own life and that's about it ... I'm the expert of nobody else.

Julia's concern about being misread as someone seeking recognition and validation as "a good little white lady" suggests not only the ubiquity of such a desire but also of the measures taken by some white settler women to quench it – issuing public declarations about their solidarity. In many ways, Julia's utterances depart from Ahmed's (2004) nonperformative speech acts where one admits to being racist in a bid to assert the contrary. Julia does not "confess" to a desire to be seen as "a good little white lady." However, in asserting the opposite, she makes a series of declarations about the flawed practice of white people who claim to be "Indigenous experts."

In contrast, Julia assured me throughout the interview that she did not seek recognition as an ally or consider herself an expert on anything but herself. However, these repeated assurances about her difference evoked Ahmed's (2004, para. 7) anxious white subject, who materializes "in its very anxiety about the effects it has on others ... Is an anxious whiteness that declares its own anxiety about its worry better, where better might even evoke the promise of 'non-racism' or 'antiracism'?" In light of Ahmed's observations, it is worth asking, does Julia's disquiet suggest a desire for exceptional/anticolonial status – as the ally who does not seek notoriety? Put differently, was Julia worried about practising (or being seen as practising) the "wrong kind" of solidarity, just as some scholars in critical whiteness studies worry about doing "the wrong kind of whiteness studies" (Ahmed 2004, para. 8)?[4] I raise these questions not to judge Julia (which would be a kind of move to exceptionalism on my part) but rather to highlight the challenges of negotiating structural privilege within solidarity work.

Julia was not alone in struggling to position herself vis-à-vis the politics of declaration in solidarity activism or in expressing a "lingering unease" (Heron 2007, 47) with how colonial relations can be reproduced via public declarations. Like Julia, Eve noted both a generalized desire among white settler activists to feel like a "great white ally" as well as the nonperformativity of associated declarations, in this example, related to decolonizing:

> Reading as much as you can. Taking people's advice. Trying to listen. Trying to be silent. All of that is really important decolonizing work, if that's how people are understanding decolonizing. Those are, obviously, so significant, but they are also so insignificant compared to the kind of decolonizing work that needs to happen in Canadian society. So me listening to some Aboriginal women and saying, "I'm decolonizing myself," makes me feel like a great white ally, when in fact what I probably should be doing is struggling against the Indian Act or supporting people trying to change the reserve systems – things that are maybe a bit more significant than me just listening.

Here, Eve starts with but goes beyond the individual to envisage collective, substantive acts of decolonization. When I asked about the role white guilt might play in this desire to feel like a great white ally, Eve repeated that declarations of decolonization can be nonperformative:

> Maybe that's part of why I say [great white ally] mockingly, because I don't feel like I'm a great white ally. I don't feel that's an important part of my struggle ... The impetus for me being an ally to Indigenous communities is not to feel like I'm a good white ally. It's for social-justice reasons, for feminist reasons, for antiracist reasons, for a bunch of stuff. But it's not to appease my own self. Maybe that's the question, when you were asking about, Have you done decolonizing work? It's very easy for white people to say, "Oh, I've decolonized myself because I read a few books." It's like, "Well, that's kind of bullshit." It's an easy out. That way I don't have to deal with my white privilege. I think I'd rather just deal with my white privilege and keep that in check, rather than say I'm decolonized because I read a few books.

Eve does not appear to be as worried as Julia does about being misidentified as someone seeking the status of great white ally. But, in mocking the "easy way out" taken by some white activists involved in decolonizing work, does she position herself as exceptional, as embodying the bona fide activist who takes action as opposed to one who makes empty declarations?

"'Why are you into solidarity?' is the thing you should be struggling with throughout this work you're doing right now." Directives like this one from Maracle have kept me vigilant in this research, persuading me to ask how my own solidarity efforts have involved attempts to prove my exceptional status vis-à-vis other white women. The irony of pronouncing on my own competitive impulses does not escape me. It could lead to nonperformative utterances (e.g., "I admit to my exceptionalism impulses") designed to exonerate me for any acts of competition in the solidarity encounter to prove my superior status.

With this caveat in mind, I begin this tale of reckoning with my reaction to Amadahy's cautionary tale about white interpreters. At the time, I commented with what now feels like barely concealed disdain: "At least my competition is mostly in my head. I don't do that shit out loud, which makes me superior, of course." (Here, I sensed a kindred spirit in Eve's mocking of the "great white ally.") Efforts at ironic humour aside, the kernel of competitiveness that has consistently germinated in my own activist practices is clearly detectable in this statement. Despite mostly keeping it to myself, my competitive streak puts me in league with "left-wing intellectuals" who "claim the right and privilege of indignation and the power to judge those cruder colonizers among [us] and attempt to use this rhetorical posture to release [ourselves] of [our] own responsibility for the colonial enterprise" (Alfred 2005, 105). In other words, judging others becomes a method for sidestepping one's accountability to Indigenous communities. The research process – especially interviews in which I was able to share experiences and hypotheses – presented me with ample opportunity to note the constancy, depth, and complexity of my own impulses to exceptionalism and competitiveness and how they spring (or not) from guilt.

A remark by Amadahy rang true for me. At one point in our conversation, she linked white guilt to a reactionary overzealousness that can accompany competitive behaviours among white women: "If someone does make an ignorant comment in public, it's really interesting to me how sometimes the white people will be angry, more impacted than the [Indigenous] people who the comment's directed at." Her insight immediately transported me back to two situations: a meeting at which a white woman took the lead during an Indigenous women's singing circle and a public symposium on reconciliation. I discussed my reactions to both events with Amadahy:

Even though I don't vocalize it, I've been that person ... getting more upset about that white woman taking the lead on the song than anybody else seemed to, for example ... Or at the symposium on reconciliation, and I just felt like a lot of the Native people there – not all of them, by any stretch – the people who were speaking and the sort of main message being conveyed was not critical enough in terms of naming colonialism. It was all about looking forward. There was one Native man who came and spoke who *was* really critical of the land claims process, and the negotiation process that was going on, and he named names, and some of the people were there in the room. Afterwards, I heard these two guys talking, two Native people ... saying things like, "Oh, that doesn't help anybody. Two steps back. He didn't need to be like that. He didn't need to be so critical." I found myself getting angry, like, why wasn't the bad stuff talked about more?

My intention here is not to evaluate the white woman in the singing circle (did she transgress some boundary?) or the symposium's focus (how do discourses of reconciliation circumscribe political debate?) but rather to point out just how much competition and self-righteousness have played a role in my disproportionate, intensely negative reactions to each moment.[5]

In journaling about my outlook on the symposium, I raised a host of questions: "Why do I feel more radical than 'the Natives'? Why is it so important for me to hold onto my anger about colonialism? Am I romanticizing Native peoples? What has white guilt got to do with this if anything?" It has become clear to me over the years that my desire to embody the good settler ally was operative in both moments. If mainstream approaches to reconciliation serve to make settlers like me feel better, as Ahmed's (2004) work suggests they might, then my overzealous attachment to criticizing these approaches is an attempt to differentiate myself from the average settler activist, whom I see as uncritically embracing reconciliation. Gada Mahrouse (2009a, 668) identifies a similar move by a white/Western citizen-journalist to present himself as an exceptional reporter given his progressive politics: "What enabled [him] to differentiate himself from professional journalists were his 'activist' intentions. He believed that because he was explicitly antiwar, he was able to transcend the seduction of sensationalism." In my case, I am claiming exceptional status due to my apparent capacity "to transcend the seduction of" mainstream reconciliation discourse.[6] By ardently opposing mainstream reconciliation discourse, I strove (and perhaps still strive) to establish myself as superior to those who embrace it, in all likelihood in a desire to overcome the white settler inertia/guilt (Lewis and Mills 2003) that has in part fuelled my solidarity work. Just like the activists Peggy described who "consider themselves the vanguard" and "everyone else a sell-out just reinforcing the colonial agenda," I sought (and perhaps still seek) to establish myself as the exceptional, more politically astute ally. Notably, the role of exceptionalism discourse in my performances as a white settler woman activist has become clear to me only in retrospect.

I end this part of my tale with one more example from my solidarity experiences. In the early stages of designing this research, the fear that an arguably more self-serving end – earning a doctorate – would overshadow my political commitment to NMS consumed me. My decision to extend the study beyond NMS was, it seems to me now, in part a strategy to remove this possibility. (That is, by separating my research from my participation in the group, I reasoned, no one could accuse me of capitalizing on the activism.) Again, in retrospect, and notwithstanding the validity of such concerns, I recognize this fear as reflective of my settler anxieties. What I feared most was becoming – or more to the point, being seen as – the bad settler ally interested in solidarity for self-serving reasons. This then-all-consuming fear reveals my own good settler ally fantasy, which in turn upholds a good–bad settler binary. As Emma Kowal (2011, 322) might say, I was caught up in managing white stigma, not wanting to be a researcher who "'builds their careers' ... while hiding their selfish motives by 'cloaking what we do in good intentions.'"[7] This anecdote highlights not only my positionality and myriad investments in the solidarity encounter but also the centrality I give to self-reflexivity in research and political activism.

Settler Status and the Limits of Self-Reflexivity

Critical race feminists among others have long pointed out that people with privilege have a responsibility to reflect on our position within systems of power that operate through interlocking categories such as race, gender, and class. In this sense, the original point of self-reflectivity was for individuals to meld the personal and the political. As I argue elsewhere, the problem is that "self-reflexivity can lose its critical impetus by re-centring the White/settler subject and obfuscating the structural conditions in which she is produced" (D'Arcangelis 2018, 342). Even so, as I illustrate above, many participants were deeply self-reflexive, especially in responding to questions about their settler status. Intriguingly, some of the most vivid claims to exceptionalism reside in these responses. For me, this is itself an indicator of the fraught nature of self-reflexivity: the same self-examination that would expose structurally derived privilege, and lead to accountability, can serve its evasion (D'Arcangelis 2018; Pillow 2003, 2015; Snelgrove, Dhamoon, and Corntassel 2014).

Indigenous participants in particular pointed to the limits of self-reflexivity as a strategy to defuse claims of exceptionalism. During our conversation about if, why, and how to acknowledge one's settler status, Amadahy swiftly identified the substance of the issue:

> I think a lot of people get stuck in that [self-reflexive] place for too long. I think sometimes when the lightbulb goes on, people are like, "Ooh my God." Canada exists because people don't think about these things. They aren't trained to think about these things. So when suddenly someone starts thinking about these things, it can be a little shocking to them. I think it's a stage that people need to go through, but I don't want to hear about it.

Crucially, in this statement, Amadahy does not dismiss self-reflexivity as unnecessary. Indeed, as Ardra suggested in regard to dealing with white guilt, context and timing are everything. Amadahy's message to white women is this: grapple with the truth but, as a rule, *not* by seeking help from Indigenous women. Put in this book's terms, do not overpursue proximity. Amadahy also pointed to what can happen when self-reflexivity is "underpinned by modernist/liberal ideologies of subjectivity" (D'Arcangelis 2018, 340) – it tends to start and stop in the individual stage. In saying this, she supports a hypothesis winding throughout this book: in prompting a heightened consciousness of our colonial complicity, the solidarity encounter can be extremely jarring and leave white women "stuck" and as prime candidates for the solidarity impulse.

Maracle was among those who valorized self-reflexivity while divesting it of too much significance and power. As alluded to in Chapter 2, for Maracle, solidarity occurs along a continuum where non-Indigenous allies would require varying levels of knowledge about colonial history and their relationship to that history. The degree to which settlers recognize their status as settlers, however, correlates to the profoundness and effectiveness of their solidarity:

> [White women] don't have to call themselves settlers ever. They are. It's sort of like saying [Spadina in Toronto] is always going to be Ishpadinaa [Ojibwe for "high place or ridge"]. You can call it Spadina if you want, but it's Ishpadinaa. It knows itself as Ishpadinaa. So they can call themselves anything they want. Dipsy-doodle. Don't care [*laughs*]. They're settlers. Now, when they recognize that they're settlers, their work will become more profound and, of course, more effective. And they'll realize the goal of decolonizing that is in the interest of Indigenous people. Otherwise, they're [just] helping us with a project.

In Maracle's assessment, white women remain settlers irrespective of our capacity to self-reflect; contemplating our positionality does not completely transform us, although we may become better allies and less likely to position ourselves as helpers. In brief, we can neither relinquish our complicity nor quickly dismantle colonial power structures with an enhanced understanding of our settler status, although we can do more profound and effective solidarity work.

From her vantage point as an Indigenous woman, Lydia observed that full awareness of being a settler does not always predate one's involvement in solidarity, nor does it need to:

> What are we going to do? Take all the allies and put them to settler ally school and say, "Once you graduate from being a settler ally then you can go and be a settler ally"? [*laughs*] They should be critically reflecting on what their role is, and that would mean a good settler ally, but they might not use that term, is what I'm getting at. They might have a better term that works for them.

In her study of twenty-two settlers' activist histories, Chris Hiller (2017, 432) echoes Lydia's point, refocusing our attention on the importance of learning (and unlearning) through taking action. Darcie, a white participant, agreed that awareness does not necessarily precede solidarity work but can emerge out of it. As you may recall from Chapter 1, she cited her own experience as an example, crediting solidarity work for the critical lens she applies to Canada's history and present. Working to improve the lives of Indigenous peoples, she believes,

> would increase people's understanding and awareness and maybe make people, particularly settlers who have been here for a couple generations or more, aware of the privilege that they have. And then I think that would make people more compassionate or more, I don't know, just like that awareness I think really needs to happen because, like I said before, you can hear people complain: "My air conditioning is broken," and it's like, "Really? If that's your biggest problem, it's a pretty good life." But a lot of people maybe aren't aware of that, and I think if we really work to try and improve things across the board then maybe that can approach that transformative moment that we kind of need.

For Lydia and Darcie, solidarity work can encourage self-reflexivity and an awareness of one's settler status. However, it is not obvious how either vision disrupts the white settler desire for belonging/innocence. In fact, Lydia urged white settlers to strive for good settler ally status, while Darcie did not explicitly define transformation as a dismantling of colonial structures.

Like the twisty turns of exceptionalism language, the limits of self-reflexivity can be subtle and difficult to spot. It is not easy to determine at what point self-reflexivity stops being useful and starts facilitating the evasion of white settler privilege and accountability. Once again, Peggy's thoughtful account of her decades of solidarity experiences sheds light on the challenges of striking that balance. It was apparent throughout our interview that Peggy had continually reexamined her white colonial privilege. When I asked if she had ever experienced white guilt and, if so, how it had affected her solidarity efforts, she described an evolution in her thinking on the matter:

> There's also forgiveness of myself. I'm not blaming myself in the way I used to. I think I feel guilty when I don't do enough. I do feel guilty about that. "Oh I should have gone to that demonstration ... I should care about those missing women" ... I think I used to feel a more amorphous guilt. I think it has played out in my relations with Indigenous people. I think that changed when I did my research ... I think it's because I didn't know what really happened, how I was implicated, what my ancestors did. I felt guilty in those situations. When I actually did the research and found out what they did ... "That was them, this was me." Sorting it out a little bit more, acknowledging the history, it changed my relations with the people I've been trying to work with. I can fully acknowledge the situation. Before the research, I thought they were exaggerating, making it up.

Here, Peggy recounts how gaining clarity about her family's colonial history impacted how she understood her positionality vis-à-vis Indigenous peoples. Her statement testifies to the value of acknowledging the specifics of one's settler status in Canada's colonial past and present: colonial structures come into clearer focus. In this case, they allowed Peggy to disentangle blame or guilt from accountability, as Barbara Applebaum (2010) would have us do. Moreover, by all accounts, and as Maracle predicted, her solidarity relationships improved as a result!

At the same time, it is worth considering to what extent, if at all, Peggy's pronouncement – "That was them, this was me" – indicates a shift to that most persistent of settler moves, claiming to be exceptional or different from more destructive settlers. In attempting to differentiate herself from her ancestors, does Peggy want the impossible as defined by Ursula, an Indigenous participant? In Ursula's words,

> But I think it's important to look at your degree of settlerhood, or whatever, especially for white people. There needs to be an honouring of your own history and your own ... how you came here. It doesn't just go away after that person died, like after your great-great-grandfather came over here, it doesn't just go away. So I think that's important to look at: your relationship to the territory which you're on and how you came to be there, and your participation in colonialism, and your grandfather's or great-grandfather's participation in colonialism.

Allow me to clarify. I am not convinced that Peggy's narrative is an example of how white settler colonial privilege "disappears from sight when it has itself in view," leaving room for the fantasy of transcendence (Ahmed 2004, para. 4). In fact, rather than seeking release from the past, Peggy seemed intent on doing just the kind of "honouring of your own history" called for by Ursula. What I want to point out is the imminent risk of slipping back into the role of liberal subject at precisely the moment of self-reflexive critique, be it of oneself, one's family, or one's community. The act of someone bracketing off their family's history from their own reveals a major unintended consequence of self-reflexivity – it can enable the white settler's quest for autonomous status and everything that that quest implies (Moreton-Robinson 2000). As Peggy's narrative suggests, the challenge is to learn about colonial history without disassociating from it, thus minimizing the chance that proximity desires and fantasies of transcendence will take hold.[8]

There is at least one more insight embedded in Peggy's story, this time about the collective benefits of self-reflexivity when done effectively. The passage ends with Peggy's admission that "before the research, I thought they were exaggerating, making it up." This parting sentiment reminds me of a point I cited earlier made by Rebeka Tabobondung (Anishinaabe), namely, "It's like white people want you to prove to them something, prove to them the impacts of colonization." Mary Louise Fellows and Sherene Razack (1998, 340) raise a similar concern in theorizing the race to innocence among women, noting, "In essence, we view other women through the lenses of our own superiority and utilize dominant explanatory frameworks to explain to ourselves the meaning of our lives" and, I would add, others' lives. Applying Fellows and Razack's lens to the solidarity encounter exposes how the central fantasy of white settler/liberal subjectivity – its own innocence – leaves Indigenous peoples having to prove their subjugation with "dominant explanatory frameworks." However, as Peggy demonstrates, self-reflexivity can temper the tendency of dominant groups to doubt or deny the validity of another group's oppression. As I discuss in the final chapter, self-reflexivity retains its utility for facilitating nonappropriative involvement in solidarity so long as the focus does not remain primarily on the white settler self and instead takes a "double turn" back toward the societal structures – economic, sociopolitical, governance, religious – that require dismantlement (Ahmed 2004; D'Arcangelis 2018).

~

As I demonstrate in this chapter, solidarity encounters are awash in the art and politics of exception, which is to say that white settler activist claims of exceptionalism are one of proximity's steadfast companions. Such claims, I contend, can serve the end goal of pursuing proximity, which is to satiate the white desire to feel welcomed or accepted by Indigenous Others. White participant efforts to claim good settler ally status, in other words, become another means of negotiating the vexing terrain of intersubjective relations in solidarity work.

I dedicated a fair amount of this chapter to analyzing how these claims work. Often, they operate as nonperformative public declarations (Ahmed 2004) or unhappy confessions (Lockard 2016) – acknowledgments of one's settler status and complicity in colonialism, past and present – that can remain divorced from anticolonial practices. While not entirely misguided, antiracist/anticolonial utterances risk remaining just that, statements decoupled from meaningful collective action that instead replicate the liberal vision of the subject as autonomous or self-determining.

Through a close analysis of participant narratives, I showed that claims of exceptionalism take a number of forms, some defying detection more easily than others. For instance, picture a white activist who describes herself as especially knowledgeable of colonial history and thus ideally positioned to help, in particular, by educating average Canadians. Settlers also claim exceptional status based on qualities such as their superior capacity to become friends with Indigenous women; their willingness to acknowledge their settler status and complicity in colonialism; an ability to identify the problem with unilateral declarations of allyship; and even acumen to see through other activists' declarations of exceptionalism! An increased awareness of our positionality, so it seems, can come with "presumptions of our own criticality [which] can be a way of protecting ourselves from complicity" (Ahmed 2012, 5). In this way, we bump up against the limits and risks of self-reflexivity (D'Arcangelis 2018; Pillow 2003, 2015). Perhaps all of this explains why Indigenous participants readily notice that the pursuit of exceptionalism can crystallize as competition among white settler activists, comingled with self-righteousness and a sense of entitlement. In these ways and more, I contend, exceptionalism discourse reflects and sustains the idea of a good–bad settler dichotomy.

I also discovered that participant descriptions of exceptionalism moves are not always gender-specific, which suggests that the desire for exceptional status is something pursued by settler subjects of all genders, albeit in different ways and at different times. For instance, white women may be more inclined to identify their exceptional capacity to make friends or help, whereas white men may be more apt to lay claim to their "Indians," as recounted in Amadahy's enthralling narration. Certainly, there is a need for more research to appreciate fully the gender dimensions of exceptionalism, along the lines of Eve Tuck and K. Wayne Yang's (2012) work on the race-specific nature of settler moves to innocence.

What I did surmise, however, was that given how whiteness works, white women in solidarity encounters are predisposed to making such claims. Drawing on concepts advanced by feminist critical race and critical whiteness studies scholars, I set the stage for my analysis by mapping the contours of whiteness in relation to the solidarity encounter. This includes a predilection among white women anywhere for reproducing white morality, goodness, and innocence (Applebaum 2010; Bush 2011; Fellows and Razack 1998; Heron 2007) alongside a drive to assuage the white guilt/stigma that appears endemic to settlerhood (Kowal 2011, 2015; Lewis and Mills 2003; Thompson 2003). Under such conditions, it is unsurprising that white women would assume that through more awareness, self-reflexivity, hard work, progressive politics, and adept friend making, we could acquire good settler ally status. In short, desiring exceptional good settler ally status is likely not an aberration but the rule.

Therefore, I did not weigh the credibility of participant claims to exceptionalism, which would be an exercise in staking my own claims. Instead, I attempted to understand how such claims reflect and perpetuate the deep inclination among, in this case, white women activists to imagine ourselves as moral, righteous, good individuals – and far removed from the "evil and racist" (Moreton-Robinson 2000) white settlers in our midst. In other words, claims of exceptionalism can be our response when the solidarity encounter forces white women to face head on our complicity in settler colonialism. These claims are evidence that, despite our concerted efforts to grapple with how colonial structures implicate us, we remain susceptible to white settler fantasies of innocence. Additionally, it is fair to say that some of us embrace exceptionalism to counter a central feature of our white settler selves – the propensity to feel white settler guilt or stigma (Kowal 2011, 2015). What enables us in our fantasies? Underneath everything lies the bedrock of white settler/liberal subjectivity. The white woman (who thinks of herself as) entering solidarity as an autonomous individual, rather than a member of a collectivity, is best poised to sustain the fantasy of overcoming colonial power relations.

Clearly, to withstand abstract individualism in the context of the solidarity encounter is a monumental task, which makes the degree to which many white participants did not succumb completely to exceptionalism tendencies all the more remarkable. In fact, most white participants embedded their claims to good settler ally status within acknowledgments of their settler positionality and/or responsibility to engage in solidarity work due to that positionality. Indeed, what stands out most to me is the willingness of many white participants to think/struggle openly and honestly, with me, about their structural privilege and the challenges it poses to solidarity work. I take Julia's determination to understand why Indigenous people so often presume white settler guilt to be a factor in solidarity encounters in this spirit. As she states clearly, "I'm trying to figure out this piece, and I want to – with you, in solidarity – tease that out. What *is* that?" Such statements lead us far beyond the realm of exceptionalism. They indicate a willingness to come to terms with both the complex desire – to live "legitimately, ethically, fully" on Indigenous land (Peggy) – lurking behind such declarations as well as the problematic pursuit of proximity to Indigenous Others that this desire can kick-start.

What would happen if white women were to stop thinking in terms of a good–bad settler binary? What if we were to reconceptualize our seemingly personal desires for friendship, belonging, and legitimacy for what they are – largely reflections of our structural position as members of a white settler collectivity? Along similar lines, how can we detangle notions of solidarity from notions of belonging? Would it then be easier to face the fact that – barring an immediate and radical exit from current colonial power structures – settlers remain settlers irrespective of our ability to connect to individual Indigenous people or communities? These are just some of the ideas sparked by my conversations with Julia, and indeed all participants, about how we might forge ahead toward non-colonizing solidarity.

5

Rewriting Colonial Scripts
Toward Non-colonizing Solidarity

> There's a massive inequity between being Indigenous and being Canadian. And the massive inequity is just that we have no country, and Canadians have our country. And the bottom line is they get to decide what happens to us and what doesn't. That's the nature of colonization. So that's the massive inequity, and that's where we begin.
> – LEE MARACLE

When I decided to look into solidarity relations between Indigenous women and white women in the Greater Toronto Area (GTA), I knew the general cause of the problems I might find, precisely the "massive inequity" Lee Maracle (Stó:lō/Métis) describes in the statement above. What I hoped for was a deeper understanding of the particulars, including how white women could better navigate the relationships that unfold – with Indigenous women and with one another – under a system that Derek Gregory (2004) aptly labels the "colonial present." Based on my own anecdotal experiences, I knew political solidarity was fraught, but I also knew it was happening, if imperfectly. Infused with this cautious optimism, I looked for paths forward, ways for white women like me to do solidarity work on more equitable, non-colonizing terms.

The story I found and tell in this book reveals some of the cracks and fault lines that white settler women often stumble on in solidarity work.

Put differently, I explore the vagaries of gendered colonial subjectivity, zeroing in on how we, white women, are prone to expressing our deep-seated desire for belonging – a defining feature of collective white settler/liberal subjectivity – by pursuing proximity to Indigenous women. Consequently, a large part of what I map in this book is the spectrum of proximity, that is, the myriad desires and related behaviours that connote, involve, or require proximity in one form or another and that figure in white women's engagement in solidarity work, including the desires for acceptance, inclusion, forgiveness, healing, purpose, empowerment, or friendship. Pursuing proximity through solidarity work, I have argued, potentially eases the discomfort of being a settler on stolen land.

As Indigenous participants noted with keen acumen, this pursuit can be self-serving and invasive, it can involve figurative or literal appropriation, and it can ultimately help white women sustain the fantasy that we are good settlers above the colonial fray. Of course, there are subplots to the story, which reveal just how much white participants wrestle with our structurally derived privilege. As long as the colonial system is intact, however, we risk drowning in the intense undercurrent of our desire for legitimacy – something even the most self-aware among us finds difficult to avoid or escape.

By thinking with (Mignolo and Walsh 2018) Indigenous and white participants alike, I paint a picture of the problem with proximity: the invasive attitudes, behaviours, and practices that ensue when white women in solidarity encounters become so entangled in our self-making pursuits that we overstep acceptable boundaries – material (physical), intersubjective (interpersonal), or epistemic (about knowledge) – as defined by Indigenous women. In the process, I have come to realize the importance of disentangling two desires on the part of white settlers that can often clash, coexist, or be conflated: a desire for legitimacy or belonging in a settler colonial context, and a desire to engage ethically with Indigenous peoples. Both are operative in the solidarity encounter. The vision of non-colonizing solidarity I have gleaned would have us understand the former to give precedence to the latter. It tasks white women with investing in solidarity in ways that keep us focused on the political project at hand – the dismantlement of settler colonial structures.

One obvious question is how to spot and disrupt the desire to practice solidarity in self-serving ways. How do white women (and people of other genders) check our solidarity impulse with its need to "do good"? How might we hold onto a sense of our structural privilege without capitulating to white settler guilt and our desire to assuage it? In a review of Lisa Slater's

Anxieties of Belonging (2019), Heike Schotten (2020, 492) challenges us to move beyond focusing on subjectivity and toward leveraging our political advantage. While I take Schotten's point, even if we were to harness our privilege, I agree with Slater that white settlers still risk giving into a "virtuous anxiety" that would reaffirm our sense of belonging à la Sara Ahmed's (2004) anxious white subject, a dynamic that is very much about subjectivity. Therefore, Slater (2019, 131) insists, "good white people" can and must process their anxiety in ways that make them/us "answerable to Indigenous peoples" and, more specifically, I would add, to Indigenous political projects. Nonetheless, both authors are onto something in suggesting ways to isolate and nurture the aforementioned political desire to engage ethically with Indigenous nations.

As Maile Arvin, Eve Tuck, and Angie Morrill (2013, 25) remind us, there is no "one proper set of decolonial practices"; indeed, there are as many paths forward as there are sociopolitical contexts. For this reason, and emboldened by Maracle's observation that white engagement itself is a non-colonizing move even if it includes "colonizing behaviours," I offer a working framework for facilitating non-colonizing political solidarity. The framework is intentionally broad – more like a scaffolding – and minimally prescriptive, which I hope makes it adaptable to different sociopolitical contexts and conditions. Anchored primarily in Indigenous participant narratives, it asks us to imagine a future beyond settler colonialism while recognizing that we are still constrained by colonial ways of thinking and doing, including paternalistic modes of helping and healing. To remind readers, I define political solidarity as a broad set of material practices that people engage in together to pursue a political goal. Below, through a synthesis of participant narratives, I flesh out non-colonizing solidarity's possible contours, the subjectivities it would produce, and the various paths that Indigenous peoples and settlers might collectively take to get there even as we interact under decidedly colonial circumstances. The framework rests on a straightforward, if difficult, idea to actualize: if the problem in solidarity work is too much proximity, then the solution involves distance or, more accurately, the renegotiation of solidarity's relational parameters.

Consistent with my approach throughout this book, I feature Indigenous participants' insights into how to move forward precisely because of their position as subjects who have been what Sara Ahmed (2012, 176) describes as "held up." For Ahmed, the "phenomenology of 'being stopped'" is what happens "when we are stopped or held up by how we inhabit what we inhabit, [and] then the terms of habitation are revealed to us. We need to rewrite the world from the experience of not being able to pass into the world." To rewrite the world this way is to bring into view the structural barriers that those of us who "inhabit a category of privilege" (Ahmed 2012, 176) cannot apprehend. As I demonstrate across these chapters, Indigenous accounts of the solidarity encounter demand that we reconceptualize political subjects, struggles, and aspirations, particularly white women and our roles as allies in political struggle with Indigenous women.[1]

In retrospect, thinking in spatial terms about the problem and its solution seems both logical and obvious. From the start, I theorized the solidarity encounter as a "contemporary mode of proximity" (Ahmed 2000, 13) in which there is a considerable, though never absolute, risk that stranger fetishism will kick in to conceal histories of domination. After all, the solidarity encounter is a microcosm of the colonial encounter, potentially replete with colonialism's characteristic invasiveness and domination of sociospatial relations in particular geographic contexts.[2] In all honesty, though, looking at the solidarity encounter through a spatial lens only dawned on me gradually over the course of the research. In what follows, I share my thoughts about what a sociospatial understanding of solidarity might accomplish. Herein lies the value of theory in relation to practice: with no illusions about erasing colonial power imbalances, I hope that theorizing the solidarity encounter as an embodied encounter taking place in space over time will bring us closer to making instances of non-colonizing solidarity the norm.

The Space of Solidarity: "Step Back, but Not Out"

When I asked Gabriela, one of this study's Indigenous participants, for advice about non-colonizing solidarity, she responded in her typically down-to-earth way: "You work together, but it's like a boundary thing." Echoing the message of Tanya Tagaq with which I open Chapter 2, Gabriela's statement epitomizes the centrality of spatial understandings of the solidarity encounter. Spatial allusions about the most effective role for white women in solidarity work abound in Indigenous participants' narratives in particular. This pervasiveness speaks both to their embodied experiences of the encounter and the importance they give to setting boundaries therein. Recall Maracle's assertion that solidarity is colonizing "when there's invasion involved and the other person has to push back to get a space ... So there's a space between us that's the cherished thing ... When you come too close and take up this space, then the cherished thing is gone." While some might interpret Maracle's reference to cherished spaces as a defence of autonomous individualism, I do not. Maracle does not deny that we become who we are in relation to others (i.e., intersubjectively). Quite the opposite. She indicts the colonizing move built into white settler/liberal subjectivity that does deny intersubjectivity and thus the possibility of invasion. Put otherwise, Maracle does not dispute the relational aspect of personhood but rather calls for settlers to exercise their personhood – and, by extension, solidarity – in nondomineering ways. Indigenous interventions such as Maracle's both demand and describe the beginnings of Indigenous–settler relationships that acknowledge difference without hierarchizing it (hooks 2000; Yeğenoğlu 1998).

While all broadly take recourse to spatial referents, Indigenous approaches to non-colonizing solidarity vary in emphasis and in how to implement non-colonizing solidarity in practice. Importantly, however, throughout their statements, Indigenous women conveyed the message that white women are to remain present. As I highlight in Chapter 2, Indigenous participants were open to working with white women despite the challenges. Admittedly, given the parameters of my study, this is a self-selected group whose amenable approach to solidarity work would not be shared by all Indigenous women, as if that were even possible. A few spoke of Indigenous people who would not work with white people. Period. Others emphasized that a lack of trust kept them from working in a predominately white group. As Rachel Flowers (2015, 38) reminds us, settlers should not be "presumptuous. Maybe some Indigenous peoples don't want or don't need settler co-resistance because we don't trust them." Still others, as I discuss in Chapter 3, admitted to needing white women allies but not necessarily wanting them.

Ardra's take on the question of whether to work with white women is fairly representative of Indigenous participant positions and consistent with my solidarity experiences:

> Well, I just think that [women's] groups should be mixed [Indigenous–non-Indigenous] because we all live in this world together, and I'm never going to be a believer of segregation ... We are at a crucial time in terms of the planet environmentally, and that isn't going to be solved unless people work together. There may have been a time where I chose to work only with [one category of women]. That doesn't make it an exclusive strategy. It may just be a temporary, necessary phase or a necessary moment in time, but at the end of the day, people are going to have to work together, so groups are going to have to be mixed, I think. We just don't have the numbers to do it on our own anyways.

Here, Ardra depicts Indigenous women as politically discerning and eminently practical, as did Danielle when she said, "We're in this together. We breathe the same air, we drink the same water, we eat the same food."

As is evident in the following exchange, Maracle also held the view that "we're in this together." She actually reproached white women who, for fear of (being seen as) appropriating Indigenous culture, refrained from taking action on the issue of MMIWG2S people. Perhaps it is no coincidence that I broached the topic with a spatial metaphor:

> CAROL LYNNE: I think some people were very cautious and concerned and wanted to step away because of this fear of appropriation or speaking for or all that kind of stuff.
>
> MARACLE: [Appropriation] involves stealing. So if you're working on an issue to stop someone from getting killed, where's the theft? That's what I want to know. What the fuck is being stolen – those guys' right to kill? And isn't that the point? It's the white boys that are killing us that you're stealing from, not me.
>
> CAROL LYNNE: What about the classic critique that "you're speaking for Indigenous women."
>
> MARACLE: No, you're not. You're speaking for yourself. Don't try to speak for me. Yeah, never speak for me. "This is my issue, I'm a white woman, and I don't want guys to go killing Indian women. This is my issue?" ... When you start speaking for me, that's ridiculous. It's comic. [Violence against Indigenous women] is a white woman's issue. It's a woman's issue. So every woman should be up there speaking against it.

Here, Maracle renders explicit the importance that gender makes to the solidarity encounter under examination in this book. For her, Indigenous women and white women are, or should be, brought together because of a common political project *as women* – to redress gender-based violence. When asked about Indigenous women's roles as allies in the struggles of other women, Wanda Whitebird (Mi'kmaq) responded, "Well, I think what we have to realize is that we are all women. We're definitely allies because we are women. So there's the fight that all women have, and then there's the fight that Indigenous women have, and there's the fight that Black women have. So we all fight as women. Equality, we fight for that." Like Maracle, Whitebird argues for the importance of women working together against violence, while pointing to the nuances of uniting with respect for the specificity of different women's struggles.

At the same time, Indigenous women gave directives about how solidarity should and should not happen. The spatial references I share next contain unambiguous instructions for how white women can be present and engage respectfully, ethically, and meaningfully in solidarity work. That is, they suggest ways for white women (and, I think, white people more broadly) to disrupt the impulse to reproduce ourselves as exceptional, innocent, and beyond the reach of power relations. Here is a sampling of four such statements.

> They should come to us and ask us, "What do you want? What can we do to help? We want to stand behind you. We want to take direction from you." (Lydia)
>
> As an Indigenous woman, as an Aboriginal woman, I don't want you to save me. I want you to stand beside me. And standing beside me does not mean that you're there to help me. We're there to help each other. We're working in partnership. I think a lot of solidarity work in quotations is, "I'm going to stand beside you and never share." (Green)
>
> There were more white women, but the speakers were 100 percent Indian, if you recall that event [around the issue of MMIWG2S people] ... and that was okay with people, and I thought that [the white] people at that meeting ... were really taking a backseat. They were really interested in learning. They were really interested in Native people speaking for Native people and taking leadership. They were not there to take any kind of leadership role. They were there really clearly as support people at that time. (Amadahy)
>
> An ally could create the space through your power, like, "Okay, I got this room here. I'm affiliated with this university ... Let's create a space where we can organically come up with the ideas of what we're going to do, because [white people] controlled everything historically, the narrative of this story. We'll just take a backseat here and learn from you, because actually you have a lot to say that's going to change this." (Tabobondung)

Each passage describes in slightly different terms how white women can position themselves in relation to Indigenous women's struggles. For example, Lydia uses "behind," Ruth Green (Kanien'kehá:ka) uses "beside," and both Zainab Amadahy (Cherokee, Seminole), and Rebeka Tabobondung (Anishinaabe) use "backseat" to denote the ideal orientation. Tabobondung also echoes Heike Schotten's (2020) recommendation to harness white settler political (and economic) capital. All passages impart the sense that Indigenous women want (indeed, require) white women to remain present but without taking over, controlling, or dominating the solidarity space in the ways described throughout this book (see especially Chapter 2).

Several white participants ascribed to this message and the metaphor used to convey it. Directly echoing Lydia, Amadahy, and Tabobondung, Eve conceptualized her ally role as one of taking direction and learning from Indigenous women:

> So shutting up is one [way to deal with white privilege], obviously. It's having compassion, listening, being open. It's trying to build the trust and solidarity. It's trying to do all of that kind of work ... It includes taking direction. It includes not necessarily leading. It includes being antivanguard, not vanguard. It includes all that kind of stuff.

Notably, Eve's take on allyship aligns with Peggy's rejection of vanguardism, discussed in Chapter 4, an approach to political struggle that carries its own spatial connotation. In lockstep with Eve's, here are Alicia's thoughts about the solidarity encounter and her role in it in terms of place:

> The identity politics around being a white woman have been an issue for me. I've struggled a lot with my place. "What is my place? Should I be doing this? What do I know? I didn't grow up on a reserve. Do I have a right to have an opinion on these things? These folks know best. I don't know what I'm talking about." There have been a lot of issues and things like that.

Throughout this book, in fact, I point to how the white participants, including me, have struggled with our place in solidarity work.

Gabriela was among those Indigenous women who most resolutely invoked the spatiality of the solidarity encounter and consequent need for boundary setting. Joining other Indigenous participants, she provided guidance about the appropriate roles for white women to assume vis-à-vis Indigenous women in that encounter: "It's really important [for white women] to step back rather than step forward ... when the struggle is around Aboriginal issues. So at the core of all of it should be Aboriginal people who are coming forward. You work together, but it's like a boundary thing." Despite her scathing critique of needy do-gooder behaviour, detailed in Chapter 2, Gabriela believed that principled relations between Indigenous and non-Indigenous women, and people more generally, can and do occur.

Gabriela described the solidarity encounter as a liminal space replete with possibilities:

> Again, using the "space" word here – creating a space to negotiate understandings, I guess, is kind of one way to say it. To negotiate understandings that really reflect an understanding of Aboriginal ways of being in the world and the major issues that we're dealing with, and that if we can have partners in a coalition, we're moving something forward. And it wasn't easy. It's never easy, that kind of space, to create, because of all that everybody brings to it. I always look at it as a little place of tension and conflict. There's a word for that – liminal space, right? – which has a possibility of going in a really positive way or a negative one. It depends on what you do with it.

I take Gabriela's definition of liminality to be akin to its use in cultural studies, "to refer to border zones and peripheries of dominant discourses, where the contestation of cultural symbols takes place" ("Liminality" 2002). In this quote, Gabriela calls on everyone in the solidarity encounter to negotiate discursive meanings "that really reflect an understanding of Aboriginal ways of being in the world and the major issues that we're dealing with." On the one hand, Gabriela's allusion to "Aboriginal ways of being in the world" is potentially risky. As discussed in Chapter 3, it could play into ahistorical, romanticized, and essentialized understandings of indigeneity and Indigenous peoples as, among other things, stuck in the past. Further, a focus on "cultural" difference – rather than on the structural power differences with which Indigenous peoples contend – threatens to set in motion the appropriation element of my proximity spectrum. On the other hand, we can interpret Gabriela's counsel differently by remembering Emma LaRocque's (2010, 138) thesis: "The Native emphasis on cultural difference reflects a strategic decolonizing response to the problem of Western intellectual dominance" (see also Weaver 1997). Read in this light, Gabriela's passage is an act of resistance and a comment on political struggle – a mandate for non-Indigenous allies to cede space to Indigenous knowledge claims and political choices, including strategies of radical resurgence (Simpson 2017).

Striking a chord with the refrains of Lydia, Amadahy, and Tabobondung, Gabriela also called on white women to take a backseat in the solidarity encounter by supporting the cultivation of Indigenous-led spaces of dialogue. By way of explanation, allow me to turn once again to my No More Silence (NMS) experience. Several years after its creation, NMS temporarily morphed into a mostly white group, which led to a protracted discussion about whether or how we should continue to organize Toronto's annual Strawberry Ceremony on February 14 to honour the MMIWG2S people of Ontario. At the time, the insistence of some white women in the group that we should no longer organize the ceremony deeply troubled me, and I struggled to articulate why. I understood (and agreed with) the reasoning behind the position – no one wanted to risk a rehearsal of white settler colonial dominance. However, I also did not want to abdicate my responsibility as a white woman to take up this issue, as per Maracle's powerful rejoinder above. Even then, I recognized the tension between acting on one's responsibility and overstepping into domineering behaviour.

For that reason, when conducting interviews, I asked participants what NMS's role should be in relation to the February 14 vigil. Here is Gabriela's response to my question about NMS and white allyship more generally. In her assessment,

> [Allies] should step back, but not out. I think that's the metaphor that works. Not step out of the picture, but step back. What [NMS members] do, what you did do, you have some key people who are connected, who are Indigenous people who you know in the community. Even if those people are not in your coalition, if those are people you've developed a relationship with, it's not just a front. It's saying, "What we want to do is we want to help here. We don't have a lot of Aboriginal people right now, but we're still doing this. Will you play these parts and be the people who come forward?"

Joining Indigenous participants across the board, Gabriela would not preclude a primarily white group from organizing around the issue of violence against Indigenous women, provided it met certain conditions. She offers the metaphor of "stepping back, but not out" to members of groups who are predominately white as a guide for how to position themselves in solidarity work. Also using a spatial metaphor, Whitebird reminds us of the negative reception awaiting white women who impose their self-serving/self-making agendas in solidarity encounters:

> Then there's the ones that I consider to be the allies. [Those] are the ones that just let us be ... When I look at No More Silence, you guys don't make a decision unless you come to the Native women who are involved. I mean, you do, but you don't have your agenda. So I guess an ally is someone who stands with me, beside me, but doesn't try to change me, and that I don't

have to defend myself to them all the time, and is going to be there just to hold me up when I can't hold myself up.

Importantly, Whitebird, like Green, could imagine Indigenous and white women working side by side. At the same time, Whitebird implicitly warned that white settler agendas can take myriad, often invasive forms and remain impervious to concerted, self-reflexive efforts by white women to unsettle their internal settler selves (Regan 2010) and disrupt those agendas.

Writing about a different context, Alyssa Rosenberg (2013) makes a similar point about whether white celebrities should make public pronouncements about racism. After asking a series of difficult questions, starting with, "Can white people speak about racism without silencing or speaking over people of color?" Rosenberg (2013, para. 6) concludes,

> The easiest answer to this set of inquiries is to drop back and drop out in the name of deference to other people. The harder, but more correct one, is to try to determine where your voice fits, knowing well that you'll be opening yourself up to criticisms both of what you say and on the grounds that your decision to speak rebounds to your own benefit.

Rosenberg's words continue to hit home as this book goes to press. With it, I have, indeed, opened myself up to criticism, which is both hard and scary. As Gabriela might say to me, however, "step back, but not out" and develop a thick skin, advice I discuss in the next section.

In various ways, all of these Indigenous participants imply that there is a rightful place for white women to assume in solidarity encounters; it involves performing a supportive, yet accountable and agentic role in political struggle. To do so, Green suggested that white women invest wholistically in the work, with the "'w' in front of 'holistic' meaning 'complete,' 'whole.'" To clarify, Green here differentiates wholistic investment from a more superficial type of activism, which "becomes almost like, 'I did a smudge. I've gone to a sweat lodge. I'm sorry.' [Indigenous people] don't brag about our spirituality. You know what I mean? It becomes like, 'I've tried it. I've tried sushi. I'm in solidarity with Japanese people. I've tried sushi.' You know what I'm saying?" Green takes aim at solidarity work that is potentially appropriative as well as reliant on the nonperformative declarations (Ahmed 2004) I analyze in Chapter 4. The question then becomes, How can white women invest in solidarity wholistically without kick-starting the pursuit of proximity that, in Maracle's poignant description, stands to transgress the sacred space that is our common breath? How do we curb the self-serving aspects of the impulse to solidarity, including the compulsion in the face of injustice "to go and do something" (Heron 2007, 39)? One answer is what we might call solidarity at a distance.

Solidarity at a Distance
So far, Indigenous participants' reflections point to the need to reconfigure the boundaries of Indigenous–non-Indigenous solidarity encounters along the lines of "stepping back, but not out." In what follows, I draw further on these narratives to offer a more precise idea of what this reorientation would involve for white women, the ultimate goal being to bring collective white settler privilege (back) into view (Ahmed 2012). With this, I suggest that the first step in stepping back for white women would be an enhanced attentiveness to Indigenous perspectives on the invasiveness of some of our solidarity performances. Moreover, in my experience with NMS, "stepping back, but not out" connotes the need to strike a balance between the extremes of proximity and distance, by which I mean too much of the wrong kind of investment in solidarity on individualistic terms versus too little or no investment at all (the latter being what Maracle might call resorting to "any colonial excuse not to do something"). Apropos here is critical race feminist and lesbian scholar Pat Parker's (2000, 73) poetic summation of the tension white women must hold in balance when negotiating racial power differences: "The first thing you do is to forget that I'm Black. Second, you must never forget that I'm Black."

I turn now to the merits of exercising white women's agency at just the right distance. Indigenous participants agreed that white women need to learn about colonialism in its historical and ongoing forms in order to grapple with our settler status. Crucial elements of this education will likely involve proximity to Indigenous groups, communities, and cultural events. Proximity per se is not the problem, to repeat a central conclusion of this book. Rather, the issue occurs when, in pursuing proximity for self-serving/self-making reasons (ultimately, to achieve settler belonging), the white woman crosses a threshold that should not be crossed. Indigenous participants directly addressed this risk and provide guidelines for alternative approaches.

I begin with Danielle, whose comments on the white woman needy do-gooder and the "celebrity Native" remain etched in my memory. Here is an excerpt from a much lengthier exchange in which I struggled to communicate my concerns around balancing proximity and distance:

> CAROL LYNNE: I've been told this by white people that in order to be an ally, you need to be involved in the community, be a part of the community. To me, there's a line there ...
> DANIELLE: It's the wrong reason.
> CAROL LYNNE: Yeah, it's like a fine line. So I have to be friends with Native people and be part of their community or I can't be an ally?
> DANIELLE: No, an ally is not ... I think an ally is that person who isn't in a conflict of interest, and once you take that emotional investment, then you're in conflict.

Here, Danielle warns of the possible negative repercussions of what I have been taking as prevailing wisdom – that effective allies must have deep ties to an Indigenous person or community. On the contrary, she recommends what I call solidarity at a distance, that is, an affiliation in which white women will not "lose their objectivity." In the next breath, Danielle clarified the underlying risk of thinking about solidarity mainly in terms of becoming part of a community: "Why would you [try to become Indigenous]? Why would you be something you're not? You can't." Here, Danielle reminds us, unprompted, that the dimensions of the proximity spectrum often interrelate: in this case, desires for Indigenous acceptance, perhaps through friendship, with the appropriation of indigeneity, the latter being a foundation of white settler/liberal nation building as I discuss in Chapter 3.

Whitebird recommended a comparable sort of distancing, for similar reasons. As I did with Danielle, when I asked Whitebird to comment on the role of white women allies, I came clean about my resistance to the idea that a non-Indigenous person would have to "make sure you have Native friends" to be an effective ally. In response, Whitebird described past situations in which she observed white women "taking over" women-only activist spaces, a transgression of Indigenous–settler boundaries to be sure. In light of this history, while she agreed that white women should "understand the plight" of Indigenous women, Whitebird also stipulated,

> I don't think you have to [experience] what [that plight] is. What [some white women] are saying is you almost have to become Native to become involved in the Native community. And to me, that's wrong, because we're fighting the exact opposite of that in our lives, because non-Native people get involved. When we had women's circles, when we first started, we decided that only Native women could go because what we found when non-Native women came, when white women came, they took over.

Listening to Whitebird's explanation, I experienced another *aha* moment. The combination of Danielle's and Whitebird's statements cleared up what has been bothering me: there can be a fine line between wanting to be involved with an Indigenous community and wanting to "become" Indigenous. Put differently, there are (at least) two desires to disentangle, and a slippery slope between them to boot: the desire to engage ethically with Indigenous peoples, which obviously requires involvement with Indigenous people and communities, and the desire for belonging in a colonial context, which can lead to appropriative and invasive attitudes and behaviours.

Rachel Flowers (2015, 27) contributed further to my *aha* moment in warning that "anticolonial resistance does not require the disappearance of difference nor should co-resistance foreclose alterity and oblige co-existence." Flowers, too, is concerned about the collapse of boundaries between Indigenous peoples and settlers, particularly when the latter co-opt Indigenous voices to impose settler visions for the future. What's more, Flowers (2015, 37) uses a spatial metaphor to challenge settlers to "find a place to stand in resistance that does not take up spaces for and appropriate the labour of Indigenous peoples (in particular, Indigenous women)." The common denominator of these messages seems to be this: white women should respect the terms and parameters of struggle and solidarity established by Indigenous peoples.

Certainly, some white participants already understood this message, as when Evelyn described the need to maintain boundaries between herself and the Indigenous people with whom she was engaged in solidarity: "I think I need to prove myself. I think I need to step up my involvement and actually have some boundaries around that too: recognizing that I do have to make my own living ... I have to watch over my health because I know that some of those people are just burning themselves out." Interestingly, Evelyn's take on distance has a prominent personal dimension. That is, her desire to "prove herself" is tempered by her recognition of the need to create "some boundaries around" her solidarity work, which is simultaneously a move to stay healthy and avoid burnout. Evelyn's perspective suggests that the task ahead for white women is to move from recognizing the various desires for proximity that beset us – for approval, acceptance, forgiveness, healing, or learning – to disrupting their unbridled pursuit.

Above all, Indigenous women's narratives teach us that there is such a thing as excessive proximity in solidarity encounters. For Danielle, when a white woman becomes embroiled in "a conflict of interest," chances are she has crossed a line. For Whitebird, the white desire to "become Native" is a telltale sign of a boundary being disrespected. In tacit agreement, a third Indigenous participant, Belinda, promoted distance – what she deems being neutral or not taking things personally – as a preventive measure. In sharing her vision of white allyship, Belinda was resolute:

> It's important to have an outsider or a neutral person, if they can be neutral. If they don't get their stuff confused with our stuff; if they just know what their place or role is, those are the most effective allies because they don't get pulled into all the conflict. They don't get confused. They know what's really playing out here; they know the colonial history ... They have to have that piece, and, uh, not to take things so personally, eh?[3]

Belinda's ideal white woman ally is a "neutral person" who does not "get pulled into all the conflict," that is, a person who can maintain a particular kind of intersubjective distance or boundary. For Belinda, as for Danielle, it is a problem when white women forget "their place or role" in Indigenous political struggles, get caught up in conflict, and "take things personally."

As I mention in Chapter 1, some white participants such as Alicia already intuited that the white tendency to take things personally is an issue. However, Belinda's intricate portrait of white ally neutrality links the capacity "not to take things so personally" with the wherewithal to acquire a knowledge of colonial history and the ability to listen or observe. This also reminds me of what Whitebird describes above as the ability to "just let us be." Belinda's message, in particular, tells me that white women are most effective as allies when we grapple not only with the damage colonialism has wrought to the fabric of Indigenous nations, but also with the effects of our structural position in that history, on us and on others – one of the ultimate mandates of self-reflexivity (Heron 2005).

Belinda provided a specific example of how white allies of any gender can "get confused" and be "pulled into the conflict." Noting that the colonially derived division in some Indigenous communities between Christians and Traditionalists can extend to solidarity circles, Belinda turned to me and asked, "But how do you be an ally in that? Well, definitely, you can't take sides and say Christians are right or Traditionalists are right. Yeah, just don't get pulled into it. I don't know, it's challenging to be a neutral party." In her experience, white settlers who "don't know their place" prolong such conflicts and perpetuate division. Belinda's example also highlights what can happen when white allies focus on cultural difference (e.g., religious beliefs) as opposed to structural oppression. I am not suggesting that the reorientation Danielle or others seek would have white women refute the significance of cultural difference, revitalization, or resurgence to political struggle. As Leanne Betasamosake Simpson (2017, 50) explains, Indigenous cultural practices have always been political; therefore, cultural resurgence in such forms as "regenerating language, ceremony and land-based practices is always political." Rather, their arguments lead me to suggest that our collective attention as settlers turn away from cultural difference and toward structural power differences, thereby retaining a focus on the broader anti-colonial political project at hand.

It bears repeating that white participants did think about their place in solidarity work. In fact, Peggy had witnessed – and tried to avoid – the kinds of "internal" conflicts Belinda identifies. In this way, Peggy echoed Indigenous participants' calls for maintaining boundaries between Indigenous women and white women. Despite knowing the importance of developing a "tough skin," Peggy had struggled to navigate this aspect of the solidarity terrain:

> Some of the most radical [Indigenous] people wouldn't have anything to do with me, even if I wanted to work with them; I'm not radical enough in their eyes. Where do you find your place, who you can ally with? What can you most productively do, who do you listen to? ... You have to be clear at what you're doing and why. You need a tough skin. There's also that phenomenon that you see amongst oppressed people particularly, which is this viciousness to each other. We [non-Indigenous people] become embroiled in that dynamic, and you can be used in that way to attack somebody else or get caught up in it. Then what?

In my interpretation, Peggy's message of "you need a tough skin" is a prescription for mitigating white women's desires for proximity to Indigenous Others. Side by side, Belinda's and Peggy's remarks suggest the importance of noting – and limiting – the degree to which difference rather than dominance remains the framework for political solidarity work (Fellows and Razack 1994).

For Danielle, Whitebird, Evelyn, Belinda, and Peggy, effective white settler ally support comes by way of boundary- or parameter-setting reflected – and effected – in the ability to take a neutral or objective stance, but, importantly, a stance nonetheless. In colloquial terms, allyship is more effective when white women do not get "their stuff confused with our stuff," Belinda's maxim-cum-mechanism for preventing the appropriation of ideas and identities (not to mention land and resources) that define settler colonialism. In making the case for neutrality, objectivity, and other distancing techniques, these participants provide a partial corrective to the misguided focus on the white settler self in solidarity encounters. As I read it, the message for white women is to bring our subject positions to bear by knowing ourselves as members of a structurally dominant group – not as "autonomous independent individuals" (Moreton-Robinson 2000) entitled to access, know, and help Indigenous Others. They ask us to recognize our "gendered colonial interpellation" in the colonial project, especially moments when we feel the need to do good.

To summarize so far, participant narratives suggest the value in reconceptualizing solidarity encounters using a spatial lens, that is, notions of proximity and distance. In what remains, I develop the point that rethinking solidarity in these terms creates fruitful ground for the production of non-colonizing attitudes and behaviours. That said, I do not claim that a reconfiguration of boundaries will eradicate white women's desires for proximity or the quest for belonging that lies underneath them. However, accepting the need for distance has the potential to forestall, however temporarily, the expression of such desires and, by extension, some of the problems with proximity. Sara Ahmed's research into diversity workers in educational institutions is transferable here. She uses a spatial metaphor to describe how people who are subordinated by, or want to change, institutional norms come up against a wall, nothing less than "the sedimentation of history into a barrier that is solid and tangible in the present ... a barrier that remains invisible to those who can flow into the spaces created by institutions" (Ahmed 2012, 175). Thus, Indigenous peoples, by virtue of the positions they inhabit and do not inhabit, are continuously bumping up against colonial power structures. In other words, heeding Indigenous participants' descriptions of the colonial walls they come up against might enable white women to invest in solidarity encounters without turning these encounters into self-servicing occasions for white settler/liberal subject formation.

Curbing the Impulse to Solidarity: The Mitigation of Healing Discourse

At the heart of my rendition of the solidarity encounter is a particular form of personhood embodied by white women that I call gendered colonial subjectivity. To recap, the normative version of this ideal turns on racial assumptions about white people as autonomous (liberal), rational, and transcendent and the white woman in particular as the "helper" of "more oppressed" Other women. In considering what had become of this figure in relation to solidarity work, I coined the phrase the impulse to solidarity. I defined this impulse as the (white woman's) drive to satisfy the settler desire for belonging through proximity to Indigenous women in the solidarity encounter. To differentiate it from Heron's (2007) overseas helping imperative, I dubbed it "helping with a twist" to convey how the solidarity impulse fuses the white desires to "help" and to "be helped by" the Indigenous Other right here on "Canadian" soil. In short, the solidarity impulse, along with the proximity spectrum concept, is my attempt to account for the self-serving/self-making reasons white women might engage, or stay engaged, in solidarity work on "home" turf. These, I argued, are the moments that most require our vigilance.

Notwithstanding the fact that we stand to be helped by the solidarity encounter, the notion that white women are preordained to rescue, save, or otherwise intervene on Indigenous women's behalf is also firmly embedded in the solidarity impulse. How might we disrupt normative forms and uses of healing discourse? After a brief review of the threat that discourse poses to solidarity work, I turn to participant narratives to consider how viewing the solidarity encounter through a spatial lens can potentially disrupt the power of hegemonic-healing discourse.

Dian Million (2013) focuses on the misuse of healing discourse and the resulting reproduction of the figure of the traumatized Indigenous subject. Million (2013, 81) is wary of the recent uptake of "the therapeutic language of trauma" by settlers in particular to discuss "'the Indian problem,' the euphemism for Canadian colonialism's systemic violence," and the intergenerational effects of residential schools. She contextualizes this uptake within a global healing discourse about Indigenous peoples that emerged out of a post-Second World War liberal human rights framework. Million (2013, 78) is most concerned about the erosion of "substantive Indigenous political empowerment" that can happen when Indigenous peoples enter this "affective discursive space." In Million's assessment, the *Final Report of the Truth and Reconciliation Commission of Canada* (2015) itself yields to the therapeutic language of trauma with the dire consequence of locating the structural dispossession and "endemic social suffering" of Indigenous peoples as a disease rooted in the past. Resultantly, "healing encompasses Canada's dialogue with Indigenous peoples, moving the focus from one of political self-determination to one where self-determination becomes intertwined with state-determined biopolitical programs for emotional and psychological self-care informed by trauma" (Million 2013, 6). In this scenario, the focus on Indigenous difference I discussed in Chapter 3 takes a particular form: healing Indigenous individuals is divorced from collective struggles for Indigenous self-determination. Applying this analysis to the solidarity encounter allows me to expand a point from Chapter 1: when white women read Indigenous women as the "traumatized" figures of this discursive landscape, we are apt to default to our historically produced role of "helper."

To reiterate, when non-Indigenous Canadians view Indigenous cultural resurgence efforts through the lens of (multi)cultural difference, we are likely to miss the (political) point entirely. Similarly, white women who employ the lens of hegemonic-healing discourse can misread Indigenous perspectives on care work in the solidarity encounter. There is no shortage of pain in this work. Ursula, Teresa, and Danielle all described the emotional labour involved in organizing around the issue of MMIWG2S people. When speaking about the role of predominately white groups (in this case NMS) in organizing around the issue, Ursula explained her hesitancy to join the group, despite having attended some vigils:

> When I go to the [NMS] rally, [people] just start crying. I can't spend my ... I can't drain my energy in that group, because that's all I would think about. It would consume me. So it's good to have [white] women who can do that work, like I said, who keep checking in, for sure, but who can lend their energy to the really hard stuff like that, the white women, because oftentimes, Native women, it's too close to home for them.

Teresa's sentiment was remarkably similar. In taking me through some of her activist experiences, she honoured the work of Amber O'Hara, one of the first Indigenous women in Ontario, if not Canada, to track the names of MMIWG2S people:

> I joined that listserv for her website, and it was all these women. They may have had dreams or visions about our sisters who had gone missing, but they were doing research. And honestly, I couldn't last on that list for longer than two years, because I wasn't strong enough at that time to see those and hear those stories.

Danielle described a comparable scenario:

> There are times when we as the Indigenous people are too close to speak, to touch the fire ... It's hard to touch the fire, because it touches you here

[*gesturing toward the heart*]. You've got to go to your core, and you experience that, and it's painful sometimes. [Patricia] Monture used to call it a boundary warrior: somebody who has to live in both worlds to interpret the one world for the other.

Importantly, all three Indigenous participants alluded to instances when white women, because of their "distance" from the oppression at hand, are in a better position to do the work that needs doing. This interpretation obviously lines up with a framework for non-colonizing solidarity that reimagines the solidarity encounter in terms of proximity and distance. However, as Million's (2013) work suggests, when hearing these statements, there is a good chance that white women in the encounter will tap into stereotypical notions of Indigenous people as psychologically scarred. If read that way, Danielle's point would reinforce dominant discourses of Indigenous women as wounded and emotionally fragile individuals instead of structurally oppressed and politically strong members of Indigenous nations – despite her calling attention to the settler responsibility to learn about colonial history and engage other settlers in the process.

There were moments in the earlier days of NMS that provided analogous opportunities for miscommunication. In my third or fourth year with the group, we talked extensively about the emotional, psychical, spiritual, and physical toll of our work on the issue of MMIWG2S people. We even went on record to say that the work is "particularly difficult for Indigenous women, who bear an unequal burden of the hurt, sorrow, and trauma inflicted by colonialism" (D'Arcangelis and Huntley 2012, 46). The idea that structurally marginalized groups bear the brunt of political struggle, or bear it differently, is a feminist idea stemming at least as far back as the Combahee River Collective (1979).[4] However, given that hegemonic-healing discourse positions Indigenous women as emotionally damaged subjects who need help, it is worth noting that our stance could have inadvertently fed into the idea that white women are rational subjects there to help more "damaged" Indigenous ones.

At the same time, Million (2013) notes that alternative conceptualizations of healing – individuals, communities, and nations – emerge out of Indigenous women's praxis. She devotes significant energy to "contrast[ing] the human development vision of healing with that of Indigenous women's activism in Canada, a movement that presents a sense of community wellness that goes beyond trauma" (Million 2013, 13). I put NMS's decision to implement, as a guiding principle, "a decolonizing politics of collective care"

(D'Arcangelis and Huntley 2012, 45–47) in this light. Our intent was to politicize the caretaking aspects of our work and resist a false dichotomy of emotion (caretaking) versus rationality (political action) (Combahee River Collective 1979; Hanisch 2006; TallBear 2016). To counter the paternalistic, appropriative bent that caretaking can assume in a colonial context, we also stressed an "anticolonial imperative" as an equally important guiding principle. In this way, we committed to centring Indigenous women's leadership while keeping white ally structural privilege in view.

Several Indigenous participants approached caretaking as a reintegration of emotional and political labour. In this way, they reconceptualize healing or caretaking work as something that enhances political struggle while suggesting ways to mitigate the invasive tendencies of helping with a twist, that is, the solidarity impulse, as detailed in Chapter 2. Their approaches conjure up other aspects of the balance white women can look to strike in solidarity work, particularly in antiviolence organizing: caretaking "wounded" Indigenous women or seeking one's own healing (too much proximity) versus negating the particular trauma experienced by Indigenous women or adopting a disembodied approach to solidarity work (too much distance). How to strike this balance? One way is to allocate particular spaces and times for white women allies to grapple with their position as settlers, thereby safeguarding solidarity encounters as spaces where the collective concerns of Indigenous women are not "hijacked" (Kellie). Teresa's thinking on the matter is illustrative. She likened doing solidarity work for the purposes of assuaging white settler guilt to a desire for healing. She soon clarified, however, that while expected, this behaviour is neither warranted nor acceptable:

> But, for Western women coming to an Indigenous circle looking for their own healing? [The solidarity encounter] is *not* the place to do it ... We understand that [desiring to be free from guilt] is a reason why many Western women are coming to the table, but not to take away space or place from an Indigenous woman at the table who's attempting to heal ... because our healing has not really been given precedence at all, so at those tables, that's what needs to be given precedence. I think that Western healing must be done kind of on an individual basis, given different time ... But when it comes time to organizing a National Day of Action, or something that's obviously giving precedence to an Indigenous cause, there's a direct mandate and it's not necessarily for giving room, time, or space for Western healing at that table, right?

Here, Teresa calls for the establishment of parameters around when, how, and where healing work is done, for whom and by whom. In fact, in a subsequent conversation years later, Teresa recounted that she holds the even firmer position that "it is not up to Indigenous women or Indigenous peoples to assist white women in healing *at all*." Admittedly, these safeguards may not trigger a sufficiently radical grappling by white women of the foundational illegitimacy of our settler status. In relation to a framework for non-colonizing solidarity, however, the hope is that enacting such boundaries will help to decentre white women's individualistic needs and recentre Indigenous women's collective political concerns in the solidarity encounter.

Building on Teresa's ideas, and her own counsel to white women "not to take things so personally," Belinda advised white women to exercise caution around the impulse to help Indigenous women who appear visibly upset. Belinda delivered her message, serious though it is, with a healthy dose of humour, "And then there is just letting people cry, just being able to listen, not be panicky and jittery or run for the Kleenex box." Filtered through my framework for non-colonizing solidarity, Belinda's statement invites white women to retain a certain intersubjective distance in the solidarity encounter. More specifically, it suggests that white women curb any overzealous and patronizing impulses we might have to comfort/help/heal Indigenous women.

Maracle seconded Belinda's point:

> To be well, to be healed, is to be entitled to express. Now, someone gets triggered ... All you need to ask is, "Are you okay," and "Do you need something?" ... It's in the moment that you take care of stuff like that. I think we need to take care of each other as much as we can without trying to be therapists ... It's part of the whole invasiveness that goes with being part of the colonial country, and that somehow you're responsible, too. Part of the patriarchy. That women are responsible for somebody else's well-being is part of the patriarchy. And then the colonial thing gets you invading.

Alluding to the spatial nature of the solidarity encounter, both metaphorical and literal, Maracle reminds us of how patriarchy and white supremacy have colluded over time to produce gendered colonial subjectivity. Lamentably, it stands to reason that some white women in the solidarity encounter will feel compelled to help Indigenous women, making the latter's approaches for mitigating that compulsion all the more timely and relevant.

Revisiting the Fraught Promise of (White Woman) Self-Reflexivity

In hindsight, the gist of the participant narratives seems obvious and simple: in theory, solidarity work is not all about us white women. However, this research suggests that lived realities are far more complicated, and praxis far more difficult. As white women, how do we press pause on our solidarity impulses and learn to recognize when our self-making or, less charitably, self-serving needs to achieve good settler status stand to supersede the political needs of Indigenous women and communities? The conundrum, as I now understand it, is how to strike a balance between not enough engagement (staying too distant) and too much of the wrong kind of engagement (getting too close) in solidarity encounters – whether in emotional, psychological, spiritual, intellectual, or material terms. This brings me to a point I cannot emphasize enough: it is the unmitigated impulse to solidarity or the untrammelled pursuit of proximity, rather than the impulse per se, that is the problem. So, putting the question another way, how do white women strike a balance between too little and too much focus on our settler selves?

Part of the answer, I believe, involves a balanced approach to self-reflexivity – hence its inclusion in my framework for non-colonizing solidarity. In the previous chapter, I refer to a range of participant statements about self-reflexivity, all of which consider it a necessary, though partial, element of the perpetual task of negotiating an ethical position as a settler in a colonial system. Also crucial to note, participants did not depict self-reflexivity as a guarantee for achieving non-colonizing solidarity nor as a self-contained, one-off action but rather as a potentially radical aspect of a broader, ongoing non-colonizing process and framework.

Take Green's narrative, in which she offers Guswenta as a model for equitable Indigenous–non-Indigenous social and political relations. In doing so, she implies the value of self-reflexivity for all settlers in and beyond the solidarity encounter. Notably, she uses a spatial metaphor to explain her point:

> Guswenta means that we walk beside each other. We travel the same road. When people say, "It shouldn't be about the settler," I'm like, "but Paulo Freire says you can't deal with oppression unless the oppressor also understands and decolonizes." So how can it not be about the settler as well, as problematic as that may be for some [Indigenous people in particular]?

Green's statement highlights a paradox that circles throughout this book: political solidarity is simultaneously about and not about the settler, which leads us back to the fraught nature of self-reflexivity as a technique for grappling with structural privilege. Given the balance we must reach, how do white women enlist self-reflexivity to "check" our power and privilege, as Eve advises in Chapter 4, and to curb the invasive, appropriative, self-making behaviours that can sustain tensions and the colonial status quo in solidarity encounters? Put squarely in the theoretical terms of this book, how can we mobilize self-reflexivity as part of a settler praxis that disrupts rather than reproduces the autonomous liberal subject imagined as capable of transcending structural power inequalities? In short, how do we create nondominating selves who respect boundaries in the ways described above by Indigenous participants?

Two other Indigenous participants, Ursula and Tabobondung, provided anecdotal evidence to explain their thoughts on how white settlers should employ – or not employ – self-reflexivity. I turn first to Tabobondung, who, at my prompting, shared how she would respond if she were asked by a white settler, "I'm from here. I'm from Canada. That's my history. What do you want me to do? Go back seven generations to Scotland?":

> Yes, definitely, that's what we're talking about, is going back, knowing who you are in Canadian history ... Non-Indigenous people are the people who need to go back the most, because their history has led to where we are today ... They need to go back to their creation story, deconstruct it. You see right within that interpretation of it is the separation from nature, the dominion of man over animals, the dominion of man over women, disempowerment of women [and] how that has evolved to patriarchy, the history of witch burnings, of all this attack on women. That's not a long history in the history of humanity ... They see it as reality now, and it's not. Because non-Native people, or white people, have so much power; if they were to deconstruct it, that would be the biggest change ... If they were to alter their ways of thinking, that would create the most change.

To be clear, Tabobondung is *not* suggesting that settlers "go back to where you came from." Instead, she describes a best-case scenario wherein self-reflexivity leads to a deconstruction of and shift in colonial power relations. Like Maracle, she also draws our attention to patriarchy's insidious part in colonial domination. In addition, by pointing out in the plural, "non-Native people or white people have some much power," she infers that self-reflexivity must have a collective component to be a viable part of non-colonizing solidarity and to facilitate a shift in colonial power relations.

Rewriting Colonial Scripts 219

Ursula touched even more directly on colonial dispossession and Indigenous struggles to reclaim land and the potential material implications of settlers reflecting deeply on these topics.[5] Halfway through the interview, I asked Ursula if solidarity is more difficult to foster around certain issues; she mentioned land without hesitation. I include the lengthy exchange that ensued to do justice to Ursula's ideas and my own interlocutory role in the conversation:

> *URSULA:* I think that's a big thing, is land reclamation, and whose land are we on. Not just giving a small, "Yes, we're on Mississauga territory," but actually really acknowledging whose territory are we on, and what does that mean. If we're on stolen land, how do we rectify that, for real, tangibly? How do we live in a good way?
>
> *CAROL LYNNE:* Yeah, I always feel really odd saying, "I'd like to recognize the traditional people of this land," just because I feel like it is an empty gesture ... Because I'm not really doing anything else concrete. It just feels like "blah, blah, blah."
>
> *URSULA:* Yeah, and I remember in one of our decolonization [class] discussions, a Japanese woman stood up, and she said, "Well, I came here for school, and my question to you is, should I go home after I've done my degree? Because I'm just trying to figure out now if I'm going to stay here and live my life here, or if I should go home, because I'm realizing I'm in a system where maybe this is not something I should take for granted." A Native Elder stood up and said, "Go home," and she did. She went home after she [graduated], and she continues to do Indigenous solidarity work there, specifically with [a First Nation] in BC.
>
> *CAROL LYNNE:* That's awesome. Did the Elder elaborate?
>
> *URSULA:* I think he did, but it was a long time ago. All I remember is everyone's, like, you could hear a pin drop when he stood up and said, "Go home." Then white people started crying. I remember one white woman started crying. Emotions were really running high. Because he's telling her to go home. What does that mean?
>
> *CAROL LYNNE:* What does that mean for everybody else? Yeah.
>
> *URSULA:* It's a hard issue. I think that issue, the most out of any one, is the most difficult.

Setting aside the necessary and worthwhile discussion we could have about the meaning and effectiveness of land acknowledgments, I want to think through what this exchange indicates about self-reflexivity as part of a framework for non-colonizing solidarity. First, it appears Ursula would agree with Tabobondung that self-reflexivity when optimally employed leads to profound alterations in settler attitudes and behaviours. Second, there are no guarantees that self-reflexivity will lead to these things. The fact that Ursula's sharpest memories consist of a "white woman who started crying" and "emotions running high" corroborates the idea that gendered colonial subjectivity in its current iteration predisposes white women to "bad feelings" (Ahmed 2004) and to seeking absolution. Indeed, a solipsistic approach to self-reflexivity – that is, one that focuses only on the self – may be what brings white women to this state or keeps us there.

The main takeaway from these narratives is that to disrupt settler subject business as usual requires a dramatic change in how settlers understand ourselves – not only, or even primarily, as individuals but as situated within a collectivity. Critical race and anticolonial studies scholar Leslie Thielen-Wilson's remedy is anticolonial agency. Validating my emphasis on the interplay between individual and collective subjectivity, Thielen-Wilson (2012, 312) writes, "The shift in consciousness required for genuine decolonization, hinges upon the settler's ability to understand that he/she (individually and as a collective) does not rightfully belong here."[6] Exercising anticolonial agency, in other words, starts with white settlers coming to grips with our illegitimate tenancy on Indigenous lands. Moreover, it requires sitting with "the discomfiting emotions" that accompany solidarity work, as Katie Boudreau Morris (2017, 469) reminds us. More than that, Elizabeth (Liz) Carlson-Manathara and Gladys Rowe (2021) suggest in their new book that it would require "living in Indigenous sovereignty."[7] In line with these thinkers and Tabobondung, among other participants, my concern here lies in how self-reflexivity can facilitate such a shift.

Emma LaRocque (2010, 6) gestures toward the historical enormity of the task. Her review of "Native-positive White constructions" in "Canada's" historical records uncovers the unfortunate reality that "even those who spoke against European cruelties or European thefts did not call for an abandonment of colonial projects." To my mind, their omission indicates an inability to link individual identity (and transformation) to colonial structures (and their dismantlement). For several participants, including Eve, Ursula, Amadahy, Tabobondung, and Whitebird, the solution lies not in words but in deeds – in the "doing" of activism and not in the confessing of privilege. Their advice to white women? Grapple with the structural illegitimacy and precarity at the core of your gendered colonial subjectivity without ending up "stuck" in the process, as Amadahy put it (see Chapter 4), and move on to the work of dismantling settler colonialism in Canada.

Following these ideas and recommendations, I propose a form of self-reflexivity that would be more akin to critical analysis than unadulterated self-discovery. My approach builds on Harjeet Badwall's work on racism and colonialism in social work education and practice. Badwall (2016, 8–10) finds that white social workers, the majority of whom are women, practise critical reflexivity in ways that reconstitute themselves as "good" and "loving" people. In such instances, critical reflexivity consists of nonperformative declarations (Ahmed 2004) described by Badwall (2016, 5) as "heroic narrations in which [white subjects'] reflections about whiteness, power, and bad practice restore their professional identities back to a place of innocence." Noting a comparable limitation of the practice, Barbara Heron (2005, 348) calls for recalibrating self-reflexivity as a process in which social workers fully examine "the constitutive effects of being in a structured position of power over other people," as opposed to simply naming their social location.

Proceeding from there, I suggest radical reflexivity as a way for white women in the solidarity encounter to withstand the discomfort of fathoming these effects, and not succumb to trying to prove our moral goodness or capacity for transcendence. In the spirit of dialogue, I offer this idea for our consideration. Radical reflexivity, understood as a combination of critical analysis plus self-reflection, might enable allies to strike a balance between an inordinate focus on the individual settler self, on the one hand, and evaporation of individual accountability, on the other. (Notably, the latter is a fantasy perpetuated by the good–bad settler binary, which I discuss in Chapter 4.) Allow me to explain. As a prefix to "self-reflexivity," "radical" denotes the fundamental structural change on whose behalf we (could) enlist self-reflexivity. In other words, radical self-reflexivity would expose the roots of the problem with proximity. It would involve a comprehensive examination of, to quote Simpson (2017, 48), "the roots of the settler colonial present – capitalism, white supremacy, heteropatriarchy, and anti-Blackness" and an explicit acknowledgment of "dispossession as the meta-dominating force" in Indigenous dealings with the Canadian state. Simpson, like Ursula and so many others, brings us back to the elephant in the room – stolen Indigenous land. Thielen-Wilson (2012, 312) further explains why understanding colonial dispossession is paramount to my framework for non-colonizing solidarity: "Settlers cannot change who we are – that is, we cannot begin to engage in human behaviour toward the other – without first recognizing and addressing how land (and its usurpation justified by a rational desire for accumulation) is central to white settler collective identity." It is again worth highlighting her focus on the collective dimension of white settler subjectivity, which we often overshadow with our individual/liberal orientation to the world.

Therefore, radical self-reflexivity earns a central place in my framework for non-colonizing solidarity. I anticipate that it could assist white women to recognize and disrupt the coconstituted desires to help and to be helped by that Indigenous women so often find invasive. More specifically, this could entail interrogating any exaggerated sense of entitlement we have to "do/be good." It could mean questioning our presumptions of unfettered access to Indigenous spaces or our capacity to "know" the Other and "fix" things. Above all, it could mean carefully considering our tendencies to claim the status of an exceptional good settler who has earned an exemption from complicity in colonial relations.

As I have discussed elsewhere, we can compare radical self-reflexivity to the autoethnographic notion of self-reflexivity as method: both require us to examine ourselves as a window into the operation, and eventual transformation, of the social structures in which we are fully entrenched (D'Arcangelis 2018). To ensure that that window opens – and stays open – I suggest performing an adapted version of the self-reflexive "double turn" Ahmed advocates in relation to whiteness studies. Ahmed (2004, para. 59) explains the double turn as follows:

> To turn toward whiteness is to turn toward and away from those bodies who have been afforded agency and mobility by such privilege. In other words, the task for white subjects would be to stay implicated in what they critique, but in turning toward their role and responsibility in these histories of racism, as histories of this present, to turn away from themselves, and toward others. This "double turn" is not sufficient, but it clears some ground, upon which the work of exposing racism might provide the conditions for another kind of work.

To take a double turn in the solidarity encounter would mean reflecting on our status as white women but not stopping there, for example, mired in guilt. Put another way, it would mean balancing the two competing spirals of non-Indigenous activist reflection and action identified by Chris Hiller (2017, 432), namely, "an upward spiral, focused outward" to acknowledge and work to dismantle settler colonial structures and "a downward spiral, focused inward ... to pull apart [our] own base assumptions, entrenched colonial mindsets, and deeply held investments in white settler privilege while also grappling with Indigenous difference." I share both Hiller's faith in critical praxis and Ahmed's guarded optimism that practising self-reflexivity in a way that "turns toward others" would deepen our critiques of white settler colonialism, in turn paving the way for different solidarity interactions.

Might a double turn open the door to a different kind of gendered colonial subject – still implicated, still marked as colonial but with non-colonizing sensibilities? I would describe her as a white woman who takes on the responsibility of tackling colonial inequities while having learned to "not take things personally" (Belinda). Ahmed (2004, para. 59) is right to remind us, "We don't know, as yet, what such conditions might be, or whether we are even up to the task of recognizing them." However, I am confident that a double turn would bring us closer to thinking past our white settler/liberal selves and toward the self–other in relation, to return full circle to Makere Stewart-Harawira's (2007) sentiment that set the tone of this book. A double turn would firmly plant us on the path to "other ways of being in relation, politically transforming all parties and our relationships with one another, and to transition toward a future ethos, the scope of which may be beyond a foreseeable progression" (Flowers 2015, 47). In sum, a double turn puts the odds more in our collective favour by promising to reveal the forest and its trees, that is, to hold in tension the white settler collectivity and the individual white women who form a part of it.

~

Perhaps to restate the obvious, this story for me is at once personal and political, which leads directly to my next point. One of the central lessons I take from this research goes something like this: the desires that individuals often register as personal (if to varying degrees) are more usefully conceptualized as political, that is, as emanating largely from our collective structural positioning, in this case, as white settler women. In no way am I disregarding the heterogeneity of white women and our experiences. Rather, I think we do a disservice to our political efficacy by relegating the structural privileges that we share to an afterthought. I wonder, what would happen if we were to keep the idea of collective structural privilege front and centre? Would it help us to refrain from engaging in the kinds of self-making behaviours that undermine solidarity work and the political projects at hand? Would it help us to disentangle the two sets of white settler desires that are easy to conflate, given that they often coexist and sometimes clash in the colonial present? Of course, I am referring to the insatiable desire for belonging in a colonial context and the desire to engage ethically with Indigenous peoples while undertaking the radical project of dismantling settler colonialism.

As a final remark, I want to revisit the paradoxical terrain of political solidarity – how to forge non-colonizing relations in a context marked by colonial inequalities. A central conundrum under these circumstances is how to foster individual- or micro-level transformations that spark collective- or macro-level transformations. As Victoria Freeman suggests, perhaps "individual and structural changes are interpenetrating," meaning that movement in one necessarily affects the other.[8] Even as I have lingered on the prevailing challenges of intersubjective relations in the solidarity encounter, I share what I take to be Freeman's optimism about the dialogical nature of change. By dialogical, I mean the inevitable back and forth between personal and structural change that for me boils down to the inescapable relationality between self and other. Alongside this hopefulness, I carry an awareness that intersubjective relations in the solidarity encounter, and beyond for that matter, are layered, contingent, and mutable – but ultimately defiant of neat theoretical description.

Notes

Introduction

1 I do not presume that all self-ascribed women in the solidarity encounter necessarily self-identify as feminist, although many of the women I cite do.
2 The Greater Toronto Area (GTA) includes the City of Toronto and the regional municipalities of Durham, Halton, Peel, and York.
3 Throughout this book, and in line with the National Inquiry, I include First Nations, Inuit, and Métis peoples in the category Indigenous. The acronym 2SLGBTQQIA stands for "two-spirit, lesbian, gay, bisexual, transgender, queer, questioning, intersex, and asexual" (NIMMIWG 2019, 7). I use an abbreviated version (2S) in accordance with the increasing prevalence of the acronym MMIWG2S among activists organizing around the issue.
4 Derek Gregory (2004) situates the colonial realities of Afghanistan, Palestine, and Iraq within broader global power relations, an argument that is equally salient to settler colonial contexts such as the United States, Australia, and Canada.
5 Several years have elapsed since I completed this research. In the interim, many have been working across differences of race, gender, class, ability, sexuality, immigration status, age, and more under many banners to demand and create a more just world. (In North America alone, these banners include Idle No More, #MMIWG2S, the Movement for Black Lives, Me Too, and Fridays for Future.) In this book, I examine a small piece of this larger puzzle by looking into the interpersonal relations – or intersubjective relations – of the solidarity encounter.
6 Plains Cree Métis feminist scholar Emma LaRocque (2010, 412) describes the lumping effect, or collapsing of diverse groups of Indigenous peoples along geographical, linguistic, cultural, religious, and political lines into one homogenous category. Māori education scholar Linda Tuhiwai Smith (1999, 27) notes the oversimplification of complex relationships into a binary.

7 Scott Morgensen (2011, 19) writes, "To say that all non-Natives are settlers may fail to explain how settler colonialism conditions non-Natives by 'race' or migrant/immigrant status, while stymieing efforts to link Native, diaspora, and critical race studies in defending Native decolonization." For more on solidarity among Black, Indigenous, people of colour (increasingly referred to as BIPOC) on Turtle Island, see Amadahy and Lawrence (2009); Jafri (2010); Kaur (2014); Khan et al. (2015); King (2019); King, Navarro, and Smith (2020); Lawrence and Dua (2005); Lee (2015); Mawani (2009); Maynard and Simpson (2020); Miles and Holland (2006); Sehdev (2010); Thobani (2007); and Tuck and Yang (2012).

8 For these statistics and more, see City of Toronto (2013). Other sources suggest that the Indigenous population was likely higher. For example, the Our Health Counts Toronto project put the Indigenous population in the City of Toronto in 2016 at about 65,832 (Smylie, O'Brien, Bourgeois, Wolfe, Maddox, and Rotondi 2019).

9 In 2019, Six Nations of the Grand River had 27,559 members, 12,892 of whom lived on reserve (Hele 2019).

10 Victoria Freeman provided invaluable assistance in framing this discussion of the GTA. Personal communication, May 5, 2021.

11 I joined NMS in 2006. It is a Toronto-based group cofounded in 2004 by an activist and documentary filmmaker of mixed Indigenous/Euro-immigrant ancestry and a white feminist educator ally of European ancestry. It works to end the impunity of the police, judiciary, and coroners' offices in cases of MMIWG2S people. Since 2006, NMS has organized an annual Strawberry Ceremony on February 14 in front of Toronto police headquarters to honour the MMIWG2S people of Ontario. For the history of this now nation-wide initiative, see the February 14 Women's Memorial March website. Since 2012, a collective of individuals and groups, including NMS, has organized the event in Toronto.

12 In less than a decade, campaigns to decolonize and indigenize settler colonial place names have taken firm hold in Toronto and beyond. Resignifying Toronto as *Tkaronto*, a Kanien'kehá:ka word meaning, "Where there are trees standing in the water," is a prominent example. See the Tkaronto Indigenous Peoples Portal website for a more comprehensive list of organizations in the GTA.

13 Idle No More (INM) emerged as a Canada-based grassroots movement of Indigenous peoples and allies in late 2012 (Coulthard 2014; Kino-nda-niimi Collective 2014; Monkman and Morin 2017; Morris 2014).

14 The Royal Canadian Mounted Police reported 1,181 cases of missing (164) and murdered (1,017) Indigenous women and girls across Canada (RCMP 2014). Comprising 4 percent of Canada's population, Indigenous women "represent 16 per cent of all murdered females between 1980 and 2012, as well as 12 per cent of all missing females on record" (Trinh 2014, May 2).

15 Simpson mentioned this at a public presentation at Memorial University in St. John's, Newfoundland. Personal communication, May 13, 2014.

16 Aware of the public discrediting of Andrea Smith's claims to Cherokee status, I cite her to be transparent about the impact of her work on my thinking, which predated that discrediting. My decision is influenced by Sámi feminist scholar Rauna Kuokkanen's (2019, 240n21) perspective. She writes, "[Smith's] contributions in the field of

Indigenous feminisms, particularly in establishing colonial, sexual violence as a central means of eroding Indigenous sovereignty, have been considerable, and therefore her work cannot be entirely omitted from the field of Indigenous feminist scholarship."

17 For example, Kanien'kehá:ka (Mohawk) scholar Taiaiake Alfred's critiques of reconciliation discourse convey strong doubts about the possibilities of Indigenous–non-Indigenous political solidarity. Nonetheless, at a University of Toronto public talk, Alfred stated that non-Indigenous allies are needed to advance Indigenous political struggles. Personal communication, February 16, 2012. See also Alfred (2010).

18 As Leanne Betasamosake Simpson (2011, 22) argues, Indigenous resistance is neutralized when institutionalized forms of reconciliation focus on past wrongs such as residential schools, "rather than the broader set of relationships that generated policies, legislation and practices aimed at assimilation and political genocide." Sherene Razack (2004) argues that reconciliation discourses generally cast Indigenous subjects as dysfunctional, traumatized, and in need of healing.

19 Maracle is the executive director of the Ontario Federation of Indigenous Friendship Centres. This point was part of her keynote address at the public forum "Challenging Racism and Appropriation in Our Classrooms and Schools," at the University of Toronto. Personal communication, November 8, 2011.

20 Frankenberg's methodological approach, similar to mine, most resembles narrative ethnography rather than personal experience narrative. David Butz and Kathryn Besio (2009, 1,665) distinguish between narrative ethnography and personal experience narrative, defining the latter as the work of "scholars who focus intensely on their own life circumstances as a way to understand larger social or cultural phenomena." See the writings of Minnie Bruce Pratt (1984) and Mab Segrest (2019) for two iconic examples of white feminist personal experience narratives of antiracist practice.

21 Despite the proliferation of critical whiteness studies in the ensuing years, many scholars insist that whiteness and white privilege in colonial contexts remains underexamined by white people (Borell et al. 2009; Denzin and Lincoln 2008; Grande 2004; Moreton-Robinson 2000).

22 Initially linked to settler and imperial women of British Empire, the category "white settler woman" has evolved to apply to any self-identified woman of European descent who would position herself, or be positioned, as white. Whenever I shorten this phrase to "white woman," I consider "settler" to be implicit.

23 Importantly, I imagine the proximity spectrum as only part of a larger constellation of self-making processes that could involve fantasies of self-discovery, transformation, and transcendence in the sense of overcoming power relations. In other words, many (if not most) white settlers do not pursue proximity through solidarity work in their bids for belonging.

24 For an introduction to Indigenous–non-Indigenous relations from the colonial past, see David A. Nock and Celia Haig-Brown's (2006) edited collection, *With Good Intentions: Euro-Canadian and Aboriginal Relations in Colonial Canada*. Contributors address both the historical limitations of white settler good intentions and the relatively progressive interventions of notable Euro-Canadians. In *Contact Zones: Aboriginal and Settler Women in Canada's Colonial Past* (Pickles and Rutherdale

2005), contributors highlight the complexity of the historically fraught relations between Indigenous women and white women. For more on Canada's fraught colonial history in general, see Miller and Upton (1991) and Miller (2000).

25 In the years since I completed my study, this scholarship has multiplied tenfold, and I cannot possibly do it justice. Nonetheless, I offer this limited snapshot organized by theme. There are case studies on topics such as the Coalition for a Public Inquiry into Ipperwash (Davis, O'Donnell, and Shpuniarsky 2007), Indigenous–non-Indigenous peace-building initiatives (Wallace 2014), the Raging Grannies (Chazan 2016), and Idle No More (Barker 2015). Some scholars focus on alliances with specific Indigenous communities such as the Lubicon First Nation (Funk-Unrau 2005; Long 1997) and the Winnemem Wintu Tribe (Bacon 2017), or on fishing and environmental struggles (Davis 2009, 2010; Lipsitz 2008). Others muse about the Occupy Movement and prospects of anarchist–Indigenous solidarity (Barker 2012; Barker and Pickerill 2012; Lagalisse 2017; Lewis 2017; Mott 2018). Still others consider decolonizing approaches to research and/or pedagogy (Bull 2010; Carlson 2017; Fortier 2017; Wallace 2011). Finally, there is also a vibrant body of literature on reconciliation since the 2008 establishment of the Truth and Reconciliation Commission on Indian Residential Schools (IRS) and the Harper government's apology to IRS survivors (Castellano 2011; Denis 2020; Denis and Bailey 2016; Henderson and Wakeham 2013; Kaye 2016; Regan, 2010; Rogers, DeGagné, Dewar, and Lowry 2012).

26 Several of the contributions to "Pathways of Settler Decolonization," a special issue of *Settler Colonial Studies* (Davis, Denis, and Sinclair 2017), consider aspects of settler subjectivity using other terms such as "settler common sense" (Hiller 2017), "settler consciousness" (Davis et al. 2017) and "settler collective identity" (Bacon 2017).

27 Davis and Shpuniarsky's (2010) list is a distillation of their findings from the Alliances Project, which consisted of three case studies.

28 Sandy Grande (2004, 9) adapts the term "whitestream," itself an adaptation by Claude Denis (1997) of feminist theory's "malestream." See also Maile Arvin, Eve Tuck, and Angie Morrill (2013, 17).

29 A key Indigenous feminist tenet is the centrality of colonialism in shaping Indigenous women's historical and ongoing oppression and resistance (see Arvin, Tuck, and Morrill 2013; Green 2007b, 2007c, 2017b; Monture-Angus 1995; Simpson 2017).

30 Many references to Indigenous–non-Indigenous solidarity appear within Indigenous feminist scholarship, which reclaims feminism as a tool for theorizing the gendered aspects of colonial oppression and envisaging change (see Arvin, Tuck, and Morrill 2013; Barker 2017; Green 2007a, 2007b, 2007c, 2017a, 2017b; Mihesuah 2003; Nickel and Fehr 2020; Suzack et al. 2010).

31 Indigenous and equity studies scholar Bonita Lawrence (Mi'kmaq) contends that the Western ideas about individualism that underpin mainstream feminist praxis are "based on the denial of even the existence of community" (Anderson 2000, 275).

32 The assertion that hierarchical gender relations in North American Indigenous nations are at least partially (if not largely) a colonial imposition is widespread (see, for example, Anderson 2000, 2016; Bourgeois 2006; Deerchild 2003; Grande 2004; Green 2007c, 2017b; Gunn Allen 1986; Henning 2007; Horn-Miller 2005; Jaimes Guerrero 1997; Johnson, Stevenson, and Greschner 1993; Ladner 2000; LaRocque 2007; Lawrence and Anderson 2005; Maracle 2006; McGowan 2006; Mihesuah 2003; Million 2008; Monture-Angus 1995; Nickel and Fehr 2020; Pyle 2020; Simpson 2011,

2017; Smith 2005a; Smith and Kauanui 2008; Stevenson 1999; Stewart-Harawira 2007; Sunseri 2008; Turpel 1993).

33 Rauna Kuokkanen (2012, 239) points out that Indigenous traditions that presumably respect women "have been employed to re-inscribe domination and patriarchal structures" (see also Kuokkanen 2019).

34 In *Warrior Life*, Pam Palmater (Mi'kmaq) (2020) provides an historical overview of these efforts. See also Kahnawake filmmaker Courtney Montour's recent documentary (2021) on the life of Mary Two-Axe Earley, a Kanien'kehá:ka woman credited for kick-starting a six-decade, ongoing movement to amend the Indian Act.

35 According to Tanana Athabascan scholar Dian Million (2008, 269), mainstream second-wave feminist struggles in Canada "were slow to recognize the double indemnity of race and sexual discrimination – much less the necessity for solidarity with sovereignty and self-determination activists." Devon Abbot Mihesuah (Choctaw) (2003) describes a similar dynamic in 1970s mainstream feminism in the United States.

36 The scholars who have most influenced my thinking, not mentioned elsewhere, include Angela Davis (1983, 1989); Enakshi Dua and Angela Robertson (1999); Chandra Mohanty (1984, 1991); Cherie Moraga and Gloria Anzaldúa (1981); Sherene Razack, Malinda Smith, and Sunera Thobani (2010); and Trinh T. Minh-ha (1989, 1997).

37 This includes cultural, critical whiteness, development, and postcolonial feminist studies scholars such as Renée Bergland (2000), Denise Ferreira da Silva (2007), Richard Dyer (1997), Anne McClintock (1995), Mary Louise Pratt (2008), María Josefina Saldaña-Portillo (2003), Andrea Smith (2013), Gayatri Spivak (1985), Ann Stoler (1995), and Sylvia Wynter (2003).

38 M/C group adherents claim that modernity/coloniality, as a new global model of power, began with the colonization of the Americas and the subsequent "Eurocentrification of world capitalism" in accordance with the "social classification of the world's population around the idea of race" (Quijano 2000, 533, 537). For more on the M/C group as a political and theoretical project in the late 1990s and early 2000s, see Asher (2013), Escobar (2007), Lugones (2010), Mignolo (2007), and Mignolo and Walsh (2018).

39 Anne McClintock (1995) and Ann Laura Stoler (1995) discuss this complexity in meticulous detail. Other works in the extensive, interdisciplinary literature on the history of gendered colonial/imperial relations include Lewis (1996), Loomba (2005), Ray (2009), Ware (1992), and Woollacott (2006). For a Canadian-focused discussion, see Pickles and Rutherdale (2005) and Rutherdale (2005).

40 Feminist historian Mariana Valverde (1992, 3) locates Canadian feminism within an ethnocentric, and increasingly racist, English-speaking international women's movement. For more on gender and coloniality in Canada, see Barman and Hare (2006), Carter (1997, 2006), Carter et al. (2005), Fiamengo (1999), Henderson (2003), Iacovetta and Valverde (1992), Perry (2001), Pickles (2002), Pickles and Rutherdale (2005), Rutherdale (2002, 2005), Strong-Boag (1977), Thobani (2007), Valverde (1991), and Van Kirk (1980).

41 Moodie is generally portrayed in benign terms as an English émigré to Canada who became the renowned author of *Roughing It in the Bush* (1852) and *Life in the Clearings versus the Bush* (1853). See Faculty of Humanities and Social Sciences, Athabasca University (2015).

42 Clare Midgley (2007, 8) cautions against anachronistically labelling someone a feminist prior to the late nineteenth century. Therefore, I use the term "protofeminist"

to refer to white women who were variously involved in the women's movement (see also Cott 1987; Offen 2000).
43 Critical race feminist scholar Sunera Thobani (2007, 306n40) singles out the Woman's Christian Temperance Union (WCTU) and the National Council of Women (NCW) as leading examples of women's groups that employed discourses of racial supremacy to further their own agendas.
44 Historian Patricia Roome (2005) warns against a simplistic reading of a monolithic racism on the part of Euro-Canadian settler feminists, as some were likely more "self-consciously oppositional" than others (Lewis 1996). For Roome (2005, 63), Henrietta Muir Edwards (1849–1931), one of the Famous Five, sits apart from other settler feminists because of her "tolerant and benevolent," if condescending, attitude toward Indigenous women. Amelia McLean Paget (1867–1922) was the daughter of an elite Hudson's Bay Company fur trader in Fort Simpson (present-day Northwest Territories). According to feminist historian Sarah Carter (2006), Paget challenged many of the misperceptions and derogatory stereotypes about Indigenous peoples in mid- to late nineteenth-century Canada. But even Paget ascribed to racial thinking by invoking "prevailing ideas about the 'vanishing race'" toward Indigenous peoples (Carter 2006, 218–9). As for Edwards, as a missionary in Canada, she embraced "motherhood and religion, the two pillars of Christian feminism" and tried to instill these beliefs in Indigenous women within her sphere of influence (Roome 2005, 68).
45 Uma Narayan (2000, 95) points out that this move obscured the exploitation and abject poverty of working-class white women in both metropole and colony. Noting that the freedom–unfreedom binary maps onto the historical construction of "East" versus "West," Narayan adds that the "'insistence on cultural difference' ... helped to cover over the sad similarities of ethnocentrism, androcentrism, classism, heterosexism, and other objectionable 'centrisms' that often pervaded both sides of this reiterated 'contrast' between 'Western culture' and its several 'Others.'"
46 Literary and cultural studies scholar Jennifer Henderson (2003, 12) depicts nineteenth-century liberal feminism in Canada similarly.
47 Ahmed's (2000) depiction of dominant self-making builds on a wealth of literature by Indigenous, postcolonial, and cultural studies scholars, including Kim Anderson (Cree-Métis) (2000), Bergland (2000), hooks (1992), and Yeğenoğlu (1998), who count the desire to consume or become the Other as a classic colonizing move.
48 I adapted antiracist feminist scholar Himani Bannerji's (1993, ix) classic title *Returning the Gaze: Essays on Racism, Feminism and Politics*, which counters the "unimaginable absence and silencing" of the critical voices of "nonwhite" women in Canadian scholarly publishing at the time.
49 While my concern with political solidarity covers some of the same issues in the literature on social solidarity associated with Emile Durkheim, including individualism and social relations, I do not share the latter's central concern over social cohesion or its breakdown (Crow 2002).
50 In the original passage, Razack (1998, 5) focuses on the "woman of colour" subject, aiming for "a gendered version of Fanon's goal [in *Black Skin, White Masks*] – the liberation of the woman of colour from herself, her release from the gaze and its consequences."

Chapter 1: The Spectrum of Proximity

1 Among other questions, I asked white participants if they used the term "white settler" to describe themselves. About one-third offered reasons for doing solidarity work without any prompting – what Carol Schick (1998, 162) describes as a significant "unbidden" response in that it could indicate, in this case, a desire on the part of white women to perform themselves and be "seen" by the interviewer in normative ways.
2 To be fair, I did not press Alicia to share more of her perspective on the history of women's/feminist struggles. Taken at face value, however, this statement accords with a rather narrow, homogenized understanding of women's movements during the so-called second wave in North America, which risks discounting the vast contributions of diverse groups of women, including working-class women, Indigenous women, and women of colour.
3 Dawn prefers the term "partnerships" to solidarity because she associates the latter with union organizing.
4 Sara Ahmed (2000, 63–64) finds a similar phenomenon in the "logic of equalization" that underpins the "democratization of ethnography" where ethnographer and informant ostensibly become coauthors of knowledge.
5 For a more fulsome understanding of the gendered aspects of the solidarity encounter, in future research I would like to interview self-ascribed settler men and non-binary people as well as Indigenous men and two-spirit or non-binary Indigenous people.
6 Sherene Razack's (2002) analysis of white settler masculine dominance is a useful touchstone for this speculation. On April 17, 1995, Pamela George, a Saulteaux woman from the Sakimay First Nation near Regina, Saskatchewan, was killed by two young white men – Steven Kummerfield and Alex Ternowetsky. In analyzing the murder, Razack (2002, 136) argues that white settler men reconstitute their dominance by moving with ease between so-called zones of respectability and degeneracy, while committing violence against Indigenous women with impunity in the latter. Razack distills her point using a spatial analysis: "For [the young white man], violence establishes the boundary between who he is and who he is not."
7 In fact, Chloe flatly rejects the insinuation that guilt has been in any way operative in her solidarity work. See Chapter 4 for a fuller treatment of the fallout of white settler guilt in solidarity encounters.

Chapter 2: Transgressing Cherished Spaces

1 Mohanty (2003) situates her commitment to centre the knowledge of marginalized communities within feminist standpoint theories on the epistemic privilege of such communities (see also Hill Collins 2000; Harding 2004). Rebecca Clark Mane (2012, 76) agrees that epistemic privilege is often a consequence of having "to critically navigate dominant worldviews and to make sense of ... alternative and marginalized experiences" but notes that critical "standpoint is achieved (and contested and constantly under revision and historically contingent) ... not guaranteed."

2 Maracle's father was from Tsleil-Waututh, and her mother was Métis.
3 In a postinterview follow-up email, Maracle broadened her response to depict a life steeped in political activism: "Politics is the extension of law, first of all. To struggle politically is to try and defeat one law with another law, and of course, that means my whole life has been one of activism, political activism." Personal communication, January 23, 2012.
4 See, for example, Barnett and Weiss (2008), Bornstein and Redfield (2011), Heron (2007), Mahrouse (2007, 2008, 2009a, 2009b, 2011), Mindry (2001), Saldaña-Portillo (2003), and Williams (2010).
5 Mary Louise Pratt (2008) developed the concept of planetary consciousness to describe a particularly European understanding of the world that emerged out of the circumnavigation and map-making practices of European explorers in the sixteenth century and one that intensified with the systematization of nature in the eighteenth century. This gave rise to an elite "European global or planetary subject [who] is European, male, secular, and lettered; his planetary consciousness is the product of his contact with culture and infinitely more 'compleat' than the lived experiences of sailors" (Pratt 2008, 29–30). Importantly, this racialized, gendered, and classed consciousness is marked by a totalizing view, a belief in the subject's capacity to know, organize, and exploit the world and its Others.
6 These words are from Wilson's public presentation that I attended at Ryerson University. Personal communication, 2012. Wilson (2008) is well known for his depiction of research as a sacred endeavour, hence his point in this talk that scholars must enter into ethical and accountable relationships with ideas as well as people.
7 Rachel Flowers's (2015, 38) similar casting of the white desire for recognition springs to mind: "In the city, in the classroom, or at a protest, there is always a settler seeking my recognition."
8 At the time, the group formed part of a broader network of Indigenous–non-Indigenous solidarity organizations across Ontario. The group has since disbanded.
9 The Oka Crisis was a seventy-eight-day standoff in 1990 between the Kanien'kehá:ka (Mohawk people) of Kanesatake, the Sûréte du Québec, and the Canadian military over the planned expansion of a golf course (Deer 2018). See also Simpson and Ladner (2010).
10 In line with Heron, Ahmed (2000) tells us that the desire to "know" the Other constitutes, rather than breaks down, the binary relationship between the "we" and those constituted as "strange/strangers."
11 I provide a detailed assessment of such unilateral self-ascriptions and other types of declarations in Chapter 4.

Chapter 3: Risky Romanticization

1 The scholarship on multiculturalism contains well-developed critiques of cultural approaches to difference. See Bannerji (2000), Burman (2016), Mackey (2002), Mahtani (2002), and Thobani (2007).
2 Erickson (2011, 21–22) describes Belaney as an "early-twentieth-century Canadian writer who achieved national notoriety in the 1930s as a proponent of wilderness

conservation" and whose accepted antics of Indian surrogacy link "the discourse of whiteness, and the field of visibility that race relies upon, to the iconic wilderness of Canada."

3 Emma LaRocque (2010, 125–27) and education scholar Susan Dion (Lenape/Potawatomi) (2009), among others, discuss the myth of the "vanishing Indian" and the damage it has wrought on Indigenous peoples.

4 See Robert Berkhofer's (1978, xiv) earlier work on how "the White image of the Indian developed over time." See also Francis (1992), Goldie (1989), and Nock and Haig-Brown (2006).

5 With this, LaRocque reminds us that the white settler desire for proximity is often a desire to be close to imagined Indigenous peoples (Francis 1992). Erickson (2011, 24) notes a prime Canadian example in Belaney, who, despite acquiring first-hand knowledge of Ojibwe, Cree, and Métis cultures, "was reluctant to abandon the images he had formed as a child [in England], including that of First Nations dancing."

6 According to Willow (2009, 59n6), one negative by-product of romanticizing Indigenous peoples' relationships to the land as inherently ecological is the failure to appreciate the ways in which Indigenous environmentalism is linked to broader struggles of Indigenous self-determination.

7 See Toni Morrison's (1993) classic work on the present absence of Africans and African Americans in the United States white literary imagination. Kobayashi, Cameron, and Baldwin (2011, 3) note a present absence in Canadian pianist Glenn Gould's ruminations on "The Idea of North," the title of his CBC radio program.

8 White feminist erasures of the specificity of violence against Indigenous women, girls, and two-spirit people stand in stark contrast to efforts in the current political moment to centre those concerns. For many, the National Inquiry into Missing and Murdered Indigenous Women and Girls is emblematic of these efforts.

9 Critical whiteness scholar Robyn Wiegman (1999) uses "identificatory mobility" slightly differently to describe the process through which white people develop progressive political positions.

10 I am indebted to Arie Molema for sharing his insights into these matters. Personal communication, October 2011.

11 Champlain is an integral player in this discourse. Saul (2008, 10) quotes Champlain as having said, "'Our young men will marry your daughters, and we shall be one people' ... With this sentence, he reveals the nature of the First Nation/European relationship – at the very least one of equals. His masters in Paris sent him constant instructions to subject the locals to French control, to assert European racial, cultural, and political superiority. He was on the spot. He knew better. He knew what reality required. That he made such a declaration suggests that he felt his colony's position to be weak. But it also suggests that he believed such a mix of the two civilizations could work."

12 Personal communication, September 2010.

13 For more on Indigenous conceptualizations of motherhood, see Anderson (2011), Lavell-Harvard and Anderson (2014), and Lavell-Harvard and Lavell (2006).

14 These women spearheaded efforts to redress gender discrimination in the Indian Act (especially the "marrying out" clause, which revoked a woman's "Indian" status if she married a man without status). Bill C-31, a 1985 amendment to the Indian

Act, permitted women and their children (but not grandchildren) to regain status and band councils to establish membership rules. In *Club Native*, Kanien'kehá:ka documentary filmmaker Tracey Deer (2008) paints a vivid picture of the stakes involved when Indigenous women (and others to a lesser degree) test membership rules. For more on gender discrimination in the Indian Act and efforts to amend it, see Eberts (2014), Lawrence (2003, 2004), Palmater (2011), Silman and Tobique Women's Group (1987), Simpson (2009, 2014), Simpson (2017), Stote (2015), and Vowel (2016).

15 In Chapter 1, I discussed choice as a defining feature of some white participants' engagement in solidarity in contrast with Indigenous participant descriptions of solidarity as sometimes a default outcome or requisite aspect of political activism.

16 Interestingly, while solidarity per se was not the goal, interpersonal friendship played a crucial role in cementing Whitebird's participation in the group. She joined at the behest of a close Indigenous woman friend. As I discuss in Chapter 4, Whitebird's description of friendship as a motivating factor for her involvement in solidarity is not akin to friendship as a technique of knowledge applied by the dominant subject (Ahmed 2000).

17 See Chapter 4 for further discussion about the roles that friendship and guilt can play in white women's impulses to exceptionalism, which, I argue, we often seek through/as proximity.

18 I have only gradually become aware of the priority Indigenous women give to solidarity work with Black people and other racialized groups. I learned a hard lesson in 2017 when creating questions for a public panel I was to moderate. The panelists included one Indigenous woman, one Black woman, and one white woman. In short, the consensus was that my questions rehearsed whiteness and needed to be changed.

19 Simpson's (2011, 27n19) work on Indigenous resurgence is also among this literature, which is but one iteration of Indigenous intellectualism and theory as developed by "Elders, Faith-Keepers, Clan-Mothers, traditional leaders, Grandmothers, Grandfathers, language-keepers and Knowledge-Holders, not western-trained academics."

20 Among other topics, scholars discuss the complex interplay between colonially imposed patriarchal "traditions," Indigenous self-determination, and cultural resurgence. See D'Arcangelis (2010), FIMI (2006), Green (2007a), Kuokkanen (2019), Ladner (2000), Starblanket (2017), and Sunseri (2000).

21 Because the non-Indigenous mainstream often depoliticizes Indigenous resurgence movements as "cultural," Simpson (2017, 50) intentionally refers to radical resurgence as a way to recoup resurgence's "revolutionary potential, that is, its potential to offer robust, ethical, and sustainable alternatives to settler colonialism." For more on Indigenous resurgence, see Alfred and Corntassel (2005), Coburn (2015), Corntassel (2008, 2012), Starblanket (2017), and Wilson (2015).

22 See Kuokkanen's (2007) formulation of the debate in relation to Sámi society.

23 In our interview, Whitebird cited a deadly example of appropriation: "I've been following the trial of the man in Sedona that had a sweat lodge, one of those new age life-coaching things they have now; that he put people into a box, and heated that box, and four people died. They keep calling it a sweat lodge. That wasn't a sweat lodge; it was a death box. We get the fall-out from that. What has changed now is

that when we organize sweat lodges, we have to have a release. So, if you get hurt, you know you've been given one of those things. During that trial, that man said he wasn't responsible for anyone in his so-called sweat. One of my first teachings was that I was responsible for anyone who goes in that door. I'm responsible for their life when they go in there. I don't take that lightly. How do you invite someone into a ceremony and not be responsible?"

Chapter 4: Claiming Exceptionalism as the Rule

1 Ahmed (2004, para. 5) uses the work of Richard Dyer (1997) and Ruth Frankenberg (1993) to cite some of the better-known critiques of critical whiteness studies: reifying whiteness into "an essential something," recentring whiteness in overall research, and refuelling the "narcissism that elevates whiteness into a social and bodily ideal."
2 Wiegman wrote at the turn of the twenty-first century. Two decades later, in the era of Black Lives Matter and campaigns to defund the police, United States white liberals may be more inclined than ever to distance themselves from overt acts of white supremacy.
3 In their introduction to "Pathways of Settler Decolonization," Lynne Davis, Jeff Denis, and Raven Sinclair (2017, 394) remind readers upfront about the limitations of friendship as a strategy for change: "Transforming social relations is not just a matter of befriending Indigenous people; it means developing long-term relations of accountability, engaging in meaningful dialogue, and respecting Indigenous laws and jurisdiction."
4 Such worries were not exclusive to white participants. Recall Kellie, a self-ascribed light-skinned Indigenous woman who worried about being misidentified as a white do-gooder: "I like my hair blonde. I don't want to be dying my hair to think that I'll get an easier ride. I deserve to be called on my privileges ... But I'm afraid of being considered one of those white do-gooders who actually ends up doing more harm than good."
5 A central critique of mainstream reconciliation discourses is that they function by demarcating past from present in a way that absolves settler subjects without redressing historical and ongoing wrongdoings. While these critiques are important and warranted, I do not review them in any detail in this book. For a recent assessment of the state of reconciliation in Canada, listen to a podcast on *Media Indigena: Indigenous Current Affairs* (Harp 2021).
6 Heron (2007, 47–8) describes the comparable struggle of a white/northern woman development worker to feel exceptional vis-à-vis other such workers: "Carol's attempt to distance herself from the more overtly altruistic, helping/saving motivations expressed by many participants actually serves at this point to place her further up on the moral high ground in her accounting to herself."
7 Kowal (2011, 316) is referring to her research participants – non-Indigenous employees at the Darwin Institute of Indigenous Health in Australia, most of whom "would comfortably identify with the label 'White antiracist' and its common associations with a middle-class background, tertiary education, and progressive political views."

8 See also Chapter 3, where I discussed the way that this fantasy can take hold, particularly as evidenced in the narratives of white participants Dawn and Chloe.

Chapter 5: Rewriting Colonial Scripts

1 While beyond the scope of this book, one prominent set of ideas is that Indigenous feminist criticism of patriarchal forms of Indigenous nationhood or self-determination struggles (Million 2013; Sunseri 2000) alongside Indigenous feminist notions of relational sovereignty (D'Arcangelis 2010; Kuokkanen 2019) could move us beyond the nation-state structure (Arvin, Tuck, and Morrill 2013; Simpson 2009, 2014; Smith 2008).
2 For more on the theory that social relations constitute place, see the seminal works of feminist geographers Doreen Massey (1994) and Linda McDowell (1999).
3 In referencing the potential for white allies to be pulled into all the conflict, Belinda alludes to the injurious power dynamics and horizontal violence that can erupt in Indigenous groups because of internalized colonialism. Other Indigenous participants – Danielle, Lydia, and Gabriela in particular – also mentioned the damage wrought by internalized colonialism in Indigenous families, organizations, and communities.
4 Here is a telling excerpt from the Combahee River Collective statement (1979, 7, "Problems," para. 3): "The psychological toll of being a Black woman and the difficulties this presents in reaching political consciousness and doing political work can never be underestimated. There is a very low value placed upon Black women's psyches in this society, which is both racist and sexist."
5 For a comprehensive look at settler colonial land dispossession in Canada as well as Indigenous struggles to "get land back," see Pasternak and King (2019).
6 Thielen-Wilson (2012, 312) defines "genuine decolonization" expansively as "the dismantling of colonial institutions, a redistribution of power and a return of land and resources to Indigenous nations."
7 I did not have the chance to read Carlson-Manathara and Rowe's book (2021) before my own went to press. I am excited to learn from the guidance on offer to settlers who want to live ethically with "Indigenous Peoples, laws and lands." This guidance is summed up as follows: "If Canadians truly want to achieve this goal ... they will pursue a reorientation of their lives toward 'living in Indigenous sovereignty' – living in an awareness that these are Indigenous lands, containing relationships, laws, protocols, stories, obligations and opportunities that have been understood and practised by Indigenous peoples since time immemorial."
8 Victoria Freeman, personal communication, April 21, 2018.

References

Ahmed, Sara. 2000. *Strange Encounters: Embodied Others in Post-coloniality*. New York: Routledge.
–. 2004. "Declarations of Whiteness: The Nonperformativity of Antiracism." *Borderlands e-Journal* 3 (2): https://www.exeley.com/journal/borderlands.
–. 2012. *On Being Included: Racism and Diversity in Institutional Life*. Durham, NC: Duke University Press.
–. 2014. *The Cultural Politics of Emotion*. 2nd ed. Edinburgh: Edinburgh University Press.
Alfred, Taiaiake. 2005. *Wasáse: Indigenous Pathways of Action and Freedom*. Peterborough, ON: Broadview Press.
–. 2010. Foreword to *Unsettling the Settler Within: Indian Residential Schools, Truth Telling, and Reconciliation in Canada*, by Paulette Regan, ix–xi. Vancouver: UBC Press.
Alfred, Taiaiake, and Jeff Corntassel. 2005. "Being Indigenous: Resurgences against Contemporary Colonialism." *Government and Opposition* 40 (4): 597–614.
Amadahy, Zainab, and Bonita Lawrence. 2009. "Indigenous Peoples and Black People in Canada: Settlers or Allies?" In *Breaching the Colonial Contract: Anti-colonialism in the US and Canada*, edited by Arlo Kempf, 105–36. New York: Springer.
Anderson, Kim. 2000. *A Recognition of Being: Reconstructing Native Womanhood*. Toronto: Sumach Press.
–. 2010. "Affirmations of an Indigenous Feminist." In *Indigenous Women and Feminism: Politics, Activism, Culture*, edited by Cheryl Suzack, Shari M. Huhndorf, Jeanne Perreault, and Jean Barman, 81–91. Vancouver: UBC Press.
–. 2011. *Life Stages and Native Women: Memory, Teachings, and Story Medicine*. Winnipeg: University of Manitoba Press.
–. 2016. *A Recognition of Being: Reconstructing Native Womanhood*. 2nd ed. Toronto: Sumach Press.

Anderson, Mark Cronlund, and Carmen L. Robertson. 2011. *Seeing Red: A History of Natives in Canadian Newspapers*. Winnipeg: University of Manitoba Press.

Applebaum, Barbara. 2010. *Being White, Being Good: White Complicity, White Moral Responsibility, and Social Justice Pedagogy*. Lanham, MD: Lexington Books.

Arvin, Maile, Eve Tuck, and Angie Morrill. 2013. "Decolonizing Feminism: Challenging Connections between Settler Colonialism and Heteropatriarchy." *Feminist Formations* 25 (1): 8–34. https://doi.org/10.1353/ff.2013.0006.

Asher, Kiran. 2013. "Latin American Decolonial Thought, or Making the Subaltern Speak." *Geography Compass* 7 (12): 832–42. https://doi.org/10.1111/gec3.12102.

Bacchi, Carol. 2005. "Discourse, Discourse Everywhere: Subject 'Agency' in Feminist Discourse Methodology." *NORA-Nordic Journal of Feminist and Gender Research* 13 (3): 198–209.

Bacon, J.M. 2017. "'A Lot of Catching Up': Knowledge Gaps and Emotions in the Development of a Tactical Collective Identity among Students Participating in Solidarity with the Winnemem Wintu." *Settler Colonial Studies* 7 (4): 441–55. https://doi.org/10.1080/2201473X.2016.1244030.

Badwall, Harjeet. 2016. "Critical Reflexivity and Moral Regulation." *Journal of Progressive Human Services* 27 (1): 1–20.

Bannerji, Himani, ed. 1993. *Returning the Gaze: Essays on Racism, Feminism and Politics*. Toronto: Sister Vision Press.

—. 2000. *The Dark Side of the Nation: Essays on Multiculturalism, Nationalism, and Gender*. Toronto: Canadian Scholars' Press.

Barker, Adam. 2010. "From Adversaries to Allies: Forging Respectful Alliances between Indigenous and Settler Peoples." In *Alliances: Re/envisioning Indigenous–Non-Indigenous Relationships*, edited by Lynne Davis, 316–33. Toronto: University of Toronto Press.

—. 2012. "Already Occupied: Indigenous Peoples, Settler Colonialism and the Occupy Movements in North America." *Social Movement Studies* 11 (3): 327–34. https://doi.org/10.1080/14742837.2012.708922.

—. 2015. "'A Direct Act of Resurgence, a Direct Act of Sovereignty': Reflections on Idle No More, Indigenous Activism, and Canadian Settler Colonialism." *Globalizations* 12 (1): 43–65. http://doi.org/10.1080/14747731.2014.971531.

Barker, Adam, and J. Pickerill. 2012. "Radicalizing Relationships to and through Shared Geographies: Why Anarchists Need to Understand Indigenous Connections to Land and Place." *Antipode* 44 (5): 1705–25. https://doi.org/10.1111/j.1467-8330.2012.01031.x.

Barker, Joanne, ed. 2017. *Critically Sovereign: Indigenous Gender, Sexuality, and Feminist Studies*. Durham, NC: Duke University Press.

Barman, Jean, and Jan Hare. 2006. *Good Intentions Gone Awry: Emma Crosby and the Methodist Mission on the Northwest Coast*. Vancouver: UBC Press.

Barnett, Michael N., and Thomas George Weiss, eds. 2008. *Humanitarianism in Question: Politics, Power, Ethics*. Ithaca, NY: Cornell University Press.

Battell Lowman, Emma, and Adam J. Barker. 2015. *Settler: Identity and Colonialism in 21st Century Canada*. Halifax, NS: Fernwood.

Beads, Tina, and Rauna Kuokkanen. 2007. "Aboriginal Feminist Action on Violence against Women." In *Making Space for Indigenous Feminism*, edited by Joyce A. Green, 221–32. Black Point, NS: Fernwood.
Bergland, Renée L. 2000. *The National Uncanny: Indian Ghosts and American Subjects*. Hanover, NH: University Press of New England.
Berkhofer, Robert F. 1978. *The White Man's Indian: The History of an Idea from Columbus to the Present*. New York: Knopf.
Bishop, Anne. 2002. *Becoming an Ally: Breaking the Cycle of Oppression in People*. 2nd ed. Halifax, NS: Fernwood.
Borell, Belinda A.E., Amanda S. Gregory, Tim N. McCreanor, Victoria G.L. Jensen, and Helen E. Moewaka Barnes. 2009. "'It's Hard at the Top but It's a Whole Lot Easier Than Being at the Bottom': The Role of Privilege in Understanding Disparities in Aotearoa/New Zealand." *Race/Ethnicity* 3 (1): 29–50.
Bornstein, Erica, and Peter Redfield, eds. 2011. *Forces of Compassion: Humanitarianism between Ethics and Politics*. Santa Fe, NM: School for Advanced Research Press.
Boudreau Morris, Katie. 2017. "Decolonizing Solidarity: Cultivating Relationships of Discomfort." *Settler Colonial Studies* 7 (4): 456–73. https://doi.org/10.1080/2201473X.2016.1243085.
Bourgeois, Robyn. 2014. "Warrior Women: Indigenous Women's Political Engagement with the Canadian State." PhD diss., University of Toronto. https://central.bac-lac.gc.ca/.item?id=TC-OTU-68238&op=pdf&app=Library&oclc_number=1033021730.
Boyd, Dwight. 2004. "The Legacies of Liberalism and Oppressive Relations: Facing a Dilemma for the Subject of Moral Education." *Journal of Moral Education* 33 (1): 3–22. https://doi.org/10.1080/0305724042000200047.
Bull, Julie R. 2010. "Research with Aboriginal Peoples: Authentic Relationships as a Precursor to Ethical Research." *Journal of Empirical Research on Human Research Ethics* 5 (4): 13–22. https://doi.org/10.1525%2Fjer.2010.5.4.13.
Burman, Jenny. 2016. "Multicultural Feeling, Feminist Rage, Indigenous Refusal." *Cultural Studies, Critical Methodologies* 16 (4): 361–72.
Burton, Antoinette M. 1994. *Burdens of History: British Feminists, Indian Women, and Imperial Culture, 1865–1915*. Chapel Hill: University of North Carolina.
Bush, Melanie E.L. 2011. *Everyday Forms of Whiteness: Understanding Race in a Post-racial World*. 2nd ed. Lanham, MD: Rowman and Littlefield.
Butz, David, and Kathryn Besio. 2009. "Autoethnography." *Geography Compass* 3 (5): 1660–74.
Calloway, Colin G. 2008. *White People, Indians, and Highlanders: Tribal Peoples and Colonial Encounters in Scotland and America*. Oxford: Oxford University Press.
Cannella, Gaile S., and Kathryn D. Manuelito. 2008. "Feminisms from Unthought Locations: Indigenous Worldviews, Marginalized Feminisms, and Revisioning an Anticolonial Social Science." In *Handbook of Critical and Indigenous Methodologies*, edited by Norman K. Denzin, Yvonna S. Lincoln, and Linda Tuhiwai Smith, 45–60. Los Angeles: Sage.

Carlson, Elizabeth. 2017. "Anti-Colonial Methodologies and Practices for Settler Colonial Studies." *Settler Colonial Studies* 7 (4): 496–517. https://doi.org/10.1080/2201473X.2016.1241213

Carlson-Manathara, Elizabeth (Liz), with Gladys Rowe. 2021. *Living in Indigenous Sovereignty*. Black Point, NS: Fernwood.

Carter, Sarah. 1997. *Capturing Women: The Manipulation of Cultural Imagery in Canada's Prairie West*. Montreal/Kingston: McGill-Queen's University Press.

–. 2006. "The 'Cordial Advocate': Amelia McLean Paget and *The People of the Plains*." In *With Good Intentions: Euro-Canadian and Aboriginal Relations in Colonial Canada*, edited by Celia Haig-Brown and David A. Nock, 199–228. Vancouver: UBC Press.

Carter, Sarah, Lesley Erickson, Patricia Roome, and Char Smith, eds. 2005. *Unsettled Pasts: Reconceiving the West through Women's History*. Calgary: University of Calgary Press.

Castellano, Marlene Brant, Linda Archibald, Mike DeGagnon, and Aboriginal Healing Foundation (Canada). 2011. *From Truth to Reconciliation: Transforming the Legacy of Residential Schools*. Vol. 1. Ottawa: Aboriginal Healing Foundation.

Chazan, May. 2016. "Settler Solidarities as Praxis: Understanding 'Granny Activism' beyond the Highly-Visible." *Social Movements Studies* 15 (5): 457–70.

–. 2020. "Making Home on Anishinaabe Lands: Storying Settler Activisms in Nogojiwanong (Peterborough, Canada)." *Settler Colonial Studies* 10 (1): 34–53. http://www.tandfonline.com/loi/csms20.

City of Toronto. 2013. "2011 National Household Survey: Immigration, Citizenship, Place of Birth, Ethnicity, Visible Minorities, Religion and Aboriginal Peoples." *Backgrounder*, May 9. https://www.toronto.ca/wp-content/uploads/2017/10/9793-2011-NHS-Backgrounder-Immigration-Citizenship-Place-of-Birth-Ethnicity-Visible-Minorities-Religion-and-Aboriginal-Peoples-.pdf.

Clark Mane, Rebecca L. 2012. "Transmuting Grammars of Whiteness in Third-Wave Feminism: Interrogating Postrace Histories, Postmodern Abstraction, and the Proliferation of Difference in Third-Wave Texts." *Signs: Journal of Women in Culture and Society* 38 (1): 71–98.

Coburn, Elaine, ed. 2015. "Introduction: Indigenous Resistance and Resurgence." In *More Will Sing Their Way to Freedom: Indigenous Resistance and Resurgence*, edited by Elaine Coburn, 24–49. Black Point, NS: Fernwood.

Combahee River Collective. 1979. "A Black Feminist Statement." *Off Our Backs: A Women's Journal* 9 (6): 6–8. https://www.jstor.org/stable/25792966.

Conway, Janet. 2004. "On Scholar-Activism." Paper presented at "Africa – The Next Liberation Struggle: Socialism, Democracy, Activism. A Conference Celebrating the Work of John Saul," York University, Toronto, October 15–16.

–. 2010. "Is the Global Justice Movement Colonial? A Troubling Tale of Indigenous Peoples at the World Social Forum." Paper presented at "Social Justice Studies Annual Lecture," University of Victoria, Victoria, BC, October 21. https://www.youtube.com/watch?v=KhetghZKxhU&t=3s.

Cordova, Viola Faye. 2004. "Ethics: The We and the I." In *American Indian Thought: Philosophical Essays*, edited by Anne Waters, 173–81. Malden, MA: Blackwell.

Corntassel, Jeff. 2008. "Toward Sustainable Self-Determination: Re-thinking the Contemporary Indigenous Human Rights Discourse." *Alternatives* 33 (1): 105–32. https://doi.org/10.1177/030437540803300106.

—. 2012. "Re-envisioning Resurgence: Indigenous Pathways to Decolonization and Sustainable Self-Determination." *Decolonization: Indigeneity, Education and Society* 1 (1): 86–101.

Cott, Nancy F. 1987. *The Grounding of Modern Feminism*. New Haven, CT: Yale University Press.

Coulthard, Glen S. 2014. *Red Skin, White Masks: Rejecting the Colonial Politics of Recognition*. Minneapolis: University of Minnesota Press.

Crenshaw, Kimberlé. 1991. "Mapping the Margins: Intersectionality, Identity Politics, and Violence against Women of Color." *Stanford Law Review* 43 (6): 1241–99. https://doi.org/10.2307/1229039.

Crow, Graham. 2002. *Social Solidarities: Theories, Identities and Social Change*. Philadelphia, PA: Open University Press.

D'Arcangelis, Carol Lynne. 2010. "Exploring Indigenous Feminist Relational Sovereignty." *Atlantis: A Women's Studies Journal* 34 (2): 127–38.

—. 2015. "The Solidarity Encounter between Indigenous Women and White Women in a Contemporary Canadian Context." PhD diss., University of Toronto. https://www.proquest.com/docview/1769022391?pq-origsite=primo.

—. 2018. "Revelations of a White Woman Settler-Activist: The Fraught Promise of Solidarity." *Cultural Studies, Critical Methodologies* 18 (5): 339–53. https://doi.org/10.1177/1532708617750671.

D'Arcangelis, Carol Lynne, and Audrey Huntley. 2012. "No More Silence: Towards a Pedagogy of Feminist Decolonizing Solidarity." In *Feminist Popular Education in Transnational Debate: Building Pedagogies of Possibility*, edited by Linzi Manicom and Shirley Walters, 41–58. London: Palgrave Macmillan.

Davis, Angela Y. 1983. *Women, Race and Class*. New York: Vintage Books.

—. 1989. *Women, Culture, and Politics*. New York: Random House.

Davis, Lynne. 2009. "The High Stakes of Protecting Indigenous Homelands: Coastal First Nations' Turning Point Initiative and Environmental Groups." *International Journal of Canadian Studies* 39: 137–59.

—. 2010a. *Alliances: Re/envisioning Indigenous–Non-Indigenous Relationships*. Toronto: University of Toronto Press.

—. 2010b. "Introduction." In *Alliances: Re/envisioning Indigenous–Non-Indigenous Relationships*, edited by Lynne Davis, 1–12. Toronto: University of Toronto Press.

Davis, Lynne, Jeff Denis, and Raven Sinclair. 2017. "Pathways of Settler Decolonization." Special issue, *Settler Colonial Studies* 7 (4): 393–97. https://doi.org/10.1080/2201473X.2016.1243085.

Davis, Lynne, Chris Hiller, Cherylanne James, Kristen Lloyd, Tessa Nasca, and Sara Taylor. 2017. "Complicated Pathways: Settler Canadians Learning to Re/frame Themselves and Their Relationships with Indigenous Peoples." *Settler Colonial Studies* 7 (4): 398–414. https://doi.org/10.1080/2201473X.2016.1243085.

Davis, Lynne, and Heather Shpuniarsky. 2010. "The Spirit of Relationships: What We Have Learned about Indigenous/Non-Indigenous Alliances and Coalitions." In

Alliances: Re/envisioning Indigenous–Non-Indigenous Relationships, edited by Lynne Davis, 334–48. Toronto: University of Toronto Press.

Davis, Lynne, Vivian O'Donnell, and Heather Shpuniarsky. 2007. "Aboriginal-Social Justice Alliances: Understanding the Landscape of Relationships through the Coalition for a Public Inquiry into Ipperwash." *International Journal of Canadian Studies* 36 (3): 95–119.

Deer, Jessica. 2018. "How the Oka Crisis has Shaped 4 Generations in Kanesatake and Kahnawake." *CBC News*, July 11. https://www.cbc.ca/news/indigenous/oka-crisis-4-generations-kanesatake-kahnawake-1.4743129.

Deerchild, Rosanna. 2003. "Tribal Feminism Is a Drum Song." In *Strong Women Stories: Native Vision and Community Survival*, edited by Bonita Lawrence and Kim Anderson, 97–105. Toronto: Sumach Press.

Deloria, Philip Joseph. 1998. *Playing Indian*. New Haven, CT: Yale University Press.

Denis, Claude. 1997. *We Are Not You: First Nations and Canadian Modernity*. Peterborough, ON: Broadview Press.

Denis, Jeffrey S. 2020. *Canada at a Crossroads: Boundaries, Bridges, and Laissez-Faire Racism in Indigenous-Settler Relations*. Toronto: University of Toronto Press.

Denis, Jeffrey S., and Kerry Bailey. 2016. "'You Can't Have Reconciliation without Justice': How Non-Indigenous Participants in Canada's Truth and Reconciliation Process Understand Their Roles and Goals." In *The Limits of Settler Colonial Reconciliation: Non-Indigenous People and the Responsibility to Engage*, edited by Sarah Maddison, Tom Clark, and Ravi de Costa, 137–58. Singapore: Springer.

Denzin, Norman K., and Yvonna S. Lincoln. 2008. "Introduction: Critical Methodologies and Indigenous Inquiry." In *Handbook of Critical and Indigenous Methodologies*, edited by Norman K. Denzin, Yvonna S. Lincoln, and Linda Tuhiwai Smith, 1–20. Los Angeles: Sage.

Dion, Susan. 2009. *Braiding Histories: Learning from Aboriginal Peoples' Experiences and Perspectives*. Vancouver: UBC Press.

Dua, Enakshi, and Angela Robertson, eds. 1999. *Scratching the Surface: Canadian, Anti-racist, Feminist Thought*. Toronto: Women's Press.

Dyer, Richard. 1997. *White*. New York: Routledge.

Eberts, Mary. 2017. "Being an Indigenous Woman Is a 'High Risk Lifestyle.'" In *Making Space for Indigenous Feminism*, 2nd ed., edited by Joyce Green, 69–102. Black Point, NS: Fernwood.

Emberley, Julia. 1993. *Thresholds of Difference: Feminist Critique, Native Women's Writings, Postcolonial Theory*. Toronto: University of Toronto Press.

Erickson, Bruce. 2011. "'A Phantasy in White in a World That Is Dead': Grey Owl and the Whiteness of Surrogacy." In *Rethinking the Great White North: Race, Nature, and the Historical Geographies of Whiteness in Canada*, edited by Audrey Lynn Kobayashi, Laura Cameron, and Andrew Baldwin, 19–38. Vancouver: UBC Press.

Escobar, Arturo. 2007. "Worlds and Knowledges Otherwise: The Latin American Modernity/Coloniality Research Program." *Cultural Studies* 21 (2–3): 179–210. https://doi.org/10.1080/09502380601162506.

Faculty of Humanities and Social Sciences, Athabasca University. 2015. "Susanna Moodie." *Canadian Writers*. http://canadian-writers.athabascau.ca/english/writers/smoodie/smoodie.php.

Fee, Margery, and Lynette Russell. 2007. "'Whiteness' and 'Aboriginality' in Canada and Australia: Conversations and Identities." *Feminist Theory* 8 (2): 187–208. https://doi.org/10.1177%2F1464700107078141.

Fellows, Mary Louise, and Sherene Razack. 1994. "Seeking Relations: Law and Feminism Roundtables." *Signs: Journal of Women in Culture and Society* 19 (4): 1048–83.

–. 1998. "The Race to Innocence: Confronting Hierarchical Relations among Women." *Journal of Gender, Race and Justice* 1: 335–52.

Ferreira da Silva, Denise. 2007. *Toward a Global Idea of Race*. Minneapolis: University of Minnesota Press.

Fiamengo, Janice. 1999. "A Legacy of Ambivalence: Responses to Nellie McClung." *Journal of Canadian Studies* 34 (4): 70–87. https://doi.org/10.3138/jcs.34.4.70.

FIMI (Foro Internacional de Mujeres Indígenas). 2006. *Mairin Iwanka Raya: Indigenous Women Stand against Violence: A Companion Report to the United Nations Secretary-General's Study on Violence against Women*. NewYork: FIMI.

Flowers, Rachel. 2015. "Refusal to Forgive: Indigenous Women's Love and Rage." *Decolonization: Indigeneity, Education and Society* 4 (2): 32–49. http://decolonization.org/index.php/des/index.

Fortier, Craig. 2017. "Unsettling Methodologies/Decolonizing Movements." *Journal of Indigenous Social Development* 6 (1): 20–36.

Foucault, Michel. 1978. *The History of Sexuality*. Vol. 1, *An Introduction*. Translated by Robert Hurley. New York: Vintage Books.

Francis, Daniel. 1992. *The Imaginary Indian: The Image of the Indian in Canadian Culture*. Vancouver: Arsenal Pulp Press.

Frankenberg, Ruth. 1993. *White Women, Race Matters: The Social Construction of Whiteness*. Minneapolis: University of Minnesota Press.

Freeman, Victoria. 2010. "'Toronto Has No History!' Indigeneity, Settler Colonialism and Historical Memory in Canada's Largest City." PhD diss., University of Toronto. https://tspace.library.utoronto.ca/bitstream/1807/26356/1/Freeman_Victoria_J_201011_PhD_thesis.pdf.

Funk-Unrau, Neil. 2005. "Construction of Relationship Frames in the Aboriginal Rights Support Movement: The Articulation of Solidarity with the Lubicon Cree of Northern Canada." In *Research in Social Movements, Conflicts and Change*, vol. 26, edited by P.G. Coy, 239–64. Bingley, England: Emerald Group Publishing Limited. https://doi.org/10.1016/S0163-786X(05)26008-1.

Gavey, Nicola. 1989. "Feminist Poststructuralism and Discourse Analysis: Contributions to Feminist Psychology." *Psychology of Women Quarterly* 13: 459–75. https://doi.org/10.1111%2Fj.1471-6402.1989.tb01014.x.

Goeman, Mishuana. 2008. "(Re)Mapping Indigenous Presence on the Land in Native Women's Literature." *American Quarterly* 60 (2): 295–302. https://doi.org/10.1353/aq.0.0011.

–. 2013. *Mark My Words: Native Women Mapping Our Nations*. Minneapolis: University of Minnesota Press.

Goldie, Terry. 1989. *Fear and Temptation: The Image of the Indigene in Canadian, Australian and New Zealand Literature*. Montreal/Kingston: McGill-Queen's University Press.

Grande, Sandy. 2004. *Red Critical Theory: Native American Social and Political Thought*. Lanham, MD: Rowman and Littlefield.

Green, Joyce A. 2007a. "Introduction – Indigenous Feminism: From Symposium to Book." In *Making Space for Indigenous Feminism*, edited by Joyce Green, 14–19. Black Point, NS: Fernwood.

–. 2007b. *Making Space for Indigenous Feminism*. Black Point, NS: Fernwood.

–. 2007c. "Taking Account of Aboriginal Feminism." In *Making Space for Indigenous Feminism*, edited by Joyce Green, 20–32. Black Point, NS: Fernwood.

–. 2017a. *Making Space for Indigenous Feminism*. 2nd ed. Black Point, NS: Fernwood.

–. 2017b. "Taking More Account of Indigenous Feminism: An Introduction." In *Making Space for Indigenous Feminism*, 2nd ed., edited by Joyce Green, 1–20. Black Point, NS: Fernwood.

Gregory, Derek. 2004. *The Colonial Present: Afghanistan, Palestine, and Iraq*. Malden, MA: Blackwell.

Grewal, Inderpal. 1996. *Home and Harem: Nation, Gender, Empire, and the Cultures of Travel*. Durham, NC: Duke University Press.

Gunn Allen, Paula. 1986. *The Sacred Hoop: Recovering the Feminine in American Indian Traditions*. Boston: Beacon Press.

Hanisch, Carol. 2006. "The Personal Is Political." https://webhome.cs.uvic.ca/~mserra/AttachedFiles/PersonalPolitical.pdf.

Harding, Sandra G., ed. 2004. *The Feminist Standpoint Theory Reader: Intellectual and Political Controversies*. New York: Routledge.

Harp, Rick, host. 2021. "The Rot of Reconciliation in Canada." *MEDIA INDIGENA: Indigenous Current Affairs*, episode 279. Podcast, December 29, 2021, https://mediaindigena.libsyn.com/the-rot-of-reconciliation-in-canada-ep-279.

Hele, Karl S. 2019. "Reserves in Ontario." *The Canadian Encyclopedia*, June 14. https://www.thecanadianencyclopedia.ca/en/article/reserves-in-ontario.

Henderson, Jennifer. 2003. *Settler Feminism and Race Making in Canada*. Toronto: University of Toronto Press.

Henderson, Jennifer, and Pauline Wakeham, eds. 2013. *Reconciling Canada: Critical Perspectives on the Culture of Redress*. Toronto: University of Toronto Press.

Henning, Denise K. 2007. "Yes, My Daughters, We Are Cherokee Women." In *Making Space for Indigenous Feminism*, edited by Joyce Green, 187–98. Black Point, NS: Fernwood Publishing.

Heron, Barbara. 1999. "Desire for Development: The Education of White Women as Development Workers." PhD diss., University of Toronto.

–. 2005. "Self-Reflection in Critical Social Work Practice: Subjectivity and the Possibilities of Resistance." *Reflective Practice* 6 (3): 341–51. https://doi.org/10.1080/14623940500220095.

–. 2007. *Desire for Development: Whiteness, Gender, and the Helping Imperative*. Waterloo, ON: Wilfrid Laurier University Press.

Hill Collins, Patricia. 2000. *Black Feminist Thought: Knowledge, Consciousness, and the Politics of Empowerment*. New York: Routledge.

Hiller, Chris. 2017. "Tracing the Spirals of Unsettlement: Euro-Canadian Narratives of Coming to Grips with Indigenous Sovereignty, Title, and Rights." *Settler Colonial Studies* 7 (4): 415–40. https://doi.org/10.1080/2201473X.2016.1243085.

hooks, bell. 1992. *Black Looks: Race and Representation*. Toronto: Between the Lines.
—. 2000. *Feminist Theory: From Margin to Center*. 2nd ed. Cambridge, MA: South End Press.
Horn-Miller, Kahente. 2005. "Otiyaner: The 'Woman's Path' through Colonialism." *Atlantis: A Women's Studies Journal* 29 (2): 57–68.
Iacovetta, Franca, and Mariana Valverde, eds. 1992. *Gender Conflicts: New Essays in Women's History*. Toronto: University of Toronto Press.
INM Collective. 2014. "#ITENDSHERE: The Full Series." http://nationsrising.org/tag/itstartswithus/.
Irwin, Kathie. 2007. "Maori Women and Leadership in Aotearoa/New Zealand." In *Making Space for Indigenous Feminism*, 2nd ed., edited by Joyce Green, 174–86. Black Point, NS: Fernwood.
Jafri, Beenash. 2010. "Indigenous Solidarity in an Anti-racism Framework? A Case Study of the National Secretariat against Hate and Racism in Canada (NSAHRC)." In *Alliances: Re/envisioning Indigenous–Non-Indigenous Relationships*, edited by Lynne Davis, 256–75. Toronto: University of Toronto Press.
Jaimes Guerrero, Marie Anna. 1997. "Civil Rights versus Sovereignty: Native American Women in Life and Land Struggles." In *Feminist Genealogies, Colonial Legacies, Democratic Futures*, edited by M. Jacqui Alexander and Chandra Talpade Mohanty, 101–21. New York: Routledge.
Johnson, Rhonda, Winona Stevenson, and Donna Greschner. 1993. "Peekiskwetan." *Canadian Journal of Women and the Law* 6 (1): 153–73.
Johnston, Anna, and Alan Lawson. 2000. "Settler Colonies." In *A Companion to Postcolonial Studies*, edited by Henry Schwarz and Sangeeta Ray, 360–76. Malden, MA: Blackwell.
Kauanui, J. Kēhaulani. 2017. "Indigenous Hawaiian Sexuality and the Politics of Nationalist Decolonization." In *Critically Sovereign: Indigenous Gender, Sexuality, and Feminist Studies*, edited by Joanne Barker, 45–68. Durham, NC: Duke University Press.
Kaur, Min. 2014. "Honoring Gaswentah: A Racialized Settler's Exploration of Responsibility and Mutual Respect as Coalition Building with First Peoples." In *Politics of Anti-racism Education: In Search of Strategies for Transformative Learning*, edited by George J. Sefa Dei and Mairi McDermott, 165–74. Dordrecht: Springer Netherlands.
Kaye, Julie. 2016. "Reconciliation in the Context of Settler-Colonial Gender Violence: 'How Do We Reconcile with an Abuser?'" *The Canadian Review of Sociology* 53, (4): 461–67. https://doi.org/10.1111/cars.12127.
Kempadoo, Kamala. (2015). "The Modern-day White (wo)man's Burden: Trends in Anti-trafficking and Anti-slavery Campaigns." *Journal of Human Trafficking* 1 (1): 8–20.
Khan, Sarah, Rochelle Allan, Jason Pennington, and Lisa Richardson. 2015. "Paying Our Dues: The Importance of Newcomer Solidarity with the Indigenous Movement for Self-Determination in Canada." *Canadian Journal of Native Studies* 35 (1): 145–53.
King, Hayden. 2016. "The Secret Path, Reconciliation and Not-Reconciliation." *Muskrat Magazine*, October 26. http://muskratmagazine.com/the-secret-path-reconciliation-not-reconciliation/.

King, Tiffany Lethabo, Jenell Navarro, and Andrea Smith, eds. 2020. *Otherwise Worlds: Against Settler Colonialism and Anti-Blackness*. Durham, NC: Duke University Press.

Kino-nda-niimi Collective, ed. 2014. *The Winter We Danced: Voices from the Past, the Future, and the Idle No More Movement*. Winnipeg: Arbeiter Ring.

Kobayashi, Audrey Lynn, Laura Cameron, and Andrew Baldwin. 2011. "Where Is the Great White North? Spatializing History, Historicizing Whiteness." In *Rethinking the Great White North: Race, Nature, and the Historical Geographies of Whiteness in Canada*, edited by Audrey Lynn Kobayashi, Laura Cameron, and Andrew Baldwin, 1–18. Vancouver: UBC Press.

Konsmo, Erin M., and A.M. Kahealani Pacheco. 2016. *Violence on the Land, Violence on Our Bodies: Building an Indigenous Response to Environmental Violence*. Toronto: Women's Earth Alliance/Native Youth Sexual Health Network. http://landbodydefense.org/uploads/files/VLVBReportToolkit2016.pdf.

Kowal, Emma. 2011. "The Stigma of White Privilege: Australian Anti-racists and Indigenous Improvement." *Cultural Studies* 25 (3): 313–33.

—. 2015. *Trapped in the Gap: Doing Good in Indigenous Australia*. Brooklyn, NY: Berghahn Books.

Kuokkanen, Rauna. 2007. "Myths and Realities of Sami Women: A Post-colonial Feminist Analysis for the Decolonization and Transformation of Sami Society." In *Making Space for Indigenous Feminism*, edited by Joyce Green, 72–92. Black Point, NS: Fernwood.

—. 2012. "Self-Determination and Indigenous Women's Rights at the Intersection of International Human Rights." *Human Rights Quarterly* 34 (1): 225–50.

—. 2019. *Restructuring Relations: Indigenous Self-Determination, Governance and Gender*. Oxford: Oxford University Press.

Ladner, Kiera L. 2000. "Women and Blackfoot Nationalism." *Journal of Canadian Studies* 35 (2): 35–60. https://doi.org/10.3138/jcs.35.2.35.

Lagalisse, Erica Michelle. 2011. "'Marginalizing Magdalena': Intersections of Gender and the Secular in Anarchoindigenist." *Signs* 36 (3): 653–78. http://www.jstor.org/stable/10.1086/657526.

LaRocque, Emma. 2007. "Métis and Feminist: Ethical Reflections on Feminism, Human Rights and Decolonization." In *Making Space for Indigenous Feminism*, edited by Joyce Green, 53–71. Black Point, NS: Fernwood.

—. 2010. *When the Other Is Me: Native Resistance Discourse, 1850–1990*. Winnipeg: University of Manitoba Press.

Lavell-Harvard, D. Memee, and Jeannette Corbiere Lavell, eds. 2006. *"Until Our Hearts Are on the Ground": Aboriginal Mothering, Oppression, Resistance and Rebirth*. Toronto: Demeter Press.

Lavell-Harvard, D. Memee, and Kim Anderson, eds. 2014. *Mothers of the Nations: Indigenous Mothering as Global Resistance, Reclaiming and Recovery*. Bradford, ON: Demeter Press.

Lawrence, Bonita. 2003. "Gender, Race, and the Regulation of Native Identity in Canada and the United States: An Overview." *Hypatia* 18 (2): 3–31.

—. 2004. *"Real" Indians and Others: Mixed-Blood Urban Native Peoples and Indigenous Nationhood*. Lincoln: University of Nebraska Press.

Lawrence, Bonita, and Kim Anderson, eds. 2003. *Strong Women Stories: Native Vision and Community Survival*. Toronto: Sumach Press.
–. 2005. "Introduction to 'Indigenous Women: The State of Our Nations.'" *Atlantis: A Women's Studies Journal* 29 (2): 1–8.
Lawrence, Bonita, and Enakshi Dua. 2005. "Decolonizing Antiracism." *Social Justice* 32 (4): 120–43.
Lee, Jo-Anne. 2015. "Non-white Settler and Indigenous Relations: Decolonizing Possibilities for Social Justice." *Lectora* 22: 13–26. https://raco.cat/index.php/Lectora/article/view/315585.
Lewis, Adam Gary. 2017. "Imagining Autonomy on Stolen Land: Settler Colonialism, Anarchism and the Possibilities of Decolonization?" *Settler Colonial Studies* 7 (4): 474–95. https://doi.org/10.1080/2201473X.2016.1243085.
Lewis, Reina. 1996. *Gendering Orientalism: Race, Femininity, and Representation*. London: Routledge.
Lewis, Reina, and Sara Mills. 2003. "Introduction." In *Feminist Postcolonial Theory: A Reader*, edited by Reina Lewis and Sara Mills, 1–21. New York: Routledge.
Lipsitz, George. 2008. "Walleye Warriors and White Identities: Native Americans' Treaty Rights, Composite Identities and Social Movements." *Ethnic and Racial Studies* 31 (1): 101–22.
"Liminality." 2002. *Dictionary of the Social Sciences*, edited by Craig Calhoun, Oxford University Press. https://doi.org/10.1093/acref/9780195123715.001.0001.
Lockard, Claire A. 2016. "Unhappy Confessions: The Temptation of Admitting to White Privilege." *Feminist Philosophy Quarterly* 2, (2): 1–20. https://doi.org/10.5206/fpq/2016.2.2.
Long, David Alan. 1997. "The Precarious Pursuit of Justice: Counter-hegemony in the Lubicon First Nations Coalition." In *Organizing Dissent: Contemporary Social Movements in Theory and Practice*, 2nd edition, edited by William K. Carroll, 151–70. Toronto: Garamond Press.
Loomba, Ania. 2005. *Colonialism/postcolonialism*. 2nd ed. London: Routledge.
Lorde, Audre. 2007. *Sister Outsider: Essays and Speeches*. Berkeley, CA: Crossing Press.
Lugones, María. 2010. "Toward a Decolonial Feminism." *Hypatia* 25 (4): 742–59.
MacDonald, David B. 2013. "Reconciliation after Genocide in Canada: Towards A Syncretic Model of Democracy." *AlterNative: An International Journal of Indigenous Peoples* 9 (1): 60–73.
Mackey, Eva. 2002. *The House of Difference: Cultural Politics and National Identity in Canada*. Toronto: University of Toronto Press.
–. 2016. *Unsettled Expectations: Uncertainty, Land and Settler Decolonization*. Halifax, NS: Fernwood.
Mahmood, Saba. 2011. *Politics of Piety: The Islamic Revival and the Feminist Subject* (Rev. ed.). Princeton: Princeton University Press.
Mahrouse, Gada. 2007. "Deploying White/Western Privilege in Accompaniment, Observer, and Human Shield Transnational Solidarity Activism: A Critical Race, Feminist Analysis." PhD diss., University of Toronto.
–. 2008. "Race-Conscious Transnational Activists with Cameras: Mediators of Compassion." *International Journal of Cultural Studies* 11 (1): 87–105.

—. 2009a. "The Compelling Story of the White/Western Activist in the War Zone: Examining Race, Neutrality, and Exceptionalism in Citizen Journalism." *Canadian Journal of Communication* 34 (4): 659–74.

—. 2009b. "Transnational Activists, News Media Representations, and Racialized 'Politics of Life': The Christian Peacemaker Team Kidnapping in Iraq." *Citizenship Studies* 13 (4): 311–31.

—. 2011. "Feel-Good Tourism: An Ethical Option for Socially-Conscious Westerners?" *ACME: An International e-Journal for Critical Geographies* 10 (3): 372–91. https://www.acme-journal.org/index.php/acme/article/view/903.

Mahtani, Minelle. 2002. "Interrogating the Hyphen-Nation: Canadian Multicultural Policy and 'Mixed Race' Identities." *Social Identities* 8 (1): 67–90. https://doi.org/10.1080/13504630220132026.

Maracle, Lee. 1993. "Racism, Sexism and Patriarchy." In *Returning the Gaze: Essays on Racism, Feminism and Politics*, edited by Himani Bannerji, 122–30. Toronto: Sister Vision Press.

—. 1996. *I Am Woman: A Native Perspective on Sociology and Feminism*. Vancouver: Press Gang.

—. 2006. "Decolonizing Native Women." In *Daughters of Mother Earth: The Wisdom of Native American Women*, edited by Barbara Alice Mann, 29–52. Westport, CT: Praeger.

Massey, Doreen B. 1994. *Space, Place, and Gender*. Minneapolis: University of Minnesota Press.

Maurantonio, Nicole. 2017. "'Reason to Hope?': The White Savior Myth and Progress in 'Post-Racial' America." *Journalism and Mass Communication Quarterly* 94 (4): 1130–45. https://doi.org/10.1177%2F1077699017691248.

Mawani, Renisa. 2009. *Colonial Proximities: Crossracial Encounters and Juridical Truths in British Columbia, 1871–1921*. Vancouver: UBC Press.

Maynard, Robyn, and Leanne Betasamosake Simpson. 2020. "Toward Black and Indigenous Futures on Turtle Island: A Conversation." In *Until We Are Free: An Edited Collection by Black Lives Matter Toronto*, edited by Syrus Ware, Sandra Hudson, and Rodney Diverlus, 75–93. Regina: University of Regina Press.

McClintock, Anne. 1995. *Imperial Leather: Race, Gender, and Sexuality in the Colonial Contest*. New York: Routledge.

McDowell, Linda. 1999. *Gender, Identity and Place: Understanding Feminist Geographies*. Minneapolis: University of Minnesota Press.

Midgley, Clare. 2007. *Feminism and Empire: Women Activists in Imperial Britain, 1790–1865*. New York: Routledge.

Mignolo, Walter. 2007. "Coloniality: The Darker Side of Modernity." *Cultural Studies* 21 (2/3): 39–49.

Mignolo, Walter, and Catherine Walsh. 2018. *On Decoloniality: Concepts, Analytics, Praxis*. Durham, NC: Duke University Press.

Mihesuah, Devon Abbot. 2003. *Indigenous American Women: Decolonization, Empowerment, Activism*. Lincoln: University of Nebraska Press.

Miles, Tiya, and Sharon Patricia Holland, eds. 2006. *Crossing Waters, Crossing Worlds: The African Diaspora in Indian Country*. Durham, NC: Duke University Press.

Miller, Christine, and Patricia Marie Chuchryk, eds. 1996. *Women of the First Nations: Power, Wisdom, and Strength*. Winnipeg: University of Manitoba Press.
Miller, J.R. 2000. *Skyscrapers Hide the Heavens: A History of Indian-White Relations in Canada*. 3rd ed. Toronto: University of Toronto Press.
Miller, J.R., and Leslie F.S. Upton. 1991. *Sweet Promises: A Reader on Indian-White Relations in Canada*. Toronto: University of Toronto Press.
Million, Dian. 2008. "Felt Theory." *American Quarterly* 60 (2): 267–72.
–. 2013. *Therapeutic Nations: Healing in an Age of Indigenous Human Rights*. Tucson: University of Arizona Press.
Mindry, Debra. 2001. "Nongovernmental Organizations, 'Grassroots,' and the Politics of Virtue." *Signs: Journal of Women in Culture and Society* 26 (4): 1187–211.
Mohanty, Chandra Talpade. 1984. "Under Western Eyes: Feminist Scholarship and Colonial Discourses." *Boundary 2* 12/13 (3): 338–58.
–. 1991. "Cartographies of Struggle: Third World Women and the Politics of Feminism." In *Third World Women and the Politics of Feminism*, edited by Chandra Talpade Mohanty, Ann Russo, and Lourdes Torres, 52–80. Bloomington: Indiana University Press.
–. 2003. *Feminism without Borders: Decolonizing Theory, Practicing Solidarity*. New Delhi: Zubaan.
Monkman, Leonard, and Brandi Morin. 2017. "5 Years after Idle No More, Founders Still Speaking Out." *CBC News*, December 10. https://www.cbc.ca/news/indigenous/idle-no-more-five-years-1.4436474.
Montour, Courtney, dir. 2021. *Mary Two-Axe Earley: I Am Indian Again*. Canada: National Film Board of Canada.
Monture, Patricia A., and Patricia D. McGuire, eds. 2009. *First Voices: An Aboriginal Women's Reader*, edited by Patricia A. Monture and Patricia D. McGuire. Toronto: Inanna.
Monture-Angus, Patricia. 1995. *Thunder in My Soul: A Mohawk Woman Speaks*. Halifax, NS: Fernwood.
–. 1999. *Journeying Forward: Dreaming First Nations' Independence*. Halifax, NS: Fernwood.
Moraga, Cherríe, and Gloria Anzaldúa, eds. 2002. *This Bridge Called My Back: Writings by Radical Women of Color*. 3rd ed. Berkeley, CA: Third Woman Press.
Moreton-Robinson, Aileen. 2000. *Talkin' Up to the White Woman: Indigenous Women and Feminism*. Queensland: University of Queensland Press.
Morgensen, Scott Lauria. 2011. *Spaces between Us: Queer Settler Colonialism and Indigenous Decolonization*. Minneapolis: University of Minnesota Press.
Morris, Amanda. 2014. "Twenty-First-Century Debt Collectors: Idle No More Combats a Five-Hundred-Year-Old Debt." *Women's Studies Quarterly* 42 (1/2): 242–56.
Morrison, Toni. 1993. *Playing in the Dark: Whiteness and the Literary Imagination*. New York: Vintage Books.
Mott, Carrie. 2018. "Building Relationships with Difference: An Anarcha-feminist Approach to the Micropolitics of Solidarity." *Annals of the American Association of Geographers* 108 (2): 424–33. https://doi.org/10.1080/24694452.2017.1385378.

Namaste, Viviane K. 2015. *Oversight: Critical Reflections on Feminist Research and Politics*. Toronto, Ontario: Women's Press.

Narayan, Uma. 2000. "Essence of Culture and Sense of History: A Feminist Critique of Cultural Essentialism." In *Decentering the Center: Philosophy for a Multicultural, Postcolonial, and Feminist World*, edited by Uma Narayan and Sandra Harding, 80–100. Bloomington: Indiana University Press.

Nestel, Sheryl. 2006. *Obstructed Labour: Race and Gender in the Re-emergence of Midwifery*. Vancouver: UBC Press.

Nickel, Sarah, and Amanda Fehr, eds. 2020. *In Good Relation: History, Gender, and Kinship in Indigenous Feminisms*. Minneapolis: University of Minnesota Press.

NIMMIWG (National Inquiry into Missing and Murdered Indigenous Women and Girls). 2019. *Reclaiming Power and Place: Executive Summary of the Final Report*. Ottawa: National Inquiry into Missing and Murdered Indigenous Women and Girls.

Nock, David A., and Celia Haig-Brown, eds. 2006. *With Good Intentions: Euro-Canadian and Aboriginal Relations in Colonial Canada*. Vancouver: UBC Press.

Offen, Karen M. 2000. *European Feminisms, 1700–1950: A Political History*. Stanford, CA: Stanford University Press.

Ouellette, Grace Josephine Mildred Wuttunee. 2002. *The Fourth World: An Indigenous Perspective on Feminism and Aboriginal Women's Activism*. Halifax, NS: Fernwood.

Palmater, Pamela D. 2011. *Beyond Blood: Rethinking Indigenous Identity*. Saskatoon: Purich.

–. 2020. *Warrior Life: Indigenous Resistance and Resurgence*. Black Point, NS: Fernwood.

Parker, Pat. 1990. "For the White Person Who Wants to Know How to Be My Friend." *Callaloo* 23 (1): 73.

Pasternak, Shiri, and Hayden King. 2019. *Land Back: A Yellowhead Institute Red Paper*. Toronto: Yellowhead Institute. https://redpaper.yellowheadinstitute.org/.

Perry, Adele. 2001. *On the Edge of Empire: Gender, Race, and the Making of British Columbia, 1849–1871*. Toronto: University of Toronto Press.

Pickles, Katie. 2002. *Female Imperialism and National Identity: Imperial Order Daughters of the Empire*. Manchester: Manchester University Press.

Pickles, Katie, and Myra Rutherdale. 2005. "Introduction." In *Contact Zones: Aboriginal and Settler Women in Canada's Colonial Past*, edited by Myra Rutherdale and Katie Pickles, 1–14. Vancouver: UBC Press.

Pillow, Wanda S. 2003. "Confession, Catharsis, or Cure? Rethinking the Uses of Reflexivity as Methodological Power in Qualitative Research." *International Journal of Qualitative Studies in Education* 16 (2): 175–96. https://doi.org/10.1080/0951839032000060635.

–. 2015. "Reflexivity as Interpretation and Genealogy in Research." *Cultural Studies ↔ Critical Methodologies* 15 (6): 419–34. https://doi.10.1177/1532708615615605.

Pratt, Mary Louise. 1991. "Arts of the Contact Zone." *Profession*: 33–40.

–. 2008. *Imperial Eyes: Travel Writing and Transculturation*. 2nd ed. New York: Routledge.

Pratt, Minnie Bruce. 1984. "Identity: Skin Blood Heart." In *Yours in Struggle: Three Feminist Perspectives of Anti-semitism and Racism*, edited by Ellie Bulkin, Minnie Bruce Pratt, and Barbara Smith, 11–62. Arlington, MA: Long Haul Press.

Pyle, Kai. 2020. "Reclaiming Traditional Gender Roles: A Two-Spirit Critique." In *In Good Relation: History, Gender, and Kinship in Indigenous Feminisms*, edited by Sarah Nickel and Amanda Fehr, 109–22. Minneapolis: University of Minnesota Press.

Quijano, Aníbal. 2007. "Coloniality and Modernity/Rationality." *Cultural Studies* 21 (2–3): 168–78. http://doi.org/10.1080/09502380601164353.

Ray, Sangeeta. 2009. *Gayatri Chakravorty Spivak: In Other Words*. Malden, MA: Wiley-Blackwell.

Razack, Sherene. 1998. *Looking White People in the Eye: Gender, Race, and Culture in Courtrooms and Classrooms*. Toronto: University of Toronto Press.

–. 2002. "When Place Becomes Race." In *Race, Space, and the Law: Unmapping a White Settler Society*, edited by Sherene Razack, 1–20. Toronto: Between the Lines.

–. 2004. *Dark Threats and White Knights: The Somalia Affair, Peacekeeping, and the New Imperialism*. Toronto: University of Toronto Press.

–. 2011. "Colonization: The Good, the Bad, the Ugly." In *Rethinking the Great White North: Race, Nature, and the Historical Geographies of Whiteness in Canada*, edited by Audrey Lynn Kobayashi, Laura Cameron, and Andrew Baldwin, 264–71. Vancouver: UBC Press.

Razack, Sherene, Malinda Sharon Smith, and Sunera Thobani. 2010. *States of Race: Critical Race Feminism for the 21st Century*. Toronto: Between the Lines.

RCMP (Royal Canadian Mounted Police). 2014. *Missing and Murdered Aboriginal Women: A National Operational Overview*. Ottawa: Government of Canada. https://www.rcmp-grc.gc.ca/en/missing-and-murdered-aboriginal-women-national-operational-overview.

Reagon, Bernice Johnson. 1983. "Coalition Politics: Turning the Century." In *Home Girls: A Black Feminist Anthology*, ed. Barbara Smith, 356–68. New York: Kitchen Table: Women of Color Press.

Rebick, Judy. 2005. *Ten Thousand Roses: The Making of a Feminist Revolution*. Toronto: Penguin Canada.

Regan, Paulette. 2010. *Unsettling the Settler Within: Indian Residential Schools, Truth Telling, and Reconciliation in Canada*. Vancouver: UBC Press.

Rich, Adrienne Cecile. 1979. "Disloyal to Civilization: Feminism, Racism, Gynephobia." In *On Lies, Secrets, and Silence: Selected Prose, 1966–1978*, edited by Adrienne Cecile Rich, 275–310. New York: Norton.

Rogers, Shelagh, Mike DeGagné, Jonathan Dewar, and Glen Lowry. 2012. *Speaking My Truth: Reflections on Reconciliation and Residential School*. Ottawa: Aboriginal Healing Foundation.

Roome, Patricia. 2005. "'From One Whose Home Is among the Indians': Henrietta Muir Edwards and Aboriginal Peoples." In *Unsettled Pasts: Reconceiving the West through Women's History*, edited by Sarah Carter, Lesley Erickson, Patricia Roome, and Char Smith, 47–77. Calgary: University of Calgary Press.

Rosaldo, Renato. 1989. *Culture and Truth: The Remaking of Social Analysis.* Boston: Beacon Press.

Rosenberg, Alyssa. 2013. "The Most Important Political Statement at the American Music Awards Last Night." *ThinkProgress*, November 25. https://archive.thinkprogress.org/the-most-important-political-statement-at-the-american-music-awards-last-night-9e08cea1febd/.

Rutherdale, Myra. 2002. *Women and the White Man's God: Gender and Race in the Canadian Mission Field.* Vancouver: UBC Press.

—. 2005. "'She was a Ragged Little Thing': Missionaries, Embodiment, and Refashioning Aboriginal Womanhood in Northern Canada." In *Contact Zones: Aboriginal and Settler Women in Canada's Colonial Past*, edited by Myra Rutherdale and Katie Pickles, 228–45. Vancouver: UBC Press.

Rutherdale, Myra, and Katie Pickles, eds. 2005. *Contact Zones: Aboriginal and Settler Women in Canada's Colonial Past.* Vancouver: UBC Press.

Said, Edward W. 1978. *Orientalism.* New York: Pantheon Books.

Saldaña-Portillo, María Josefina. 2003. *The Revolutionary Imagination in the Americas and the Age of Development.* Durham, NC: Duke University Press.

Saul, John Ralston. 2008. *A Fair Country: Telling Truths about Canada.* Toronto: Viking Canada.

Schick, Carol. 1998. *"By Virtue of Being White": Racialized Identity Formation and the Implications for Anti-racist Pedagogy.* http://hdl.handle.net/1807/11914.

Schotten, Heike. 2020. "Good White People: Lisa Slater's *Anxieties of Belonging.*" *Theory and Event* 23 (2): 409–92.

Segrest, Mab. 2019. *Memoir of a Race Traitor: Fighting Racism in the American South.* 2nd ed. New York: The New Press.

Sehdev, Robinder Kaur. 2010. "Lessons from the Bridge: On the Possibilities of Antiracist Feminist Alliances in Indigenous Spaces." In *This Is an Honour Song: Twenty Years since the Blockades – An Anthology of Writings on the "Oka Crisis,"* edited by Leanne Simpson and Kiera L. Ladner, 103–23. Winnipeg: Arbeiter Ring.

Silman, Janet, and Tobique Women's Group, eds. 1987. *Enough Is Enough: Aboriginal Women Speak Out.* Toronto: Women's Press.

Simpson, Audra. 2009. "Captivating Eunice: Membership, Colonialism, and Gendered Citizenships of Grief." *Wicazo Sa Review* 24 (2): 105–29.

—. 2014. *Mohawk Interruptus: Political Life across the Borders of Settler States.* Durham, NC: Duke University Press.

Simpson, Leanne Betasamosake. 2011. *Dancing on Our Turtle's Back: Stories of Nishnaabeg Re-creation.* Winnipeg: Arbeiter Ring.

—. 2017. *As We Have Always Done: Indigenous Freedom through Radical Resistance.* Minneapolis: University of Minnesota Press.

Simpson, Leanne Betasamosake, and Kiera L. Ladner, eds. 2010. *This Is an Honour Song: Twenty Years since the Blockades – An Anthology of Writings on the "Oka Crisis."* Winnipeg: Arbeiter Ring.

Slater, Lisa. 2019. *Anxieties of Settler Colonialism: Australia, Race and Place.* New York: Routledge.

Smith, Andrea. 2005. *Conquest: Sexual Violence and American Indian Genocide.* Cambridge, MA: South End Press.

—. 2008. "American Studies without America: Native Feminisms and the Nation-State." *American Quarterly* 60 (2): 309–15.

—. 2013. "Unsettling the Privilege of Self-Reflexivity." In *Geographies of Privilege*, edited by France Winddance Twine and Bradley Gardener, 263–79. New York: Routledge.

Smith, Barbara, ed. 1983. *Home Girls: A Black Feminist Anthology*. New York: Kitchen Table: Women of Color Press.

Smith, Linda Tuhiwai. 1999. *Decolonizing Methodologies: Research and Indigenous Peoples*. New York: St Martin's Press.

Smylie, Janet, Kristen O'Brien, Cheryllee Bourgeois, Sara Wolfe, Raglan Maddox, and Michael Rotondi. 2019. *2016 Indigenous Population Estimates for the City of Toronto*. http://www.welllivinghouse.com/wp-content/uploads/2019/12/OHC-Toronto-Population-Estimate.pdf

Snelgrove, Corey, Rita Kaur Dhamoon, and Jeff Corntassel. 2014. "Unsettling Settler Colonialism: The Discourse and Politics of Settlers, and Solidarity with Indigenous Nations." *Decolonization: Indigeneity, Education and Society* 3 (2): 1–32.

Spivak, Gayatri. 1985. "Three Women's Texts and a Critique of Imperialism." *Critical Inquiry* 12 (1): 243–61.

St. Denis, Verna. 2007. "Feminism Is for Everybody." In *Making Space for Indigenous Feminism*, edited by Joyce Green, 33–52. Black Point, NS: Fernwood.

Stevenson, Winona. 1999. "Colonialism and First Nations Women in Canada." In *Scratching the Surface: Canadian, Anti-racist, Feminist Thought*, edited by Enakshi Dua and Angela Robertson, 49–80. Toronto: Women's Press.

Starblanket, Gina. 2017. "Being Indigenous Feminists: Resurgences Against Contemporary Patriarchy." In *Making Space for Indigenous Feminism*, 2nd ed., edited by Joyce Green, 21–41. Black Point, NS: Fernwood.

Stewart-Harawira, Makere. 2007. "Practising Indigenous Feminism: Resistance to Imperialism." In *Making Space for Indigenous Feminism*, edited by Joyce Green, 124–39. Black Point, NS: Fernwood.

Stoler, Ann Laura. 1995. *Race and the Education of Desire: Foucault's History of Sexuality and the Colonial Order of Things*. Durham, NC: Duke University Press.

Stote, Karen. 2015. *An Act of Genocide: Colonialism and the Sterilization of Aboriginal Women*. Halifax, NS: Fernwood.

Strong-Boag, Veronica Jane. 1977. "'Setting the Stage': National Organization and the Women's Movement in the Late Nineteenth Century." In *The Neglected Majority: Essays in Canadian Women's History*, edited by Alison L. Prentice and Susan Mann, 87–103. Toronto: McClelland and Stewart.

Sudbury, Julia, and Margo Okazawa-Rey, eds. 2009. *Activist Scholarship: Antiracism, Feminism, and Social Change*. Boulder, CO: Paradigm.

Sullivan, Shannon. 2006. *Revealing Whiteness: The Unconscious Habits of Racial Privilege*. Bloomington: Indiana University Press.

—. 2014. *Good White People: The Problems with Middle-Class White Anti-racism*. Albany: State University of New York Press.

Sullivan-Clarke, Andrea. 2020. "Decolonizing 'Allyship' for Indian Country: Lessons from #NODAPL." *Hypatia* 35: 178–89. https://doi.org/10.1017/hyp.2019.3.

Sunseri, Lina. 2000. "Moving beyond the Feminism versus Nationalism Dichotomy: An Anti-colonial Feminist Perspective on Aboriginal Liberation Struggles." *Canadian Women's Studies/Les Cahiers De La Femme* 20 (2): 143–48.

—. 2008. "Sky Woman Lives On: Contemporary Examples of Mothering the Nation." *Canadian Woman Studies* 26 (3/4): 21–25.

Suzack, Cheryl, Shari M. Huhndorf, Jeanne Perreault, and Jean Barman, eds. (2010). *Indigenous Women and Feminism: Politics, Activism, Culture*. Vancouver: UBC Press.

TallBear, Kim. 2016. "Badass (Indigenous) Women Caretake Relations: #NoDAPL, #IdleNoMore, #BlackLivesMatter." *Society for Cultural Anthropology*, December 22. https://culanth.org/fieldsights/badass-indigenous-women-caretake-relations-no-dapl-idle-no-more-black-lives-matter.

Thielen-Wilson, Leslie. 2012. "White Terror, Canada's Indian Residential Schools and the Colonial Present: From Law towards a Pedagogy of Recognition." PhD diss., University of Toronto.

Thobani, Sunera. 2007. *Exalted Subjects: Studies in the Making of Race and Nation in Canada*. Toronto: University of Toronto Press.

Thompson, Audrey. 2003. "Tiffany, Friend of People of Color: White Investments in Antiracism." *International Journal of Qualitative Studies in Education* 16 (1): 7–29. http://resolver.scholarsportal.info/resolve/09518398/v16i0001/7_tfopocwiia.

Thorpe, Jocelyn. 2005. "Indigeneity and Transnationality?" *Women and Environments International Magazine* 68/69 (Fall): 6–8.

Trask, Haunani-Kay. 1999. *From a Native Daughter: Colonialism and Sovereignty in Hawai'i*. Rev. ed. Honolulu: University of Hawai'i Press.

Trinh, T. Minh-Ha. 1989. *Woman, Native, Other: Writing Postcoloniality and Feminism*. Bloomington: Indiana University Press.

—. 1997. "Not You/Like You: Postcolonial Women and the Interlocking Questions of Identity and Difference." In *Dangerous Liaisons: Gender, Nation, and Postcolonial Perspectives*, edited by Anne McClintock, Aamir Mufti, and Ella Shohat (for the Social Text Collective), 415–19. Minneapolis: University of Minnesota Press.

Trinh, Theresa Do. 2014. "RCMP Confirm Report of More Than 1,000 Murdered Aboriginal Women." *CBC News*, May 2.

Tuck, Eve, and K. Wayne Yang. 2012. "Decolonization Is Not a Metaphor." *Decolonization: Indigeneity, Education and Society* 1 (1): 1–40.

—. 2014. "Unbecoming Claims: Pedagogies of Refusal in Qualitative Research." *Qualitative Inquiry* 20 (6): 811–18.

Turpel, Mary Ellen. 1993. "Patriarchy and Paternalism: The Legacy of the Canadian State for First Nations Women." *Canadian Journal of Women and the Law* 6 (1): 174–92.

Valverde, Mariana. 1991. *The Age of Light, Soap, and Water: Moral Reform in English Canada, 1885–1925*. Toronto: McClelland and Stewart.

—. 1992. "When the Mother of the Race Is Free: Race, Reproduction, and Sexuality in First-Wave Feminism." In *Gender Conflicts: New Essays in Women's History*, edited by Franca Iacovetta and Mariana Valverde, 3–26. Toronto: University of Toronto Press.

Van Kirk, Sylvia. 1980. *"Many Tender Ties": Women in Fur-Trade Society in Western Canada, 1670–1870*. Winnipeg: Watson and Dwyer.
Vera, Hernán, and Andrew M. Gordon. 2003. *Screen Saviors: Hollywood Fictions of Whiteness*. Lanham, MD: Rowman and Littlefield.
Veracini, Lorenzo. 2011. "On Settlerness." *Borderlands e-Journal* 10 (1): 1–17.
Vickers, Jill. 2002. "Thinking about Violence." In *Gender, Race, and Nation: A Global Perspective*, edited by Vanaja Dhruvarajan and Jill Vickers, 222–46. Toronto: University of Toronto Press.
Vowel, Chelsea. 2016. *Indigenous Writes: A Guide to First Nations, Métis and Inuit Issues*. Winnipeg: Highwater Press.
Walia, Harsha. 2012. "Decolonizing Together." *Briarpatch* 41 (January-February): 27–30.
Wallace, Rick. 2011. "Power, Practice and a Critical Pedagogy for Non-Indigenous Allies." *Canadian Journal of Native Studies* 31 (2): 155–72.
–. 2014. *Merging Fires: Grassroots Peace-Building between Indigenous and Non-Indigenous Peoples*. Halifax, NS: Fernwood.
Ware, Vron. 1992. *Beyond the Pale: White Women, Racism, and History*. New York: Verso.
Waters, Anne, ed. 2004a. *American Indian Thought: Philosophical Essays*. Malden, MA: Blackwell.
–. 2004b. "Language Matters: Nondiscrete, Nonbinary Dualisms." In *American Indian Thought: Philosophical Essays*, edited by Anne Waters, 87–96. Malden, MA: Blackwell.
–. 2004c. "Ontology of Identity and Interstitial Being." In *American Indian Thought: Philosophical Essays*, edited by Anne Waters, 153–70. Malden, MA: Blackwell.
Weaver, Jace. 1997. *That the People Might Live: Native American Literatures and Native American Community*. New York: Oxford University Press.
Wente, Jesse. 2017. "Canada Can't Look Away after 2017: We Won't Let It." *CBC News*, December 21. http://www.cbc.ca/2017/canada-can-t-look-away-after-2017-we-won-t-let-it-1.4350376.
Wiegman, Robyn. 1999. "Whiteness Studies and the Paradox of Particularity." *Boundary 2* 26 (3): 115–50.
Williams, Randall. 2010. *The Divided World: Human Rights and Its Violence*. Minneapolis: University of Minnesota Press.
Willow, Anna J. 2009. "Clear-Cutting and Colonialism: The Ethnopolitical Dynamics of Indigenous Environmental Activism in Northwestern Ontario." *Ethnohistory* 56 (1): 35–67.
Wilson, Alex. 2015. "Afterward: A Steadily Beating Heart: Persistence, Resistance and Resurgence." In *More Will Sing Their Way to Freedom: Indigenous Resistance and Resurgence*, edited by Elaine Coburn, 255–64. Black Point, NS: Fernwood.
–. 2018. "Skirting the Issues: Indigenous Myths, Misses, and Misogyny." In *Keetsahnak: Our Missing and Murdered Indigenous Sisters*, edited by Kim Anderson, Maria Campbell, and Christi Belcourt, 161–74. Edmonton: University of Alberta Press.

Wilson, Shawn. 2008. *Research Is Ceremony: Indigenous Research Methods*. Winnipeg: Fernwood.
Wolfe, Patrick. 2006. "Settler Colonialism and the Elimination of the Native." *Journal of Genocide Research* 8 (4): 387–409. http://doi.org/10.1080/14623520601056240.
Woollacott, Angela. 2006. *Gender and Empire*. New York: Palgrave Macmillan.
Wynter, Sylvia. 2003. "Unsettling the Coloniality of Being/Power/Truth/Freedom: Towards the Human, after Man, Its Overrepresentation – An Argument." *New Centennial Review* 3 (3): 257–337.
Yeğenoğlu, Meyda. 1998. *Colonial Fantasies: Towards a Feminist Reading of Orientalism*. New York: Cambridge University Press.

Index

Note: In subentries, NMS stands for No More Silence.

Aboriginal Legal Services (Toronto), 7
acceptance/inclusion by Indigenous peoples/communities, white settler desire for, 37, 57, 117–18; as element of proximity spectrum, 12–13, 56, 74, 92, 154, 195, 207; through friendship, 165–66, 206; and need for forgiveness, 13, 56, 154, 157–58, 195, 207
Ahmed, Sara, 212, 221–22, 230n4, 231n10, 234n1; and author's proximity spectrum, 27–28, 54–57, 73–75; on colonial encounters of both distance and proximity, 27–28, 54–55, 67, 96; on *Dances with Wolves*, 63, 65, 68–69, 120–22; on friendship as way to achieve proximity, 165; on "going strange, going native," 28, 69, 70–71, 149; on Indigenous peoples as having been "stopped"/"held up," 196–97; on "learned whites," 177; on politics of antiracist declarations, 162–64, 174–75, 176, 179, 182, 185; on stranger fetishism, 27–28, 55, 63, 73, 96, 163, 197, 229n46; on white fantasies of "becoming Native"/transcendence, 37, 57, 64, 65, 68–71, 74–75, 112, 149, 165. *See also* appropriation of Indigenous culture/identity, by white settlers; "going strange, going native" (Ahmed); stranger fetishism (Ahmed)
Alfred, Taiaiake, 16, 226n17
Alicia (white study participant), 31; as acknowledging her white settler status/privilege, 41, 43; on *Avatar*, 124–25; claims of exceptionalism by, 59, 169, 171–73, 174, 175, 176; and cultural appropriation, 127, 128; and distancing from Indigenous women, 65, 66, 67, 68; on friendships with Indigenous women, 168–69; as helper, 64–65, 66, 124–25; on her involvement in solidarity work, 41, 43; and narrative of "becoming Native," 58–61, 62, 63, 71, 75, 119; and need to be helped by Indigenous

women, 124–56; on need to educate other white people, 172–73, 174, 175; and negative reaction from Indigenous woman, 64, 166; on second-wave feminism, 41, 231*n*2; self-discovery/transformation of, 63, 64–66, 67, 68; on taking direction from Indigenous women, 202; on violence against Indigenous women, 47–48; on Western lack/white sociocultural deficiencies, 117–18, 123, 125–26; on white settler guilt, 162; on white tendency to "take things personally," 60, 209
allies, Indigenous women as, 34–35, 40, 42, 148, 200. *See also entry below*
allies, white settler women as: and author's experiences, 9–10, 54, 144–45, 186–87, 226*n*11; and claims of exceptionalism, 144–45, 171–87, 192–94; competition among, 177–80, 185–86, 193; and desire to belong on Indigenous land, 106, 109; doubts/misgivings of, 60–61, 107; friendships of, ix, 169–70, 207; gender as factor for, 60–63, 64, 179; and genuine desire to help, 60–61; and helper-beneficiary binary, 34–35; identification of, 50–51; as important to Indigenous causes, 8, 135–36, 226*n*17; Indigenous women's willingness to work with/ appreciation of, 8, 9–10, 80, 108; and need to confront colonialism, 15–16; and need to "step back, but not out," 198–206; as needy do-gooders, 88, 141; and non-colonizing solidarity, 4–5, 36–36, 198, 199–11, 221; as not always wanted, 135, 199, 120; parameters for, 53–54, 84, 110–11; and privilege of liberal individualism, 40–43, 46; as seeking care/healing from Indigenous women, 95–96, 215–16; as seeking company of Indigenous women, 53–54; and

solidarity at a distance, 206–13, 235*n*3; transgressive behaviour by, 90, 100–2; and white self-reflexivity, 189–90, 221; and white settler guilt, 15, 159–62
Amadahy, Zainab (Cherokee, Seminole) (study participant), 31; on "celebrity" status, 147, 149; on claim of settler status, 176–77; on competition between white activists, 178–79, 181, 185–86, 193; on need for white women to "step back, but not out," 201, 202, 203; on solidarity work with white women, 99, 135; on specific nature of violence against Indigenous women, 144–45; on white self-reflexivity, 187–88, 218, 220–21; on white tokenization of Indigenous peoples, 97–98; on white view of Indigenous women as healers/ caretakers, 95–96
Anderson, Kim, 71–72, 74, 131, 143–44
Applebaum, Barbara, 160–61, 164, 190
appropriation of Indigenous culture/ identity, by white settlers, 36, 111–53, 196, 203; Ahmed on, 28, 38, 58, 64, 66, 69–72, 75–76, 73, 113, 150, 166; and Canadian nation building, 36, 115–17, 126–29, 144, 153, 207; in *Dances with Wolves*, 64, 66, 69–70, 121–23; at Indigenous events, 90, 92–93, 102, 158–59; and need to learn about white settler ancestry, 140; participants' discussion of, 68–69, 81, 83–84, 89–94, 111–53, 154–55, 177–78, 181, 200, 207, 110–11, 234*n*23; and participants' narratives of "becoming Native," 58–63, 69–71, 75, 119, 235*n*8; and settler precarity, 112–15; and Western lack, 66, 117, 121–23, 126, 150; and white/settler liberal subjectivity, 36, 111, 112–14, 151–52; and white settler need to belong on Indigenous land, 28, 111, 112, 113–14, 116, 121–29, 150–51

appropriation of Indigenous land, by white settlers. *See* land, Indigenous, as stolen land, *and entry following*
Ardra (Indigenous study participant), 31; on crises faced by Indigenous peoples, 84; on need for mixed activist groups, 199–200; on "radical" white women as more likely to seek Indigenous women's friendship, 106–7, 166; on white settler guilt, 102, 158–59, 188; on white women's need for proximity, 53, 55, 106–7
Arvin, Maile, Eve Tuck, and Angie Morrill, 197. *See also* Tuck, Eve
attraction to Indigenous culture/tradition/spirituality, 36, 58–59, 63, 111–53; and allure of "authentic Indian," 146–50; and Canadian nation building, 115–17, 126; and collective survival of Indigenous women, 129–35; consuming nature of, 71–72, 87–88, 91, 113; as element of proximity spectrum, 57, 75; and Indigenous women's deconstruction of white depictions, 141–46, 152–53; and Indigenous women's resistance/reaffirmation discourse, 137–41, 152; and Western lack, 111, 112, 116–21, 150–51; and white settler claims to national belonging in Canada, 121–29, 151; and white settler cultural appropriation, 66, 117, 121–23, 126, 150; and white settler precarity/desire for emplacement, 112–14
Avatar (film), 124–25

Badwall, Harjeet, 221
Bannerji, Himani, 230*n*47
Barker, Adam, 15, 16; Emma Battell Lowman and, 15, 22, 23–24, 40, 155
"becoming Native": narratives of, 58–63, 64, 66, 69–73, 75–76, 119, 121–23, 235*n*8; and settler subjectivity, 122–23, 126; as technique of "going strange, going native," 28, 56, 70–72, 76, 113; white fantasies of, 38, 58, 64, 66, 69–71, 75–76, 113, 166
Belaney, Archibald (Grey Owl), 113, 116, 232*n*2, 233*n*5
Belcourt, Christi, 7
Belinda (Indigenous study participant), 31; on Indigenous peoples' tolerance/inclusivity, 138–39; on inevitability of white involvement in solidarity work, 43, 209; on internalized colonialism, 149–50, 235*n*3; on need for boundaries in solidarity work, 84, 140, 209–11, 216, 223; on seeking white-dominated solidarity work, 149; on survivalist aspect of activism, 131; on white women's allyship, 84
belonging, on Indigenous land, 28, 111, 112, 113–14, 116, 121–29, 150–51. *See also* land, Indigenous, white settler need to belong/live "legitimately" on
Bergland, Renée, 113–14, 123, 126
Black Lives Matter, 225*n*5, 235*n*2
Boudreau Morris, Katie, 220
boundaries, of solidarity work, 10, 12; respect for, 216, 218; transgression of, 14, 28, 36, 77–110, 196, 215–16; and white women's need to maintain distance, 206–11, 235*n*3; and white women's need to "step back, but not out," 198–206. *See also* parameters
Bourgeois, Robyn, viii, 130
Boyd, Dwight, 22–23, 27, 67, 161
burden of proof, on Indigenous peoples/women, 96–103, 191; and white supremacist thinking, 98–100
Bush, Melanie, 156

Calloway, Colin G., 114
caretaking/healing by Indigenous peoples, white settler desire for, 49, 159; as element of proximity spectrum, 13, 57, 75, 93–96, 108–9, 196, 208; through Indigenous culture/spirituality, 116, 140; and need for boundaries, 215–16

Carla (white study participant), 31; on claims of exceptionalism/white settler guilt, 160, 161–62, 180–81; on family history/settler status, 44, 45

Carlson-Manathara, Elizabeth (Liz), and Gladys Rowe, 220, 235*n*7

Castellano, Marlene Brant, 8

"celebrity" Elders/Indigenous spokespeople, 146–48, 206

challenge, white settler desire for. *See* learning/being challenged, white settler desire of

Champlain, Samuel de, 127, 233*n*11

Chazan, May, 15

Chloe (white study participant), 31, 235*n*8; on being valued/respected for solidarity work, 62–63, 64; and denial of white settler guilt, 51–52, 231*n*7; on healing power of solidarity work, 62, 69; as "a little ahead" of Indigenous women, 70–71, 114; and narrative of "becoming Native," 69–71; on white settler admiration of Indigenous peoples, 127–28, 129

Clark Mane, Rebecca, 51, 231*n*1

Combahee River Collective, 214, 235*n*4

competition, among white settler activists, 177–80, 185–86, 193

consuming: and "eating the Other," as prelude to appropriation of Indigenous land/resources, 71–72, 113; as technique of "going strange, going native," 28, 56, 70–72, 76, 113; and white needy do-gooder as leech/succubus, 87–88, 91

Conway, Janet, x, 96, 97

Cordova, Viola Faye, 142, 143

Council Fire Native Cultural Centre (Toronto), 7

cultural appropriation. *See* appropriation of Indigenous culture/identity, by white settlers

cultural attraction. *See* attraction to Indigenous culture/tradition/spirituality

"culture shopping," 154–55

Dances with Wolves (film), 64, 66, 69–70, 121–23. *See also* "becoming Native"

Danielle (Indigenous study participant), 31, 135, 138–39, 141, 200, 206–8, 209–10; on "celebrity Elders," 146–48, 206; on emotional labour of solidarity work, 213–14; on internalized colonialism, 235*n*3; on legitimacy of Canadian state, 128–29; on reasons for political activism, 132, 133–34; on white needy do-gooders, 89–91, 128, 206

Darcie (white study participant), 31; as acknowledging her white settler status/privilege, 115–16, 174–75, 189–90; anger/anticolonial stance of, 48, 49; and changed view of Canada, 115–16, 189–90; claim of exceptionalism by, 166–68, 169, 174–75, 176; on friendships with Indigenous women, 167–68, 169; on need to educate other white people, 174–75, 176; on reasons for participating in solidarity work, 48; on white women's need for proximity, 53–54, 55, 115

Dawn (white study participant), 31, 235*n*8; and "challenge" of solidarity work, 67; and distancing from Indigenous women, 66–67, 68; on "partnerships" rather than "solidarity," 51, 231*n*3; and refusal to invoke colonialism, 50–51, 52; and self-making/appropriation of Indigenous culture, 119–20, 123, 125–27, 129; on sister's drug use, 66–67; and use of false equivalences, 51, 52, 66–67, 70–71, 122; on violence against Indigenous

women/environmental violence, 120–22, 134
decolonizing, 127, 144, 172, 184, 203; by No More Silence, 16, 214–15; vs non-colonizing, 4–5
Deer, Tracey, 233n14
distance: as needed in solidarity work, 206–11, 235n3; and proximity, in colonial encounters, 27–28, 55–56, 68, 97
distancing, by white settler women: from Indigenous women, 65, 66–67, 68; from racism/colonialism, 18, 54, 67, 157, 161
Downtown Eastside (DTES) (Vancouver), 66–67, 145–46
Dyer, Richard, 235n1

Edwards, Henrietta Muir, 230n43
environment: respect for, as linked to Indigeneity/Indigenous spirituality, 115, 117, 122, 126, 171–72, 233n6; violence against, as linked to violence against Indigenous women, 118, 120–22, 125, 134
Erickson, Bruce, 113, 114, 116, 119, 232n2, 233n5
Eve (white study participant), 31; on choices in solidarity work, 42–43; on declarations of white settler status/ allyship, 175–76, 177, 181, 183–84, 218; on importance of deeds over words, 184, 220; on taking direction from Indigenous women, 202
Evelyn (white study participant), 31; as acknowledging her white settler status/privilege, 44, 45; on being valued/respected for solidarity work, 62, 63, 64; as both critical and proud of Canada, 115–16; on Canadian colonial affairs, 44–45; and narrative of "becoming Native," 61–62; on need for boundaries in solidarity work, 208, 120; and need for Indigenous women's acceptance, 118–19; on non-colonizing solidarity work, 61–62; and self-making/appropriation of Indigenous culture, 118–19, 122–23, 125–26; on transformation through Indigenous spirituality/ solidarity work, 122–23, 140; on violence against Indigenous women/ environmental violence, 120–21
exceptionalism, claims of, by white settler women, 13, 21, 36, 59, 144–45, 154–94; art/politics of, 163–66; and belief in white morality/goodness/ innocence, 156–58; in declarations, 171–81; and friendships in solidarity work, 180–81, 192, 193, 194, 234n17; and gendered colonial subjectivity, 36, 46, 166, 171–72; Heron on, 156, 164, 235n6; and limits of self-reflexivity, 187–93; participants' self-examination of, 182–87; Schick on, 165, 174; and self-making, 163–81; and white settler guilt/need for forgiveness, 36, 153, 155–56, 158–63, 169–70, 177, 186–87, 194, 234n17

false equivalences, 145, 151; participants' use of, 51, 52, 66–67, 70–71, 122
Fee, Margery, and Lynette Russell, 123
Fellows, Mary Louise, and Sherene Razack, 21; on "race to innocence," 157, 191–92. *See also* Razack, Sherene
femininity, Indigenous: and balance with masculinity, in spiritual teaching, 120; and earth/ environment, 120–21, 134. *See also* environment; women, Indigenous
feminism, Indigenous, 143–44, 152, 228n30, 235n1; and Black feminism, 20, 200, 234n18; and emphasis on colonialism, 19–20, 28–29, 122, 228n29; and Indigenous women's roles as caretakers, 130–31; self-determination struggles of, 130.

See also entries below; women, Indigenous, and entry following feminism, white: colonial roots of, 12, 24–25, 26, 78–79; failures of, 62; second-wave, 41, 229n35, 231n2; third-wave, 51. See also entry below; women, white settler, and entry following feminism, "whitestream," Indigenous women's criticisms of, 17–21, 51, 79–80, 229n35; and colonial impulse to "help"/"save" Indigenous women, 17, 24–27; and focus on gender/ patriarchal oppression, 17, 18–19; and insufficient analysis/recognition of colonialism, 17, 18–20, 21, 122

First Nations House (University of Toronto), viii, 4

Flowers, Rachel, 8, 199, 208, 232n7

forgiveness of Indigenous peoples, white settler desire for, 13, 57, 155, 158–59, 196, 208. See also acceptance/ inclusion by Indigenous peoples/ communities, white settler desire for

Foucault, Michel, 129

Frankenberg, Ruth, 11, 226n20, 235n1

Free Trade Area of the Americas, 6

Freeman, Victoria, 6, 224

friendships, in solidarity work, ix, 28, 166–70, 207; and acceptance/inclusion of white women, 166–67, 207; and claims of exceptionalism, 180–81, 192, 193, 194, 234n17; Indigenous women's experience of, 207, 234n16; as more likely to be sought by "radical" white women, 106–7, 166

Gabriela (Indigenous study participant), 31; on internalized colonialism, 235n3; on liminal space of solidarity work, 203; on need for white women to "step back, but not out," 202–5; on non-colonizing solidarity, 198; on white needy do-gooders, 89, 91; on white settler guilt, 161–62

gendered colonial subjectivity. See subjectivity, gendered colonial

George, Pamela, 231n6

Goeman, Mishuana, 56, 87

ghosts, Indigenous peoples as, 113–14. See also "vanishing Indian," myth of

"going strange, going native" (Ahmed), 28, 70, 71–72, 150; consuming, becoming, and passing, as techniques of, 28, 56, 70–72, 76, 113. See also Ahmed, Sara; appropriation of Indigenous culture/ identity, by white settlers; "becoming Native"; consuming; stranger fetishism (Ahmed)

Grahn, Judy, 123

Grande, Sandy, 18, 51, 228n28

Green, Ruth (Kanien'kehá:ka) (study participant), 31; on Guswenta, 132, 217; on need for white women to "step back, but not out," 201; on need for white women's "wholistic investment" in solidarity work, 205; on white settler guilt, 94–95, 98, 177; on white women's need to be educated by Indigenous women, 96, 97, 99, 101; on white women's personal outrage/emotional responses, 49, 75, 85, 87–88, 94–95

Gregory, Derek, 4, 195, 225n4

Grewal, Inderpal, 25–26

Grey Owl (Archibald Belaney), 113, 116, 232n2, 233n5

guilt, white settler, 9, 11, 15, 16, 36, 45, 71, 102, 234n17; author on, 9, 155–56, 185–87, 194, 222; claims of exceptionalism and, 36, 155–56, 158–63, 186–87, 234n17. See also entry below

guilt, white settler, discussion of, 76, 158–63; by Indigenous study participants, 82–83, 87–88, 94–95, 98–99, 102, 158–60, 177, 185, 188, 215; by white study participants, 51–52, 160, 161–63, 174–75, 180–81, 184, 190, 194, 231n7

Guswenta (Two Row Wampum Treaty), 132, 217

Harper, Stephen, 115
Hassan, Ali, 7
healing/caretaking by Indigenous peoples, white settler desire for, 49, 159; as element of proximity spectrum, 13, 57, 75, 93–96, 108–9, 196, 208; through Indigenous culture/spirituality, 116, 140; and need for boundaries, 215–16
"helping" Indigenous women, 8–9, 28, 64–65, 72, 80–86, 102, 192–93; colonial roots/aspects of, 12, 13, 17, 24–27, 34–35, 65, 78–79, 157, 176, 189, 197, 213, 214; and desire to be helped by Indigenous women, 13, 35, 66, 79, 85, 88–89, 90, 103–10, 124–25, 188, 211–12, 222; from position of privilege/dominance, 34–35, 41, 47, 70, 90–91; in positive/non-colonizing way, 60–61, 84, 201, 204, 216; and white women's saviour mentality, 10, 25–26, 41, 88, 107, 124–25. *See also entries below*
"helping imperative" (Heron), 13, 17, 79, 85–86, 103–6, 107, 117, 151, 211–12
"helping with a twist," 9, 79, 103–10, 123, 211–12
Heron, Barbara: study by, of Canadian white women development workers in Global South, 11, 13, 47, 57, 89, 90, 172; on claims to exceptionalism, 156, 164, 235n6; compared to solidarity work on "Canadian" soil, 105–6, 107; on continuities of colonial behaviour/attitudes, 49, 85, 100, 103; on "helping imperative," 13, 17, 79, 85–86, 103–6, 107, 109, 117, 151, 175, 212; and impulse to solidarity, 103–6, 107, 109, 117, 151, 212; and self-reflexivity in social work, 221; on white desire to know/learn from Other, 100, 232n10; on white women's right to do solidarity work, 85, 172

Hiller, Chris, 15, 189, 222–23
hooks, bell, 20, 21, 71, 113
Huntley, Audrey, 16

Idle No More, 7, 225n5, 226n13, 228n25
Indian Act, 19, 184, 229n34, 233n14
Indigenous peoples: burden of proof placed on, 96–103, 191; as ghosts, 113–14; as having been "stopped"/"held up," 197–98; and massive inequity of settler colonialism, 141–42, 195; participants on, 84, 127–28, 129, 138–39; and "vanishing Indian" myth, 119, 124, 230n43; white tokenization of, 97–98. *See also* acceptance/inclusion by Indigenous peoples/communities, white settler desire for; caretaking/healing by Indigenous peoples, white settler desire for; forgiveness of Indigenous peoples, white settler desire for; Other, Indigenous
Indigenous Solidarity Week (Toronto), 61
Indigenous women. *See* feminism, Indigenous; women, Indigenous, *and entry following*

Johnston, Anna, and Alan Lawson, 5
Julia (white study participant), 31; as acknowledging her white settler status/privilege, 45–46; on "culture shopping" by white women, 154–55, 182; on educating oneself about settler colonialism, 96; on her involvement in Indigenous solidarity work, 48, 154; and negative reaction from Indigenous woman, 162; on white needy do-gooders, 92–93; on white settler guilt, 162–63, 194; on white women's declarations of solidarity, 182–84, 194

Kellie (Indigenous study participant), 31; on benefits of participation in Indigenous activism, 140–41; on "celebrity" Indigenous spokespeople,

148; on white needy do-gooder, 89–90; on white settler appropriation/hijacking of solidarity space, 89–91, 93–94, 140
Konsmo, Erin M., and A.M.K. Pacheco, 120–21
Kowal, Emma, 17, 157–58, 177, 187, 235*n*7
Kuokkannen, Rauna, 121, 130, 226*n*16, 229*n*33

land, Indigenous, as stolen land, 7, 16, 23, 46–47; reclamation of, 30, 43–44, 219. *See also entry below*
land, Indigenous, white settler need to belong/live "legitimately" on: and claims of exceptionalism/white settler guilt, 155, 160, 169–70, 194; and cultural appropriation, 28, 111, 112, 113–14, 116, 121–29, 150–51; and desire for proximity, 37, 38, 76, 196; and impulse to solidarity, 103, 104, 106, 108, 109; and non-colonizing solidarity, 220, 221–22, 235*n*7; and white/settler liberal subjectivity, 23–24, 28, 38, 72–73, 78, 106, 109, 112, 196
LaRocque, Emma, 139, 146, 150, 203, 225*n*6; on "civilized"–"savage" binary, 114, 128, 129, 137; on colonization as "active toxin," 81; on Indigenous political resistance as act of survival, 132, 152; on myth of "vanishing Indian," 233*n*3; on white concept of "noble savage," 55, 116, 137; on white desire for proximity to Indigenous people, 55, 74, 233*n*5; on white failure to dismantle colonial projects, 220
Lavell, Jeannette Corbiere, 133
Lawrence, Bonita, 130, 143–44, 146, 159, 228*n*31
learning/being challenged, white settler desire of: and desire to be knowledgeable/superior, 97–101, 178; as element of proximity spectrum, 57, 67, 75, 108–9, 155, 168, 208; as inappropriate in solidarity work, 101; in participants' narratives, 154–55, 167–68; salvific benefits of, 124; and white stigma/guilt, 157–58
Lewis, Reina, and Sara Mills, 158, 159, 160
Lockard, Claire A., 164, 165, 177
Lorde, Audre, 20
Lovelace, Sandra, 133
Lowman, Emma Battell, and Adam Barker, 15, 22, 23–24, 40, 155. *See also* Barker, Adam
Lydia (Indigenous study participant), 31; on her own activist work, 82, 131–32; on Indigenous women's responsibilities to their communities, 132–33; on internalized colonialism, 235*n*3; on need to take direction from Indigenous women, 201, 202, 203; on survivalist aspect of activism, 131–32; on white awareness of settler status, 189–90; on white needy do-gooders, 85, 87–89, 91, 94–95; on white settler guilt, 82–83, 87–88; on white women's challenges in negotiating privilege, 101–2

MacDonald, David, 128, 129
Mahmood, Saba, 33
Mahrouse, Gada, 85, 86, 96–97, 124, 141, 186
Mair, Charles, 55
Maracle, Lee (Stó:lō/Métis) (study participant), 31; background of, 4, 81, 226*n*19, 232*nn*2–3; on class as factor in white women's privilege, 11, 25; on colonial origins of feminism, 24–25, 26; on "decolonizing" vs "non-colonizing," 4; on interpretation of participants' narratives, 69; on massive inequity of settler colonialism, 141–42, 195; on patriarchy, 24–25, 216, 218; on reasons for solidarity work, 184–85; on solidarity work as non-colonizing/necessary, 81–84, 108,

197, 200, 204; on solidarity work as taking precedence over relationships, 135; on white self-reflexivity, 188–89, 190; on white settler guilt, 160, 164; on white women's desire for proximity, 92; on white women's pursuit of proximity in "cherished spaces," 77–78, 86–87, 105, 110, 198–199, 205–6; on white women's transgressive behaviour, 137–38
Maracle, Sylvia, 8
masculine discourse, white: distancing perspective of, 66, 68; of self-discovery, 66. *See also* men, white settler
masculinity: and balance with femininity, in Indigenous teaching, 120. *See also* men, Indigenous; men, white settler
McCue, Duncan, 7
McIvor, Sharon, 132–33
men, Indigenous, 54, 59, 63, 68, 91, 122, 168; author's interaction with, 65–66; as celebrities, 148; and concept of "noble savage," 55, 116–17, 137; and confrontation with transgressive white woman, 90; preparation of food by, at NMS ceremony, 179
men, white settler, 45, 65, 71, 90, 91, 149; and competition between activists, 179, 193; distancing perspective of, 66, 68; dominance of, and violence against Indigenous women, 72, 231*n*6; and narrative of "becoming Native," 64, 66, 69–70, 75–76, 121–23; transgressive behaviour by, at Indigenous events, 94, 95; white women's modeling of themselves after, 68
Mignolo, Walter, and Catherine Walsh, 36
Million, Dian, 212, 214, 229*n*35
Missing and Murdered Indigenous Women and Girls, National Inquiry into (NIMMIWG), 3, 7, 233*n*8. *See also* No More Silence (NMS)

missing and murdered Indigenous women, girls, and two-spirit (MMIWG2S) people, 3, 7, 9, 144, 200, 201, 204; advocacy of NMS for, viii, 6; annual Strawberry Ceremony honouring, 6, 29, 30, 144, 203–4, 226*n*11; participants' solidarity work for, 46, 49, 67, 84, 135, 213–14. *See also* No More Silence (NMS)
Mississaugas of Scugog First Nation, 5–6
modernity/coloniality (M/C) group (Latin America), 24, 229*n*37
Mohanty, Chandra, 5, 80, 231*n*1
Monture, Patricia, 19, 214
Moodie, Susanna, 25, 229*n*40
Moreton-Robinson, Aileen: study by, of white feminist academics in Australia, 17–18, 27, 51, 127; on Indigenous women's feminist/self-determination struggles, 130; on Indigenous women's life writings/knowledge, 79; on Indigenous women's subordinate subject position, 33, 132; on white women's distancing from/disavowal of racism, 18, 67, 157, 161; on white women's dominant subject position, 33, 39, 76; on white women's self-serving behaviour, 86
Morgensen, Scott, 23, 112–13, 123, 126, 225*n*7
Morrison, Toni, 233*n*7

Na-Me-Res (Native Men's Residence, Toronto), 7
Namaste, Viviane K., 164–65, 177
Narayan, Uma, 230*n*44
nation building, Canadian, 36, 115–17, 126–29, 144, 153, 207
national belonging, as white settler desire/goal, 28, 111, 112, 113–14, 116, 121–29, 150–51
Native Canadian Centre of Toronto, 6
Native Women's Resource Centre (Toronto), 6–7, 37

"needy do-gooder," figure of, 87–93, 128, 141, 202, 206; as compared to leech/succubus, 87–88, 91; and gendered colonial subjectivity, 85, 86, 87–88, 89–90, 93; transgressive/attention-getting behaviour of, 78, 86–87, 89–90, 91, 93, 99–100, 139; and underside of desire to help, 85, 103, 108; and white settler guilt, 158–59
Nestel, Sheryl, 79–80
No More Silence (NMS), viii, 42, 226n11; author as member of, viii, x, 6–7, 8, 30, 47, 54, 206, 226n11; and author's research, 9–10, 16, 29, 30, 187; decolonizing politics of, 16, 214–15; and Indigenous women's spirituality, 140; men's solidarity with, 179–80; Strawberry Ceremony of, 6, 29, 30, 144, 203–4, 226n11; white women in, 203–5, 206, 213
"noble savage," white concept of, 55, 116–17, 137
non-colonizing solidarity, proposal for, 14, 36–36, 195–224; and need to curb solidarity impulse, 211–16; and need to "step back, but not out," 198–206; and solidarity at a distance, 206–13; and use of "non-colonizing" rather than "decolonizing," 4–5; and white self-reflexivity, 217–23
nostalgia: environmentalism and, 117; salvific benefit and, 123–24, 126, 128, 151. See also salvific benefit

O'Hara, Amber, 213
Oka Crisis, 232n9
Ontario Institute for Studies in Education (OISE), 6, 9
Other, Indigenous, 155; "eating" of, as prelude to appropriation of land/resources, 71–72, 113–14, 230n46; friendship with, 28; helping, 28, 35; "helping with a twist," 9, 79, 103–10, 123, 211–14; identification with, 123; knowing/learning from, 28, 56, 97, 100, 125, 222, 232n10; saviour mentality and, 41; stranger fetishism/self-making and, 56, 58, 69–72, 76, 88, 97, 125

Paget, Amelia McLean, 230n43
parameters: of solidarity work/relationships, 84, 167–68, 197, 208, 215–16; of white allyship, 53–54, 84, 210–11; of white settler knowledge production, 97–98. See also boundaries, of solidarity work
Parker, Pat, 206
passing: as technique of "going strange, going native," 28, 56, 70–72, 76, 113
Peggy (white study participant), 31; as acknowledging her white settler status/privilege, 44, 45, 72, 75, 174, 175, 177–78, 190–92; on competition/judgmental behaviour among white activists, 177–78, 186, 202; on friendships with Indigenous women, 169–70; on her involvement in Indigenous solidarity work, 43–44, 45; "in-between" subject status of, 68–69; on need for boundaries in solidarity work, 120; on white settler guilt, 174–75, 190; on white settlers' need to belong/live "legitimately" on Indigenous land, 72–73, 106, 155, 169–70, 194
Pratt, Mary Louise, 4, 232n5
Pratt, Minnie Bruce, 226n20, 232n5
proximity, to Indigenous women/feminists, as pursued by white women/feminists: and attraction to Indigenous culture/tradition/spirituality, 36, 57, 58–59, 63, 75, 111–53; consuming nature of, 71–72, 87–88, 91, 113; in context of Indigenous–non-Indigenous alliances, 14–17; and gendered colonial subjectivity, 10, 13, 28, 33, 36, 55, 104, 196, 211–12, 216; impulse

to, 12–14; Indigenous women's frustration/anger with, 17–21; Indigenous women's perception of, as transgressive, 10, 36, 77–110; and proposal for non-colonizing solidarity, 14, 36–36, 195–224; and pursuit of exceptionalism, 13, 21, 36, 154–94; in solidarity work, 27–28, 32–35; spectrum of, 12–13, 35–36, 37–76; and white/settler liberal subjectivity, 28, 38, 72, 78, 86. *See also entries below*; solidarity, between white and Indigenous women/feminists; *specific topics*

proximity, spectrum of, 12–13, 35–36, 37–76; Ahmed's work and, 27–28, 55–58, 74–76; author's explanation of, 55–58, 226*n*23; and Indigenous/collective vs white/individual approaches to solidarity work, 38–43; and self-discovery/transformation/transcendence fantasies, 63–69; and white women's challenges as members of political collectivity, 43–52; and white women's narratives of "becoming Native," 58–63, 69–73; and white women's self-making goals, 52–73, 212, 226*n*23. *See also entry below*

proximity, spectrum of, five elements comprising, 12–13, 57, 75–76, 93, 196, 208. *See also* acceptance/inclusion by Indigenous peoples/communities; attraction to Indigenous culture/tradition/spirituality; caretaking/healing by Indigenous peoples, white settler desire for; learning/being challenged, white settler desire of; self-empowerment/worth/purpose, white settler desire for

radical self-reflexivity, 16, 221–22
"radical" white activists: desire for proximity by, 106–7, 109; self-righteousness of, 178

Razack, Sherene, 21, 35, 226*n*18, 230*n*49; on "playing primitive," 113; on white innocence, 156; on white settler masculine dominance, 231*n*6. *See also* Fellows, Mary Louise, and Sherene Razack
Reagon, Bernice Johnson, 20
Regan, Paulette, 16
Roome, Patricia, 230*n*43
Rosenberg, Alyssa, 205

salvific benefit, 123–25; nostalgia and, 123–24, 126, 128, 151. *See also* nostalgia
Sarah (white study participant), 31; anger/anticolonial stance of, 48, 49; on immigrants fleeing racism/violence, 46–47, 52; on issue of stolen land, 46–47; on violence faced by Indigenous women, 48
Saul, John Ralston, 127–29, 233*n*11
saviour mentality, of white women, 10, 41, 88, 107; colonial origins of, 25–26; and saviours vs helpers, 124–25. *See also* "helping" Indigenous women, *and entries following*
Schick, Carol: study by, of white pre-service teachers, 39, 57, 231*n*1; on collective exceptionalism, 165, 174; on white awareness of collective privilege, 39; on white desire for proximity to Indigenous people, 54, 55, 74; on white "imperialist nostalgia"/salvific benefit, 123–24, 126, 128, 151
Schotten, Heike, 197, 201
Segrest, Mab, 226*n*20
self-empowerment/worth/purpose, white settler desire for, 62; as element of proximity spectrum, 13, 57, 75–76, 93, 196; and narratives of becoming/self-worth, 58–63
self-making, by white settler women, 4, 9, 10–11, 13, 18–36, 37–76; and Canadian nation building, 36, 115–16;

and claims of exceptionalism, 163–81; and cultural appropriation, 36, 111–53; and impulse to solidarity, 78–79, 103–10, 123, 212; and neediness, 78–79, 85, 87–93, 95; and non-colonizing solidarity, 204–5, 217–18, 223–24; as ongoing process, 34; and proximity spectrum, 52–73, 212, 226n23; and settler colonialism, 23–25, 27–28, 124; and transgressive behaviour, 196, 204–5, 206; and white settler guilt, 102, 159

self-reflexivity, by white settler women, 12, 16, 61, 107, 164–66, 205, 210; Amadahy on, 187–88, 218, 220–22; limits of, in context of exceptionalism, 187–93; Maracle on, 188–89, 190; and non-colonizing solidarity, 36–36, 217–23; as radical, 16, 221–22; in social work, 221

self-worth: Amadahy's solidarity work and, 147; narratives of becoming and, 58–63; white settler desire for, 57, 75–76

settler colonialism, ix, 160, 120–11; and attraction to Indigenous culture/ tradition/spirituality, 36, 111–53; and cultural appropriation, 36, 111–53, 196, 203; dismantling of, 7–9, 15, 35, 36, 78, 85, 110, 189–90, 192, 196–97, 220–24; and Indigenous burden of proof, 96–103, 191; vs Indigenous resistance, 234n21; and "race"/migrant status, 225n7; and white self-making, 23–25, 27–28, 124; white complicity in, 11, 13, 15, 16, 18, 20, 21, 38, 39, 47, 52, 74, 79, 106, 156, 161, 164, 165, 171, 174–76, 180–81, 188, 189, 192–94, 222; and white/settler liberal subjectivity, 24–27, 199. *See also* appropriation of Indigenous culture/identity, by white settlers; guilt, white settler, *and entry following*; "helping" Indigenous women, *and entries following*; land, Indigenous, as stolen land, *and entry following*; men, white settler; subjectivity, gendered colonial, *and entries following*; women, white settler, *and entry following* settler subjectivity. *See* subjectivity, gendered colonial, *and entries following*

Simpson, Leanne Betasamosake: and critique of Western knowledge production, ix–x; on Indigenous resurgence/resistance, 143, 144, 146, 149–50, 152, 120, 226n18, 234n19, 234n21; on issue of stolen land, 7, 221; on Moodie, 25; on subjectivity, 22; on violence against Indigenous women/environmental violence, 121

Six Nations of the Grand River, 6, 226n9; women of, 120

Slater, Lisa, 23, 196–97

Smith, Andrea, 226n16

Smith, Linda Tuhiwai, 225n6

Snelgrove, Corey, 5, 163; with Rita Dhamoon and Jeff Corntassel, 15

solidarity, between white and Indigenous women/feminists, 3–36; author's experience of/academic research on, in Toronto, 5–7, 9–12; author's study of, 3–4, 28–35; in colonial landscape, 7–9; and gendered colonial subjectivity, 9, 10, 13, 21, 22–27, 28, 33–34, 36–36; impulse to, 79, 103–10, 123, 212; and Indigenous women's frustration/anger with "whitestream" feminism, 17–21; and need to maintain distance, 206–11, 235n3; as problematized by settler colonialism/white settler anxieties about belonging, 23–24; and proposal for non-colonizing solidarity, 14, 36–36, 195–224; proximity in, 27–28, 32–35; scholarship on, 14–17; and white/settler liberal subjectivity, 9, 14, 23–24, 28, 36. *See also* proximity, to Indigenous women/feminists, as

pursued by white women/feminists; *specific topics*
spectrum of proximity. *See* proximity, spectrum of
spirituality, Indigenous, 62, 94, 120, 139–41, 205, 214; attraction to, 36, 57, 58–60, 63, 75–76, 88, 107, 111, 124–27, 150, 151, 217; author's experience of, 65–66; respect for environment, as linked to, 115, 117, 122, 126, 171–72, 233n6; white desire to be healed through, 116, 140; white women's transformation through, 122–23, 140–41, 142
Spivak, Gayatri, 26, 53
Stevenson, Winona, 19
Stewart-Harawira, Makere, 3, 130, 223
stolen land. *See* land, Indigenous, as stolen land, *and entry following*
stranger fetishism (Ahmed), 27–28, 56, 64, 74, 97, 164, 198, 230n46; and "going strange, going native," 28, 70, 71–72, 150
Strawberry Ceremony (NMS), 6, 29, 30, 144, 203–4, 226n11
subjectivity, gendered colonial: about, 9, 21, 22–27; and "becoming Native," 122–23; and claims of exceptionalism, 36, 46, 166, 171–72; complexities of, 27, 46, 50, 74, 171–72; and desire for proximity through solidarity work, 10, 13, 28, 33, 36, 55, 104, 196, 211–12, 216; and liberal individualism, 74–75; and neediness/transgressive behaviour, 85, 86, 87–88, 89–90, 93; and non-colonizing solidarity work, 36–36, 217–23. *See also entries below*
subjectivity, settler: and "becoming Native," 126; collective aspects of, 55, 102–3, 112, 158, 221–22; and desire for proximity, 12–13; and learning/knowing, 97; scholarship on, 15–16, 23–24, 228n26; and white settler guilt, 158

subjectivity, white/settler liberal: collective aspects of, 72, 111, 112–14, 151; colonial roots of, 24–27, 199; and cultural appropriation, 36, 111, 112–14, 151–52; and desire for legitimacy/belonging on Indigenous land, 23–24, 28, 38, 72–73, 78, 106, 109, 112, 196; and desire for proximity to Indigenous women, 28, 38, 72, 78, 86; as gendered, 9, 21, 22–27; and Indigenous women's burden of proof, 191–92; and neediness/transgressive behaviour, 78, 86, 90; and non-colonizing solidarity work, 14; as personal/individualistic, 38, 43, 67, 194; scholarship on, 24; and white activism, 141; and white settler guilt/exceptionalism, 153, 158, 177, 194
Sullivan, Shannon, 59–60, 164
Sunseri, Lina, 130
survival, collective, of Indigenous women, 129–35; political activism and, 131–34, 152

Tabobondung, Rebeka (Anishinaabe) (study participant), 31; on Indigenous peoples' burden of proof, 99, 191; on need for white women to learn about their own ancestry, 140, 218, 220; on white supremacist thinking/"Westerness," 98–99, 112, 114; and white women's need to take direction from Indigenous women, 101, 135, 201, 202, 203
Tagaq, Tanya, 77–78, 198
Teresa (Indigenous study participant), 31; on danger of solidarity work as too inclusive, 139; on emotional labour of solidarity work, 213; on inherent politicization of Indigenous women, 131, 139; on importance of collective activism, 40, 83; on white needy do-gooders, 99–100, 102–3, 159, 215–16; on white settler guilt, 215; on white supremacist thinking,

99–100, 102–3; on white women's grounding in liberal individualism, 40, 99; on white women's motives for solidarity work, 63, 83
Thielen-Wilson, Leslie, 220, 221–22, 235n6
Thobani, Sunera, 230n42
Thompson, Audrey, 165, 166, 168, 178
Tkaronto (Toronto), 6, 226n12
transcendence: white settler capacity for, 23, 161, 221; white settler fantasy of, 27, 63–64, 113, 163, 170, 191, 226n23; and white women's claims of exceptionalism, 170, 174–77; white women's desire for, as underpinning solidarity work, 15; and white women's need for belonging, 58, 69–73
transgressive nature of proximity, as seen by Indigenous women, 10, 36, 77–110; author's thoughts on, 79–80; and gendered colonial subjectivity, 85, 86, 87–88, 89–90, 93; and impulse to solidarity work, 103–7; and invasive behaviour in cherished spaces, 86–87; and value/limits of caring, 80–86; and white demands for Indigenous caretaking, 93–96; and white demands to be educated in settler terms, 96–103; and white needy do-gooders, 87–93; and white supremacist thinking, 98–101
Trudeau, Justin, government of, viii
Truth and Reconciliation Commission of Canada, 45, 228n25; final report of, 7, 212
Tuck, Eve: with Maile Arvin and Angie Morrill, 197; and K. Wayne Yang, 5, 28, 158, 159, 193
two-spirit, lesbian, gay, bisexual, transgender, queer, questioning, intersex, and asexual (2SLGBTQQIA) people, 3, 225n3. *See also* missing and murdered Indigenous women, girls, and two-spirit (MMIWG2S) people

United Nations Mission in Guatemala (MINUGUA): author's experiences on, 65–66, 141
University of Toronto, viii, 4, 6, 56, 84, 130
Ursula (Indigenous study participant), 31; on emotional labour of solidarity work, 213; as having light-skinned privilege, 148–49, 235n4; and importance of being recognized as an ally, 181; and need to honour personal/family history, 191; on stolen land, 219, 221; on white self-reflexivity, 218, 219–20; on white women's guilt/need for care, 94–95, 219–20

"vanishing Indian," myth of, 119, 124, 230n43. *See also* ghosts, Indigenous peoples as
violence, against Indigenous women: as linked to environmental violence, 118, 120–22, 125, 134; participant as unaware of, 47–48; specific nature of, 144–45; white settler male dominance and, 72, 231n6. *See also* Missing and Murdered Indigenous Women and Girls, National Inquiry into (NIMMIWG), *and entry following*; No More Silence (NMS)

Walia, Harsha, 16
Waters, Anne, 131
Wente, Jesse, 7
Western lack, 111, 112, 116–21, 150–51; components of, 117; and concept of "noble savage," 116–17; and nostalgia/salvific benefit, 123–24, 151; and white settler claims to national belonging in Canada, 121–29, 151; and white settler cultural appropriation, 66, 117, 121–23, 126, 150
white supremacism, 24, 25, 96–103, 114–15; and burden of proof, 98–100
white/settler liberal subjectivity. *See* subjectivity, white/settler liberal

Whitebird, Wanda (Mi'kmaq) (study participant), 31; on cultural appropriation project with fatal consequences, 234*n*23; on expectations of Indigenous authenticity, 146; on friendships in solidarity work, 207, 234*n*16; on her own solidarity work, 49, 134–35, 135; on Indigenous women's roles in other women's struggles, 200; on men's role at women's events, 179; on need for white women to "step back, but not out," 204–5; on solidarity at a distance, 207–9, 120; on white desire to "become Native," 207–9; on white self-reflexivity, 220; on white settler guilt, 160; on white women's declarations of allyship, 181; on white women's hijacking of Indigenous events, 101, 137, 207; on white women's saviour mentality, 41–42
Wiegman, Robyn, 169, 233*n*9, 235*n*2
Willow, Anna J., 117, 123, 233*n*6
Wilson, Shawn, 87, 232*n*6
Wolfe, Patrick, 23, 46
women, Indigenous: and "authentic" Indigeneity, 146–50; burden of proof on, 96–103, 191; collective survival of, 129–35, 152; criticisms of "whitestream" feminism by, 17–21, 51, 79–80, 229*n*35; and deconstruction of white depictions, 141–46, 152–53; and internalized colonialism, 149–50, 235*n*3; life writings/knowledge of, 79; political activism of, 130–35, 139, 152; resistance/reaffirmation discourse of, 137–41, 152; responsibilities of, to their communities, 132–33; spirituality of, 62, 94, 120, 139–41, 205, 214; subordinate subject position of, 33, 132; violence against, 47–48, 72, 118, 120–22, 125, 134, 144–45, 231*n*6. *See also entry below*; feminism, Indigenous; missing and murdered Indigenous women, girls, and two-spirit (MMIWG2S) people
women, Indigenous, in solidarity work: as allies, 34–35, 40, 42, 148, 200; caretaking role of, 130–31; emotional labour of, 213–14; negative reactions by, 64, 166; and other women's struggles, 200; white desire for acceptance/inclusion by, 37, 58, 118–19; white desire for care/ healing by, 49, 95–96, 159, 215–16; white desire for company of, 53–54; white desire for forgiveness by, 13, 57, 155, 158–59, 196, 208; white desire to be educated by, 96, 97, 99, 101; white desire to be helped by, 103–10, 124–25; white desire to "help"/"save," 17, 24–27, 35; white distancing from, 65, 66–67, 68; white friendships with, ix, 28, 166–70, 207; white need to take direction from, 101, 135, 201, 202, 203; and willingness to work with white women, 8, 9–10, 80, 108. *See also* proximity, to Indigenous women/feminists, as pursued by white women/feminists; solidarity, between white and Indigenous women/ feminists
women, white settler, 11, 21, 22; definition of, ix, 226*n*22; Moodie as representative of, 25, 229*n*40. *See also entry below*; feminism, white, *and entry following*; settler colonialism
women, white settler, in solidarity work: as acknowledging settler status/privilege, 41, 43–46, 72, 75, 115–16, 174–75, 177–78, 189–92; claims of exceptionalism by, 13, 21, 36, 154–94; competition among, 177–80, 185–86, 193; as "helping with a twist," 9, 79, 103–10, 123, 211–12; as needing to learn their own ancestry, 140, 218, 220; as "needy do-gooders," 87–93, 128, 141, 158–59, 202, 206; as "radical"

activists, 106–7, 109, 178; saviour mentality of, 10, 25–26, 41, 88, 107, 124–25; self-making by, 4, 9, 10–11, 13, 18–36, 37–76, 78–79, 103–10; self-reflexivity by, 12, 16, 61, 107, 164–66, 187–93, 205, 209, 221–22; transgressive behaviour by, 10, 36, 77–110; on white settler guilt, 158–63; and white supremacism, 24, 25, 96–103, 114–15. *See also* allies, white settler women as;

exceptionalism, claims of, by white settler women; guilt, white settler, *and entry following*; proximity, to Indigenous women/feminists, as pursued by white women/feminists; solidarity, between white and Indigenous women/feminists

World Social Forum, 96

Yeğenoğlu, Meyda, 24, 26, 53, 68, 230*n*46